Cambridge Studies in Chinese History, Literature, and Institutions

General Editor, Denis Twitchett

Women, Property, and Confucian Reaction in Sung and Yüan China (960–1368)

Bettine Birge
University of Southern California

CAMBRIDGE
UNIVERSITY PRESS

PUBLISHED BY THE PRESS SYNDICATE OF THE UNIVERSITY OF CAMBRIDGE
The Pitt Building, Trumpington Street, Cambridge, United Kingdom

CAMBRIDGE UNIVERSITY PRESS
The Edinburgh Building, Cambridge CB2 2RU, UK
40 West 20th Street, New York, NY 10011-4211, USA
477 Williamstown Road, Port Melbourne, VIC 3207, Australia
Ruiz de Alarcón 13, 28014 Madrid, Spain
Dock House, The Waterfront, Cape Town 8001, South Africa

http://www.cambridge.org

First published 2002

Printed in the United States of America

Typeface Baskerville 10/12 pt.   *System* QuarkXPress™ [BTS]

A catalog record for this book is available from the British Library.

Library of Congress Cataloging in Publication Data available

ISBN 0 521 57373 4   hardback

To my father, Robert Walsh Birge,
and my late mother, Ann Chamberlain Birge

The publication of this book was made possible, in part, by generous grants from the Chiang Ching-kuo Foundation and the Pacific Cultural Foundation.

Contents

Contents

Contents

List of Maps, Figures, and Tables

xiv

Tables

Chronology of Chinese Dynasties

Shang	1766?–1067 B.C.
Chou	1067–221 B.C.
Spring and Autumn period	722–481 B.C.
Warring States period	403–221 B.C.
Ch'in	221–206 B.C.
Han	202 B.C.–A.D. 220
Six Dynasties period	A.D. 220–589
Sui	589–618
T'ang	618–906
Five Dynasties period	906–960
Northern Sung	960–1127
Southern Sung	1127–1279
Yüan	1260–1368
Ming	1368–1644
Ch'ing	1644–1911

Abbreviations

CMC	*Ch'ing-ming chi*, or *Ming-kung shu-p'an ch'ing-ming chi*
c.s.	*chin-shih* (highest degree in the civil service examinations)
HCP	*Hsü tzu-chih t'ung-chien ch'ang-pien*
SHT	*Sung hsing-t'ung*
SHY	*Sung hui-yao chi-kao*
SKCS	Ssu-k'u ch'üan-shu
SPTK	Ssu-pu ts'ung-k'an
SPPY	Ssu-pu pei-yao
SYHA	*Sung-Yüan hsüeh-an*
TCTK	*T'ung-chih t'iao-ko*
TSCC	Ts'ung-shu chi-ch'eng
YTC	*Yüan tien-chang*, or *Ta-Yüan sheng-cheng kuo-ch'ao tien-chang*
YTCHC	*Yüan tien-chang hsin-chi*, or *Ta-Yüan sheng-cheng tien-chang hsin-chi chih-chih t'iao-li*

Acknowledgments

During the years I have worked on this book, I have benefited greatly from the help and expertise of many colleagues and friends. The Sung portion of the book began as my Ph.D. dissertation at Columbia University, and I thank foremost my dissertation advisor Robert P. Hymes. I had the honor of being his first research student, and I have benefited enormously over the years from his broad learning, cogent criticisms, and careful reading of my work. I am also deeply indebted to Wm. Theodore de Bary and the late Wing-tsit Chan for their instruction and example. People who read all or part of the manuscript or the dissertation before that and generously took time to provide written or oral comments include Barand ter Haar, Charlotte Furth, Richard von Glahn, Ann Waltner, Paul Smith, Brian McKnight, Patricia Ebrey, John Chaffee, Morris Rossabi, Yao Dali, and an anonymous reviewer for Cambridge University Press. Special thanks go to Barand ter Haar, who sent me copious comments on the entire manuscript. Paul Smith first suggested that I look at the *Statutes and Precedents of the Yüan*, which became a major source for my conclusions. Brian McKnight sent me texts at timely moments, shared drafts of his own work, and kindly discussed translations by post and e-mail. I am deeply grateful for invaluable advice and comments from Frederick W. Mote in frequent correspondence and from Herbert Franke during a long afternoon at his home in Munich in June of 1996. I have also benefited from comments and camaraderie from Beverly Bossler, Ellen Neskar, and Ari Borrell. Finally, I thank the students in my graduate seminar on Women and the Family in China for their insightful comments, especially Constance Orliski, George daRoza, and David Bello.

The main research for this book was carried out at the Academia Sinica in Taipei, Taiwan, in the spring of 1994. Foremost I thank my two official sponsors Huang K'uan-ch'ung and Lau Nap-yin. They not only arranged for my appointment as a visiting scholar and extended every professional courtesy but also steered me to sources and offered invaluable advice during my stay. This book owes a further debt to Lau Nap-yin for his ongoing assistance and illuminating comments in the years since. I am deeply grateful to Hung Chin-fu for allowing me to join his graduate seminar at Ch'ing-hua University, where by a marvelous coincidence the students were reading the *Yüan tien-chang*, and for subsequently spending many hours answering my numerous queries. Other members of the Academia Sinica gave me help and welcomed me into their community. I am grateful to each of them.

My dissertation research was carried out in Kyoto, Japan, and my teachers and colleagues there have continued to offer me guidance and encouragement. My sponsors Chikusa Masaaki and Kinugawa Tsuyoshi helped me in countless ways both during my stay in Japan and in the years since. Sugiyama Masaaki taught me much about Yüan history and the reading of Yüan texts during our meetings in both Japan and the United States. In Tokyo, Shiba Yoshinobu, Yanagida Setsuko, and Ihara Hiroshi repeatedly took time from their busy schedules to meet with me to discuss my work and guide me to sources. I cannot thank them enough. Other scholars who deserve special thanks are Tonami Mamoru, Morita Kenji, Nakamura Yonoe, Saeki Tomi, and Umehara Kaoru.

The materials for this book were collected from a number of libraries in several countries. I thank the entire staff of the following libraries, with special thanks to Mr. Lin Ding-Tzann of the Fu Ssu-nien library at the Academia Sinica in Taipei; Mr. Mori of the library of the Research Institute of Humanistic Studies in Kyoto; Yamakami Teruo of the library of the Faculty of Letters, Kyoto University; Kenneth Harlin of the C. V. Starr East Asian Library at Columbia University; Kenneth Klein of the East Asian Library, University of Southern California; and James Cheng formerly of the East Asian Library at the University of California, Los Angeles, now at the Harvard-Yenching Library in Cambridge, Massachusetts.

The main research for this book was supported by a research grant in 1994 from the Joint Committee on Chinese Studies of the American Council of Learned Societies and the Social Science Research Council with funds provided by the Chiang Ching-kuo Foundation (with possible additional funds from the Ford Foundation and the National Endowment for the Humanities). Additional support came from the James H. Zumberge Faculty Research and Innovation Fund at the University of Southern California. I received research assistance of various kinds, both paid and unpaid, from Shaoyi Sun, Mei-ch'in Lin, and Itsuko Nishikawa. David Bello and Rebecca Harz helped get the manuscript into final form, and Sean O'Connell helped with the maps. Mr. Jiang Jianyuan provided invaluable assistance from finding information and checking sources to discussing translations with me. Special thanks go to my dear friends Lynn Chancer and Suzanne Leonora for their steadfast support and encouragement over many years.

I am deeply grateful to Denis C. Twitchett for his help and encouragement over the years of preparation of this manuscript, and I am honored to be included in his series of Cambridge Studies in Chinese History, Literature, and Institutions. I have had the good fortune to work with two wonderful editors at Cambridge University Press. Elizabeth Neil guided the manuscript quickly through the review and acceptance stage, and Mary Child worked with me with endless patience and understanding through the revision and production process. This book was completed with subsidies from the Pacific Cultural Foundation and from the Chiang Ching-kuo Foundation. I thank both foundations for their generous support.

My husband Peter R. Lee could not have done more, from attending to the household and caring for our infant son, to drawing maps and filling in Chinese characters, to providing unconditional moral support. My young son Henry provided inspiration and much comic relief. Despite the ample help I have received from teachers, colleagues, and friends, the book necessarily has many remaining shortcomings, for which I alone am responsible.

Characters for all Chinese words are given in the Glossary-Index, except for the names of otherwise anonymous people who appear in legal cases and other primary documents. Chinese characters are given in the text for a few terms of particular importance.

Introduction

This book describes a transformation of gender and property relations that occurred in China between the tenth and fourteenth centuries, a period of rapid social and economic change and expanding foreign occupation. During much of this time, women's property rights were steadily improving, and laws and practices affecting marriage and property were moving away from Confucian ideals of patrilineality. Then the Mongol invasion of the thirteenth century and the subsequent confrontation between nomadic and sedentary culture precipitated a re-Confucianization of the law and a swing back toward patrilineal principles that deprived women of their property rights and reduced their legal and economic autonomy.

By using gender and property as its focus, this book provides a reevaluation of the Mongol invasion and its influence on Chinese law and society. It also presents a new look at the changing position of women in premodern China and explores the changing meaning of gender with all its contradictions as it was continually reinvented and reinforced. The transmission and control of property was an area of tension between government laws, Confucian ideology, social practice, and ethnic norms. It was a site at which gender constructions, moral standards, and ethnic identity were both defined and challenged, such that new sets of meanings emerged over time. Such themes are the subject of this book.

The Mongol conquest of China, completed in 1276, marked the culmination of a process of foreign encroachment begun by the Khitan Liao in the tenth century and continued by the Jurchen Chin in the eleventh and twelfth. The widespread destruction of life and property in North China, especially during the prolonged Mongol attacks, has been well documented, but it is generally accepted that the conquest of China by its nomadic steppe neighbors did not appreciably affect basic Chinese social institutions such as marriage and inheritance. This book argues that on the contrary the Mongol invasion was instrumental in

1

bringing about a fundamental change in gender relations that altered the legal and economic position of women for centuries.

In the Sung dynasty (960–1279), previous to the Mongol invasion, property law affecting women was undergoing ferment and change, as described in Chapter 2. At a time of unprecedented commercialization that eroded social stability, property took on new importance, especially for women. More property was transferred to women than at any time previously in Chinese history. Most strikingly, traditional law that was originally meant to keep inheritance along the agnatic male line was reinterpreted to allow considerable assets to pass out of the patriline to daughters. Other laws protected a woman's property within marriage and allowed her to take all of it into a remarriage in case of widowhood or divorce. These developments gave elite women unprecedented economic independence and encouraged the remarriage of widows. Patrilineal principles were further eroded by state policies that deprived agnates of family property and granted considerable benefits to daughters and nonrelatives when no sons survived in a household. In response, newly developing agnatic kin groups devised ways to keep property in the male line at the expense of women.

During these same centuries, influential philosophers sought to revitalize the Confucian tradition and apply its precepts more rigorously to the family and household. Property devolving to women conflicted with Confucian ideology, which tied succession to property to the ritual duties of ancestral sacrifices and an unbroken line of male descendents to carry on these sacrifices. As described in Chapter 3, Confucian reformers challenged women's customary and legal rights to property. At the same time, however, they granted faithful wives and chaste widows considerable financial authority within the household as they rethought issues of gender roles, male–female identity, and the preservation of patrilineal descent. Although Confucian philosophers opposed Sung laws that granted elite women considerable financial autonomy, they did not succeed in changing these laws, nor did their ideas upset customary notions of marriage, property control, personal autonomy, and widow remarriage. This was to change under Mongol rule.

Chapter 4 details how indigenous social change combined with foreign invasion to create a new constellation of property and gender relations that curtailed women's financial and personal autonomy and promoted widow chastity. The Mongol conquest of China during the thirteenth century confronted the Chinese with new forms of marriage and property relations that were radically different from their own. Practices such as the levirate, which allowed a man to marry his father's or brother's widow and prevent her from returning home, challenged

Chinese notions of incest, personal autonomy, and marriage exchanges, and they upset traditional power relations within a household. The lack of a comprehensive legal code during the Yüan and frequent reversals of rulings by both local magistrates and central ministries caused further confusion and disagreement around issues of marriage and property. By the 1270s, issues of marriage, incest, property control, personal autonomy, control of reproduction, and widow chastity had entered a contested sphere of conflicting values, seen in legal challenges and court battles. This atmosphere created the opportunity for a radical rethinking of traditional Chinese values and practices surrounding women, marriage, and property. The result was a transformation of the law and social attitudes at the expense of women's property rights and personal autonomy, which endured for the remainder of the imperial period.

The men and women who are the primary subjects of this study held property in some amount. Often they owned only small amounts of land or occasionally only movable property. They appeared on the government registers as members of taxable households, and while they might not have been well off, they were not people of servile status. This group represented a majority of the population, not just the elite. The women who are discussed in this book were usually (though not always) principal or first wives. Concubines and maids, who themselves could be bought and sold, sometimes appear in the pages below, but they are important to the narrative more for what they represented to free women: the potential fate of any woman without property.

Property and related social standing were major sources of agency for women. The pages below bring to life many strong women who exercised power and authority within the household and beyond. They show women going to court to defend their property rights, sometimes even against members of their family. At the same time, this book is concerned primarily with changes over time in the parameters within which women's agency had to operate. Laws, social structures, and ideology informed and limited the possibilities of action for both men and women. Individual challenges to these structures determined their parameters but also opened fissures and instabilities in them over time. Lawsuits and other sources used in this study demonstrate differing expectations around gender roles on the part of male and female litigants, individual judges, and the state. It is precisely these areas of disagreement that reveal the limits created by laws and social structures, the areas of their instabilities, and the evolution of all of these over time. The study of these themes reveals the changing and contested meaning of gender and ethnicity in middle-period China and shows how these both informed and were informed by other historical developments.

Historical Context

The Sung dynasty (960–1276) was a time of economic development, social transformation, and cultural brilliance. Its sophisticated arts were famous around the world and delight visitors to museums to this day. Overshadowing the richness of the society, though, was the constant threat of foreign war with powerful neighbors. Periods of uneasy peace were punctuated by border wars, leading finally to the Jurchen invasion of North China completed in 1127, which ended the Northern Sung, and the Mongol invasion of all of China, by 1276, which ended the Southern Sung. (See Map 1.)

Contours of Change at the National Level

Sung society was fundamentally different from that of the T'ang, which preceded it.[1] The T'ang was basically an aristocratic (or to some an oligarchic) society, where high office was dominated by a small number of "great clans." Membership in these clans was determined by birth, making marriage into a powerful family the best way to achieve wealth and high status.[2] Elite status was closely tied to government service, and officials were chosen from a proportionately small pool of elites. This privileged group all but disappeared during the upheavals at the end of the T'ang, eventually being replaced in the Sung by a broader and less stable elite, variously called the literati or gentry (in Chinese, *shih*).

The new elites of the Sung maintained their status through a range of activities including government service, community leadership, learning, and wealth. In the Northern Sung, a relatively small segment of the elite, which Robert Hartwell has called the "professional elite,"

1 The general outlines of this difference and its significance were first described in the early twentieth century by the Japanese scholar Naitō Konan (Torajirō, 1866–1934). For a summary, see Naitō Torajirō, "Gaikakuteki Tō-Sō jidai kan," *Rekishi to chiri* 9:5 (1922): 1–12. For an English overview of Naitō's thesis, see Miyazawa Hisayuki, "An Outline of the Naitō Hypothesis and Its Effects on Japanese Studies of China," *Far Eastern Quarterly* 14:4 (1955): 533–52. For a critical appraisal of Naitō and the context of his work, see Joshua Fogel, *Politics and Sinology: The Case of Naitō Konan* (Cambridge, Mass.: Harvard University Press, 1984).

2 David Johnson, *The Medieval Chinese Oligarchy* (Boulder, Colo.: Westview Press, 1977); David Johnson, "The Last Years of a Great Clan," *Harvard Journal of Asiatic Studies* 37:1 (June 1977): 5–102; Patricia Ebrey, *The Aristocratic Families of Early Imperial China* (Cambridge: Cambridge University Press, 1978).

Map 1. Northern and Southern Sung borders superimposed on the provinces of modern China.

still dominated the highest government offices and used the capital as their power base. But the majority of officialdom was recruited from the much larger *shih* class, and by Southern Sung times, the small professional elite had been subsumed within this. The members of this larger *shih* group concentrated on securing their positions in their home prefectures. They accomplished this through landholding, marriage ties, community relief work, temple and shrine building, bridge and dam repair, other public works, participation in the examination system, and occasional appointment to office.[3] Women played a significant role in these endeavors.

While members of the Sung elite had to employ various strategies to maintain or improve their status, participation in the examinations (by the males of the household), and the possibility of government service that it offered, continued to be preeminent. An important factor in the transformation of the elite from T'ang to Sung was the expanded and revised system of civil service examinations under the Sung, which recruited as many as half of all new officials by anonymous competitive examinations based on literary ability and knowledge of the Confucian classics.[4] Figures for the numbers of candidates sitting for the civil service examinations provide an estimate of the size of the *shih* class. The number of adult males taking the prefectural (lowest level) examinations was as much as 3 to 5 percent of the total male population (in some areas as much as 10 percent) and was increasing over the course of the dynasty.[5] This represents a portion of the population considerably larger than the elite class of Europe during the same centuries. It reflects the expansion of literate culture and economic opportunity in the Sung

3 Robert Hartwell, "Demographic, Political, and Social Transformations of China," *Harvard Journal of Asiatic Studies* 42 (1982): 383–94; Robert P. Hymes, *Statesmen and Gentlemen: The Elite of Fu-chou, Chiang-hsi, in Northern and Southern Sung* (Cambridge: Cambridge University Press, 1986). Conclusions about changes in marriage strategies and residence patterns are also shown by Ihara Hiroshi; see esp. "Sōdai kanryō no kon'in no imi ni tsuite," *Rekishi to chiri* 254 (1976): 12–19; and "Nan-Sō Shisen ni okeru teikyo shijin: Seidofu ro, Shishū ro o chūshin to shite," *Tōhōgaku* 54 (1977). For more on elite strategies and the importance of kinship (both agnatic and affinal), see Beverly Bossler, *Powerful Relations: Kinship, Status, and the State in Sung China (960–1279)* (Cambridge, Mass.: Harvard University Press, 1998). For the localist orientation in religion, see Ellen Neskar, "The Cult of Worthies: A Study of Shrines Honoring Local Confucian Worthies in the Sung Dynasty (960–1279)" (Ph.D. dissertation, Columbia University, 1993).

4 John Chaffee, *Thorny Gates of Learning in Sung China: A Social History of Examinations* (Cambridge: Cambridge University Press, 1985); Thomas H. C. Lee, *Government, Education, and Examinations in Sung China* (Hong Kong: Chinese University Press, 1985); E. A. Kracke, *Civil Service in Early Sung China: 960–1067* (Cambridge, Mass.: Harvard University Press, 1953).

5 Chaffee, *Thorny Gates*, 36–8, esp. Fig. 3, and 219 n. 75; and John Chaffee, "Education and Examinations in Sung Society" (Ph.D. dissertation, University of Chicago, 1979), 57–9. These numbers vary considerably by geographic region.

compared to the less commercialized, more aristocratic society of the preceding T'ang dynasty.[6]

The belief by some scholars that the examinations fostered social mobility, regularly bringing "new blood" into the bureaucracy,[7] has been tempered by the realization that the examinations drew almost exclusively from among those who already had elite status in their communities, and who usually had other examination candidates or officeholders in their extended families.[8] Moreover, over the course of the Sung, examinations became less important as a means of recruitment, providing 57 percent of officials in 1046 and only 27 percent in 1213.[9] The rest of officialdom gained office through a combination of hereditary appointment (*yin*, literally "shadow" privilege), government schools, and special, less competitive examinations given to selected groups.[10] The most important of these, hereditary appointment, was based on family connections, which could be through affinal relatives. Thus connections through women, cemented by marriage ties and the exchange of dowry, were an important part of elite male strategies.

Ironically, even as the standard examinations became less important as a means of government recruitment, more and more literati flocked to take them. Competition for even the lowest degree increased

6 The "aristocrats" of the T'ang represented a very narrow segment of the population, much like the knights and feudal elite of medieval Europe. See Johnson, *Medieval Chinese Oligarchy*. The elite of the Sung are much more comparable to the "gentry" of Tudor and Stuart England, who comprised a comparable portion (4–5%) of the population. For England, see e.g., Peter Laslett, *World We Have Lost* (London: Methuen and Co., 1979), 27–8. The connection between learning and the elite, found in China, is made for the later period in Europe by Lawrence Stone, "The Education Revolution in England, 1560–1640," *Past and Present* 28 (July 1964): 41–80.

7 E. A. Kracke, "Family versus Merit in Chinese Civil Service Examinations under the Empire," *Harvard Journal of Asiatic Studies* 10 (1947): 105–23; Sudō Yoshiyuki, *Sōdai kanryōsei to daitochi shoyū* (Tokyo: Nihon hyōronsha, 1950), 33–76; Ping-ti Ho, *The Ladder of Success in Imperial China: Aspects of Social Mobility, 1368–1911* (New York: Columbia University Press, 1962).

8 Hymes, *Statesmen*, esp. chs. 1 and 2. There were various limits on who could sit for the examinations, and each candidate had to be recommended by local officials; Chaffee, *Thorny Gates*, 53–61. There is disagreement over the extent to which local elites could exclude candidates from the prefectural examination halls and thus limit competition and social mobility; see Chaffee, *Thorny Gates*, 60 and 223 n. 97; and Hymes, *Statesmen*, 42–6. The qualification of some candidates to sit the examinations was at times contested in court; see for example *Ming-kung shu-p'an ch'ing-ming chi* (Beijing: Chung-hua shu-chü, 1987), 97–8 [hereafter cited as CMC].

9 Chaffee, *Thorny Gates*, 26–7.

10 For the relative importance of different recruitment methods at different times, see Chaffee, *Thorny Gates*, esp. ch. 2; and Umehara Kaoru, *Sōdai kanryō seido kenkyū* (Kyoto: Dohosha, 1985). Officeholding through the *yin* privilege shows that hereditary advantage did not completely disappear in the Sung.

dramatically over the Sung, rising to a pass ratio of about 1 in 100 or more.[11] As the population increased dramatically in the Sung, fewer men per capita could become officials. This meant that the vast majority of elites could no longer depend on the state for their status, in the form of actual government service or an examination degree that provided a sinecure and the promise of eventual appointment. Nevertheless, participation in the examinations in itself became ever more important as a marker of elite status. It confirmed a certain level of wealth, education, and local connection, and it validated the privileges that these had already conferred. As success on the examinations grew more remote, a schism developed between government service and the education that prepared one for it. Education in the Confucian classics by itself became a trapping of status. In this context, a fellowship of Confucian reformers, led in the Southern Sung by Chu Hsi (1130–1200), promoted learning as an end in itself. Having seen factionalist politics at court and the failure of central government action to improve local conditions, they stressed the value of direct knowledge of the classics for personal cultivation and community rejuvenation, separate from government service. In essence, they promoted as a virtue what had become a necessity for most elites: the pursuit of study without regard to obtaining office thereby. They stressed the broad, even cosmic, relevance of education, toward a goal of comprehensive social reform.[12]

The economic changes taking place in the Sung, with which the elite had to contend, have been appropriately described as an "economic revolution."[13] Technological advances in agriculture and transportation transformed daily life and produced a society that dazzled the few Europeans who observed it just after the Sung.[14] New strains of early ripening Champa rice were introduced from Southeast Asia early in the Sung dynasty, and innovations in fertilizers, irrigation, seed strains, and

11 Chaffee, *Thorny Gates*, 35–7. The ratios differed greatly by prefecture, as government quotas lagged behind population growth. In some areas, especially in the Southeast and Fukien, only one in several hundred candidates was granted a degree.

12 For discussions of these developments, see Peter Bol, "The Sung Examination System and the *Shih*," *Asia Major*, 3rd series, 3:2 (1990): 149–71; Peter Bol, "Chu Hsi's Redefinition of Literati Learning," and Wm. Theodore de Bary, "Chu Hsi's Aims as an Educator," both in *Neo-Confucian Education: The Formative Stage*, ed. Wm. Theodore de Bary and John Chaffee (Berkeley: University of California Press, 1989).

13 Mark Elvin, *The Pattern of the Chinese Past* (Stanford, Calif.: Stanford University Press, 1973).

14 See for instance the account of Marco Polo (though he may have been reporting second hand information); Ronald Latham trans., *The Travels of Marco Polo* (New York: Penguin Books, 1980), esp. chs. 4 and 5.

cropping contributed further to huge increases in agricultural output.[15] These increases made it possible to support a vastly larger population. The population of China doubled between the eighth and eleventh centuries, with nearly all of the increase in the rice-growing south.[16] The T'ang dynasty had already sought to tap the agricultural wealth of the rice-growing areas with its system of canals, bringing tax grain from the lower Yangtze up to the capital at Ch'ang-an.[17] The placing of the Sung capital far to the east at Kaifeng, nearer by canal to the lower Yangtze region, reflects the growing economic importance of the Southeast in the economy of that time.

Commercial expansion of the Sung went far beyond anything seen in the T'ang. The T'ang system of price controls and strictly regulated markets broke down as commerce burst the confines of government regulation.[18] Even far-flung rural areas were drawn into market networks, stimulating commercial agriculture and sideline production, though this development was highly uneven even in the economically advanced Lower Yangtze.[19] Commercial taxes and income from state monopolies became a major source of income for the Sung government as land tax revenues stagnated. Merchants delivered an extraordinary range of products to urban centers.[20] Trade

15 Ping-ti Ho, "Early Ripening Rice in Chinese History," *Economic History Review*, 2nd series, 9:2 (1956): 200–18. Elvin, *Pattern*, 121–4. Advances in agriculture were by no means universal, and regional variation in cropping and technology was striking. See Sudō Yoshiyuki, *Sōdai keizaishi kenkyū* (Tokyo: Tōkyō daigaku shuppankai, 1962), 73–206; and Shiba Yoshinobu, *Sōdai Kōnan keizaishi no kenkyū* (Tokyo: Tōkyō daigaku Tōyōbunka kenkyūjo, 1988), esp. 137–65, 365–449.

16 Ping-ti Ho, "An Estimate of the Total Population of Sung and Chin China," *Etudes Song*, 1st series, no. 1 (The Hague: Mouton, 1970), 33–53; Hans Bielenstein, "Chinese Historical Demography: A.D. 2–1982," *Bulletin of the Museum of Far Eastern Antiquities*, no. 59 (1987): 1–288; Hartwell, "Demographic, Political, and Social Transformations of China," 383–94.

17 Denis Twitchett, *Financial Administration under the T'ang Dynasty* (Cambridge: Cambridge University Press, 1963).

18 Kato Shigeshi, "On the Hang or the Associations of Merchants in China," *Memoirs of the Research Dept. of the Tōyō Bunko*, no. 9 (1936); Denis Twitchett, "Merchant, Trade, and Government in Late T'ang," *Asia Major*, new series, 14:1 (1968): 63–93.

19 Shiba Yoshinobu, *Commerce and Society in Sung China*, trans. and ed. Mark Elvin (Ann Arbor: Center for Chinese Studies, University of Michigan, 1970); Shiba Yoshinobu, "Urbanization and the Development of Markets in the Lower Yangtze Valley," in *Crisis and Prosperity in Sung China*, ed. John Haeger (Tucson: University of Arizona, 1975); and Shiba, *Sōdai Kōnan keizaishi*.

20 Jacques Gernet, *Daily Life in China on the Eve of the Mongol Invasion*, trans. H. M. Wright (Stanford, Calif.: Stanford University Press, 1962), esp. 44–51; Shiba, *Commerce and Society in Sung China*; Shiba Yoshinobu, *Sōdai shōgyōshi kenkyū* (Tokyo: Kazama shobō, 1968); Colin Jeffcott, "Government and the Distribution System in Sung Cities," *Papers on Far Eastern History* 1 (March 1970): 119–52.

was facilitated by the use of money: gold, silver, and especially copper coins, and by private and, from the twelfth century, government issue of paper currency – the first in the world.[21] Strings of "1,000" copper cash (actual numbers varied to as low as 770) became the standard medium of exchange, as quotes from Sung sources show. Transportation networks and the diversification of production allowed the unprecedented growth of towns and cities in the Sung. Urban centers like Hangchow may have had populations exceeding 1 million, representing urbanization rates that were not surpassed until the twentieth century. These towns and cities in turn became centers of industrial production.[22]

Towns and cities were also centers of learning. The invention of printing in the seventh century and its rapid spread in the Sung gave many more people the opportunity to become educated.[23] When education became more widely available, more people over a wider area of the empire could aspire to Confucian training that might lead to success in the state examinations and an official career. This also helped increase the size of the elite, and gave its members the character of literati. The printing and book-making industry flourished, expanding beyond government printing of the Confucian classics. Especially in the last half of the dynasty, commercial publishers produced many types of books on a wide range of topics such as agriculture, medicine, family advice, legal precedents, miscellaneous notes, and local history. Research on the Sung today is facilitated by these many volumes that were printed.

Another major change from the T'ang was the irreversible development of a free market in land. Already in the late T'ang, government attempts to control land tenure, with periodic redistributions under the "Equal Field System," had broken down. The Sung government made a few localized attempts to limit large landholdings but in general placed

---

21 Lien-sheng Yang, *Money and Credit in China: A Short History* (Cambridge, Mass.: Harvard University Press, 1952); Robert Hartwell, "The Evolution of the Early Northern Sung Monetary System," *Journal of the American Oriental Society* 87 (1967): 280–9; Richard von Glahn, *Fountain of Fortune: Money and Monetary Policy in China, 1000–1700* (Berkeley: University of California Press, 1996).

22 G. William Skinner, "Introduction: Urban Development in Imperial China," in *The City in Late Imperial China*, ed. G. Wm. Skinner (Stanford University Press, 1977), 9–31; Robert Hartwell, "Markets, Technology, and the Structure of Enterprise in the Development of the Eleventh-Century Chinese Iron and Steel Industry," *Journal of Economic History* 26:9 (1966): 29–58; Robert Hartwell, "A Revolution in the Chinese Iron and Coal Industries," *Journal of Asian Studies* 21 (1962): 153–62.

23 Thomas Carter, *The Invention of Printing in China and Its Spread Westward* (New York: Columbia University Press, 1925); Denis Twitchett, *Printing and Publishing in Medieval China* (New York: Frederic Beil, 1983).

few restraints on the exchange of private lands.[24] Land was a major commodity and source of wealth.[25] Government registers, called *chen-chi-pu*, recorded the owners of land, and written contracts stamped with government seals made mortgage or change of ownership legally verifiable. Regular updating of the registers proved impossible, so private contracts came to be relied on by judges to document land ownership.[26] Such contracts always recorded whether property belonged in the category of "dowry property" (women's property), which enjoyed special treatment under the law. In addition to jewelry, maidservants, and movable household items, land was a regular item of personal dowry taken into marriage by elite Sung women.

Land was often sold together with the tenants or field hands who worked it. Various degrees of servility existed in the Sung. Servile status ranged from the extreme bondage of agricultural and domestic slaves to the freer type of obligation of a tenant farmer, who might have contractual rights to cultivate some lands and who might himself own others. The view that one type of "manorial system" pervaded all of Sung China has been replaced by a view, first articulated by Yanagida Setsuko, that a range of status distinctions was found in the Sung and different systems of land tenure dominated in different geographic areas.[27]

---

24 Sudō Yoshiyuki, *Chūgoku tochi seidoshi kenkyū* (Tokyo: Tōkyō daigaku shuppansha, 1954), 537–602; Sudō Yoshiyuki, *Tōsō shakai keizaishi kenkyū* (Tokyo: Tōkyō daigaku shuppankai, 1965), 233–320. When land was sold, priority was given to buyers who were relatives or neighbors, but this did not necessarily affect the fluidity of the land market. For general information on the development of private land holdings, see Niida Noboru, *Chūgoku hōseishi kenkyū*, Vol. IV, *Hō to kanshū, hō to dōtoku* (Tokyo: Tōkyō daigaku shuppankai, 1964; reprint 1991), hereafter cited as *Hōseishi* IV. For an excellent English summary of the issues, see Denis Twitchett, *Land Tenure and the Social Order in T'ang and Sung China* (London: Oxford University Press, 1962), esp. 25–9.

25 Peter Golas, "Rural China in the Sung," *Journal of Asian Studies* 39:2 (Feb. 1980): 299–300. A recent study on the Sung that reinforces the importance of land for the elite is Ch'i Hsia, "Sung-Yüan shih-ch'i P'u-yang Cheng-shih chia-tsu chih yen-chiu," in *Ryū Shiken hakushi shōju kinen Sōshi kenkyū ronshū*, ed. Kinugawa Tsuyoshi (Tokyo: Dōhōsha, 1989), 159–66. A study that systematically examines the importance of landholding for the elite after the Sung is Hilary Beattie, *Land and Lineage in China: A Study of T'ung-ch'eng, Anhwei, in the Ming and Ch'ing Dynasties* (Cambridge: Cambridge University Press, 1979).

26 For the evolution from reliance on government registers to private contracts to prove land ownership, see Valerie Hansen, *Negotiating Daily Life in Traditional China* (New Haven, Conn.: Yale University Press, 1995).

27 Yanagida Setsuko, "Sōdai tochi shoyūsei ni mirareru futatsu no kata: senshin to henkyō," *Tōyō bunka kenkyūjo kiyō*, 29 (1963): 95–130. Yanagida's work has been carried forward by Peter Golas, "Rural China in the Sung"; and her simple dichotomy between "advanced and frontier" areas has been refined by Joseph McDermott, "Charting Blank Spaces and Disputed Regions: The Problem of Sung Land Tenure," *Journal of Asian Studies* 44:1 (1984): 13–41. The old view that a manorial system of large amalgamated holdings worked by servile tenant-serfs dominated the countryside was put forward

Rapid economic development was overshadowed by economic insecurity for people of every stratum. The expansion of the market brought new opportunities but also new dangers. Families could rise to affluence or more likely fall into poverty in a very short time, sometimes just one generation. Even high officials could not guarantee that their immediate descendants would enjoy the same prosperity as they had.[28] A new genre of family advice books reflects the emphasis that elite families placed on sound household finances and their concern with preserving wealth and status.[29] Wives played an important role in household fiscal management and family discipline. (Chapter 3 examines the growing emphasis Confucian authors placed on such female responsibilities.)

Women were especially vulnerable to loss of status. The growing elite class created an expanding market for concubines and maids.[30] When orphaned or otherwise separated from property, a woman could easily fall into servile status. Unscrupulous brokers sold girls into slavery without asking their background or origin. Men could be sold as bondservants or slaves as well, but a man from the educated class was unlikely to fall into servitude. He could usually expect to find some employment based on his literary skills, perhaps as a tutor or clerk. A literate woman was more likely to become a concubine, or a courtesan if she had the looks.

Another development of great significance for women was the spread of footbinding. Traditional accounts place its origin in the early tenth century (prior to the Sung), among palace dancers. During the eleventh

---

most fully by Sudō (see esp. his *Chūgoku tochi seidoshi kenkyū*), and was adopted for English readers by Mark Elvin, *Pattern*, 69–83. The counterargument that contractual relations between owners and tenants working fragmented landholdings were the norm is set forth by Miyazaki Ichisada, "Sōdai igo no tochi shoyū keitai," in *Ajia shi kenkyū*, Vol. 4. (Kyoto: Tōyōshi kenkyūkai, 1964), 87–129. Yanagida's work reconciled these two extremes.

28 This point is emphasized by Beverly Bossler, though the possibility of rising may not have been as great as she suggests; *Powerful Relations*, esp. chs. 2, 4, 5, 9, Concl.

29 The most famous of these has been translated, by Patricia Ebrey, *Family and Property in Sung China: Yüan Ts'ai's Precepts for Social Life* (Princeton, N.J.: Princeton University Press, 1984). See her introduction, esp. pp. 41–4, for a discussion of others, and Joseph McDermott, "Family Financial Plans of the Southern Sung," *Asia Major*, 3rd series, 4:2 (1991): 15–78.

30 Patricia Ebrey, *The Inner Quarters: Marriage and the Lives of Chinese Women in the Sung Period* (Berkeley: University of California Press, 1993), 217–35; 265–70; Patricia Ebrey, "Concubines in Sung China," *Journal of Family History*, 11 (1986): 1–24; and Patricia Ebrey, "Women, Money, and Class: Ssu-ma Kuang and Sung Neo-Confucian Views on Women," in *Papers on Society and Culture of Early Modern China* (Taipei: Institute of History and Philology, Academia Sinica, 1992). These works include many examples of high-born girls in the Sung getting sold into slavery. See also Hill Gates, "The Commoditization of Chinese Women," *Signs* 14:4 (Summer 1989): 799–832.

and twelfth centuries the practice began to spread be͵
ment circles to elite households, where it was practiced ͵
and maids. Evidence from archeology reveals that footbͺ
nearly universal among the southern elite by the thirteenth cenͺ
around this time we also find a protest by one essayist against thͺ
ble pain it caused little girls.[31] Confucian reformers, who called foɾ
seclusion of women, have been blamed for footbinding but in fact seeͺ
not to have promoted it. There is no direct evidence that they approved
of what unquestionably began as an erotic practice, and consistent with
this attitude, the female descendants of Ch'eng I (1033–1107), a patri-
arch of the Confucian reform movement, did not bind their feet as late
as the early Yüan period.[32] It is intriguing to speculate on the possible
connection between footbinding and ethnic confrontation that might
parallel the developments in property law that I describe in this book.
Footbinding, it can be argued, came to be associated with the refine-
ment of Chinese culture in contrast to that of the Mongols and China's
other steppe neighbors, whose women never bound their feet. Unfortunately, however, the extant sources do not allow for any meaningful
connection between footbinding and the developments in women's lives
described in this book. Reference to footbinding is entirely absent from
legal records and other data used herein, and the issue must be left aside
until more information can be found.

Changes in Sung economy and society stimulated changes in
family organization of considerable relevance to issues of women and
property, namely the development of organized descent groups.
While the large corporate estates of late imperial China do not appear
yet in the Sung and Yüan, the tenth to fourteenth centuries saw
the growth of a repertoire of activities and institutions that promoted
agnatic group ties. One of the earliest to appear was the practice of
group sacrifices at graves. These began in the T'ang among commoners, likely influenced by Buddhist funerary rituals, but became more
elaborate and important in the Sung. Ties to more distant agnatic kin

31 *Chiao-ch'i chi* (Pai-pu TSCC ed.), 1:22a; Ebrey, *Inner Quarters*, 40. For more discussion, see Howard Levy, *Chinese Footbinding: The History of a Curious Custom* (New York:
Walton Rawls, 1966); and Ebrey, *Inner Quarters*, 37–43. One woman, Huang Sheng
(1227–1243) from Fu-chou, Fukien, was buried with bindings and tiny shoes on her
feet; five other pairs of shoes were buried with her, measuring 5.3–5.6 inches long and
less than 2 inches wide; Fu-chien sheng po-wu kuan, ed., *Fu-chou Nan-Sung Huang Sheng
mu* (Peking: Wen-wu ch'u-pan she, 1982) 8, 9, 19, plate 62. For more archaeological
evidence, see Chiang-hsi sheng wen-wu k'ao-ku yen-chiu so, et al., "Chiang-hsi Te-an
Nan-Sung Chou-shih mu ch'ing-li chien-pao," *Wen-wu* (1990): 1–13; and Ch'ü-chou
shih wen-kuan hui, "Che-chiang Ch'ü-chou chih Nan-Sung mu ch'u-t'u ch'i-wu," *K'ao-
ku*, no. 11 (1983): 1007.
32 *Chan-yüan ching-yü* (TSCC ed.), 1:1b–2a.

were created by worshiping older ancestors, often the earliest to be buried in an area, and meeting all together on the same day. New attention was paid to burying agnatic relatives together in patrilineal formation (a feat that might conflict with the dictates of geomancy) and preserving old grave sites. By Southern Sung times, we find frequent reference to communal lands set aside to keep up grave sites and support graveside rituals.[33]

Parallel to these popular developments were attempts by elites to promote descent-group solidarity and Confucian rituals. Confucian revivalists put renewed emphasis on ancestor worship and tried to displace Buddhist and Taoist death rites with Confucian oriented ones.[34] A few even argued for the revival of a (supposedly) ancient system of family organization – the descent-line system (*tsung-fa*) where office and resources were dominated by the senior line of a lineage, but this idea led nowhere.[35] More significant was genealogy writing, which quickly spread from a few national elites in Northern Sung to any who could afford it in Southern. By Yüan times, these had become printed documents graced with prefaces by distinguished authors that listed a broad group of agnates to create wide public networks of connections.[36] Communal ancestral halls further advertised a lineage's prestige and local standing. More ambitious was the founding of charitable estates. Pioneered by Fan Chung-yen (989–1052) as an institution to promote Confucian religious, moral, and family welfare activities, its fate is instructive. Even with tax exemptions and other state support, the early charitable estates of Fan and others tended to fail, leaving member families to fend for themselves economically, usually turning to daughters and affines

33 These issues are best described in Patricia Ebrey, "The Early Stages in the Development of Descent Group Organization," in *Kinship Organization in Late Imperial China, 1000–1940*, ed. Patricia Ebrey and James Watson (Berkeley: University of California Press, 1986), 16–61. For post-Sung lineage types, see other essays in this volume, and for classic accounts of corporate lineages, see Maurice Freedman, *Chinese Lineage and Society: Fukien and Kwangtung* (London: Athlone Press, 1966; reprint 1971); Maurice Freedman, *Lineage Organization in Southeast China* (London: Athlone Press, 1958), and Hugh Baker, *Chinese Family and Kinship* (New York: Columbia University Press, 1979).
34 See introduction to Patricia Ebrey, trans., *Chu Hsi's "Family Rituals": A Twelfth-Century Manual for the Performance of Cappings, Weddings, Funerals, and Ancestral Rites* (Princeton, N.J.: Princeton University Press, 1991); and Patricia Ebrey, *Confucianism and Family Rituals in Imperial China: A Social History of Writing about Rites* (Princeton, N.J.: Princeton University Press, 1991), 68–102.
35 Patricia Ebrey, "Conceptions of the Family in the Sung Dynasty," *Journal of Asian Studies* 43:2 (Feb. 1984): 219–46.
36 Robert Hymes, "Marriage, Descent Groups, and the Localist Strategy in Sung and Yüan Fu-chou," in *Kinship Organization in Late Imperial China*, ed. Ebrey and Watson, 95–136; Morita Kenji, "SōGen jidai ni okeru shūfu," *Tōyōshi kenkyū* 37:4 (1979): 27–53. Hugh Clark has found many genealogy manuscripts from the Southern Sung in Fukien. I thank him for discussing his unpublished findings with me.

for help.[37] More successful were the limited efforts to pool lineage resources in communally owned grave sites and endowment lands to support group rituals.

Taken together, these institutions and practices created new descent-group consciousness and ties among agnates in a local area, especially in South China. Such agnates were loath to let property go to daughters who married outside the descent group, and they became more willing and able to claim property that would previously have gone to natal daughters. The word of lineage elders, even distant relatives, gained standing in courts of law, as lineage identity and communal action became more common. By the end of the Yüan dynasty, the foundations of corporate lineage estates were firmly in place in the South. For much of the southern population, family affairs became lineage affairs as members participated in a broad spectrum of descent-group activities and institutions. This widened the group with interests in how property devolved, which adversely affected women.

The Sung state faced a constant threat from the peoples beyond its borders. It was surrounded by a number of non-Chinese states, whom it had to acknowledge as equals on the world stage, and who variously occupied territory controlled by previous Chinese dynasties. As early as 937, sixteen northern prefectures, including the region of modern Peking, had been ceded to the non-Chinese Khitan dynasty of the Liao. Like other steppe regimes to follow, the Khitan fielded a powerful cavalry that posed a serious threat to the Chinese heartland. In 1004, the Sung ended hostilities and agreed to a humiliating treaty that required large annual payments of silk and silver and acknowledged the equal standing of the Sung and Liao emperors.[38] In the Northwest, the Buddhist state of Hsia (or Hsi Hsia, Western Hsia) was ruled by the Tanguts, a Tibetan peoples. The Sung failed to conquer this territory in war, and in 1006 concluded a treaty lasting into the 1040s.

---

37 Denis Twitchett, "The Fan Clan's Charitable Estate, 1050–1760," in *Confucianism in Action*, ed. David Nivison and Arthur Wright (Stanford, Calif.: Stanford University Press, 1959), 97–133; Linda Walton, "Kinship, Marriage, and Status in Sung China: A Study of the Lou Lineage of Ningbo c. 1050–1250," *Journal of Asian History*, 18:1 (1984): 35–77.

38 Jing-shen Tao, *Two Sons of Heaven: Studies in Sung-Liao Relations* (Tucson: University of Arizona, 1988); Wang Gungwu, "The Rhetoric of a Lesser Empire: Early Sung Relations with Its Neighbors," in *China among Equals*, ed. Morris Rossabi (Berkeley: University of California Press, 1983), 47–65. For more on the Liao, see Karl A. Wittfogel and Feng Chia-sheng, *History of Chinese Society: Liao* (Philadelphia: American Philosophical Society, 1949); and Denis Twitchett and Klaus Peter Tietze, "The Liao," in *Cambridge History of China*, ed. Herbert Franke and Denis Twitchett, Vol. 6, *Alien Regimes and Border States, 907–1368* (Cambridge: Cambridge University Press, 1994), 43–153.

Against external threats, the Sung government was forced to maintain a large standing army. To prevent internal threats from regional militia, the Sung funded and commanded its armies from the capital. The pressures of war and the needs of the military created unprecedented demands for government revenues, which spurred government reform movements of the eleventh century. The most significant was that of Wang An-shih (1021–1086), who served as chief councillor from 1068–1076. Wang and the young emperor Shen-tsung initiated a campaign called the New Policies that sought to expand the economy and increase state revenues by economic activism and intervention on the part of the government.[39] Despite fierce opposition, and a counterreform during 1085–1100, Wang's policies were promoted in some form until 1126, leading to debilitating factional struggles at court and a general loss of confidence in central government during the Southern Sung. Anti-Wang opinion was much bolstered by the loss of North China in 1127, which was blamed on a pro-Wang chief minister.

In the early twelfth century, a Tungusic people from the area of Manchuria, the Jurchens, became powerful enough to found their own dynasty, the Chin. The Jurchens practiced a mixed mode of production based on hunting, fishing, cattle raising, and agriculture. Though horseriding was an important part of their culture, they were not nomadic. The Jurchens soon threatened the Liao state, and the Sung, hoping to regain lost territory, sought a military alliance with them. The extent of this miscalculation became apparent when Liao resistance quickly collapsed and the last Liao emperor was captured in 1225. The Chin then launched a full-scale attack on the Sung and in 1126 laid siege to the capital of Kaifeng. Kaifeng fell in early 1127, with the humiliating capture of much of the royal family and countless officials and courtiers, ending the period of the Northern Sung. The Jurchens continued their attack, making incursions south of the Yangtze and even into Chekiang. A Sung prince was set up as the new emperor, beginning the era of the Southern Sung, but for some fifteen years the remains of the Sung government were forced to flee from place to place to avoid the Jurchen advances. Finally, in 1238, the court was able to establish a secure capital at Hangchow, and in 1142 a peace treaty with the Chin was established that fixed the boundary of

---

39 James T. C. Liu, *Reform in Sung China: Wang An-shih (1021–1086) and His New Policies* (Cambridge, Mass.: Harvard University Press, 1959). Wang's economic activism, its connection to military and security needs, and its aftermath are well described by Paul Smith, *Taxing Heaven's Storehouse: Horses, Bureaucrats, and the Destruction of the Sichuan Tea Industry, 1074–1224* (Cambridge, Mass.: Harvard University Press, 1991).

the two states at the Huai river, between the Yellow and Yangtze rivers.[40] (See Map 1.)

During the Southern Sung, the capital was located in the heartland of Chinese prosperity, and despite the periodic wars with the Chin, large indemnity payments, and control of only half of the country, the Southern Sung dynasty generally flourished as the Northern Sung had. Continued external threats to the Chinese state combined with rapid social and economic development to create the context for a rethinking of social policy and cultural values that characterized intellectual life of the Southern Sung. This rethinking set the stage for national changes that took place during the Yüan.

The Chin dynasty in the North was soon faced with external threats of its own from the formidable Mongols, who were in the process of conquering all of Asia. In 1211, Chinggis khan turned his attention to North China and in a series of invasions successively occupied large parts of Chin territory. By 1234 (after the death of Chinggis khan in 1227) the Chin dynasty fell to the Mongols.[41] Further conquest of the South was delayed more by internal Mongol affairs than by effective Sung resistance, and by 1276 the Mongols had gained control of all of South China. The last Sung emperor died at sea in 1279.

The magnitude of the clash between Mongol and Chinese social practices can be appreciated if we understand that it represented a confrontation between two basic world systems of production and reproduction: what the social anthropologist Jack Goody calls the African and the Eurasian, corresponding to the nomadic and the sedentary.[42] The Eurasian model, exemplified by the Chinese, was dominated by fixed agriculture, complex social hierarchies and class distinctions,

---

40 For these developments, and accounts of the Mongols and their conquests, see Frederick W. Mote, *Imperial China 900–1800* (Cambridge, Mass.: Harvard University Press, 1999), chs. 9, 10, 12, 18; and Franke and Twitchett, eds. *Cambridge History of China*, Vol. 6, esp. chs. 3–5. For relevant studies on the Chin, see also Herbert Franke and Hok-lam Chan, *Studies on the Jurchens and the Chin Dynasty*, Variorum Collected Studies Series: CS591 (Aldershot, England: Ashgate Publishing Ltd., 1997); Jing-shen Tao, *The Jurchen in Twelfth Century China* (Seattle: University of Washington Press, 1976); and Hoyt Cleveland Tillman and Stephen H. West, eds. *China under Jurchen Rule* (Albany: State University of New York Press, 1995).

41 For the Sung response to these events, see Charles A. Peterson, "Old Illusions and New Realities: Sung Foreign Policy, 1217–1234," in *China among Equals*, ed. Rossabi, 204–39.

42 Goody first put forth the difference between Africa and Eurasia (India in this case) in Jack Goody and S. J. Tambiah, *Bridewealth and Dowry* (Cambridge: Cambridge University Press, 1973). Goody developed it further in *Production and Reproduction: A Comparative Study of the Domestic Domain* (Cambridge: Cambridge University Press, 1976); and most thoroughly, including China in the analysis, in *The Oriental, the Ancient and the Primitive* (Cambridge: Cambridge University Press, 1990).

and a system of dowry whereby property routinely devolved to women (a system Goody calls "diverging devolution"). The African model by contrast, corresponding to Mongol society, was marked by nomadism or shifting agriculture, relative economic equality, a lack of strict class distinctions, marriage relations dominated by brideprice (that is, payments made from the groom's to the bride's family), and a relative absence of dowry. The Chinese recognized complex land rights, and the government emphasized taxation on the proceeds of land; the Mongols in contrast thought in terms of control over people rather than control over land. This led to different forms of taxation under the Yüan (such as greater emphasis on labor services and the establishment of hereditary soldier households) that had profound implications for women.

Local Conditions: The Prefecture of Chien-ning, Fukien

The national conditions of the Sung and the Mongol invasion form the general context of this book, but much of the evidence used is connected to the region of Northern Fukien, in particular the prefecture of Chien-ning. The two collections of legal cases, one from the Southern Sung and one from the Yüan, on which I rely for many of my conclusions, were both produced in Chien-ning, a center of commercial publishing during this period. Chien-ning was also a major center of the Confucian revival that is so important to our story. It was the home of the most influential leader of this revival, Chu Hsi (1130–1200). And Chu's son-in-law Huang Kan (1152–1221), whose teachings most influenced Yüan Confucianism, served as a prefect there. Likewise the authors of many of my sources were connected to this place. For all these reasons, the local conditions in Chien-ning deserve special attention. In many respects they mirror the developments just described for the whole country.

The area of Chien-ning became a prefecture in 621,[43] and in the Sung comprised seven counties: Chien-an, Chien-yang, Ch'ung-an, Ou-ning, P'u-ch'eng, Sung-ch'i, and Cheng-ho.[44] (See Map 2.) The prefecture was

43 Northern Fukien was not fully integrated into the Han Chinese cultural sphere until waves of migration in the seventh century, by which time there were flourishing trade routes through the area of Chien-ning up the Min river from the coast; Hans Bielenstein, "The Chinese Colonization of Fukien until the End of the T'ang," in *Studia Serica Bernhard Karlgren Dedica*, ed. Soren Egerod (Copenhagen: Ejnar Munksgaard, 1959), 102–11; Hugh Clark, *Community, Trade, and Networks: Southern Fujian Province from the Third to Thirteenth Century* (Cambridge: Cambridge University Press, 1991), 7–18; Billy Kee-long So, "Economic Developments in South Fukien, 946–1276" (Ph.D. dissertation, Australian National University, 1982), 12.

44 Some of these changed their names over the course of the Sung and Yüan. See Hope Wright, *Alphabetical List of Geographic Names in Sung China* (Paris: École Pratique des Hautes Études, 1956), 21.

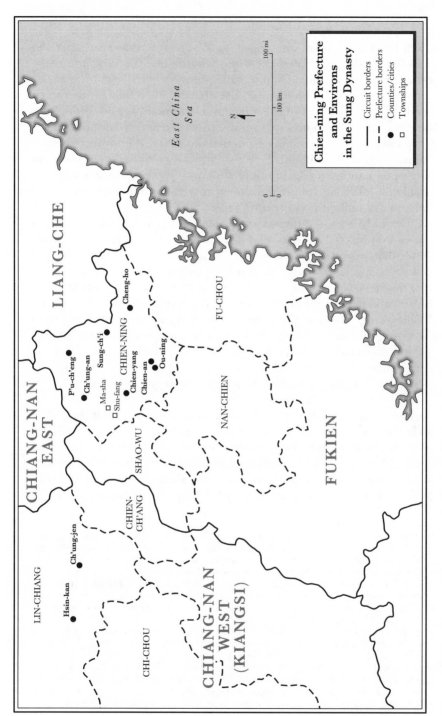

Map 2. Chien-ning prefecture and environs in the Sung dynasty.

raised from a "regular" one (*chou*) to a "superior" one (*fu*), after the emperor Kao-tsung resided there temporarily in 1162, and the name was changed from Chien-chou to Chien-ning-fu.

The population of Chien-ning, like that of all of Fukien, increased rapidly in the early part of the Sung, and continued to rise throughout the dynasty. Census figures that survive from 980 and 1080 show a more than doubling of Chien-ning's population in these hundred years to almost 200,000 households.[45] According to the 1162 census, Chien-ning's population had again doubled to over 400,000 households. The population of Fukien showed a similar increase of fourfold during the Sung, to 1.7 million households in 1225.[46]

Chien-ning was a mountainous inland district, far from Fukien's coastal commercial centers of Fu-chou and Ch'üan-chou. But trade routes that passed through the prefectural seat saved it from being a backwater and kept its elite in touch with developments in the rest of the empire. Tea from the area was prized throughout the empire, and timber, silk, paper, and porcelain were all exported from the region.[47]

Chien-yang county, in Chien-ning, was the center of a flourishing commercial publishing industry. Books on every subject were produced at the printing centers of Ma-sha and Shu-fang, in Chien-yang, and the trade extended throughout East Asia.[48] The large number of books that survive from these publishing houses accounts for the provenance of many of the sources for this study.

Chien-ning had a strong tradition of scholarship and education. The prefecture produced more metropolitan graduates (*chin-shih*), 809 in all, than any other prefecture during the Northern Sung. It continued to do well in the Southern Sung, with a total of 1,318 over the course of the entire Sung dynasty, second only to its Fukien neighbor Fu-chou.[49] As the home of the famous philosopher Chu Hsi, it became a natural

---

45 These figures are from the *T'ai-p'ing huan-yü chi* and *Yüan-feng chiu-yü chih*; see Clark, *Community, Trade, and Networks,* 74–5; and Bielenstein, "Historical Demography," 75. Population statistics for the Sung are incomplete and not yet fully understood, but they are reliable in revealing basic trends like those described here.

46 Population figures are found in *Sung shih* (Peking: Chung-hua shu chü, 1977), ch. 88–90. Additional provincial totals for the Southern Sung, mostly from the *Sung hui-yao*, are reproduced in Clark, *Community, Trade, and Networks,* 74, and Bielenstein, "Historical Demography," 77–9.

47 Shiba, *Commerce and Society in Sung China,* 183. For the later tea production in this area, see Robert Gardella, *Harvesting Mountains: Fujian and the China Tea Trade, 1757–1937* (Berkeley: University of California Press, 1994).

48 See Lucille Chia, "Printing for Profit: the Commercial Printers of Jianyang, Fujian (Song-Ming)" (Ph.D. dissertation, Columbia University, 1996). Remnants of the Ma-sha and Shu-fang works remain today, and some have been reconstructed for visitors.

49 Chaffee, *Thorny Gates,* 149, 197. Fu-chou, Fukien, had 2,799 *chin-shih* in the Sung.

center of the Confucian revivalist, Learning of the Way movement. Its teaching was spread through private academies, as many as seven being founded in Chien-yang county alone, of which the most important was K'ao-t'ing shu-yüan, where Chu Hsi taught. Numerous shrines to Confucian worthies, often within the academies, further promoted Confucian ritual, religion, and study.[50]

Religion of all kinds flourished in Fukien.[51] Prior to the Sung, the area was controlled by the Kingdom of Min (A.D. 879–978), a Buddhist state, and after the Sung conquest, the strength of the Buddhist establishment persisted. In the Northern Sung as much as one-third, and in the Southern Sung as much as one-fifth, of the total cultivated land in Fukien was controlled by Buddhist temples.[52] The number of Buddhist monks was also high, especially in the cities of the southeast coast, perhaps reflecting the pressure of population growth.[53] In Chienning, away from the Buddhist centers of the coast, lay Buddhist movements flourished. The White Lotus society was especially strong in Chien-yang toward the end of the Sung and into the Yüan; followers built halls of worship as well as bridges and other public works.[54] Manichaeanism had many adherents throughout Fukien, as did other popular religious movements. Uninformed officials lumped together followers of various cults as dreaded Manichaeans or "vegetable eaters and demon worshipers," whom they feared could inspire local rebellions.[55] Fukien was also known in Sung times (as it is today) for a major school of geomancy.[56]

---

50 Thomas H. C. Lee, "Neo-Confucian Education in Chien-yang, Fu-chien, 1000–1400: Academies, Society, and the Development of Local Culture," in *Kuo-chi Chu-tzu hsüeh-hui i-lun wen-chi* (Taipei: Academia Sinica, 1993), 945–96; and Wing-tsit Chan, "Chu Hsi and the Academies," in *Neo-Confucian Education*, ed. de Bary and Chaffee, esp. 400–1. For more on Confucian shrines, see Neskar, "The Cult of Worthies"; and for Chien-ning's reputation for scholarship, see Shiba, *Commerce and Society in Sung China*, 181–2.

51 This tradition continues today. The revival of Christianity is thought to be stronger there than in any other province in China. (Personal communication from officials and clergy in Chien-yang, Fukien, Sept. 1988.)

52 Chikusa Masaaki, *Chūgoku bukkyō shakaishi kenkyū* (Kyoto: Dōhōsha, 1982), 151. For pre-Sung, see Edward Schafer, *The Empire of Min* (Rutland, Vt.: Charles E. Tuttle, 1954).

53 Chikusa argues that monks comprised as much as 0.5% of the male population; *Bukkyō*, 158.

54 Barend J. ter Haar, *The White Lotus Teachings in Chinese Religious History* (Leiden: E. J. Brill, 1992), esp. 80–2, 93–6.

55 Chikusa, *Bukkyō*, 199–260; ter Haar, *White Lotus Teachings*, 48–55. See also Gernet, *China on the Eve of the Mongol Invasion*, 208–10; and Daniel Overmyer, *Folk Buddhist Religion* (Cambridge, Mass.: Harvard University Press, 1976), 77 (citing Hung Mai, d. 1202).

56 Ebrey, *Confucianism and Family Rituals*, 140. Chu Hsi himself praised the Fukien and Kiangsi schools of geomancy.

What little evidence we have suggests that the mountainous areas of Northern Fukien were cultivated largely by small proprietors. Tenancy was also common, and land frequently changed hands through sale or mortgage (or inheritance). The manor system with indentured field-workers that characterized the more peripheral areas of the upper Yangtze was not present in Chien-ning.[57] The land was intensely cultivated, and hillsides were probably terraced in much of the prefecture.

Under good conditions, Chien-ning could produce enough rice for local needs and transport some to the coastal prefectures, which also imported rice by sea.[58] Early ripening Champa rice grew well in the poor, hilly soil of the area, but farmers had to cultivate or purchase less gluti-nous, late-ripening varieties to pay taxes and rents.[59] Floods from the Wu-i mountains and unreliable weather, as well as low capital inputs, made the margin of subsistence narrow. Monocrop agriculture among the poor, unstable harvests, and dependence on the market caused violent price fluctuations, which plunged families into debt and explains the frequent mortgaging of land.[60] Salt smuggling was a chronic problem in Chien-ning, and the prefecture was known in the Sung as a place where infanticide was rife.[61]

The insecure agricultural economy meant there was a constant threat of famine and uprisings. During the Southern Sung, harvest shortfalls occurred in Chien-ning in 1150 and 1167–8. Major food riots broke out in 1187, 1191, 1194, and 1207, when starving peasants seized granaries of the rich and killed any found hoarding grain. Philosopher Chu Hsi witnessed a bloody rice riot in his home county of Ch'ung-an in 1188.[62] Sung government attempts to provide relief and control prices through charitable granaries (*i-ts'ang*) and ever-normal granaries (*ch'ang-p'ing-*

---

57 Joseph McDermott, "Charting Blank Spaces," 30; Gudula Linck, *Zur Sozialgeschichte der Chinesischen Familie im 13. Jahrhundert* (Stuttgart: Franz Steiner Verlag, 1986), 221.

58 Shiba, *Sōdai shōgyōshi kenkyū*, 161–2; Shiba, *Commerce and Society in Sung China*, 61.

59 The government demanded taxes in high-quality, low-gluten rice since it could be stored longer.

60 Richard von Glahn, "Community and Welfare: Chu Hsi's Community Granary in Theory and Practice," in *Ordering the World: Approaches to State and Society in Sung Dynasty China*, ed. Robert Hymes and Conrad Schirokauer (Berkeley: University of California Press, 1993), 225 and n. 4.

61 *Sung hui-yao* (Peking: Chung-hua shu-chü, 1957; reprint 1987), hsing-fa Pt. 2, 49:49b, 56b (Vol. 7, pp. 6520, 6523). See also Niida Noboru, *Chūgoku hōseishi kenkyū*, Vol. 3, *Dorei nōdohō, kazoku sonrakuhō* (Tokyo: Tōkyō daigaku shuppankai, 1962; reprint 1991), 389, 391 n. 6; and Shiba, *Sōdai shōgyōshi kenkyū*, 429, 430 n. 2. Shiba cites a number of other Sung officials who complain about infanticide in Northern Fukien.

62 Watanabe Hiroyoshi, "Junki matzunen no Kenneifu: shasōgome no konrai to tairyō to," in *Nakajima Satoshi sensei koki kinen ronshū* (Tokyo: Kaimeidō, 1981), 204–6; von Glahn, "Community and Welfare," 223, 243.

ts'ang) failed to solve the problems. Then in the Southern Sung, public spirited officials and residents (including Chu Hsi) tried to establish private "community granaries" (*she-ts'ang*) to lend to the poor.[63] These worked in some areas for a time, but in Chien-ning the institutions broke down after a decade or two. Influential families would borrow grain under false names, then refuse to repay. Local officials were powerless to force them to do so.[64] By the early thirteenth century the system had collapsed, and following this, in 1232, there was a major uprising in the Wu-i Mountains, which was put down at great cost.

The problems just described explain why northern Fukien was considered hard to govern. In a memorial assessing the successes and failures of the community granary system, Chu Hsi's son-in-law Huang Kan, while a prefect of Chien-ning, had this to say:

> Of all the customs I have seen in Fukien, Chien-ning-fu's are the worst, making it the hardest area to govern. The mountains are steep and the rivers are dangerous; thus the common people like to quarrel and they treat human life lightly. The soil is bad, and the hillside fields are cramped; thus the great families lack a sense of charity and are miserly about donating grain [to the poor]. They take five or six pints [of grain] to make a peck.[65] The price of a peck is not more than 50–60 cash, but if there is a drought, within one month the price goes up to 100. The great families close their granaries and wait for the highest price. The commoners get together and kill people to get at their grain. The rural villages are thrown into a panic, but the officials are hard pressed to punish [the perpetrators]. [The rioters] withdraw to strongholds, and when there is a risk of being captured, they signal each other by whistling and change their hideouts.[66]

Chien-ning was not the only prefecture that was hard to govern – all of northern Fukien was notorious, – and Huang's doom and gloom

---

63 von Glahn, "Community and Welfare"; Hoyt Tillman, "Intellectuals and Officials in Action: Academies and Granaries in Sung China," *Asia Major*, 3rd series, 4:2 (1991): 8–14; and Watanabe, "Junki matzunen no Kenneifu," 195–217. Foundling granaries were also established to prevent infanticide, but these in themselves were not supported by Chu Hsi; von Glahn, "Community and Welfare," 240–2.

64 Watanabe, "Junki matzunen no Kenneifu," 196–9. For accounts from officials about their helplessness against local magnates, see Hymes, *Statesmen*, 206–9. This includes comments by Huang Kan from Chien-ning (during his tenure in Fu-chou, Kiangsi). Local powerbrokers often had official connections themselves; see Chikusa Masaaki, "HokuSō shidaifu no tokyo to baiden: omoni Tōhan sekitaku o shiryō toshite" *Shirin* 54:2 (1971); and Chikusa Masaaki "Sōdai kanryō no kikyo ni tsuite" *Tōyōshi kenkyū* 41:1 (1982), 28–57.

65 A peck (*tou*) was about 9 liters of dry measure but could vary widely (going as low as 6 liters). In modern times a peck was standardized to 10 liters and contained ten Chinese pints (*sheng*). Note that according to Huang, in Sung Chien-ning a peck contained only "five or six" pints.

66 *Mien-chai chi* (SKCS chen-pen ed.), 18:19b.

description may convey an exaggerated impression of the problems of the day. Nevertheless, his comments give us some idea of the importance of land to the people of Chien-ning and elsewhere, and the uncertain economic situation in which many of them found themselves. This helps to explain the many disputes over land and the importance of women's inheritance of it, for themselves and for others around them.

Chu Hsi (1130–1200) and the Learning of the Way (Tao-Hsüeh)

The Sung dynasty is perhaps best known for a revival of Confucianism as the dominant intellectual influence in the lives of the literati. After several centuries during which Buddhism had gained a permanent place in Chinese society, a number of prominent scholar-officials began to attack it and to redefine classical Confucianism to respond to the challenges of Buddhism. The Confucian revival had already begun in the T'ang with men like Han Yü (768–824) and Li Ao (d. ca. 844). But it gained popularity and vigor in the Northern Sung, and different approaches and emphases began to emerge, with men like Ou-yang Hsiu (1007–1070), Wang An-shih (1021–1086), and Ssu-ma Kuang (1019–1086). One branch concerned itself with issues of cosmology and personal salvation, and this emerged as the dominant form of Confucianism from Yüan times on. This branch, which grew out of the thought of the Northern Sung philosopher Ch'eng I (1033–1107) and his brother Ch'eng Hao (1032–1085), and whose main interpreter was Chu Hsi, developed into what followers called *tao-hsüeh*, or the "Learning of the Way," sometimes translated "Neo-Confucianism" or "Orthodox Neo-Confucianism."[67] It is also known as the Ch'eng-Chu school, or Ch'eng-Chu Confucianism, after its two founders.

67 "Neo-Confucianism" was used to translate *tao-hsüeh* by Derk Bodde translating Fung Yu-lan, *A History of Chinese Philosophy*, Vol. 2 (Princeton, N.J.: Princeton University Press, 1953), chs. 10–13. Since then, Wm. Theodore de Bary has argued for the narrower term "Orthodox Neo-Confucianism" to distinguish the broader Confucian revival in the Sung from the more narrow Chu Hsi school that developed at the end of the dynasty; "Introduction," in *The Rise of Neo-Confucianism in Korea*, ed. Wm. Theodore de Bary and JaHyun Kim Haboush (New York: Columbia University Press, 1985), 4–17; and Wm. Theodore de Bary, *The Liberal Tradition in China* (Hong Kong and New York, 1983), 5–6. To avoid confusion, I have chosen the more literal "Learning of the Way" as the English rendering of *tao-hsüeh*. But it should be kept in mind that the term *tao-hsüeh* too was understood differently over time and by different contemporary authors, as the movement developed from a broad fellowship to a narrow orthodoxy, and eventually back to a broad social movement in the late Sung and Yüan; see esp. Hoyt Tillman, *Confucian Discourse and Chu Hsi's Ascendancy* (Honolulu: University of Hawaii Press, 1992). For a brief discussion of problems with the term *tao-hsüeh*, see Conrad Schirokauer and Robert Hymes, "Introduction," in *Ordering the World: Approaches to State*

The term *tao-hsüeh* reflects the emphasis that Ch'eng I and his followers gave to the concept *tao*, "the Way." The *tao* represented for these Confucians a path of moral action, dictated by study of the Confucian classics and religious self-awareness, together termed self-cultivation (*hsiu-shen*). The emphasis on moral action was part of a self-conscious effort to shift the focus of literati endeavor from what can broadly be called "culture" (*wen*) to a more narrow morality, or *tao*.[68] The goal was to realize in contemporary society the moral path found in the Confucian classics through a fundamentalist reading of the ancient texts. To this end, Learning of the Way Confucians founded schools and academies to spread their teaching and established shrines to Confucian worthies who were deemed to have transmitted the true *tao* (a process called *tao-t'ung*).[69] The direct appeal to a new fundamentalist interpretation of the classics provided a source of authority and intellectual legitimacy independent of contemporary government institutions or the immediate historical past. This allowed radical solutions that broke from long tradition to be couched in terms of a "return" to ancient values and true Confucian morality. Such was their approach to the role of women and interpretation of marriage law.

The *tao-hsüeh* movement began in the twelfth century as a loose fellowship of literati influenced by several intellectual giants, primarily Lü Tsu-ch'ien (1137–1181).[70] After Lü's death, Chu Hsi emerged as the dominant figure, and the scope of the fellowship shrank as Chu articulated a more narrow orthodoxy of ideas. Chu's many writings synthesized the thought of earlier philosophers and formed the core of the *tao-hsüeh* teaching for later generations. His principal disciple was his son-in-law Huang Kan, who studied with him in Chien-ning and served in office there. By the late Southern Sung, Learning of the Way

and Society in Sung Dynasty China, 9–12. For discussion of the appropriateness of terms like "Neo-Confucianism," see Hoyt Cleveland Tillman, "A New Direction in Confucian Scholarship: Approaches to Examining the Differences between Neo-Confucianism and *Tao-hsüeh*," *Philosophy East and West* 42:3 (July 1992): 455–74; Wm. Theodore de Bary, "Uses of Neo-Confucianism: A Response to Professor Tillman," *Philosophy East and West* (Jan. 1993); Hoyt Cleveland Tillman, "The Uses of Neo-Confucianism, Revisited: A Reply to Professor de Bary"; and Wm. Theodore de Bary, "Reply to Hoyt Cleveland Tillman," *Philosophy East and West* 44:1 (1994): 135–44. See also Peter K. Bol, *"This Culture of Ours": Intellectual Transitions in T'ang and Sung China* (Stanford, Calif.: Stanford University Press, 1992), 27–31. Readers should note that in modern scholarship on the Yüan and beyond, the Confucian school that I call here "Learning of the Way" is routinely termed "Neo-Confucianism;" see for instance Franke and Twitchett eds., *The Cambridge History of China*, Vol. 6, and Martina Deuchler, *The Confucian Transformation of Korea* (Cambridge, Mass.: Harvard University Press, 1992).

68 This essential point about Sung *tao-hsüeh* is developed by Peter Bol in *"This Culture of Ours"*.

69 See Neskar, "The Cult of Worthies."   70 Tillman, *Confucian Discourse*.

Confucianism had blossomed into an intellectual, religious, and social movement that had broad appeal to much of the southern scholarly elite. It offered a justification for the elite to concentrate on local prestige through community action instead of high official position at the capital, which was unattainable for most with the increased competition on the civil service examinations. The teaching also provided moral and social justification for elite dominance of local society, independent of government authority.

After the Mongol conquest of the South, Chu's teachings spread north and quickly gained adherents at the Mongol court. In 1313, the Mongol-Yüan government made Chu Hsi's commentaries on a newly defined Confucian canon the basis of the reinstituted civil service examinations,[71] and this new government-sponsored orthodoxy thereafter dominated Chinese intellectual life. The penetration of Chu Hsi's thought into North China can be traced to three intellectual lineages. All three of these originated with Chu Hsi's disciple Huang Kan, and Huang's interpretation of the Learning of the Way thus became the standard for Yüan and later dynasties.[72] This had bearing on marriage and property law (See Chapter 4).

The Learning of the Way had special meaning for daily life, and for women as a result. Transformation of society began with the individual and the family. The individual sought spiritual rejuvenation akin to religious salvation through moral self-cultivation. The family was the setting for moral cultivation and served as a model for the society and state. Moreover, proper ritual relations and moral purity within the family connected the individual to the universal principles of the cosmos. Just as in some schools of Ch'an Buddhism daily life took on religious overtones, the household was the holy temple of the religion of the Learning of the Way.[73] What to most people had once seemed mundane and routine took on the nature of sacred action that now had to accord with duty and principle.

The Confucian tradition stressed an exaggerated differentiation of sex roles and set up relational boundaries between men and women to

71 Wm. Theodore de Bary, *Neo-Confucian Orthodoxy and the Learning of the Mind and Heart* (New York: Columbia University Press, 1981), 1–66. The Mongols had cancelled the examinations when they came into power.
72 Wing-tsit Chan, "Chu Hsi and Yüan Neo-Confucianism," in *Yüan Thought: Chinese Thought and Religion under the Mongols*, ed. Hok-lam Chan and Wm. Theodore de Bary (New York: Columbia University Press, 1982).
73 For an elaboration of these points, see Theresa Kelleher, "Confucianism," in *Women in World Religions*, ed. Arvind Sharma (Albany: State University of New York Press, 1987); and Theresa Kelleher, "Reflections on Persons at Hand: The Position of Women in Ch'eng-Chu Neo-Confucianism," paper presented at Annual Meeting of the Association for Asian Studies, March 22–4, 1985, Philadelphia.

divide both physical space and social function. It separated women and men conceptually by proclaiming their "natural" realms to be the "inner" (*nei*) and the "outer" (*wai*), respectively. Women were understood to be uniquely suited for the inner sphere of domestic and reproductive labor: taking care of food, clothing, birth, and child rearing. Early writings assigned women attributes that rendered them unsuited for public leadership or work outside the home. Throughout history they were thus excluded from government schools, private academies, officeholding, the civil service examinations, and almost any kind of legitimate political power.[74] Men were assigned the public sphere, or "outside," sphere of scholarship, government, and commerce.

The Confucian classics equated the functional distinction between the two spheres with a spatial one: "They built the mansion and its apartments, distinguishing between exterior and interior parts. The men occupied the exterior; the women the interior. . . . The men did not enter the interior; the women did not come out into the exterior."[75] Promoters of the Confucian revival in the Sung reiterated the physical separation of the sexes and made it a foundation of their philosophy. Philosophers like Ssu-ma Kuang boasted of a strict Confucian household, where even female servants were forbidden to move beyond the inner courtyards, let alone the young mistresses. According to this prescription, when women did have to venture out, they were to be veiled.[76] In reality we know that poorer women in the Sung worked in the fields, sold goods in the market, acted as matchmakers and midwives, and carried on multifarious activities that precluded any strict seclusion

74 For sex roles and misogyny in the Confucian classics, see for instance Richard Guisso, "Thunder over the Lake: the Five Classics and the Perception of Woman in Early China," in *Women in China*, ed. Richard Guisso and Stanley Johannesen (Youngstown, N.Y.: Philo Press, 1981). See also Ebrey, *Inner Quarters*, 23–7. Of course other traditions, including the Western, assigned similar differences to gender roles. A good overview is found in Michelle Rosaldo, "Women, Culture, and Society: A Theoretical Overview," and Sherry Ortner, "Is Female to Male as Nature Is to Culture?" both in *Women, Culture, and Society*, ed. Michelle Rosaldo and Louise Lamphere (Stanford, Calif.: Stanford University Press, 1974). For the wider significance of these binary constructs, see for instance, Joan Scott, *Gender and the Politics of History* (New York: Columbia University Press, 1988), esp. 28–52.

75 Legge trans., *Li Chi* (1885; reprint New York: University Books, 1967), I, 470–1; *Hsiao-hsüeh chi-chieh*, by Chu Hsi (Kuo-hsüeh chi-pen ts'ung-shu ed.; reprint, Taipei: Commercial Press, 1968), 33–4. See also Bettine Birge, "Chu Hsi and Women's Education," in *Neo-Confucian Education*, ed. de Bary and Chaffee, 331–3; and discussion in Ebrey, *Inner Quarters*, 21–7.

76 *Ssu-ma shih shu-i* (TSCC ed.) 4:43. Men slept in the inner "women's" quarters at night, but were to avoid entering them during the day. As Ssu-ma's prescription shows, there were always exceptions to the separation.

as envisaged by Confucian idealists.[77] As for elite women in the Sung, it is hard to tell how much the rhetoric of seclusion affected the majority of them. Paintings show very few women on the streets, but these may represent the ideal more than reality.[78] After the Sung, however, in later imperial times, the seclusion of women became an important mark of family virtue such that, where a family's resources allowed, elite women ventured into the streets only in carefully chaperoned outings.[79]

Chu Hsi and others in the Learning of the Way fellowship paid considerable attention to a woman's domestic role. Their writings on the subject appear mostly in the form of funerary inscriptions (*mu-chih-ming*), eulogistic biographies written after a person's death. These documents include only selective information about a person's life and are filled with standard comments of praise. Often the author did not know the subject personally and was writing from second- or third-hand information. While funerary inscriptions cannot be trusted to tell the whole story, they nevertheless reveal what was considered praiseworthy and virtuous in a woman's behavior. They represent models of ideal behavior that were to be emulated by others, and thus accurately reveal the Learning of the Way agenda for women.[80] I rely on these

77 For instance, a late Sung commentator in Shao-wu, Fukien, claimed that more market stalls were run by women than by men, and another described female brokers dominating commerce in the county seat. See Shiba, *Sōdai shōgyōshi kenkyū*, 429; Shiba, *Commerce and Society in Sung China*, 187.

78 Valerie Hansen, *The Beijing Qingming Scroll and Its Significance for the Study of Chinese History* (Albany, N.Y.: Journal of Sung-Yuan Studies, 1996), 4–5; Ebrey, *Inner Quarters*, 21–2. As in other societies, seclusion probably operated mostly as a series of mutual behaviors between men and women that minimized contact between members of the opposite sex, especially strangers; see Bettine Birge, "Review of *Chu Hsi's Family Rituals: A Twelfth-Century Manual for the Performance of Cappings, Weddings, Funerals, and Ancestral Rites*, trans. by Patricia Ebrey," *Chinese Literature: Essays, Articles Reviews* 16 (1994): 160. By late Sung times and after, bound feet also limited a woman's mobility.

79 For seclusion in the late imperial period, see Francesca Bray, *Technology and Gender: Fabrics of Power in Late Imperial China* (Berkeley: University of California Press, 1997); Susan Mann, *Precious Records: Women in China's Long Eighteenth Century* (Stanford, Calif.: Stanford University Press, 1997); and Dorothy Ko, *Teachers of the Inner Chambers: Women and Culture in Seventh-Century China* (Stanford, Calif.: Stanford University Press, 1994). Comments from poetry suggest that separation of the sexes and the seclusion of women were more intense in the later period. See Robert Hymes, "Review of *The Inner Quarters: Marriage and the Lives of Chinese Women in the Sung Period*, by Patricia Ebrey," *Harvard Journal of Asiatic Studies* 57:1 (June 1997): 236.

80 Funerary inscriptions also give accurate and invaluable biographical data, such as birth and death dates, year of marriage, spouse's name, and offices held; see list of items to include by Ssu-ma Kuang (*Ssu-ma shih shu-i* 7:80). For more detail about the composition of funerary inscriptions and an analysis of those of Chu Hsi, see Birge, "Chu Hsi and Women's Education." For the accuracy of inscriptions, see also Angela Schotten-

heavily in Chapter 3, where I describe the Confucian reaction to women's property rights.

The descriptions in funerary inscriptions of the activities of exemplary women bring out for us today the artificiality of the inner–outer binary. The boundaries between male and female, inner and outer activity necessarily shifted, so that behavior that fit into the masculine/outer category in one context could switch to the feminine/inner in another. (Space inside the home could also shift in this way.) This shifting nature of gender roles is evident from the writings of Sung Confucians on a woman's duties in the household. Chu Hsi and others associated with the Learning of the Way stressed obedience and subordination as exemplified in the "Three Obediences," which taught that women should obey their fathers when at home, their husbands after marriage, and their sons in old age.[81] Nevertheless, Chu Hsi and others called on a wife to be her husband's helpmate, and this extended to advising her husband on problems in the "outside" world, such as those encountered in resolving lawsuits or dealing with bureaucratic corruption.[82]

Going beyond advising her husband, Chu Hsi and other Sung Confucians assigned women an independent and vital role as household managers. In this arena, the boundary between inner and outer appears especially ambiguous. Sung writers eulogized senior wives for managing large households with a strong hand, including acting as household bursar.[83] Such activities went beyond supervising

hammer, "Characteristics of Song Epitaphs," in *Burial in Song China*, ed. Dieter Kuhn (Heidelberg: Edition Forum, 1994); and for their placement in graves, see Dieter Kuhn, "Decoding Tombs of the Song Elite," in *Burial in Song China*, ed. Kuhn, 38–9. For T'ang, see Denis Twitchett, *The Writing of Official History under the T'ang* (Cambridge: Cambridge University Press, 1992), 71–5.

81 Chu Hsi includes this in his prescriptive text, the *Elementary Learning*, see *Hsiao-hsüeh*, 35–6. The doctrine was first made popular in the Han dynasty; Albert O'Hara, *The Position of Women in Early China: According to the* Lieh-nü chuan, *"The Biographies of Eminent Chinese Women"* (Westport, Conn.: Hyperion Press, 1945, reprint 1981), 42. Similar obedience was called for by Pan Chao (A.D. 45–114?) in her "Lessons for Women," which Chu Hsi much admired; Nancy Lee Swann, *Pan Chao: Foremost Woman Scholar of China* (New York: Century Co., 1932). The doctrine of filial piety counteracted the Three Obediences. Filial piety dictated that a man obey his parents, including his mother, and mothers thus had considerable influence and authority over their sons at any age.

82 *Chu Wen-kung wen-chi* (SPTK ed.), 90:19b; 92:3b. For more on these cases, see Bettine Birge, "Woman and Property in Sung Dynasty China" (Ph.D. dissertation, Columbia University, 1992), 298–300.

83 A woman's authority over others varied of course according to her life-cycle position. While a young wife had to give devoted service to her mother- and father-in-law and obey their every command, after they died she moved into the position of mistress of the household. When her own sons brought brides into the house, she gained the power of a mother-in-law herself.

household servants and advising their husbands in office to include arranging marriages, conducting funerals, hiring farm laborers, buying and selling land, keeping household accounts, collecting rents, aiding relatives in need, and distributing relief to the community. The activities of women were considered to be in the realm of "inner" (*nei*) only in relation to the complementary activities of men. The writings of Chu Hsi stand out for his approval of men *not* paying careful attention to household affairs and money matters. Men could better spend their time on education, moral self-cultivation, and "outside" affairs like serving in office. It was preferable for men not to burden themselves with household management or sully themselves with matters of money. This gender dynamic relegated considerable authority to women, including the power of the purse and control of property.

The emphasis on women as household managers made the position of the widow especially important to followers of Chu Hsi. A widow had to hold the household together and ensure the survival of the family line. It was in the capacity of widow that women might gain total responsibility for a household's income and expenditure. The ability of a widow to overcome the hardships facing her and be able to educate her sons and get them established was the highest achievement for a woman. A widow had to take over for her husband and make possible the continuance of his line of descendants, who would sacrifice to him after death. The loyalty of a widow to her husband also took on metaphorical significance. A wife who served two husbands by remarrying was akin to the minister who abandoned his ruler and served another. Uncompromising loyalty was an important virtue for Confucian revivalists, and the chaste widow represented such virtue. This stance would dictate their reaction to Sung property law, which in many respects encouraged the remarriage of widows.

For the family and society to be reformed, women had to be part of the process. The interconnectedness and dependence between men and women, both ideologically and materially, explains why Chu Hsi and Learning of the Way reformers gave considerable attention to women in their vision of a new and transformed social order. Society could not be in order for men unless women were also in their proper place, with appropriate rules and restrictions dictating their actions. These attitudes extended to women's property rights, and eventually, through a complicated process of social change, affected women's economic independence.

Women's Property: Conceptions, Language, and Significance

The Language of Minimization

Property attached to a woman was a conceptual anomaly in a patrilineal society where the family line and theoretically the patrimony passed only through men. The language to describe women's property reflects this conceptual gap. Terms used for married women's property tend to minimize its importance and reduce any consciousness of it as an economic force. They stress the private and personal nature of it, and give the impression that it was movable not real.[84]

The most common term in the Sung for property that a bride took into marriage is *chuang-lien* (粧奩).[85] The word *chuang* means "to adorn" and refers to a woman's personal toilette. In the Sung, the ideograph was usually written with the rice radical, signifying the white rice powder of makeup. The character *lien* means simply box or case. The great Sung dictionary *Kuang-yün* defines it as a box for incense or perfume; it could also mean a mirrored box, used for combs and makeup.[86] The term *chuang-lien* thus literally means "makeup box," an item for adornment of the wife's own body, and the term was sometimes used in medieval China with this basic meaning.[87] More often, however, it was used as a synecdoche to refer to all of a married woman's property, which can be seen from earliest surviving records to have included much more than cosmetics. In the Sung, words like *chuang-lien* often denoted landed property.[88]

An array of other words also signified women's property, landed or movable, with similar euphemistic usages. The single word *chuang* 裝 (to be distinguished from the preceding word also pronounced *chuang*) has the meaning of "to wrap or tie in a bundle," thereby deriving from the

---

84 In early times before land was easily exchanged, dowry was always movable.

85 Variant characters were sometimes used for *chuang*. I have not found the common modern term *chia-chuang* in any Sung text. For the equation of both these terms with "dowry," see Tai Yen-hui, "Divorce in Traditional Chinese Law," in *Chinese Family Law and Social Change*, ed. David Buxbaum (Seattle: University of Washington Press, 1978), 105.

86 Morohashi, *Dai kanwa jiten* (Tokyo: Taishūkan, 1960), Vol. 3, 606. For examples, see *Fei-jan chi*, 26:15b; *T'ao-shan chi*, 16:186.

87 See Morohashi, *Dai kanwa jiten*, Vol. 3, 653 for a T'ang example.

88 For a few examples, see *Chiang-su chin-shih chih* (reprint *Shih-k'o shih-liao hsin-pien*, Vol. 13), 14:27a (p. 9781); CMC 10:365; Shiga Shūzō, *Chūgoku kazokuhō no genri* (Tokyo: Sōbunsha, 1967; reprint 1981), 516–17 [hereafter cited as *Genri*].

same root meaning as the English word trousseau.[89] Both the European and Chinese terms have a connotation of baggage prepared for traveling; in both cases the traveler is a bride leaving her parents and going to a new home.[90] (See Figure 1.) Appropriately, another meaning for *chuang* is to load, pack, or store.

Boxes, bags, and baskets are used to store personal belongings, and specific words with these meanings are found in Sung and Yüan sources to mean a bride's possessions. *Nang* 囊 denotes a large sack, while *t'o* 橐 means a small one.[91] Sometimes they were used together, and sometimes they were combined with other words to mean property brought with the bride (e.g., *t'o-chung* 橐中 or *nang t'o* 囊橐).[92] Bamboo boxes or baskets are suggested by the words *ch'ieh* 箧 or *fei* 篚. Again, the context of many Sung usages makes it clear that these words in combinations like *lien-fei* 奩篚 or *nang-ch'ieh* 囊箧 denoted a woman's private property whether real or movable.[93] All of these words underscore the personal, private nature of a woman's property in marriage. The suggestion therein that it could not be simply appropriated by her husband will be confirmed in the chapters below.

When a wealthy family in the Sung or Yüan sent their daughter out in marriage, they typically outfitted her lavishly with both movable items for her conjugal "room" (*fang*) and real property that could include land, buildings, and even businesses. In contexts where it mattered, such as during the marriage negotiations or in the final dowry list, Sung Chinese used language that specified whether the property was movable or not. For example, they might say *tzu-sui-t'ien* 自隨田, meaning "fields brought along" or "lands that followed [the bride into marriage]," or *sui-chia t'ien-t'u* 隨嫁田土 "land brought along into marriage."[94] Even landed property picked up associations with the inner boudoir in common expressions like *lien-t'ien* 奩田, literally

---

89 Morohashi, *Dai kanwa jiten*, Vol. 10, 226. For Chinese usages, see for instance Chu Hsi, *Chu Wen-kung wen-chi*, 90:15a, 92:3b. Variant forms with different radicals are found in Sung texts. The word "trousseau" derives from the medieval French word "trussel" meaning "bundle" or "parcel."

90 Of course the destination of the move was different in the two cases. In Europe new-lywed couples set up a new household, while in China the bride moved to the home of her husband's parents.

91 Morohashi, *Dai kanwa jiten*, Vol. 2, 1187; Vol. 6, 550. Another gloss gives the meanings as sacks with and without bottoms.

92 E.g., CMC 10:365; *Chu Wen-kung wen-chi*, 90:15a, 91:14a. Ssu-ma Ch'ien (145–90? B.C.) in his *Records of the Historian* used the expression *t'o-chung chuang* to mean money and jewels stored in a sack or purse; *Shih chi* (Peking: Chung-hua shu-chü, 1959; reprint, 1982), 97:2698.

93 E.g., *Tung-hsüan pi-lu* 12:90; CMC 10:366.

94 E.g., CMC 8:258, 259, 366; *Meng-liang lu*, 20:304. Conversely, terms like *lien-chü* were sometimes used to indicate that property was movable.

"cosmetics-box fields." *Lien* always indicated property of a married woman. Words like *nü-t'ien* 女田, "daughter's fields," indicated fields owned by a woman who was probably unmarried.[95] All of these terms were common in the Sung and Yüan and appear along with others in later times.[96]

Conceptually and linguistically these different kinds of property were lumped together. Sung writers made no systematic distinction between movable and immovable property, or between property that was purely for the woman (like jewelry and cosmetics), and that which might be used jointly with the husband (like land). Different terms with different degrees of association with the boudoir could be used interchangeably to denote a woman's private property in any form. Only when a word like *t'ien* 田, "fields," or *chü* 具, "objects," appears in the term can we be sure that the property was immovable or movable. Thus *nang-ch'ieh* 囊篋 or *nang-t'o* 囊橐 (literally "sacks and boxes" or "big and small sacks") could just as well mean land cultivated by servile tenants, as personal jewelry or quilts.[97]

A Sung letter-writing guide distinguishes between "major numbers" (*ta-shu* 大數), namely land and servants listed in an "agreement card" (or "betrothal card" *ting-t'ieh* 定帖) at the early stages of the marriage negotiation, and the "minor numbers" (*hsi-shu* 細數), consisting of cloth, jewelry, and items "for the room" that were detailed in a trousseau list (*lien-chü chuang* 奩具狀) delivered right before the wedding with the dowry items themselves.[98] We can hypothesize that the first list described the dowry as a whole for purposes of negotiation, while the other identified every item the bride took into her marital home to distinguish it in the future from property of the husband and to prevent any misunderstandings with his relatives. A surviving record of a Sung agreement card and the corresponding trousseau list supports this conclusion. The agreement card dated 1260

95 E.g., CMC 8:258; *Yüan tien-chang* (photo reprint of Yüan edition: Taipei: Ku-kung po-wu kuan, 1976), 14:35; *Liang-che chin-shih chih*, 14:8b. For more on unmarried women owning property, see Yanagida Setsuko, "Sōdai no joko," in *Yanagida Setsuko sensei koki kinen Chūgoku no dentō shakai to kazoku*, ed. Ihara Hiroshi (Tokyo: Kyūko shoen, 1993).

96 Shiga, *Genri*, 516–17 provides other terms used in the twentieth century. Shiga argues elsewhere that except in the Sung, landed dowries were rare, *Genri*, 440.

97 E.g., CMC 10:365–6.

98 *Han-mo ch'üan-shu* (1307 ed.), i 18:6b; as cited in Patricia Ebrey, "Shifts in Marriage Finance," in *Marriage and Inequality in Chinese Society*, ed. Rubie Watson and Patricia Ebrey (Berkeley: University of California Press, 1991), 106. I thank Prof. Ebrey for expanding on this reference in a personal communication, when the original source was inaccessible. These "agreement cards" are described in *Meng-liang lu*, 20:304, and *Tung-ching meng-hua lu*, 5:30. See also Ebrey, *Inner Quarters*, 83–4.

Figure 1. Delivering the dowry to the groom's household. From Nakagawa Tadahide, *Shinzoku kibun* (1799), courtesy of Marquand Library of
Art and Archaeology, Princeton Univerisity Library.

lists three general categories and their total value: 500 *mou* of land
(about 90 acres), movable property (*lien-chü* 奩具) worth 100,000 strings
of cash, and things to "tie the marriage" (*ti-yin* 締姻) worth 5,000 strings.
The detailed list, compiled twenty-six months later, gives a breakdown
of the movable property, describing the various kinds of cloth, utensils,

Figure 1. *(cont.)*

ritual books, and other objects.[99] Such lists provided legal protection for a wife's dowry.

One reason for there being no systematic distinction between movable and immovable property might be that they were frequently exchanged for one another. Sung sources contain many references

99 *Shui-tung jih-chi*, 8:4a–5b (SKCS ed.). This huge dowry could not have been typical (which may explain why it was recorded in a Ming note), but references to such large dowries among the Sung elite are not rare; see for instance *Lü Tung-lai wen-chi*,

to women using the jewelry or silk from their trousseau to buy land or other productive enterprises. One couple in the thirteenth century bought 47 *chung* of land with the wife's dowry money to add to the mere 23 *chung* that the husband previously owned.[100] In an incident told by Hung Mai (1123–1202), a woman whose husband divorced her in favor of a prostitute used her dowry to set up a shop, which according to the story grew in value to 100,000 strings of cash.[101] Liu Tsai (1166–1239) tells us in a funerary inscription how his wife sold "plates, bowls, ceremonial cups and curtains" in the market to help his father buy a piece of land.[102]

Sung evidence confirms that, as in other premodern societies, cash, jewelry, and movable property were relatively more valuable compared to land than they are today, and thus easily traded for one another. A woman in Suchou in the early thirteenth century sold 136 *mou* of dowry land for about 14 strings per *mou*, a price similar to that found in other late Sung documents.[103] At this exchange rate, the movables worth 100,000 strings of cash in the dowry list of 1260 could buy more than 7,000 *mou*, or considerably more than the 550 *mou* of land brought into the marriage with the movables.[104] We know that in other societies movables depreciated more slowly than today, thus keeping

---

8:201. For the imperial family, see John Chaffee, "The Marriage of Sung Imperial Clanswomen," in *Marriage and Inequality*, ed. Watson and Ebrey, 142–3; and for a reference in fiction from the late Sung or early Ming, see Yang Xianyi and Gladys Yang, trans., *The Courtesan's Jewel Box: Chinese Stories of the 10th to 17th Centuries* (Beijing: Foreign Languages Press, 1981), 18. "Things to tie the marriage" were probably gifts for the husband's family; Ebrey, "Shifts," 106. For a similar term, *hsi-ch'in* (gifts to "join relatives"), see *Sung shih*, 115:2732.

100 CMC 10:365–6. A *chung* was a unit of land whose exact dimensions are not known today, but which is thought to have been fairly large.

101 *I-chien chih* (Peking: Chung-hua shu-chü, 1981), ping-chih 14:484; Ebrey, *Inner Quarters*, 11.

102 *Man-t'ang chi* (SKCS chen-pen ed.), 32:17a.

103 *Chiang-su chin-shih chih*, 14:6a. CMC 8:170 records the same price of about 14 strings per *mou* for a conditional sale in 1218; while another reference to a conditional sale in 1206 (CMC 9:315) gives about 10 strings per *mou*. Of course the price of land varied according to the quality, location, and year; moreover, most exchanges in the Sung were conditional sales representing limited ownership. A *mou* was a bit less than one-sixth of an acre in Sung.

104 Recall that the 1260 list also included an additional 5,000 strings worth of movables to "tie the marriage"; *Shui-tung jih-chi*, 8:4a–5b; Ebrey "Shifts," 106. This high value of movable property compared to land corresponds to England from the late middle ages to the mideighteenth century, when a house might not be more valuable than the bed, furniture, and utensils in it, and a son's landed inheritance was often balanced by cash or movable property to his sisters. Amy Louise Erickson, *Women and Property in Early Modern England* (London: Routledge, 1993), 64–78. For a similar situation in the American colonies, see Carole Shammas, Marylynn Salmon, and Michel Dahlin, *Inheritance in America from Colonial Times to the Present* (New Brunswick, N.J.: Rutgers University Press, 1987), 32, 64–7.

their value relative to land.[105] This was likely the case in middle period China as well.

The Chinese terms for property held by a woman do not distinguish whether she obtained it before, at the time of, or after her marriage.[106] There was no conceptual distinction in Chinese between "dowry," which a woman received at the time of marriage, and "inheritance," which she might receive at other times. Wealth that passed to a minor (because of the death of her parents and the premature division of her household) might be referred to more generally as "property," but when a girl reached marriageable age, any assets that had accrued to her were lumped together and relabeled as "dowry."[107] Any property that a woman obtained after her marriage was similarly labeled "dowry." This could be a further bequest from her parents, profits generated from her previous assets, or land purchased by her husband and intentionally registered as "dowry land" (to keep it away from his brothers or other relatives, sometimes fraudulently). The Chinese terms used for women's property make no distinction between assets acquired in these different ways. Instead, these terms stressed the different treatment under the law afforded to women's property as compared to men's. As this study will show, a wife's property was always carefully distinguished from other property in a household, and the special labeling as "dowry" in Chinese denoted the separate treatment it received, rather than when or how the woman obtained it.

The Economic Significance of Women's Property

The language of the boudoir, which minimized the economic importance of women's property, contrasts with the documentary evidence of

105 For example, Erickson, *Women and Property*, 64–78.
106 The word "dowry" in English connotes property that came to a woman only at the time of her marriage and can thus be misleading. Moreover, historically, under English Common Law, a woman's dowry was merged with her husband's estate and put under his control (though with some limits, particularly for land; see Erickson, *Women and Property*, 24–5; Goody, *Oriental*, 85). The Chinese words for "dowry" are thus perhaps best translated into English as "property of a wife," or "a woman's personal property," and in some places I have used such phrases. But for readability I mostly use "dowry" or "trousseau" in my translations.

There has been much debate in modern scholarship over the nature of women's property and the difference between dowry and inheritance. This includes a famous exchange between the Japanese scholars Niida Noboru and Shiga Shūzō; see, e.g., Shiga, "Chūgoku kazokuhō hokō," *Kokka gakkai zasshi* Pt. 1–4 67–8 (Nov. 1953–Mar. 1955); Shiga, *Genri*, esp. 437–65; and Niida, *Hōseishi* III, esp. 381–93. For a review of the literature, see Birge, "Women and Property," 36–41.

107 For an example, see CMC 7:217, where in family division the portion going to women of marriage age is labeled "dowry" (or "marriage endowment" *chia-tzu* 嫁資), while that going to minors is called simply "property" (*ts'ai-ch'an* 財產).

women as owners and disposers of property. Sung sources reveal that women of all ages could be significant economic players in society and that, from the inner quarters, their presence was felt in the outside world.

Women appear as owners of land in Sung contracts. For instance an inscription dated 1206 describes the purchase of land by a school in Wu county, Suchou, under the direction of a new professor, Mr. T'ang. The inscription contains several contracts in which a number of parcels of land are clearly identified as belonging to women. One contract was for the purchase of the land of a Madam T'ao, daughter-in-law of an unnamed official in the Ministry of Personnel, for the large sum of 1,908 strings and 550 cash. The land was fragmented into 17 parcels, with a total area of 136 *mou*, 3 *chiao*, and 14 *pu*, and a total income of 123 piculs, 1 peck of rice.[108] Moreover, the land came with a tenant, Wu Seventy-five, and the tenancy contract appended to the bill of sale named Madam T'ao as the sole landlord.[109] We can understand from this entry that the land appeared on government registers in Madam T'ao's name, with an indication of her father-in-law as head of the household that paid taxes on the land.[110] The sixteenth of the seventeen parcels bordered to the south on land described as "own property" (*chi-ch'an* 己產), which presumably referred to other land of Madam T'ao. The names of women appear repeatedly as property owners in the descriptions of parcels: as owners of neighboring acreage in each of the four directions, as previous owners, and so on.[111] Other inscriptions in the same collection have similar entries that list women as sellers, mortgagers, occupants of neighboring lands, or previous owners of land. Some of these seem to be unmarried girls.[112]

---

108 *Chiang-su chin-shih chih,* 14:6a, 8a. See also Yanagida Setsuko, "NanSōki kasan bunkatsu ni okeru joshōbun ni tsuite," in *Ryū Shiken hakushi shōju kinen Sōshi kenkyū ronshū,* ed. Kinugawa Tsuyoshi (Tokyo: Dōhōsha, 1989), 239. A *mou* was a bit less than one-sixth of an acre in Sung; there were 10 *chiao* and approximately 240 *pu* to a *mou.* A picul (*shih*) was about 72 kilograms, and a peck (*tou*) was approximately 9 liters, but all of these measures could vary; see for instance Ogawa Tamaki et al., *Shinjigen* (Tokyo: Kadokawa shoten, 1968), 1224–5; and Brian McKnight and James T. C. Liu, *The Enlightened Judgments: Ch'ing-ming Chi, The Sung Dynasty Collection* (Albany: State University of New York Press, 1999), 498.

109 *Chiang-su chin-shih chih,* 14:9a.

110 Yanagida, "Joshōbun," 239. These registers were the *chen-chi pu,* land tax registers, that were established in 1142 to make tax assessments more accurate. They told the size, boundaries, location, and character of each parcel of land in a canton. See Brian McKnight, *Village and Bureaucracy in Southern Sung China* (Chicago, Chicago University Press, 1971), 51–2. This Su-chou inscription seems to be quoting from these registers.

111 *Chiang-su chin-shih chih,* 14:6b–7b (Vol. 13, 9781–2).

112 Yanagida, "Joshōbun," 239–40.

Other records show women contributing to public works with large donations given in their own names. A rare stele records the names of people who donated money to lay paving stones down the main road of Suchou city in 1179. Several women appear on the list. One of them, "Fourth Sister Chu" (Chu-shih ssu-niang) gave 20 strings of cash to purchase 10,000 stones. The size of this donation can be appreciated when we note that a county magistrate got a monthly salary of about 30 strings, and that this was enough to support a household of several dozen people. As in the land contracts, some of the names, like "Eighteenth sister Hu" (Hu shih-pa mei), seem to be names of unmarried girls.[113] In neighboring Chiang-nan West circuit (Kiangsi), just over the Wu-i mountains from Chien-ning, a widow née Wang (d. 1191) undertook the yearly rebuilding of a dam near her home that was noted for the large area it irrigated (20 *ch'ing* or 2,000 *mou*).[114]

Women are most visible in our sources by their contributions to religious establishments. Numerous funerary inscriptions recorded how women gave generously to Buddhist temples, and steles erected by the temples themselves celebrated women among the names of benefactors. For instance, soon after the founding of the Sung, several women in Ch'ang-chou (modern Kiangsu) contributed to the carving of two octagonal sutra pillars in T'ai-p'ing temple.[115] In 1134 twenty-three women provided funds to a temple in nearby Chiang-yin prefecture for a devotional stele of the 500 arhats. An additional sixty-two women are named as lesser benefactors to the temple.[116] In 1157 a splendid hall was built in a monastery in Hu-chou (modern Chekiang) to house a statue of the bodhisattva Kuan-yin, which was said to perform miracles. Women appear in the list of donors by themselves or together with their husbands or sons.[117] Temples to popular deities were also patronized by

---

113 *Chiang-su chin-shih chih*, 13:12b–13a (pp. 9754–5); Ihara Hiroshi, *Chūgoku chūsei toshi kikō* (Tokyo: Chūō kōron sha, Chūkō shinshō, 1988), 77–9; and Ihara Hiroshi, "Sōdai shakai to zeni: shomin no shisanryoku o megutte," *Ajia yūgaku*, no. 18 (July 2000): 14. I thank Prof. Ihara for first calling my attention to this reference. An official of the lowest level received about 12 strings per month; see Kinugawa Tsuyoshi, "Shushi shōden," in *Kōbe Shōka daigaku jinbun ronshū*, 15:1 (1979), part 1, p. 10. For more information on official salaries, see Kinugawa Tsuyoshi, "Sōdai no hōkyū ni tsuite: bunshin kanryō o chūshin toshite," *Tōhō gakuhō* (Tokyo) 41 (1970); and Kinugawa Tsuyoshi, "Kanryō to hōkyū: Sōdai no hōkyū ni tsuite zokkō," *Tōhō gakuhō* 42 (1971).

114 *Chiang-hu wen-chi* (SKCS chen-pen ed.), 35:13a–16a; Hymes, *Statesmen*, 169. The involvement of women in community charity is discussed further in Chapter 3.

115 *Chiang-su chin-shih chih*, 8:1a–b (*Shih-k'o shih-liao hsin-pien*, Vol. 13, 9613).

116 *Chiang-su chin-shih chih*, 11:17a–20a (*Shih-k'o shih-liao hsin-pien*, Vol. 13, 9697–9).

117 *Wu-hsing chin-shih chi*, 8:20b–25a (*Shih-k'o shih-liao hsin-pien*, Vol. 14, 10770–73). The miracles were triggered when a woman née Chang repaired the arm of the statue and then found her own arm cured by the bodhisattva; Valerie Hansen, *Changing Gods in*

women. In 1227 a major effort was launched by devotees in I-hsing county (Kiangsu) of the Chin dynasty hero-turned-god Chou Ch'u to provide a permanent endowment of land for his temple. Of seventeen listed donors, one was a woman, née Chuang, who gave 10,000 strings in paper money and 1 picul, 6 pecks of rice.[118]

These random examples reveal that women had considerable independent control of property. The chapters that follow examine how women obtained property and to what extent they controlled it at different times of their lives. The book will show how women's relation to property changed over time before and especially after the Mongol invasion.

Medieval China, 1127–1276 (Princeton, N.J.: Princeton University Press, 1990), 167–70.

118 *Chiang-su chin-shih chih*, 15:23b (Vol. 13, 9818). The final endowed income of the temple was 560,000 strings worth of paper money and 19 piculs of rice (about 1,800 liters); Valerie Hansen, "Popular Deities and Social Change in the Southern Song Period (1127–1276)" (Ph.D. dissertation, University of Pennsylvania, 1987), 35–6.

1

Women and Property before the Sung: Evolution and Continuity

From earliest times for which records survive, we find a remarkable continuity of concepts and practices that governed women's relations to property over the centuries. Sung practices, discussed in the next chapter, must be understood within this long tradition. In essence, the bonds of blood for daughters as well as sons carried with them a certain expectation of material support, commensurate with the wealth of the parents. Thus despite long-term political and social evolution that dictated considerable changes in forms of property, marriage laws, and inheritance patterns, certain basic contours of women's property rights can be discerned in almost every age before the Sung. Sung laws also, while new in many respects, did not contradict these. These contours included several key points: (1) A woman of nonservile status could expect to marry with dowry property attached to her. (2) A married daughter might receive additional property from her parents sometime after the marriage on top of her previous dowry portion. (3) Within marriage, a wife's property was conceptually distinct from that of her husband. Although the husband or his family invariably benefited directly or indirectly from the wife's property, it was her own in that she could take it with her out of the marriage in case of divorce or widowhood. (4) In the absence of sons, daughters married or unmarried, stood to inherit all of their parents' estate. (5) Widows in particular often gained considerable power over households and property and enjoyed certain protection of their authority. While evidence for the early periods is scarce, the sources show a basic consistency of practice that gave

41

women, especially of the elite, considerable control over assets of various types. Despite a lack of legal guarantees for women's inheritance, women routinely gained access to personal property that could help support them for their lifetimes and supply sacrifices to them after their deaths.

The historical reality of women's control of property has been hidden by the language of Confucian ideals. Elite men who authored the documents surviving today were steeped in the ideology of classical Confucianism, which necessitated a veneer of Confucian propriety when describing elite practices. Even some modern scholars have been so influenced by this bias in the sources that the reality of women's property rights has been obscured.[1] In the pre-T'ang period, Confucian thought had very little effect on law or persisted in the realm of women's property rights, and women's property prevailed even when it conflicted with Confucian ritual demands and concepts of lineage organization. Even in the T'ang and after, when laws consciously upheld patriarchal power, traditional practices that gave women property persisted and remained legal.

In the following pages I attempt to separate Confucian ideals from historical reality in describing the contours of women's relation to property in early China. The chapter explores the contradictions between religious, social, and legal concepts and actual historical practice. It traces historical change in the laws governing property for women before the Sung, noting the areas of continuity. This brief overview shows that strong property rights enjoyed by women in the Sung, while new in many respects, were consistent with long-established practices.

Chou Feudalism and Confucian Ideals

Chinese, from at least the Shang period (second millennium B.C.), traced their descent patrilineally. The ruling house claimed descent through the male line from powerful ancestral deities whom it alone was allowed to worship. Elaborate ancestral sacrifices, royal burials, and divination to communicate with ancestors established the political and religious authority of the ruling house.[2] In the succeeding Chou dynasty, the ancestral cult had spread to aristocrats and commoners but was

1 See for instance Ch'en Tung-yüan, *Chung-kuo fu-nü sheng-huo shih* (Taipei: Commercial Press, 1986); Ch'en Ku-yüan, *Chung-kuo ku-tai hun-yin shih* (Shanghai: Commercial Press, 1933); Ch'ü T'ung-tsu, *Law and Society in Traditional China* (Paris: Mouton and Co., 1965); Shiga Shūzō, *Chūgoku kazokuhō no genri* (Tokyo: Sōbunsha, 1967); and Esther Yao, *Chinese Women: Past and Present* (Mesquite, Texas: Ide House, 1983).

2 David Keightley, "Early Civilization in China: Reflections on How It Became Chinese," in *Heritage of China: Contemporary Perspectives on Chinese Civilization*, ed. Paul Ropp (Berkeley: University of California Press, 1990), 15–54.

strictly limited according to political rank. (Commoners could sacrifice only vegetables, no meat, for instance.)

Political power was passed down through the male line. In a loose system of feudal organization, the Chou state made the first son of the principal wife heir to the fiefdom and ritual head of the lineage. A system of hierarchy within the family, superiority of first-born sons over their brothers, seniors over juniors, men over women, was part of a combined religious and political order centered around patrilineality. Ruling aristocrats needed male offspring to continue the family line and inherit the fief, and to fulfill the ritual obligations of the ancestral cult. Women were excluded from political power and from the ritual family line. They could not sacrifice to their own natal ancestors, and they themselves became ancestors only in their husband's line. Only the principal wife of the family head had an official role in the sacrifices; according to the ritual texts, the sacrifices were incomplete without her participation.[3]

The ideals of the Confucian school reflect their genesis at the time of this religious and political order, and Confucius and his followers articulated the philosophical and religious underpinnings of this order. Filial piety and attention to station and hierarchy were foundations of Confucian thought. Ancestor worship and rituals were also stressed by Confucians, who came to be experts on court ceremonies and mourning practices. The Confucian philosopher Mencius expressed the absolute need for male progeny in his famous dictum that the greatest of unfilial acts is to have no posterity.[4]

The Confucian ritual classics, compiled from documents of the late Chou and early Han, provide a detailed picture of the ideal form of the aristocratic lineage structure, as it was to operate within Chou dynasty feudalism. Since these texts were to be influential in the Sung, the family structure they describe deserves presentation here. The family was organized into a "descent line" (*tsung* 宗). The eldest son of the senior line was the "descent-line heir" (*tsung-tzu* 宗子), who was the ritual head of the lineage and the successor to the political office and fief of his father. The senior line comprised the "main descent line" (*ta-tsung* 大宗), while the collateral lines of younger sons were called "lesser descent lines" (*hsiao tsung* 小宗), each lasting for five generations. Stem family units usually lived separately, but together they made up the *tsu* 族 or lineage.[5] Land was not privately owned in this period, and theoretically its profits

---

3 Legge, *Li Chi*, "Tseng-tzu wen," I, 316.   4 *Mencius* 4A:26
5 Ch'ü, *Law*, 31–6; Legge, *Li Chi*, esp. Bk. 14, "Ta chuan"; John Steele, trans., *The I-li or Book of Etiquette and Ceremonial*, 2 vols. (London: Probsthain & Co., 1917) II, Sec. 11, esp. 18–20; Patricia Ebrey, "Conceptions of the Family," *Journal of Asian Studies* 43:2 (Feb. 1984): 221–2.

belonged only to the feudal lord to whom it was enfeoffed. Though members of the *tsu* did not all live together, resources of the *tsu* were to be controlled by the ritual head of the family, the descent-line heir (*tsung-tzu*), and distributed according to need.[6] But even the *Record of Rites* (*Li-chi*) acknowledges that younger brothers living apart might have more wealth and higher noble rank than their ritual superiors in the descent-line system. Such members are exhorted to leave their carriages, attendants, and signs of nobility outside when visiting the household of the descent-line heir.[7]

Sons living with their parents were forbidden to keep private property and so were their wives: "A son and his wife should have no private goods, nor animals, nor vessels."[8] The ritual classic *Record of Rites* (*Li-chi*) spelled out rules for how the son or daughter-in-law should handle immovable property that fell into their possession. The wife was to present it to her in-laws, and even if they gave it back was to keep it aside for their later request.[9] These passages suggest that, Confucian strictures notwithstanding, it was not unusual for individuals to keep some personal possessions in the household.

Other sources from the Chou period confirm the reality that women did indeed keep personal property. We know that women went into marriages with slaves and material goods. A story from the legalist text *The Han Fei-tzu*, written in the third century B.C., when the *Record of Rites* was also put into its present form, confirms this. The legalist Han Fei (280–233 B.C.) opposed many of the doctrines of the Confucians, but he accepted the system of family hierarchy and filial piety, since it fostered the loyalty and obedience needed in his authoritarian organization of society. He did not generally write about domestic affairs. The following passage is meant to chastise officials for enriching themselves in office, but it incidentally speaks of women and property:

A man from Wei married off his daughter and told her, "You must accumulate for yourself as much [private property] as you can (*pi ssu chi-chü*), for it is common for wives to be expelled and it is only a matter of luck to live with your husband your whole life." His daughter thus accumulated [property] for herself, but her mother-in-law considered her to have too much and expelled her. When the girl returned home, she had twice as much [property] as when she had married. Her father did not blame himself for teaching her badly, but consid-

---

6 Steele, *I-li* II, 17. These rules also appear in the Later Han Confucian ritual manual *Pai-hu t'ung*; Ch'ü, *Law*, 34.

7 *Li-chi* (Shanghai: Ku-chi ch'u-pan she, 1987), "Nei-tse," 5:156; Legge, *Li Chi* I, 458–9; Ch'ü, *Law*, 36. (I follow Ch'ü's translation, which differs significantly from Legge's.)

8 *Li-chi*, 5:156; Legge, *Li Chi* I, 458.   9 *Li-chi*, 5:156; Legge, *Li Chi* I, 458.

ered himself clever that she had increased her wealth. The way officials manage their offices nowadays is just like this.[10]

We see several points from this passage. First, a woman took property into her marriage as dowry.[11] Second, within the marriage she kept such property as her personal possession. Third, she took this property with her out of the marriage in the case of divorce, and it was intended to protect her in just such an event. And fourth, her personal wealth could increase during the marriage. We also see a general disapproval of too much private property within marriage lurking in the background (so much so that the story could be an analogy of officials' acting in their own private interests), and that property could be the source of tension between mother- and daughter-in-law, or even be grounds for divorce.[12]

The Confucian classic *Record of Rites* itself indicates that wives kept private property and could take it with them out of a marriage. The chapter "Miscellaneous Records" dictates the procedure for expelling a wife and states that the articles sent with her at marriage were to be returned.[13] Commentators have understood these dowry items to include male and female attendants and movable property.[14]

The Ch'in legal code similarly dating to the third century B.C. (fragments of which were unearthed in Hupei in 1975) provides additional

10 *Han Fei-tzu chiao-chu,* Yang Ching-chao et al., eds. (Chiang-su province: Jen-min ch'u-pan she, 1982), "Shuo-lin" Pt. 1, 249.

11 This point follows from the words, "When the girl returned home, she had twice as much property as when she had married."

12 I disagree with modern scholars who believe this passage illustrates that the keeping of private property by daughters-in-law was tantamount to theft and was grounds for divorce. See Ch'en Ku-yüan, *Chung-kuo ku-tai,* 46; Tai, "Divorce in Traditional Chinese Law," 88. Ch'en and Tai link this passage to the "Seven Conditions of Divorce" (*ch'i ch'u*) in traditional Confucian literature, one of which was "stealing." There is nothing in the *Han Fei-tzu* text to link it to the "Seven Conditions" or even to the idea of stealing. Moreover, the "Seven Conditions for Divorce" come to us only from Han texts, written several centuries after Han Fei lived, and even in the Han they were rarely cited as grounds for divorce; see Jack Dull, "Marriage and Divorce in Han China," in *Chinese Family Law and Social Change,* ed. David Buxbaum (Seattle: University of Washington Press, 1978), 52–3, 57. Ch'ü T'ung-tsu in his treatment of the "Seven Conditions" makes no connection between a wife's private property and stealing; *Han Social Structure* (Seattle: University of Washington Press, 1991), 40. The "Seven Conditions" are found in the *Family Sayings of Confucius* (*K'ung-tzu chia-yü*); the *Rites of the Elder Mr. Tai* (*Ta-Tai li-chi*); and the Ho Hsiu commentary of the *Kung-yang chuan,* all of the Han dynasty. The Seven Conditions were copied into the T'ang code and appeared in commentaries on the Confucian ritual texts; *T'ang-lü shu-i* (Beijing: Chung-hua shu-chü, 1983), 14:267–8. See also Tai, "Divorce in Traditional Chinese Law," 85; Niida, *Tō Sō hōritsu bunsho no kenkyū* [hereafter cited as *Bunsho*] (Tokyo: Tōhō bunka gakuin, 1937; reprinted Tōkyō daigaku shuppankai, 1983), 483.

13 *Li-chi,* "Tsa-chi" Pt. II, 7:239; Legge, *Li Chi* II, 170–1. The text also suggests that women could seek divorce on their own initiative.

14 Niida, *Bunsho,* 499 and 505 n. 60.

45

evidence that a wife's dowry was distinguished under the law from her husband's property. The code states that when a man committed a crime warranting arrest and confiscation of his property, his wife could prevent confiscation of "the male and female slaves, clothes, and vessels of her dowry" if she denounced him to the authorities before his apprehension. (Presumably if she did not denounce him, she was seen to have colluded with him and lost her property.) The code also reveals the expectation that dowry benefited the couple together and that it was to some extent seen to be under the control of the husband, for when the wife was arrested for a crime, her dowry was not confiscated but stayed behind with the husband.[15]

Han Dynasty Developments:
Communal Living, Common Property

We cannot know whether the Confucian descent-line system ever operated as described in the ritual texts, but we do know that by the beginning of the Han dynasty (202 B.C.–A.D. 220) it was no longer practiced. During the Spring and Autumn and the Warring States periods (eighth to third centuries B.C.), as land tax and rent gradually replaced labor services to a feudal lord, the household became an independent economic unit among the peasantry.[16] With the further demise of feudalism, a system of individual households, called *chia* 家, in which brothers lived together with their parents, gradually became the universal pattern for all social classes in China. From then on, the descent-line system, with its ritual and material inequality between brothers, was an abstract ideal that never again operated in its original form, despite later efforts to revive it.[17]

The concept of the *chia* as it developed in the Han dynasty was based on a formula of "communal living, common property" (*t'ung-chü kung-ts'ai*). We find this term in both legal documents and others as early as the Han, and with great frequency thereafter.[18] According to the

15 Anton F. P. Hulsewé, *Remnants of Ch'in Law* (Leiden: E. J. Brill, 1985), 168–9; Ch'eng T'ien-ch'üan, "Hun-yin yü ch'in-shu," in *Chung-kuo min-fa shih*, ed. Yeh Hsiao-hsin (Shanghai: Jen-min ch'u-pan she, 1993), 149–50.
16 Hsü Cho-yün, *Ancient China in Transition* (Stanford, Calif.: Stanford University Press, 1965), 107–39.
17 The *tsung* system was not without influence on later lineage organizations. Even in the twentieth century, anthropologists have identified lineage solidarity in North China based on kinship relations that formally resemble the *tsung* system of antiquity. See, for instance, Myron Cohen, "Lineage Organization in North China," *Journal of Asian Studies* 49 (Aug. 1990): 510 and n. 5.
18 Shiga Shūzō, "Family Property and the Law of Inheritance in Traditional China," in *Chinese Family Law and Social Change*, ed. David Buxbaum (Seattle: University of

formula, sons stayed with their parents in joint families while women married out, entering the homes of their husbands to serve their parents-in-law (as in pre-Han times). Property within the family (the *chia*) was to be held communally under the direction of the household head, who could delegate another household member to be manager. Conjugal units of a man, wife, and his children had their own quarters (*fang*) within the household, but were to pool their labor and income while receiving an allowance for their living needs from the common budget of the *chia*. The entire *chia* took meals together, and a *chia* was commonly defined as a household sharing one stove. The traditional ideal was to have a joint household with five generations of *fang* living under one roof, but both historical and modern data show us that households usually had to divide after the death of the parents. From the Han to the twentieth century the average household size in China was only four to six people. At the time of household division, the family property was divided equally among the sons, and each son succeeded to a position as head of a new household. Governments from the Ch'in on held the household heads responsible for tax payments and gave them legal authority over members of the household. Thus the *chia* was a formal economic and legal entity. Remarkably, this model of household organization has persisted in Chinese society up to the present day, among poor and rich alike.[19]

The origins of the rule of partible inheritance are not known, but this new Chinese familism contradicted the Confucian principles of the descent-line system. Materially and legally all the sons succeeded equally to the father's position. Even more importantly, each son had the right

Washington Press, 1978), 111–12. As Shiga shows, even in Han times the qualifications for "communal living," *t'ung-chü*, did not necessarily require physical presence in the household. For modern times, see also Myron Cohen, "Developmental Process in the Chinese Domestic Group," in *Family and Kinship in Chinese Society*, ed. Maurice Freedman (Stanford, Calif.: Stanford University Press, 1970); James Watson, *Emigration and the Chinese Lineage: The Mans in Hong Kong and London* (Berkeley: University of California Press, 1975). In some cases, the law only recognized residents in the household as members of the *t'ung-chü* group. See discussion of T'ang code in this chapter. See also Shiga, *Genri*, 50–107; Nakada Kaoru, "Tōsō jidai no kazoku kyōsan sei," in *Hōseishi ronshū* (Tokyo: Iwanami Shoten, 1943; reprint 1985), Vol. 3, Pt. 2, 1295–1360.

19 There is abundant historical and anthropological data on the joint family system in China. For historical work, see for instance Shiga, *Genri*, chs. 1 and 2; and Shiga, "Family Property and the Law of Inheritance." For seminal anthropological works, see Fei Hsiao-t'ung, *Peasant Life in China* (London: Routledge and Kegan Paul, 1939, reprint 1980); Olga Lang, *Chinese Family and Society* (New Haven, Conn.: Yale University Press, 1946). The most systematic modern study is Myron Cohen, *House United, House Divided: the Chinese Family in Taiwan* (New York: Columbia University Press, 1976). I agree with his assertion that his Taiwan model applies to virtually all of China. The idea of the common stove is described well in Margery Wolf, *The House of Lim* (Englewood Cliffs, N.J.: Prentice-Hall, 1968) ch. 3.

and duty to sacrifice to his father and carry on a new family line. There was no distinction between main lines and collateral ones. Shiga Shūzō argues that "inheritance" or more appropriately "succession" in China had three meanings: succeeding to the father in a line linking ancestors to descendants, succeeding to sacrifices to the father and his ancestors, and succeeding to the property that ensured both sacrifices and descendants.[20] Vestiges of the Confucian doctrine that the eldest son had extra sacrificial duties are seen in later legal codes (including in Taiwan in the twentieth century) and some lineage practices,[21] but such practice was undermined by the rule of equal inheritance that was upheld by law and custom. From the T'ang on, even the father could not circumvent the basic intent of this rule either during his lifetime or in a will.[22]

The ideal of "communal living, common property" seems to have been in the minds of the Chinese as early as the Warring States period, but historical documents show us that it was far from a reality even in the Han. The great history *Shih-chi* records two fourth century laws from the state of Ch'in discouraging joint households: one imposed a double tax on households with more than two adult sons, the other forbade fathers and sons to "live in one room."[23] These laws were copied into the Han code and stayed on the books until the Wei dynasty (A.D. 220–265). Sources indicate that they were no longer effective in the Later Han, but they were enforced in parts of China during the Former Han. The aim of such laws was to reduce the power of large families, but Ch'ü T'ung-tsu argues that they forced both rich and poor to live apart from their adult sons. The poor "pawned" their sons to other households, while the rich distributed property to their sons at the time of marriage and sent them off to form new households.[24]

Like sons in the Han, daughters also received property at the time of marriage. Dowries could be substantial, and property given to a daughter could be equal to the share given a son. A famous case is that of Cho Wen-chün, the widowed daughter of a rich iron manufacturer, Cho Wang-sun, who married the poet Ssu-ma Hsiang-ju (179–117 B.C.). As

---

20 Shiga, *Genri*, 108–48; Shiga, "Family Property and the Law of Inheritance," 121–7.
21 Fei, *Peasant Life in China*, 66–8; and esp. Cohen, "Lineage Organization in North China," 510ff.
22 Shiga, "Family Property and the Law of Inheritance," 125. Ebrey, in an historical overview, suggests that eldest sons had extra ritual responsibilities in Han times, but Shiga argues that this was probably not true. Ebrey, "Women, Marriage and the Family," in *Heritage of China*, ed. Ropp, 205.
23 *Shih-chi* (Peking: Chung-hua shu-chü, 1959; reprint 1982), 68:2230, 2232; Ch'ü T'ung-tsu, *Han Social Structure*, 4–5. Translations of the documents are provided, 252–4.
24 Ch'ü, *Han Social Structure*, 5–8.

described in the *Shih-chi* and *Han shu*, she fell in love with Hsiang-ju at a banquet her father gave for him, and eloped with him that night. Her father was furious that she married without his consent and at first refused to give her "a single cash." After the couple opened a wine shop to support themselves and relatives pleaded with the father, he relented and "dividing his property, he gave Wen-chün one hundred slaves, a million cash, and the clothing, coverlets, *and other property she had had in her first marriage*" (emphasis mine). She and her husband then sold these riches and purchased land in his home of Ch'eng-tu, where they established a comfortable life for themselves. After Ssu-ma Hsiang-ju had become a high official, the father reconsidered again and, "he generously divided his property and gave his daughter a portion equal to that of his son."[25]

This story shows that people expected fathers to give daughters dowry in proportion to their wealth. The industrialist Cho Wang-sun was shamed into giving his daughter property, despite her disobedience. We also see that she had brought property back from her first marriage. Finally, Wen-chün eventually received a portion equal to her brother's, but the text calls this "generous" (*hou*), suggesting that it was unusual. Wen-chün had one sister and one brother: we do not know what the other sister received.

Other documents from the Han and just after confirm that elite women routinely received large dowries. In the *Debates on Salt and Iron* (*Yen-t'ieh lun*), an official complained that "patrimonies are wasted to provide sumptuous funerals and dowries by the cartload for marrying daughters."[26] In the reign of Emperor Hsüan (r. 73–47 B.C.), there was a similar complaint that dowries and betrothal gifts were given without restraint, making it impossible for the poor to compete.[27] Wang Fu (ca. 90–165), in his *Discourses by a Man in Hiding (Ch'ien-fu lun)*, complained that the rich competed to outdo each other in lavish dowries, while the poor felt ashamed at not measuring up.[28] In another late Han text two women are described as taking seven or eight slaves and valuable property into a marriage.[29] The nonconformist Tai Liang of the first century, who flouted ritual by taking wine and meat when in mourning for his

---

25 *Shih-chi*, 117:3000, 3047. These passages are translated by Ch'ü, *Han Social Structure*, 271–3. The same story appears in *Han shu* (Peking: Chung-hua shu-chü, 1962; reprint 1975), 57A:2530–1; 57B:2581.
26 Cited in Dull, "Marriage and Divorce," 46. Dull discusses only betrothal gifts, but in his argument he mixes together evidence of dowries with that of betrothal gifts, assuming they were about equal. I make no such assumption and only use his data on dowries.
27 *Han shu*, 72:3064; Dull, "Marriage and Divorce," 46.
28 *Ch'ien-fu lun* (TSCC ed.), 3:77.
29 *Hua-yang kuo-chih* (Taipei: Shang-wu yin-shu kuan, 1976), 10C:172.

mother, further went against custom by marrying off his five daughters with only "plain garments, simple bedding, and wooden shoes." This meager dowry was celebrated for its rarity, though even Tai Liang could not dispense with dowry completely.[30] The scholar Pao Hsüan complained to his wife that she had come with too much dowry, and that he could not match her wealth. The wife sent her servants, clothes, and jewelry back to her father, and her selfless act earned her a mention in the dynastic history.[31]

The personal nature of dowry is revealed in the story of Li Ch'ung of the Later Han. Li lived with his mother and five brothers in a communal household. His wife, finding their poverty unbearable, secretly told him, "I have [substantial] personal property (*ssu-ts'ai*). Why don't we live separately?" Li pretended to go along with this suggestion and told his wife to arrange a farewell banquet. When the guests had assembled, Li knelt before his mother and described how his wife had shamelessly wanted him to leave his mother and brothers. Then he expelled her.[32] This story illustrates the inequality and discord between brothers that a wife's property could cause (a theme raised throughout Chinese history in Confucian texts). Li's wife was not willing to share her property with the whole family and intended to keep it even from her husband until the family had divided. Her dowry property was firmly under her control. This issue gained prominence in the Sung.

Han law stipulated that, in case of a divorce, the property went with the woman back to her natal family. According to law, these property rights applied to divorces instigated by either the husband or the wife.[33] Some scholars even argue that children born to the serving maids of the wife went back with her at the time of divorce.[34]

Han documents provide examples of women disposing of property, including buying and selling land (which had become common for some types of land by Han times). A contract dated A.D. 176, preserved on a tile, states, "Liu Yüan-t'ai of Lo-ch'eng village of Kuang district buys from the wife of Liu Wen-p'ing of the same prefecture a parcel of grave mound land in Tai-yi village. The price is 20,000 cash."[35] In a document

---

30 *Hou-Han shu* (Peking: Chung-hua shu-chü, 1965; reprint 1973), 83:2773.
31 *Hou-Han shu*, 84:2781–2. The examples cited are all mentioned in Dull, "Marriage and Divorce," 48. The last is in Ch'ü, *Han Social Structure*, 283.
32 *Hou-Han shu*, 81:2684. See also Nakada, *Hōseishi ronshū*, Vol. 3, Pt. 2, 1343 n. 16.
33 Niida, *Bunsho*, 498–9; Tai, "Divorce in Traditional Chinese Law," 105 and n. 173.
34 Tai, "Divorce in Traditional Chinese Law," 105. Tai does not specify clearly his source regarding the serving maids, and I have not found it in a primary text. The point is interesting since (in later times at least) children of a wife's serving maids could be fathered by her husband.
35 Hugh Scogin, "Between Heaven and Man: Contract and the State in Han Dynasty China," *Southern California Law Review* 63:5 (July 1990): 1344.

from Loyang dated A.D. 188, a woman sells another woman one *mou* of uncultivated land for 3,000 cash.[36] Evidently, a widow could dispose of the estate of her late husband. A story from the first century B.C. includes a detailed contract for the sale of a slave. The slave is owned by a widow, and the contract describes the slave as "the bearded male slave, Pien-liao, of her husband's household."[37] There is further evidence in the Han to suggest that a widow could inherit her husband's estate and take it into a remarriage.[38] This probably happened when the couple had been living away from the husband's parents or when the parents were deceased, as was often the case.

Data for the Han are scarce, but the preceding examples and others suggest that dowry was a customary right enjoyed by daughters, and that it was not very different from property given to sons if they left home at marriage or when a household divided. Moreover, parents might distribute more of their wealth to their daughters after marriage, just as to their sons. While the conjugal unit as a whole benefited from dowry, and many husbands undoubtedly gained access to their wives' property, dowry was legally separate from other household property. Theoretically, a wife could dispose of her dowry without interference from her husband, and in case of divorce, a woman kept her property.

Finally, widows were able to take possession of the property of their late husbands, and data reveal them disposing of it. In some cases, they might take these assets into a remarriage.

Dowry versus Betrothal Gifts

The foregoing discussion shows that a married woman's private property was not merged with property held by her husband or his family. The loss of property that parents experienced when a daughter married was not strictly an exchange between families. Rather the property stayed with their daughter, and in some circumstances could come back to them.

In this regard, betrothal gifts given by the groom's family to the bride's were quite different from dowry. According to Confucian ritual texts, a

---

36 Scogin, "Between Heaven and Man," 1345.
37 C. Martin Wilbur, *Slavery in China during the Former Han Dynasty* (Chicago, 1943), 122; Scogin, "Between Heaven and Man," 1357. For a discussion of how this fictitious account must have corresponded to actual circumstances, see Anton F. P. Hulsewé, "Contracts of the Han Period," in *Il Diritto in Cina*, ed. Lionello Lanciotti (Florence: Leo S. Olschki, 1978), 30.
38 See the evidence presented by Jennifer Holmgren, "Economic Foundations of Virtue: Widow Remarriage in Early and Modern China," 5–6 (taken mostly from Dull, "Marriage and Divorce," and Ch'ü, *Han Social Structure*).

proper marriage required an exchange of property from the groom's family to the bride's parents. Such an exchange was one of the Six Rites of Marriage, which were to be followed for a marriage to be ritually complete. Without the proper rites, a woman became a mere concubine.[39] Jack Dull has shown that during the Han, the Six Rites were rarely observed, with precisely the exception of the fourth, the presentation of betrothal gifts (*na-cheng*).[40] Already in Han times, the transfer of betrothal gifts "was the key feature of the marriage ceremony."[41] Not only did the Confucian classic *Record of Rites* stress the mandatory nature of the betrothal gifts, but the other texts of the Han Confucian schools also agreed on their prime importance.[42] The prescriptions of the *Record of Rites (Li-chi)* were codified into law by the seventh century, and possibly well before. According to the T'ang code, once the bride's family received the betrothal gifts, no matter how meager or lavish they were, the engagement could not be broken off and the marriage was final. The code explains that accepting the gifts was legally the same as returning a formal written marriage agreement.[43] The *Classic of Etiquette and Ritual (I-li)* prescribes gifts of "a bundle of black and red silks and a pair of deer skins."[44] People in the Han disregarded the literal message of this passage and the families of elite brides demanded gifts of great extravagance.[45]

The betrothal gifts per se were not reciprocated; rather, the bride herself came to the husband's home with her own possessions. Legally and theoretically, no dowry was required to make a marriage complete, in contrast to betrothal gifts, which could not be dispensed with in a proper marriage. This meant that marriage customs in early China required a transfer of property from the groom's family to the bride's, but not vice versa. In contrast, the property that a bride's parents did sacrifice did not go directly to the husband's family. It was meant to be inherited by a woman's children, and these children could expect to have unlimited access to it only after their mother's death, when it could be used to support sacrifices to her spirit.

Even with the limited evidence available for the early period, we can already discern a conceptual barrier that stood between the resources of the wife and her natal family and those of her husband and his

39 Steele, *I-li* I, 18–41; Legge, *Li Chi* II, 428–30, and I, 78.
40 Dull, "Marriage and Divorce," 42–9.   41 Dull, "Marriage and Divorce," 45.
42 Both the *Huai-nan tzu* and the *Ta-Tai li-chi* stressed that licentiousness ensued without betrothal gifts; Dull, "Marriage and Divorce," 45.
43 *T'ang-lü shu-i*, 13:253–4. Even the acceptance of food and wine made the engagement legally binding. The penalty for breaking this law was 60 strokes of the bamboo.
44 Steele, *I-li* I, 21.   45 Dull, "Marriage and Divorce," 45–8.

household into which the wife moved at marriage. This barrier prevented the complete transfer of property from the wife's family to the husband's in their generation, and maintained the wife as a quasi-independent economic entity within her husband's household. This conceptual barrier and the practices that supported it continued in later dynasties.

T'ang Inheritance and Property Law

By the T'ang dynasty (618–906), the principle of "communal living, common property" in a joint household (*t'ung-chü kung-ts'ai*), under the patriarchal authority of the family head, had become the foundation of elite and commoner family values. It had become in effect the new Confucian ideal. The T'ang government encouraged joint families and supported the authority of the family head. To this end it promulgated laws and statutes that worked to enforce the rule of joint family living and curtail the freedom of family members, both male and female.

Several revisions of the law code were made in the early T'ang. The most authoritative version is attributed to T'ai-tsung's (r. 627–649) brother-in-law Ch'ang-sun Wu-chi (?–659), but all extant editions of the code are based on a revision of 737.[46] This compilation, known as *The T'ang Code*, was the basis of all subsequent law codes in China and the model for those of Japan, Korea, and Vietnam.[47] Its provisions, including those on the family and inheritance, were enormously influential.

The code itself as it comes down to us consists of 502 articles, each containing the main clause of code (*lü* 律), with commentaries (*chu* 註) and subcommentaries (*shu* 疏) appended.[48] The first section

[46] There is no evidence of significant change between the 653 and 737 revisions. In 653 Ch'ang-sun and his committee added the subcommentary (*shu*) to the articles of code (*lü*) and produced the most celebrated edition of the code. It was assumed that all extant versions of the code were based on Ch'ang-sun's edition, until in 1931, Niida Noboru and Makino Tatsumi proved that all extant versions are in fact from a text dated 737, the year that is now the accepted date of the T'ang code. Wallace Johnson, *The T'ang Code*, Vol. I, *General Principles* (Princeton, N.J.: Princeton University Press, 1979), 39–40. From the Yüan on, the title has been *T'ang lü shu-i* (literally: "The T'ang code with subcommentary and explanations").

[47] Johnson, *T'ang Code* I, 9. For more information, see Niida Noboru, *Chūgoku hōseishi kenkyū*, Vol. I, *Keihō* (Tokyo: Tōkyō daigaku shuppankai, 1959; reprint 1991), 301–596.

[48] See *T'ang lü shu-i*. The commentaries (*chu*) contain essential elements of the code and are thus seen to be an integral part of the code itself. They are often printed in smaller type appended to each article of code. The subcommentaries are helpful explanations and expansions of the code written by Ch'ang-sun's committee. Johnson, *T'ang Code* I, 43.

of the code, comprising 57 articles, sets forth General Principles (*ming-li* 名例), which are largely explanations of status differences, social hierarchy, and gradations of punishment. Seniors are given authority over juniors, commoners over slaves and bondsmen (*chien-min*), and men over women. Certain heinous offenses, labeled "The Ten Abominations," are highlighted by inclusion in the General Principles (under Article 6) as well as being covered in more detail in the body of the code.[49] Under the heading "Lack of Filial Piety" (the seventh of the Ten Abominations) are several injunctions designed to buttress the family system and the hierarchy of status within it. In one example, sons and grandsons may not register as a separate household or maintain separate property as long as their parents are alive.[50] Later, in the main body of the code, Article 155 addresses this issue more concretely, prescribing three years of penal servitude for sons and grandsons who set up separate households or divide property without their parents' permission.[51]

To find more detail on inheritance and family division, we must look beyond the provisions of the code itself to the more specific rules of administration spelled out in the Statutes (*ling* 令).[52] The Statutes were almost as important for the daily administration of justice as the code itself.

The statute on inheritance, issued in 719 and again in 737, had five main sections with important commentary. The five sections are translated in full as follows:[53]

1. All fields, houses, and movable property involved in the family division should be divided equally among older and younger brothers.
Commentary: After the parents and grandparents have died, brothers who have been living separately with a separate stove for more than three years, or those who have run away for more than six years, even though they did not receive any of their parents' or grandparents' fields, houses, shops, mills, retainers, or

---

49 These "Ten Abominations" are mostly crimes that threaten the authority of the state or the family. See discussion in Johnson, *T'ang Code* I, 17ff.
50 *T'ang lü shu-i*, 1:12; Johnson, *T'ang Code* I, 33, 74.
51 *T'ang lü shu-i*, 12:236. The process of household registration and changes in the system is described by Ikeda On, "T'ang Household Registers and Related Documents," in *Perspectives on the T'ang*, ed. Arthur Wright and Denis Twitchett (New Haven, Conn.: Yale Univeristy Press, 1973); 135 discusses family division.
52 The Statutes do not survive as a whole, but they have been reconstructed from quotations and fragments by the Japanese legal scholar Niida Noboru in his *Tōryō shūi* (1933; reprint Tokyo: Tōkyō daigaku shuppankai, 1983). Two other forms of T'ang law were the Regulations (*ko*) and Ordinances (*shih*). The translations I use for these terms are found in Johnson, *T'ang Code* I, 5.
53 Niida, *Tōryō*, 245. See also Niida, *Bunsho*, 583; Shiga, *Genri*, 245.

slaves[54] which are now being divided, may not [return and] request shares of the estate.[55]

2. Property from the wife's family is not to be part of the division.

Commentary: If the wife has died, her natal family may not seek to dispose of any of her assets or slaves (*tzu-ts'ai chi nu-pi*).

3. If any one of the brothers has died, his sons inherit their father's portion.

Commentary: This also applies to an adopted heir.

4. If all of the brothers have died, the property is divided equally among all of their sons [i.e., grandsons of the head of household].

Commentary: The father's and grandfather's permanent lands and imperial gift lands should also be equally divided. The personal share lands should be distributed according to the age-status rules [of equal field distributions].[56] Even if the land is limited in quantity, it should be divided according to this rule.

5. Any sons who have not yet obtained wives should receive a separate portion for their betrothal gift. Any unmarried daughters or aunts [father's sisters] should receive portions equal to half the amount of the son's betrothal gift. Any widowed wives without sons should receive their husband's share. If all of the husband's brothers have died, the widow should receive the same portion as one of the sons.

Commentary: If the widow has a son, she does not get a separate portion, assuming she stays in her husband's house as a chaste widow. If she remarries, she may not dispose of the retainers, slaves, fields, and houses [of her husband], but [must leave them] to be divided equally among the remaining coparceners (*ying-fen jen* 應分人).

Sections 1, 3, and 4 of this statute pertain to inheritance by sons. The statute clearly states the concept of equal division among brothers. The coparceners are those who reside in the joint family household, and residence is the primary qualification for inheritance. If a son has left the

54 Retainers (*pu-ch'ü*) and slaves (*nu-pi*) are two of three categories of servile people mentioned in the code. The third is bondsmen (*k'o-hu*), either government (*kuan-hu*) or general (*tsa-hu*). Many other degrees of bondage existed in the T'ang, but the four characters *pu-ch'ü nu-pi* seem to have referred to them all. For a complete discussion, see Niida Noboru, *Chūgoku mibunhō shi* (1942; reprint, Tokyo: Tōkyō daigaku shuppankai, 1983), 858–997 [hereafter cited as *Mibunhō*]. The history of the term *pu-ch'ü* is discussed in Yang Chung-i, "Evolution of the status of 'Dependents,' " in *Chinese Social History*, ed. E-tu Zen Sun and J. de Francis (Washington D.C.: American Council of Learnied Societies, 1956), 142–56.

55 The implication here is that the property division would already have taken place without the missing brothers and they could not then request a redivision (*pu-te ch'e-keng lun fen*).

56 The different categories of land in this passage reflect the "equal field" (*chün-t'ien*) distribution system of the T'ang dynasty. For an excellent English summary, see Denis Twitchett, *Financial Administration under the T'ang* (Cambridge: Cambridge University Press, 1963; reprint 1970), 1–23; and Wan Kuo-ting, "The System of Equal Land Allotments in Medieval Times," in *Chinese Social History*, ed. Sun and de Francis.

household, after a three- or six-year period (depending on the circumstances of his leaving) his claim on any inheritance from family division is lost. The commentary in Section 1 addresses the practice left over from earlier times where a son might receive a portion of property and set up a new household while his parents still lived. The T'ang statute assumes that a son who lives separately with parental permission has already received property, and it prohibits "double dipping" by such a person. If a son runs away without permission, after six years he can no longer be forgiven and receives nothing. If all the sons die, the various grandsons constitute a new joint family with the grandparents and divide the property equally among themselves, regardless of the shares previously due their fathers. The cousins now form the first line generation of cohabitors and thus are coparceners. Each will establish a new household (*chia*) and a new descent line.

Women were not officially part of the coparcener group. A wife who married into the family shared her husband's portion. As seen in Section 5, if her husband died, she received his inheritance. The widow represented the imaginary, potential descent line of her dead husband. As long as she did not remarry, remaining a chaste widow, she could keep and dispose of her husband's property in a household that she now headed. (The family was being divided, so presumably no parents- or brothers-in-law remained in her household.) As Shiga Shūzō has emphasized, the idea was that the widow would transmit the property to an heir (adopted if necessary) who could perpetuate the family sacrifices. She was like a place-holder link in her husband's family line.[57] If the widow remarried, she would break the descent line. In this case her husband's patrimony was transferred to her agnatic nephews, who gave sacrifices to her husband's ancestors and formed their own descent lines, which had not been broken. The widow's first husband would have no progeny and no official sacrifices unless the widow had sons who stayed behind when she remarried (a common occurrence).

Section 2, in prominent position, instructed that a wife's property was not part of the family division. The husband's joint family establishment could not dispose of the property that a woman brought into her marriage. This dowry was for her own personal use both before and after the division. But what happened to the wife's personal property after she died? The customary barrier between the property of the wife and her family and that of her husband and his, which I have described above, might raise the possibility of the widow's family reclaiming the dowry. The commentary specifically forbids this, suggesting

57 Shiga, *Genri*, 415–33.

that it may have happened in past cases. If a woman had sons or daughters, her property went to them. But if she had none, the disposition of her dowry was complicated and was not clearly specified in T'ang or Sung law.

Section 5 shows that daughters and aunts received property at the time of family division, if this took place before they got married and moved out of the household. There was a parallel between the residence requirement for a son and the practice of giving daughters property either at family division or at marriage, whichever was first. When a daughter married, she stopped being resident in the household, and thus her claim to a share of the later division was weakened or eliminated. As a result, her portion of property was given to her at the time of marriage, as dowry. Daughters may have routinely inherited less property than sons, but they had a strong customary and legal right to some share of their father's estate.

A manuscript from Tunhuang dating to the T'ai-ho period (827–836) verifies this point. Appended to one of a few surviving family division contracts is a more general document where a father who is terminally ill enjoins his two sons and one daughter to divide the family property fairly (following their mother's instructions) and not fight over it after his death. He explicitly includes his daughter as a beneficiary of the family division.[58]

Much has been made of the clause in Section 5 that gives sons a betrothal gift twice the size of their sisters' dowry; and it may indicate that betrothal gifts were usually larger than dowries among the T'ang elite.[59] We cannot tell from the statute how large either a dowry or a betrothal gift was likely to be in comparison to a man's entire estate. As in earlier times, a father in the T'ang could give his daughter a dowry of any amount he wished. Dowry, like the betrothal gift, was subject to negotiation between the parties at the time of a marriage (though this was officially frowned on), and among the upper classes both dowries and betrothal gifts could be enormous. In 642 T'ai-tsung bemoaned the commercial nature of marriage arrangements. He complained that the great clans demanded huge dowries or betrothal gifts that humiliated whichever partner had paid out the most for the marriage.[60] In 659

58 Stein #6537; Lionel Giles, *Descriptive Catalogue of the Chinese Manuscripts from Tunhuang in the British Museum* (London: British Museum, 1957), 185; reprinted in Niida Noboru, *Hōseishi* III, 582 (and Plate 7, which reproduces part of the original).
59 This position is argued by Patricia Ebrey, and this statute is a key piece of evidence; "Shifts," 107.
60 *T'ang hui-yao* (Taipei: Kuo-hsüeh chi-pen ts'ung-shu, 1968), 83:1528; Johnson, *Medieval Chinese Oligarchy*, 50.

his successor Kao-tsung further attempted to reform marriage practices by prohibiting marriages between certain aristocratic clans and forbidding the exchange of extravagant betrothal gifts. Significantly, his same edict of 659 had the effect of supporting women's rights to personal property. Kao-tsung demanded that betrothal gifts in elite marriages all be given to the bride as part of her dowry, so that her family did not make a net profit on her marriage, and he further proclaimed that the husband's family was not to appropriate this dowry property.[61] Kao-tsung's words provide further evidence of the already long tradition of giving elite daughters considerable property at the time of their marriage. They could receive this property directly from their parents or indirectly from their new in-laws through their parents. (If all of the betrothal gifts indeed went to the bride as dowry, as Kao-tsung instructed, it might explain why the dowry portion guaranteed in the statutes was just half the betrothal gifts.) The edict also reinforces the concept of a barrier between the personal resources of a wife and those of the family into which she married, even when her personal property came indirectly from her in-laws in the form of betrothal gifts. Though granted, Kao-tsung's words suggest that the barrier was easily breeched and needed continual legal reinforcement.

In some circumstances daughters could receive another form of inheritance above and beyond dowry or post-marriage gifts. If a woman had no brothers, when both her parents died the family line was considered to be extinct, or "cut off" (*hu-chüeh* 戶絕). The statute of 719 and 737 translated above does not address this situation, but another of 737 speaks to it explicitly. It specifies that in case someone dies leaving a cut-off household (*hu-chüeh*), once appropriate burial and funeral services are paid for, the rest of the estate goes entirely to the surviving daughters. If no daughters survive either, the property should go to the next nearest relatives. If no relatives can be found, the state confiscates the property; but if the deceased leaves a testament, his wishes are honored and the statute is null.[62] This statute shows that T'ang law recognized a

---

61 *T'ang hui-yao*, 83:1528–9. Ebrey, "Shifts," 100, cites this but gives the date as 657. Ebrey uses this edict to argue that more complaints were made about large betrothal gifts than dowries in the T'ang, and thus betrothal gifts were larger than dowries. Kao-tsung like T'ai-tsung seems to have been concerned about mercenary marriages generally, and if betrothal gifts went largely or entirely toward the dowry, dowries must have been large too. Johnson, *Medieval Chinese Oligarchy*, 50, cites this edict to say that Kao-tsung was limiting "dowries," but I agree with Ebrey that the text reads that limits are being placed on betrothal gifts.

62 Niida, *Tōryō*, 835; *Hōseishi* III, 381; *Mibunhō*, 478–9; Shiga, *Genri*, 396. Though I have no direct evidence for the T'ang period, I would assume that a sole surviving woman could also leave a testament.

certain "right of survivorship," as Niida calls it,[63] separate from the concern, strong as it was, to preserve sacrifices in an endless line of descendants. Daughters as blood relatives could inherit all of their parents' property when sacrifices were no longer an issue.

A commentary on the statute states that if the government registers indicate the deceased is still part of a joint family, but in fact division has already taken place, the statute still applies and the daughters get the property.[64] This has been interpreted to mean that the statute held only if family division in the father's generation had taken place and the deceased father (or mother) had been the head of a household. If her father had still been in a joint household when he died, a daughter would not receive his portion as a son would, but would get only a dowry portion, the rest going back into the communal pool for her uncles (father's brothers) and their sons to inherit.[65] Again the residence test was crucial to the disposition of property. If agnatic cousins lived in the household, they could claim some of the property that would have gone to the natal daughters. Daughters had inheritance rights that took precedence over agnatic cousins only if family division had taken place and they lived separately from these cousins.

Marriage may also have affected inheritance by daughters in a cut-off household. The 737 statute did not specify that the daughters had to be unmarried to inherit, and presumably many did get such inheritance after their marriage. But in the opinion of some officials, marriage could weaken their claims on the property. In what was probably a hypothetical problem given to exam candidate Wang Yüeh (fl. 904–905), a wealthy man was said to have died after his only daughter had married. The government tried to confiscate his property, but the married daughter sued to recover it. The father's younger brother also sued. In a written response called a "judgment" (*p'an* 判)[66] candidate Wang Yüeh

---

63 *Hōseishi* III, 381.

64 Niida, *Tōryō*, 835. This commentary incidentally confirms that the government registers were routinely out of date and inaccurate.

65 Niida, *Hōseishi* III, 381 n. 3, 382. Shiga, *Genri*, 396. Niida and Shiga disagree slightly on the interpretation of this commentary. Niida follows Nakada to understand the "separate [living]" to apply to the daughter not to the deceased father; *Hōseishi* III, 381 n. 3. This would affect married daughters. See next paragraph.

66 The genre *p'an* in the T'ang consisted of responses to hypothetical cases given to candidates for promotion as a test of their literary abilities. They were written in flowery and allusive language, and there is no evidence that they had anything to do with real applications of the law. See David McMullen, *State and Scholarship in T'ang China* (Cambridge: Cambridge University Press, 1988), 26, 231; Ch'en Chih-ch'ao, "Ming k'o-pen *Ming-kung shu-p'an ch'ing-ming chi* chieh-shao," appendix to *Ming-kung shu-p'an ch'ing-ming chi* (CMC) (Peking: Chung-hua shu-chü, 1987), 659–61; Niida Noboru, "*Meikō shohan seimeishū* kaidai," Postface to *Meikō shohan seimeishū* (Tokyo: Koten kenkyūkai, 1964), 3.

decided in favor of the younger brother, on the grounds that he was of the same surname as the deceased and could carry on essentially the same family line, whereas the daughter had entered another lineage (*tsu*) and her property would not benefit her father's line.[67] This judgment shows that it was probably possible for a married daughter to inherit her father's estate after marriage, but that some officials were concerned enough about patriline continuation to give agnatic relatives advantages over daughters.

Conclusion

Early Confucian texts laid out patriarchal principles that gave men authority over women and dictated that succession to status and transmission of property follow male patrilines. Ancestor worship, always along agnatic lines as defined in Confucian ritual texts, further tied property to men and male descendants. Nevertheless, evidence from early China presents a very different picture and allows us to discern the general contours of traditional practices whereby Confucian morality adapted to the times, and considerable property devolved to women.

Confucian ethics, as seen in elite values, legal codes, and ritual and philosophical texts, evolved with changing social structures, such that the idea of the descent-line system that supported a clanwide patriline appropriate to an idealized version of Chou feudalism was replaced by the concept that each son, not just the eldest, carried on a family line into eternity. This meant that each son succeeded to sacrifices, and each son had the legal right to a share of the family patrimony. By Han times, if not well before, the communal economic unit did not extend beyond the *chia*, usually a group of brothers living with their parents and wives, and within this the right of a son to a share of the family assets equal to that of his brothers was firmly entrenched in law and practice.

Women were excluded from the ritual patriline and thus had no legal guarantees to family property. Nevertheless, the evidence shows that in fact property was routinely passed down through women. In the highly class-stratified, agrarian society of traditional China, social status was supported by material wealth. When a woman entered a marriage, she brought her family status with her, in large part confirmed by the size of her dowry. Customary practice ensured that a daughter enter marriage with personal property appropriate to her family's social and mate-

67 *Ch'üan T'ang wen* (Beijing: Chung-hua shu-chü, 1983), 821:8653 (Vol. 9); Wong Sunming, "Confucian Ideal and Reality: Transformation of the Institution of Marriage in T'ang China" (Ph.D. dissertation Univ. of Washington, 1979), 253.

rial position. Scattered evidence from the Han and after further shows that married women might continue to receive gifts and inheritance from their parents before or after the parents' death. The strict requirements of Confucian ritual, and even the more popular practices of ancestor worship and continuation of the male family line, had minimal effect on family decisions about property transmission. Parents were as much concerned with the well-being of their daughters and alliances formed through good marriages in this life as they were with less tangible concerns of patrilines and rituals for the after life. A deceased couple needed sons to feed their hungry ghosts, but this did not mean that natal daughters had to be disinherited.

Once married, a woman's physical presence in the home of her husband meant that her property benefited her new family, and her husband undoubtedly exercised certain control over it. But a wife's property always had a personal nature to it that kept it legally and practically distinct from the communal estate of the larger household. Before the Sung, when women's property consisted largely of jewelry, movables, and personal attendants, the private nature of the assets was especially clear. As seen in the introduction to this book, the vocabulary of women's property – often denoting boxes, cases, or even cosmetics – reinforced the personal, private nature of it. When women left marriages, their dowry property went with them. Laws on divorce required property to be returned with the woman, even if she were expelled with legal cause. While many women may have been prevented from enjoying their rights to property, both within a marriage and when leaving it, the understanding that dowry was attached to the woman herself, whether married, divorced, or widowed, was embodied in legal norms and customary practice. This gave women recourse to natal family members, courts of law, and social pressure to try to enforce rights to their property. The demographic fact that most couples lived in nuclear family households meant that often when the husband died, the wife additionally gained control of her husband's estate. Widows are seen defending their assets in court from Han times on, just as male heads of household did; and while widows without powerful connections may have had trouble exercising their legal rights to property, state support for these rights in court provided at least one significant source of redress.

From T'ang times on, we have much more detailed evidence of inheritance and property law. The great T'ang code is the first Chinese legal code to survive in full, and it is our earliest record of formal inheritance statutes. The T'ang was a period when scholar-officials were making conscious efforts to inject Confucian morality into social practice. The code reflected these efforts, encouraging the ethic of filial piety through communal living and descent-line sacrifices. Classical injunctions about marriage were enforced for the first time, and ritual manuals designed to make the ancient classics usable in the present were produced.[68] With regard to succession, the rule of equal inheritance among brothers, which had long since become customary, was written into law. The law placed emphasis on coresidence as a requirement for inheritance, reflecting the relatively uncommercialized economy of the T'ang and the government's attempts to preserve a stable agrarian population regulated by the equal field system (an attempt that was already unrealistic in T'ang times).

By longstanding customary practice, women continued to receive a portion of the family assets. The residence test can be seen to have applied by analogy to them as well: a daughter left the household at marriage, and accordingly she received her portion at that time as dowry or at the time of family division, whichever was first. Orphaned daughters were given certain legal rights to the dowry they had become accustomed to receiving, while orphaned sons were ensured a betrothal gift. The law stipulated that the latter was twice the size of the former, perhaps reflecting the practice of families using betrothal gifts to outfit the bride. Within a joint household in the T'ang, an orphaned daughter with no brothers did not receive her father's share of property, rather it went to the coresident agnates. Dowry was determined by the new household head, and orphaned daughters received nothing beyond their dowry portion, even if they had no brothers. After family division had occurred, however, a family line was considered to be "cut off" if no sons survived, and the daughters could inherit all of their parents' estate. The law made no distinction between married or unmarried daughters who could thus inherit, but claims of married daughters to this property may have been weakened.

T'ang law clearly stated the rule that the wife's assets were not part of family division and were thus not combined into the communal estate. Within a marriage, it was referred to as "dowry," but it may have come to her as a dowry portion at the time of her marriage, as a portion of the communal estate at the time of family division, or even as straight inheritance when her parents died if she had no brothers. While the law codified the barrier between the wife's property and that of her

68 See Wong, "Confucian Ideal"; Patricia Ebrey, *Confucianism and Family Rituals in Imperial China: A Social History of Writing about Rites* (Princeton, N.J.: Princeton University Press, 1991), 38–9; and David McMullen, "Bureaucrats and Cosmology: The Ritual Code of T'ang China," in *Rituals of Royalty*, ed. David Cannadine and Simon Price (Cambridge: Cambridge University Press, 1987).

husband, imperial exhortations against the husband's family appropriating dowry property may indicate the difficulty of enforcing rights
to personal property within marriage. Nevertheless, as in times past,
a woman could take her assets out of the marriage, though if she
died, her family could not reclaim her dowry; it had to be left to her
husband's heirs.

A widow was responsible for her husband's line of succession. As long
as she remained in his household, she represented his actual or potential heirs, and thus had rights to the husband's share at the time of family
division. (If she had sons, the share went to them to be managed by her
as household head if they were minors, or jointly with her if they were
adults.) If a widow remarried, she was no longer part of the agnatic line,
and could not claim any of her husband's assets, though she could still
claim her dowry. In this way, succession to a place in the patriline was
legally tied to transmission of agnatic property. Dowry property stood
outside of agnatic transmission and stayed with a woman. Widows who
did not remarry still formed a link in the patriline and as such could
legally control considerable assets.

The enormous prestige of the T'ang and the Chinese veneration of
the past ensured that the T'ang code would be copied in large part into
all later law codes. The basic provisions of marriage and inheritance survived intact. As society underwent inevitable change, however, some
injunctions of T'ang law became obsolete. Later governments were left
to enact additional legislation to respond to contemporary needs, and
a thick layer of edicts, statutes, and ordinances obscured the original
intent of some of the T'ang provisions. I will show in the next chapter
how the Sung state responded to historical change and popular practice
with legal activism that in several respects worked in favor of women.

2
Women and Property in the Sung: Legal Innovation in Changing Times

The Sung can be seen as a high point for women's property rights in China. Whereas Sung women's relation to property was broadly consistent with earlier tradition, in rapidly changing times and unstable economic conditions, women's property took on new importance and received new protections. Detailed laws dictated the devolution of property to daughters under various conditions and protected a wife's property within marriage and after widowhood. A plethora of legislation allowed considerable wealth to pass to families of different surnames through daughters or be taken into second and third marriages by widows. Most significantly, legal language originally intended to protect the agnatic line was reinterpreted to justify the transfer of property to daughters. These developments represented the culmination of a trend, already underway before the Sung, away from patrilineal principles and toward protection of women's property rights.

Social and economic changes during the Sung that affected the dynamic between state and society also affected the evolution of property rights and our knowledge of these. The spread of literacy and printing of law books gave more people the ability to go to court. The scope of litigation expanded as men and women in large numbers disputed property in court or appealed to the state for protection of property rights. Additionally, a wealth of records produced by the new Sung printing industry make it possible to fill in details of legal developments left unknown for earlier periods.

Property was fundamental to maintaining elite status in the Sung, for both men and women. The presence or absence of dowry determined whether a bride entered her marital family as a principal wife or a concubine, as a free woman or in servitude. If her parents had died, a woman needed property to keep from falling into servile status. New laws aimed at protecting orphaned girls are especially noteworthy in the Sung. Beyond status for the woman herself, dowry cemented marriage ties between families, which were another vital component of elite social strategies in the Sung. Without a large dowry, a woman could not marry into an influential household and serve as a link to powerful relatives. Affinal connections helped men gain education, sit for the examinations, or obtain office through hereditary ("shadow," *yin*) privilege. More fundamentally, parents often turned to their daughters and affinal kin for financial support. The dowry they had earlier provided could be their own safety net.[1] Links to the right affines provided insurance for desperate times, which could befall even wealthy official families in the fluid and diversified economy of the Sung.

Large dowries became a hallmark of the Sung elite, causing hardship on parents who had to generate them. Reflecting the loosening of controls on land sales and ownership, Sung dowries often included large amounts of land. Landed dowries are not recorded in earlier periods and were rare or nonexistent in later periods. Their regular appearance in the Sung, even among peasants of moderate means, was a unique feature of the times.

The prominence of dowry, complex land rights, strong affinal ties, and fine gradations of status all place Sung society firmly within Jack Goody's model of sedentary Eurasian society, as described in the Introduction. These features point to how Sung China represented a prime example of the Eurasian mode of production in sharp contrast to the Mongols, who were to invade in the thirteenth century.

Several themes are discernible in the material that follows. Each illustrates an historical trend in the Sung that affected legislation and practice surrounding women's property, and men's. First, even though Confucian ideals of patrilineality continued to provide the vocabulary for property law in the Sung as in the T'ang, women gained from a reinterpretation of this language and flexible application of the law. Second, from early in the dynasty the Sung state asserted its authority to intervene in inheritance matters. Changes in the laws of inheritance and confiscation reflect official efforts to prevent land aggrandizement by rich families and to secure income for the imperial treasuries to fight border wars.

---

1 On the importance of affines, see Walton, "Kinship, Marriage and Status in Sung China"; and Bossler, *Powerful Relations*. For examples of large dowries in the Sung and men borrowing to pay for them, see Ch'en P'eng, *Chung-kuo hun-yin shih-kao* (Peking: Chung-hua shu-chü, 1990), 137–42.

Third, the spread of organized agnatic kin groups created challenges to women's expanding inheritance and property rights. Even as women controlled more property, in particular landed property, during the Sung than at any other time in Chinese history, their property rights came to be encroached upon by the state on one side and by lineages on the other.

Finally, even as Sung law gave new protection to women's property that lasted for the duration of the dynasty, the development of Learning of the Way Confucianism led to a new discourse of disapproval over women's property. Confucian reformers attempted to apply classical Confucian ideals to contemporary society, including the ideal of strict patrilineality, which cut women out of inheritance. A more thorough exploration of the Confucian response to the changing relation between women and property is left for Chapters 3 and 4, but it will also be evident in some of the material below.

Sung Law and the Legal System

In its effort to unify and then hold on to the Chinese empire, the Sung government codified laws and supplementary legislation to create judicial norms that were universal, consistent and widely applicable. To this end, the founder Chao K'uang-yin hurried to promulgate a law code and in 963 issued the *Collected Penal Laws of the Sung (Sung hsing-t'ung,* hereafter *Sung Penal Laws*).[2] This code was largely copied from that of the Later Chou dynasty (950–965), the *Collected Penal Laws of the Great Chou (Ta-Chou hsing-t'ung)*, which in turn was based on the T'ang code of 737. Many of the provisions in the *Sung Penal Laws* were copied verbatim from T'ang laws, illustrating the Sung desire to promote an image of continuity with the past even as innovation swept away old practices.[3] The main difference in the form of the two codes is that the *Sung Penal Laws* gathered pieces of later legislation (statutes, edicts, etc.) and appended them to the relevant items of code, making the document a more useful legal reference work.

2 Hereafter cited in the text as *Sung Penal Laws* and in the notes as SHT. All references are to *Sung hsing-t'ung,* Tou I et al. (Peking: Chung-hua shu-chü, 1984). I give the traditional *chüan* number followed by a colon, then the page number in the modern edition.

3 This introduction to Sung law is based on Miyazaki Ichisada, "The Administration of Justice during the Sung Dynasty," in *Essays on China's Legal Tradition,* ed. Jerome Cohen, Randle Edwards, and Fu-mei Chang Chen (Princeton, N.J.: Princeton University Press, 1980); Brian McKnight, "From Statute to Precedent: An Introduction to Sung Law and its Transformation," in *Law and the State in Traditional East Asia,* ed. Brian McKnight (Honolulu: University of Hawaii Press, 1987); and Brian McKnight, "Chinese Law and Legal Systems: Five Dynasties and Sung," draft chapter for Cambridge History of China (1989 version). I thank Brian McKnight for letting me cite his unpublished manuscript.

The Sung state solved the problem of updating codified law to respond to changing times by issuing large numbers of legal directives in the form of statutes (*ling* 令), regulations (*ko* 格), ordinances or administrative rules (*shih* 式), and edicts (*ch'ih* 敕).[4] Precedents (*li* 例) and "clarified instructions" (*shen-ming* 申明, also called "explanatory edicts") were also used.[5] These were compiled into works such as "Collections of Edicts" (*Pien-ch'ih*) and "Classified Laws" (*T'iao-fa shih-lei*), which were meant to supersede the outdated code and guide officials in the application of the law. An example of the latter survives from the Ch'ing-yüan period (1195–1200), understandably titled *Classified Laws of the Ch'ing-yüan Period* (*Ch'ing-yüan t'iao-fa shih-lei*). Unfortunately, the other collections do not survive, but legal documents, including statutes and memorials, were preserved in an administrative compilation, *Important Documents of the Sung* (*Sung hui-yao*), and in official and unofficial histories. These cover legal developments up to about the 1220s.[6]

Of most interest for this study, a different genre of legal writing developed in the Sung, which unlike the documents just mentioned shows us how laws were applied to actual cases. This genre was called "written judgments" (*shu-p'an* 書判). These are short essays, written by a presiding judge, that summarize the facts of a case and pronounce the verdict.[7]

4 The translations of these terms have been inconsistent between T'ang and Sung scholars and between different scholars of the Sung. T'ang scholars have consistently translated these words as: *lü*: code; *ling*: statute; *ko*: regulation; *shih*: ordinance; see Johnson, *Tang Code* I, 5; Twitchett, *Financial Administration*; Denis Twitchett, "The Fragment of the T'ang Ordinances of the Department of Waterways," *Asia Major* 6:1 (1957); Endymion Wilkinson, *The History of Imperial China: A Research Guide* (Cambridge, Mass.: Harvard University Press, 1973), 132. The major Western interpreter of Sung law, Brian McKnight, departs from these usages, arguing that the meanings changed over time. He translates as: *lü*: statute; *ling*: ordinance; *ko*: regulation; *shih*: specification or administrative rule; see "From Statute to Precedent" esp. 112–13, and "Chinese Law and Legal Systems." The Sung scholar Miyazaki Ichisada in a 1980 article used a formula closer to the T'ang: *lü*: original statute; *ling*: administrative statute; *ko*: regulation; *shih*: ordinance; see "Administration of Justice." Everyone agrees that *ch'ih* translates as "edict," and *ko* is noncontroversial as "regulation" (though in the Yüan, the term is closer to "statute"; see Chapter 4). I follow T'ang usage in this chapter, as in Chapter 1. My frequent indication of the Chinese original should prevent any confusion.

5 McKnight, "From Statute to Precedent," 113–17; McKnight, "Chinese Law and Legal Systems," 10–12.

6 See Wang Yün-hai, *Sung hui-yao chi-kao k'ao-chiao* (Shanghai: Ku-chi, 1986). All citations are to *Sung hui-yao chi-kao* (Peking: Chung-hua shu-chü, 1987); hereafter cited as SHY.

7 These should not be confused with the earlier genre of *p'an*, which was a category of writing on selection and promotion tests in the T'ang known for its obscure and allusive style (McMullen, *State and Scholars in T'ang China*, 26, 231). The straightforward writing and moralistic tone of Sung dynasty *shu-p'an*, by contrast, supports the contention of Peter Bol that moral correctness superseded literary accomplishment in the Sung as the goal of literati endeavor (Bol, *"This Culture of Ours"*). The evolution of *shu-p'an* as a genre can also be understood in the context of developments like the statecraft movement; see Ch'en Chih-ch'ao, "Chieh-shao," 661–4.

A collection of these judgments survives from the Southern Sung, covering the years 1210 to 1260; it is the *Collection of Decisions by Famous Judges to Clarify and Enlighten*, or the *Collected Decisions* (*Ming-kung shu-p'an ch'ing-ming chi* or *Ch'ing-ming chi*).[8]

Until recently, the only extant edition of the *Collected Decisions* was a small part of the Southern Sung original (preface dated 1261), preserved in the Seikadō library in Tokyo. It contains 4 *chüan* and 136 cases, mostly on family issues, that represent about one-third of the total work.[9] Then in 1984, a virtually complete edition from the Ming dynasty was uncovered in the Shanghai Municipal library, containing 14 *chüan* and 473 cases, with material on nearly every aspect of daily life and legal procedure. This complete edition was published in 1987.[10]

The author of the *Collected Decisions* cannot be positively identified, except that he was from Chien-ning, Fukien (the home prefecture of the philosopher Chu Hsi and an area of importance to this study).[11] The Sung edition, preserved in Japan, includes a fragment of a preface written by the compiler of the work. The date is 1261, and he signs himself with a four-character sobriquet that can be made out to read "Great-grandson of the curtained pavilion" (*Man-t'ing tseng-sun*). (See Figures 2 and 3.) The Chinese scholar Ch'en Chih-ch'ao has traced the classical allusions in this expression to mean a person from Ch'ung-an county in the Wu-i Mountains of Chien-ning.[12] Further, he has found another text by an author using the same sobriquet, who can be identi-

---

8 About half of this work has been translated by Brian McKnight and James T. C. Liu, under the title *The Enlightened Judgments: Ch'ing-ming Chi, The Sung Dynasty Collection* (Albany: State University of New York Press, 1999).

9 *Meikō shohan seimeishū* (Tokyo: Koten kenkyūkai, 1964). Umehara Kaoru has translated this edition with useful notes; *Meikō shohan seimeishū yakuchū* (Kyoto: Dōhōsha, 1986).

10 *Ming-kung shu-p'an ch'ing-ming chi* (Peking: Chung-hua shu-chü, 1987). All references to the *Ch'ing-ming chi* are to this edition, hereafter cited as CMC. The Ming edition was copied from the *Yung-lo ta-tien* and printed in 1569 by a man named Chang Ssu-wei. He took the 14 *chüan* of Sung material out of a 17-*chüan* work that included cases from the Yüan. Until 1984 it was thought that both the 14-*chüan* version and the 17-*chüan* version were lost (bibliographies and fragments from the *Yung-lo ta-tien* indicated their former existence). The 4-*chüan* version in the Tokyo Seikadō library, believed to date to the Sung, agrees almost completely with the complete Ming edition from Shanghai. The editors of the 1987 edition conveniently indicate in notes any differences between the two texts. Unfortunately, the three *chüan* of Yüan material that made up the complete *Yung-lo ta-tien* version are still missing.

11 The following discussion is based on Ch'en Chih-ch'ao, "Chieh-shao," 645–85; Ch'en Chih-ch'ao, "Ming k'o-pen *Ming-kung shu-p'an ch'ing-ming chi* shu-lüeh," *Chung-kuo shih yen-chiu*, no. 4 (1984), 137–52; and two postfaces to the Seikadō edition, *Meikō shohan seimeishū* (Tokyo: Koten, 1964): Niida Noboru, "*Meikō shohan seimeishū* kaidai"; and Nagasawa Noritsune, "Hampon kaisetsu." See also Niida Noboru, "Eiraku Taitenbon 'Seimeishū' ni tsuite," in *Hōseishi* IV, 437–41.

12 Ch'en, "Chieh-shao," 650–1; Ch'en, "Shu-lüeh," 184.

fied. This work dates to 1216, forty-five years before the *Collected Decisions*, and is a Taoist compendium by an unemployed literatus named Chan Yen-fu. In this earlier work Chan Yen-fu also calls himself "descendant of Hsien-ye" (*Hsien-ye hou-jen*). Chan Hsien-ye was a prefectural exam graduate of 1026 who never took up office but lived in retirement in Ch'ung-an. The later Chan would seem to have had a similar career, and might understandably have identified with this ancestor. The reference to Hsien-ye further identifies the author as someone from Ch'ung-an. Nevertheless, the question remains, was Chan Yen-fu the same "Great-grandson of the Curtained Pavilion" as the person who compiled the *Collected Decisions*? Ch'en Chih-ch'ao suspects he was not, because of the forty-five-year gap between the dates of the two works with this name attached. Although forty-five years may seem to a modern scholar a long time between books, it does not in my opinion eliminate the possibility that the authors of the two books were the same person. Moreover, other books no longer extant may have been published in between. Conclusive identification awaits further evidence.

While the exact identity of the author may remain a mystery, we *can* conclude that he was from Ch'ung-an county in the Wu-i mountains of Chien-ning. This information helps explain the contents of the work. A large number of the cases are by local Chien-ning men or by officials who served in Chien-ning. The remaining ones are mostly by famous officials whose collected works (*wen-chi*) included written judgments, or whose decisions are likely to have been published already. The compiler of the *Collected Decisions* seems to have collected written judgments that were available in the yamen archives at Chien-ning or that he got through personal connections with Chien-ning officials, then added in extras that were already in print.[13] That the collection was published in Chien-ning, a center of the commercial printing industry, points to a likely financial motive for production of the work.[14]

---

13 For instance, written decisions by the judge Fan Ying-ling (c.s. 1205) had been published in a collection no longer extant, titled *Tui-yüeh chi*. Ch'en Chih-ch'ao suggests the CMC cases were copied from this; "Chieh-shao," 662. Liu K'o-chuang's and Chen Te-hsiu's judgments survive partly in their collected works, though CMC has some not included there. Liu K'o-chuang, in a postface to the two *chüan* of *shu-p'an* in his works, says they are taken from a larger selection, and he laments that some documents left behind in the yamen archives of previous posts had been destroyed; *Hou-ts'un chi* (SPTK ed.) 193:18b–19a (pp. 1730–1); CMC Appendix 3:632. See also Ian Burns, "Private Law in Traditional China (Sung Dynasty): Using as a Main Source of Information the Work *Ming-kung shu-p'an ch'ing-ming chi* (Ph.D. dissertation, University of Oxford, 1973) 15–16.

14 On the Chien-ning publishing industry, see Lucille Chia, "Printing for Profit: the Commercial Printers of Jianyang, Fujian (Song-Ming) (Ph.D. dissertation, Columbia University, 1996).

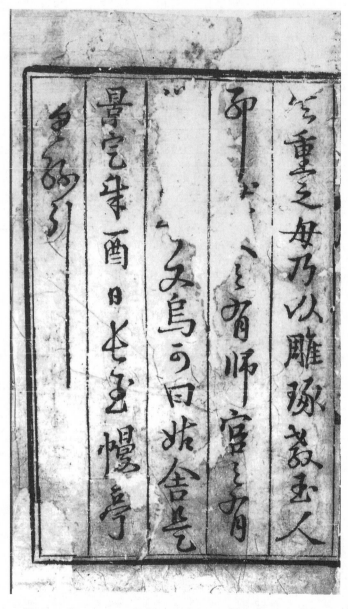

Figure 2. Extant fragment of the preface to the Sung edition of the *Collected Decisions*. The preface ends with the Chinese characters *ching-ting sui yu jih ch'ang-chih*, indicating the day of the solstice in 1261,

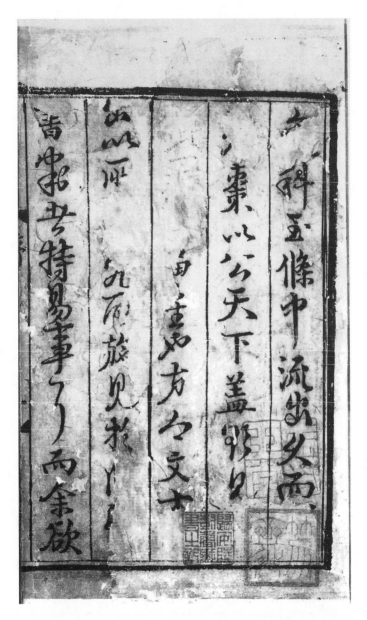

Figure 2. *(cont.)* followed by the four-character sobriquet *Man-t'ing tseng-sun*, "Great-grandson of the curtained pavilion." (Courtesy of the Seikadō Bunko, Tokyo, Japan.)

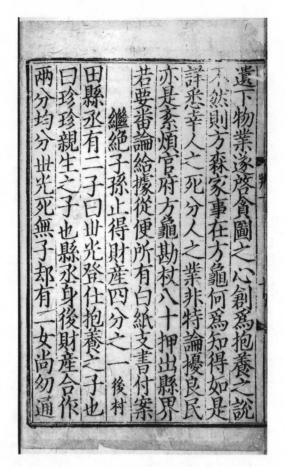

遺下物業遂啓貪圖之心創為抱養之說
不然則方森家事在方龜何為知得如是
亦悉幸人之死分人之業非特論擾良民
許是素煩官府方龜勘杖八十押出縣界
若要番論給據從便所有白紙文書付案
繼絕子孫止得財産四分之一　後村
田縣丞有二子曰世光登仕抱養之子也
口珍珍親生之子也縣丞身後財産合作
兩分均分世光死無子却有一女尚勿通

Figure 3. Excerpt from the Sung edition of the *Collected Decisions*. (Courtesy of the Seikadō Bunko, Tokyo, Japan.)

The contents of the collection, and what evidence we do have of authorship, point to the almost accidental nature of the selection of cases. I find nothing to suggest that the work is tendentious or that it is a collection of model cases.[15] The title, I would argue, was meant to sell

---

15 For a different opinion, see Gudula Linck, *Zur Sozialgeschichte der Chinesischen Familie im 13. Jahrhundert: untersuchungen am Ming-gong shu-pan qing-ming ji* (Stuttgart: Franz Steiner Verlag, 1986), 27–31; and for a critique, see Bettine Birge, "*Zur Sozialgeschichte der Chinesischen Familie im 13. Jahrhundert: untersuchungen am Ming-gong shu-pan qing-ming ji*, by Gudula Linck, review article," *Journal of Sung-Yuan Studies* 24 (1994): esp. 279–80.

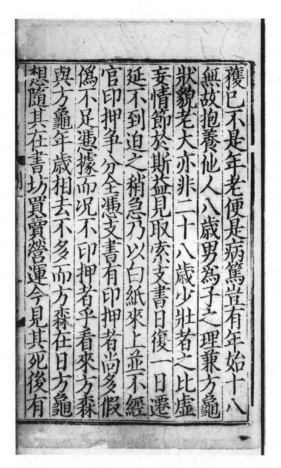

Figure 3. *(cont.)*

books and intentionally misleads us as to the exemplary nature of the decisions. The judges themselves represent a spectrum of legal opinion; some are unnamed or identified only by the name of a low-level government office. Inconsistencies between judgments preclude any predetermined plan by the compiler. In the thirteenth century, debates over Learning of the Way Confucianism continued to simmer in South China (not least in Chien-ning), but our reclusive Ch'ung-an compiler shows no concern with them. The nineteen judges of the *Collected Decisions* whom we can identify fall both inside and outside the Learning of the Way camp. It has recently been argued that the work was meant as

73

a writing aid, in the genre of almanacs or encyclopedias (*lei-shu*) for which there was much consumer demand at the time.[16] This may well be the case, and would further attest to the value of the collection as a representative sample of legal proceedings in the late Southern Sung, reflecting the complexities and contradictions that plagued Sung law and society.

Cases can be found in the *Collected Decisions* from nearly all circuits of the Southern Sung. The areas corresponding to modern Chekiang, Kiangsi, Fukien, Hupei, and Hunan are especially well represented. For this reason, and because judges frequently cite statutes (*ling*) and other nationally promulgated laws to support their points, I do not agree with the contention that the *Collected Decisions* demonstrates local variation in inheritance practices.[17] The new expanded version shows general consistency in law over a large area of the country. Inconsistencies between decisions are usually the result of mitigating circumstances (many of the cases are very complex), or sometimes even of conscious disagreement with laws or customs as articulated by the judges themselves.[18] They also demonstrate the latitude given Sung magistrates in settling disputes.

Judges in the Sung had a difficult task made worse by structural characteristics of the legal system. The parties to a civil case could appeal any decision ad infinitum; and since officials at almost any level in any post could hear cases, the possibilities were many.[19] Plaintiffs were supposed

16 Christian de Pee, "Cases of the New Terrace: Canon and Law in Three Southern Song Verdicts," *Journal of Sung-Yuan Studies* 27 (1997): 52–7.

17 E.g. Patricia Ebrey, "Women in the Kinship System of the Southern Song Upper Class," in *Women in China: Current Directions in Historical Scholarship*, ed. Richard Guisso and Stanley Johannessen (Youngstown, N.Y.: Philo Press, 1981), 118 n. 13. Niida makes the argument that the statutes and verdicts found in the CMC reflected Southern practices, to which the Sung state felt obliged to conform; *Hōseishi* III, 387–91. Burns, *Private Law*, 275–7, summarizes this argument with Shiga's objections. Linck, *Zur Sozialgeschichte*, 119–20, adopts Niida's position.

18 A few may have resulted from a judge's unfamiliarity with the law, but in general I doubt such explanations. For legal training of officials and clerks and the many resources they had for adjudicating cases, see Brian McKnight, "Mandarins as Legal Experts: Professional Learning in Sung China," in *Neo-Confucian Education: the Formative Stage*, ed. Wm. Theodore de Bary and John Chaffee (Berkeley: University of California Press, 1989), 493–516; Hsu Dau-lin, "Separation between Fact-finding (Trial) and Law-Finding (Sentencing) in Sung Criminal Proceedings" *Sung Studies Newsletter* 6 (1972); Miyazaki, "Administration of Justice." On forensic expertise, see Brian McKnight, *The Washing Away of Wrongs: Forensic Medicine in Thirteenth-Century China* (Ann Arbor: Center for Chinese Studies, University of Michigan, 1981).

19 Civil cases never went all the way to the central government as penal ones could do, thus no decision was unambiguously final; Miyazaki, "Administration of Justice," 66. For the separation of judicial and administrative functions (or lack thereof), see Hsu Dau-lin, "Separation," and Miyazaki, "Administration of Justice."

to bring their suits first to the county magistrate – the lowest level court – and only if his judgment went against them were they allowed to appeal to a higher level administrator such as a prefect or circuit intendant. In practice, however, wily litigants sought out judges at all levels or in neighboring jurisdictions whom they thought would be sympathetic. Some even launched "appeals" of a case while it was still ongoing in a lower court or different county. The lament of a judge in the *Collected Decisions* describes this problem:

At a time when this prefect had not yet concluded their case, [the Tsengs] took it to the fiscal intendant. The fiscal intendant was just asking for the files when they took it up to the military intendant. The military intendant had just sent down word about it when they took it to the judicial intendant.[20]

To prevent suits from going to higher courts, judges had to resolve cases to everyone's satisfaction. This nearly impossible task involved mediating between the various parties to a suit and between written law and what judges called "human feelings," and it explains the need for latitude in settling cases.[21] The Sung state allowed each judge to find his own balance between popular expectation (put in terms of "human feelings"), codified regulations, and Confucian ideals.

The spread of literacy and the growth of the printing industry made the courts more accessible to the common people.[22] These included women, and the *Collected Decisions* records females of all ages initiating lawsuits.[23] Almanacs published sample forms for all kinds of plaints, and books described how to pursue lawsuits. The famous literatus Shen Kua (1030–1095) complained that these books also taught people how to falsify documents and bring fraudulent charges.[24] The majority of

---

20 CMC 8:281. Translation follows McKnight and Liu, *Enlightened Judgments*.
21 For further discussion, see Sadachi Haruto, "Seimeishū no 'hōi' to 'ninjō': Soshō tōjisha ni yoru hōritsu kaishaku no konseki," in *Chūgoku kinsei no hōsei to shakai*, ed. Umehara Kaoru (Kyōto: Kyōto daigaku jinbun kagaku kenkyūjo, 1993), 293–334.
22 The Sung government forbade private publishing of the law codes to prevent litigiousness, but this did not stop a precipitous rise in lawsuits in the eleventh century; Miyazaki Ichisada, "SōGen jidai no hōsei to saiban kikō: Gentenshō seiritsu no jidaiteki shakaiteki haikei," in *Ajiashi kenkyū*, Vol. 4, (Kyoto: Dōhōsha, 1975), 237–8; Miyazaki, "Administration of Justice," 58–9, 71–2.
23 See CMC 12:479 for a girl of 12 bringing a plaint. Only pregnant women and people over 70 could not be chief plaintiffs, because they were excused from the beatings that were the punishment for bringing a false accusation; Miyazaki, "Administration of Justice," 60.
24 *Meng-ch'i pi-t'an* (SPTK ed.) 25:7a. For sample forms from the Yüan, see *Yüan-tai fa-lü tzu-liao chi-ts'un* (Hang-chou: Chekiang ku-chi ch'u-pan she, 1988), 214–37. For Chu Hsi's complaints of fraudulent suits and his efforts to stem excessive litigation, see Ron-guey Chu, "Chu Hsi and Public Instruction," in *Neo-Confucian Education*, ed. de Bary and Chaffee, 268–70. See also CMC Appendix 6:640.

people, who were illiterate, would go to scriveners who helped them submit the required documents and pursue their case. These scriveners operated both with and without government sanction, and were perennially accused of fomenting excessive litigation.[25]

The Sung government made strenuous efforts to disseminate and enforce consistent laws throughout the country. Inevitably, however, different judges harbored different opinions and practiced different judicial philosophies. Conflicting verdicts in multiple appeals of the same case were common. The relentless pace of change in Sung society made the law especially fluid and presented the legal system at every level with all the challenges and complexities we find in our own, modern society. Property law is thus best seen as a process of tension and evolution, rather than as representing consistent, stagnant, or universal norms.[26]

Transmission of Wealth to Women

As in the T'ang and before, a daughter in Sung times typically left her family at marriage and received at this time property in her name in the form of dowry. Fathers in the Sung legally had complete discretion to endow their daughters with as much or as little as they chose. Nevertheless, consistent with earlier practices, custom dictated that elite brides receive considerable assets, and by the tenth century, daughters had strong claims to a significant portion of the ancestral patrimony. Developments in the Sung gave daughters new customary and legal inheritance rights both in the presence and the absence of sons. These operated within the traditional laws of family division, despite the original intent of these laws to support patrilineality and exclude women from formal inheritance.

Daughters and Sons in Family Division

THE HALF-SHARE RULE

The T'ang statute on inheritance from 737 prescribed "equal division among brothers" at the time of family division. In this prescription for patrilineal succession, daughters were excluded from the division and

---

25 CMC 12:479–80; 8:280; Appendix 6:640; *Tso-i tzu-chen* (SPTK ed.), 8:40a–41b; Kuo Tung-hsü, "Sung-tai chih sung-hsüeh," in *Sung-shih yen-chiu lun-ts'ung*, ed. Ch'i Hsia (Pao-ting: Hopei ta-hsüeh ch'u-pan she, 1990), 133–47; Miyazaki, "Administration of Justice," 59–60.
26 See my remarks in Birge, "Linck review article," 283–5.

from any formal inheritance in the presence of sons. Property transmission to daughters is mentioned only in the context of marriage
endowments needed for unmarried boys or girls in the household.
Unmarried boys were to receive an extra portion of family property
as betrothal gifts, and unmarried girls were to receive a dowry
portion equal to half of the betrothal gifts given a boy. The official law
code of the Sung dynasty (the *Sung Penal Laws*) issued in 963 repeats all
five points of the 737 T'ang statute on inheritance, including archaic
references to the equal field system, which had long since ceased to
exist.[27] But there is evidence that as early as the tenth century, when the
Sung code was published, the half-share formula for a daughter's dowry
was being used to *include* daughters in family division, giving them half
of a son's total inheritance, instead of half of an arbitrarily small
betrothal gift.

The earliest testimony of this change comes from the biography of
Chang Yung (styled Kuai-yai, 946–1015), an official renowned for his
administrative and judicial skills. In 999 he became the prefect of Hangchow, where, as the Sung dynastic history recounts, he resolved a dispute
between a young man and his sister's uxorilocal husband. The sister and
her husband had documentation that the father had left 70 percent of
the property to them and only 30 percent to his son, who was only three
when the father died. Chang Yung read the will and ordered that 70
percent of the property go to the son and 30 percent to the daughter
and her husband. He said to the husband, "Your wife's father was a good
judge of people. Since his son was young, he entrusted him to you. Had
he given 70 percent to the son, the boy would have died at your hands."[28]

Chang's legal judgments were particularly famous and were collected
and published in Szechwan, where he served intermittently during
troubled times as an administrator.[29] This verdict was well known and

---

27 SHT 12:197. The only difference between the T'ang statute and the SHT is the addition of the word *ch'ieh* 妾 "concubines," in the last section, which in the SHT could
be read literally: "Widowed wives and concubines without sons should receive their
husband's share." This is most likely a two-word term meaning "wives." Nakada Kaoru
argues that the additional character is a mistake, since in other sources concubines are
explicitly excluded from receiving family property; *Hōseishi ronshū*, Vol. 3, Pt. 2, 1342.
See also Shiga, *Genri*, 262 n. 16. I agree with Nakada that the statute was meant to refer
only to legal wives. Concubines in the Sung did not receive their master's property,
though concubines and even maids did sometimes control such property on behalf of
a son or daughter; see for instance CMC 8:251–3; 7:238–9 and examples in this chapter.
28 *Sung shih*, 293:9802 (Vol. 28).
29 *Sung shih*, 293:9800–9804 (Vol. 28); Umehara Kaoru, "Chang Yung" in *Sung Biographies*, ed. Herbert Franke (Wiesbaden: Franz Steiner Verlag, 1976), 48–50; Paul Smith,
*Taxing Heaven's Storehouse: Horses, Bureaucrats, and the Destruction of the Sichuan Tea
Industry, 1074–1224* (Cambridge, Mass.: Harvard University Press, 1991), 99.

served as a precedent for later decisions. We find it cited three centuries later in the *Collected Decisions* by a local sheriff to justify a two-thirds/one-third division of the family estate between a son and daughter in the household.[30] (We also see that a father could leave 70 percent of an estate to his daughter and her husband and only 30 percent to his son, though a challenge to such a distribution could get a favorable hearing in court.)

The general practice of daughters inheriting through family division in the presence of sons is revealed in a text a century later by the Vice Chancellor of the Directorate of Education Kao K'ang (1097–1153; *chin-shih* 1131). In a thirty-two-chapter book on ritual, Kao advocated a return to the classical descent-line system (whereby the first son of the principal line controlled all property on behalf of clan members) and criticized the long-established practice of equal division among brothers. He incidentally confirms that sisters were included in this "equal division" and even participated in distributions of real property by lot:

Today people do not understand the principle by which the ancients lived separately, and thus when they separate their residences they also divide the family property. Is this not a misunderstanding? Furthermore, the law on dividing the patrimony specifies equality (*chün-p'ing* 均平) merely to prevent disputes, but it does not distinguish between principal heirs and lesser heirs (older and younger sons). This is a mistake by those who wrote the code (*lü*). When a man dies, he should not have to worry that the household will be without a family shrine.

If the brothers draw lots to divide the patrimony, then it cannot be determined who will get the family shrine. Moreover, the code also has articles that say: "A wife inherits her husband's portion," and "a daughter inherits her father's portion." If by chance a woman drew the lot for the family shrine, there would be no one to perform the sacrifices. What of it then![31]

Division of family property by drawing lots is mentioned as early as the second century B.C. Taoist text, the *Huai-nan tzu*, and was practiced up to modern times by both literati and peasant families. As explained in the *Huai-nan tzu*, drawing lots was to ensure fairness and strict equality in the division of estates, a principle that was entrenched in Chinese custom by Han times.[32] Other Sung literati must not have shared Kao's concerns, for Kao's warning went unheeded, and distribution of shares

30 CMC 8:278.
31 *Chieh-tzu t'ung-lu* (SKCS chen pen ed.), 6:13b; Niida, *Bunsho*, 597. Part of this passage is also found in Niida, *Hōseishi* III, 382; and Ebrey, "Conceptions," 231.
32 Niida, *Hōseishi* III, 386 n. 8; Niida, *Bunsho*, 597, 603 n. 78.

by lot and daughters' inheritance of land remained common during the Sung.[33]

Kao refers to an "article of code" (*lü*) that says, "A daughter inherits her father's portion" (*nü ch'eng fu fen* 女承父分), and he was referring to households divided between brothers *and* sisters. Such a law would have been the most explicit that is known regarding a daughter's claims to family property in the presence of sons. The preeminent Japanese legal scholar Niida Noboru conjectures that these words appeared not in the Sung code (*lü*) but in a later statute (*ling*) of the Shao-hsing period (1131–1162),[34] which is far more likely since the code was left untouched in the Sung. The T'ang law, repeated in the Sung code, states more generally "sons (or children) inherit the father's portion" (*tzu ch'eng fu fen* 子承父分).[35] Niida argues that the word *tzu* 子 (child or son) means "sons and daughters" in this part of both the T'ang and Sung codes,[36] and indeed judgments in the *Collected Decisions* a century later quote the phrase to support daughters' inheritance.[37] It is not clear if Kao was interpreting the original wording of the Sung code to apply specifically to daughters, or if he was citing the more precise wording of a later statute no longer extant. In either event, his testimony shows that daughters were assumed to be beneficiaries of inheritance by family division in the presence of sons by the early Southern Sung.

The basic inheritance law of the T'ang and Sung codes specified "equal division" (*chün fen* 均分) among brothers, and Kao K'ang referred to "equality" (*chün-p'ing* 均平) in family division. Words like "*chün*" or *chün-p'ing*" also mean more broadly "equitable," "fair," or "impartial," and in the Southern Sung they were applied with this meaning to divisions between sons *and* daughters. Twelfth-century judges interpreted "equal division among brothers" to mean "equitable division among brothers and sisters" based on a half-share rule. By the late Southern Sung the two-to-one ratio of division between orphaned sons and daughters seen in Chang Yung's famous decision of 999 was dictated by law.

33 See Niida, *Bunsho*, 597, for numerous examples of division by lot. From 1092 on, the government allowed families to exclude sacrificial lands from family division, SHY shih-huo 61:61 (p. 5904). Kao may have been making a rhetorical point to support a return to the descent-line system; his essay is extant only because it was included in a later anthology by Learning of the Way advocate and Chu Hsi collaborator Liu Ch'ing-chih (1130–1195) in support of the descent-line system.

34 Niida, *Hōseishi* III, 382–3, 388.

35 Niida, *Tōryō*, 246, 245; SHT 12:197. Kao's line "A wife inherits her husband's portion" (*fu ch'eng fu fen*) also does not appear in the code. The closest is a reference to a widow without sons receiving her husband's share; SHT 12:197.

36 Niida, *Bunsho*, 583. Burns disagrees with this; "Private Law," 260.

37 For instance CMC 8:280–1; 8:255.

Several judgments from the *Collected Decisions* quote a statute (*ling*) giving daughters whose parents had both died not just an undefined "dowry portion" as in the wording of T'ang and early Sung law, but a share of the communal estate equal to half that of a son. After centuries during which women routinely received substantial property from their parents, by the late Sung the Chinese government seems to have caught up with practice and provided them certain guarantees to that property.

Two of three judgments that directly quote a statute are by Liu K'o-chuang (1187–1269), a prominent official from P'u-t'ien county on the Fukien coast. Liu gained office through family connections and became magistrate of Chien-yang, Chien-ning prefecture, in 1209. His many written judgments were published both in his collected works and in the *Collected Decisions*. The two cases in question took place on the shores of P'o-yang lake (modern-day Kiangsi), and date to between 1244 and 1246 while Liu served as Judicial Intendant (*t'i-hsing*) of Chiang-nan East circuit (see Map 3).[38]

In the first case, Liu K'o-chuang opens with an unambiguous statement of the law: "According to the law, when the mother and father have died, the sons and daughters divide the property, and a daughter gets half as much as a son."[39] In a written judgment that resonates with Chang Yung's division of land between an infant son and his uxorilocally married sister, and which includes the apportionment of land to daughters by lot as seen in Kao K'ang's complaint, a man named Chou Ping from P'o-yang county was survived by his daughter, her uxorilocal husband, and a posthumously born son. Liu writes, "After Chou Ping's death, his property should have been divided into three, with the posthumously born son receiving two shares and his daughter Ssu-i-niang receiving one share. Such a division would be in accordance with the law." Instead, the daughter's uxorilocal husband had falsely claimed to other lineage members that the parents had allocated half the land to their daughter (instead of a third). Liu K'o-chuang upheld

38 Internal evidence and a notation in Liu K'o-chuang's collected works (*Hou-ts'un chi* 192:1a) tell us that all these cases date to his tenure as Judicial Intendant, and we learn from his biographical essay (*hsing-chuang*) the dates he served in this office; *Hou-ts'un chi* 194:6b–7a. (Some scholars have mistakenly read a colophon by Liu [*Hou-ts'un chi* 193:18b; CMC Appendix 4:632] to suggest that his written judgments date to 1249–1258.) Liu himself was proud of these judgments and picked them out as his best to be included in his collected works; *Hou-ts'un chi*, 193:18b; CMC Appendix 4:632.

39 CMC 8:277. See also Niida, *Hōseishi* III, 381; Shiga, *Genri*, 612; Yanagida, "Joshōbun," 237; Ebrey, "Kinship," 117; Linck, *Zur Sozialgeschichte*, 118; Yüan Li, "Sung-tai nü-hsing ts'ai-ch'an-ch'üan shu-lun," in *Chung-kuo fu-nü shih lun-chi hsü-chi*, ed. Pao Chia-lin (Taipei: Tao-hsiang ch'u-pan she, 1991), 178. A full translation of the case is found in McKnight and Liu, *Enlightened Judgments*.

the half-share rule, citing a "statute currently in effect (*hsien-hsing t'iao-ling* 見行條令)," and reprimanded the son-in-law for his illegal encroach-ment. He then ordered the participants in family division – that is, the daughter and the son – to draw lots for their shares of the movable and immovable property.

Liu's verdict upheld an earlier decision by the sheriff, who cited the precedent of Chang Yung in 999: "When the county sheriff made ref-erence to the story of Chang Kuai-yai [Yung] giving 30 percent to the uxorilocal son-in-law, his meaning was the same as the statute currently in effect that daughters receive half of what the son does."[40] Liu's words confirm that the one-half rule was known for centuries and was applied by low-level officials such as the sheriff.[41]

In the second case, Liu K'o-chuang explicitly applies the term "equal division" (*chün fen*) to divisions between sons *and* daughters, using the one-half rule for a daughter's share.[42] A low-level official from Tu-ch'ang county (on the northern shore of lake P'o-yang, Chiang-nan East; see Map 3) Vice Magistrate T'ien and his concubine wife Madam Liu had a son adopted in infancy, Shih-kuang, a natural son, Chen-chen, and two daughters left unnamed (see family tree, Figure 4).[43] Shih-kuang like his father never formally married, but produced two daughters by a maid named Ch'iu-chü (Autumn Chrysanthemum). Sometime after Vice Magistrate T'ien's death, the adopted son, Shih-kuang, also died, and T'ien's younger brother T'ung-shih tried to set up his own son as heir, disinheriting Shih-kuang's two daughters. Madam Liu filed a lawsuit to retain control over the patrimony and prevent the naming of an heir, and the first verdict, by the previous Judicial Intendant Ts'ai, went in her favor. Liu K'o-chuang initially concurred in this decision; but he reversed himself when information from the lineage convinced him that

---

40 CMC 8:278. As in the exactly comparable Chang Yung case of 999, we see here the residence principle at work. The daughter is already married, but since she lives in her father's home with her husband, she probably did not previously receive dowry and is a participant in family division.

41 County sheriffs (*hsien-wei*) did not normally decide cases, but they had a wide range of police duties, including criminal investigations, and might take over at times for the magistrate; Brian McKnight, *Law and Order in Sung China* (Cambridge: Cambridge University Press, 1992), 147–67, esp. 157, 166.

42 CMC 8:255.

43 CMC 8:251–7; *Hou-ts'un chi*, 93:10a–17b. Madam Liu is by law a "concubine" (*ch'ieh*), because T'ien did not marry her formally, a point emphasized by Judge Liu in his verdict. Nevertheless, the use of her last name and her savvy in filing a lawsuit suggest nonservile birth, and indeed she herself claimed status as a principal wife (*ch'i*). See discussion in Niida *Hōseishi* III, 385; and Yanagida, "Joshōbun," 237. Within the verdict, the family home is given as Tu-ch'ang county, whereas in the title of the case in Liu's collected works, it is given as nearby Chien-ch'ang.

Diagram 1
T'ien Family Tree

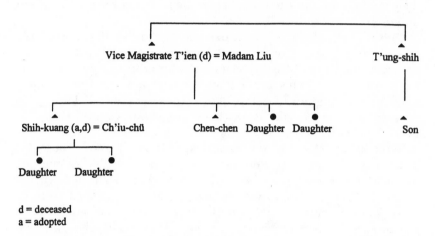

d = deceased
a = adopted

Figure 4. Diagram of T'ien Family Tree.

Madam Liu was trying to disinherit Shih-kuang's two daughters (whom she had not mentioned in her suit) and was squandering the patrimony that should pass to her children. He ordered a division of the property and allowed the heir to be named.[44]

The division was complicated, and Liu K'o-chuang rendered several decisions on the case as new information kept coming to light.[45] Each time he reconsidered the ruling, he applied the one-half rule. Like most cases, this one did not fit neatly into the categories covered by the law, but Liu carefully articulated the laws to be applied at every turn, thus educating both us and his contemporary readers. His first of many references to the one-half rule is especially telling, for he links it to the law of "equal division":

When I previously judged this case, I did not know that Madam Liu had two daughters. These two girls are the natural daughters of Vice Magistrate T'ien. If

44 T'ung-shih's son, as a cousin of the deceased, was of the wrong generation to be heir, but Liu allowed it at the request of the lineage elders, who claimed no suitable heir was available.

45 The structure of the text and Judge Liu's own words tell us that the decision was written in two parts at two different times. The second part, that which interests us most here, is found only in Liu's collected works, not in the *Collected Decisions.* This suggests that the first part of the text may have circulated separately, perhaps even before the rest was written.

his [adopted] son T'ien Shih-kuang were still alive, the property would be divided between him and Chen-chen, and the two daughters would each get half of what the sons received. But now Shih-kuang has already died, and we can only rely on the law of "equal division among children [*tzu*]."[46] The Vice Magistrate's two daughters and his son Chen-chen together receive their father's portion. Out of ten shares, Chen-chen receives five, and the two girls receive five between them.[47]

Liu goes on to note that since the adopted son Shih-kuang has progeny, the property should actually be divided into thirds: one-third to Shih-kuang's branch, one-third to the natural son Chen-chen, and one-third to the two daughters. (Shih-kuang's portion was to be further divided according to the laws on extinct households, with one-fourth going to the posthumous heir and three-fourths going to the two daughters. See discussion of these laws at the end of this section, under Daughters and Posthumous Heirs.) He repeatedly states that such a division would be to the letter of the law. One example reads:

If we pronounce it according to the law, we ought to take the movable and immovable property of Vice Magistrate T'ien and divide it all into three big equal portions. Shih-kuang and Chen-chen should each get one portion, and the two daughters together should get one.[48]

Nevertheless, Liu notes that Madam Liu controls all the movable property, that Shih-kuang has not been buried, and that if the various daughters get unequal portions there will surely be additional lawsuits. Thus, in the end, Liu chooses to bend the law to find a solution acceptable to all parties, including the T'ien lineage (though he laments that Madam Liu, who has the law more on her side, may not accept it).[49] He allows Madam Liu to retain control of all the movable property, which he figures cannot be pried away from her, then orders that all the landed property be divided into eight equal parts. Under the supervision of the county, these are to be distributed by drawing lots: the natural son Chen-chen gets two shares, his sisters each get one (according to the formula that they each receive half of a son's share), and the remaining four

---

46 "*Chu-tzu chün-fen.*" Note the difference between this and the T'ang statute, which says "equal division among brothers" (*hsiung-ti chün-fen*). As discussed by Niida, "*tzu*" can mean "sons and daughters" (*Bunsho*, 583), and indeed here and elsewhere in Sung texts, daughters are included in the term.

47 CMC 8:255. *Hou-ts'un chi*, 93:10a. See also Niida, *Hōseishi* III, 385; Shiga, *Genri*, 455; Yanagida, "Joshōbun," 237.

48 CMC 8:255.

49 Recall that the earlier decisions were more in her favor. Liu K'o-chuang emphasizes her status as a "mere" concubine in going against laws that prevented both family division and the naming of heirs without the widow's consent.

shares go to Shih-kuang's branch. These latter were distributed with the posthumous heir receiving one share, the two daughters each receiving one (making their portions equal to those of their aunts), and one going to pay for Shih-kuang's burial expenses. Such a decision cleverly granted the posthumous heir one fourth of Shih-kuang's estate in line with the law on extinct households, while leaving the two daughters portions no larger or smaller than those of their aunts.[50] At every turn of this complicated case, Liu applied the half-share rule. Both these cases draw attention to daughters participating in family division by lot and thereby receiving land. Liu explicitly refers to daughters as "participants in division" or "coparceners" (*he-fen jen* 合分人).[51] Such language further suggests that the term "equal division" had come to mean "equitable division" or "fairness" between sons *and* daughters in dividing the patrimony. Having equal shares that could be distributed by lot to males or females meant that real property could not be limited to male heirs. Daughters might receive any type of property that a son did – movable or immovable, and "fairness" dictated that their share be half of a son's.

We do not know exactly when the new statute about half shares took effect, but we have evidence that it started as a local ruling. (Such local rulings were often the basis for national statutes.) Reference to the one-half rule as a "precedent (*li* 例) in other prefectures" (or "another prefecture")[52] comes in a judgment by Fan Ying-ling (c.s. 1205), for a case that probably came to court between 1219 and 1224 in Ch'ung-jen county (modern Kiangsi), where Fan was serving as magistrate.[53] Ch'ung-jen was about 120 km. southwest of P'o-yang, in neighboring Chiang-nan West circuit (see Map 3), and my dating would place this case at least twenty years before Liu K'o-chuang's

---

50 The final division, giving Shih-kuang's branch half the property, may have been influenced by the fact that Liu K'o-chuang had previously divided the estate in half between the two brothers, before he knew of Madam Liu's two daughters. This is the division he makes in the first half of the judgment, and if the second half was written later, as I believe, such a distribution of property may have been in effect for some time, giving Liu incentive to devise a final ruling that preserved it.

51 CMC 8:278.

52 For discussion of the term *li*, see Burns, *Private Law*, 275–7.

53 Later in his career Fan served as Vice Prefect of Fu-chou, Kiang-nan West, and of Ch'i-chou, directly north in Huai-nan East. He was also Judicial Intendant of Kuang-hsi circuit in the South. Ch'en, "Chieh-shao," 682, and *Sung-shih*, 410:12344. This case could have come from any one of these areas, but Fan was noted for the many exemplary verdicts he rendered as Magistrate of Ch'ung-jen, and other cases of his in the CMC can be identified from this area; see Hymes, *Statesmen*, 266 n. 76. This case appears to be from the same group. Fan hailed from just north of Ch'ung-jen, in Feng-ch'eng county, Lung-hsing prefecture (modern Kiangsi), very close to the site of Liu's two cases.

judgments. Like Liu, Fan applies the term "equal division" to a distribution of property among sons and daughters, with daughters receiving half shares.

As described in the judgment, a man named Cheng Ying-jen had two daughters and no son. He adopted a stepson, Hsiao-hsien, from among his agnates, and died leaving 3,000 *mou* of land and ten storehouses. In his last instructions (either written or oral) Cheng left each daughter just 130 *mou* and one storehouse, with the rest going to the adopted heir. Even so, after Cheng's death the latter tried to seize all the property for himself. Judge Fan noted the parsimony of the bequest to the daughters and expressed outrage at the son's attempt to deny it to them. The father had already left the daughters a very small portion of his property; had there been no testament, Fan suggested, they would have received much more: "If the case were handled according to the equal division precedent in other prefectures, the two daughters [on one hand] and the adopted son [on the other hand] would each receive half the property."[54] Later in the case, Fan stated strongly that daughters had a right to property, and he criticized a ruling by the previous county magistrate for ignoring this point and concentrating only on the veracity of Cheng's testament:

When the county magistrate decided this case, he did not consider the extent of the family estate, or the amount apportioned to the daughters. In vain he tried to determine the validity of the will and whether the plaintiffs were acting out of a sense of duty (*i*) or desire for profit (*li*).[55] He did not consider that the son is adopted and the total inherited land is 3,000 *mou*, while the amount apportioned [to the daughters] does not exceed 260 *mou*. What is there to discuss regarding the validity of the will?

The two daughters are born of the father himself. If the ancestral property provides them no benefit, but instead is given entirely to someone adopted from agnates, where is the choice between duty and profit? If one rejects the wrong

54 CMC 8:290. For the use of precedents from other prefectures to decide cases, see CMC 9:303, McKnight and Liu, *Enlightened Judgments*, 312–13. On the significance of this case see especially Yanagida Setsuko, "Sōdai joshi no zaisanken," *Hōseishi gaku* 42 (1990), 326. See also Niida, *Hōseishi* III, 386; Shiga, *Genri*, 441; Yanagida, "Joshōbun," 236; Ebrey, "Kinship," 119, Linck, *Zur Sozialgeschichte*, 118–19. Some scholars mistakenly take Fan's words to mean that in a household with an adopted son, all daughters, no matter how many, would divide half of the estate, with the son receiving the other half; see Kathryn Bernhardt, "The Inheritance Rights of Daughters: the Song Anomaly?," *Modern China* 21:3 (July 1995): 282; and Yeh Hsiao-hsin et al., *Chung-kuo min-fa shih* (Shanghai: Jen-min ch'u-pan she, 1993), 416–17. This ignores the fact that in all of Sung law, a son adopted before the father's death had the same legal status as a natural son. Yeh et al. conclude that between this judgment and Liu K'o-chuang's the law changed to give *each* daughter half of a son's share; *Min-fa shih* 417.
55 Cf. *Mencius* 1A:1 and 6B:4.

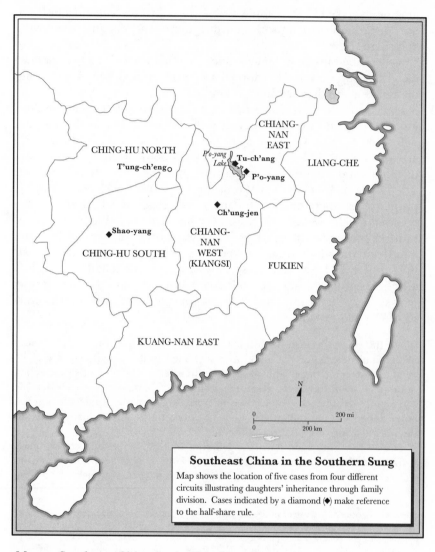

Map 3. Southeast China in the Southern Sung.

and follows the right, can one either give or not give the land [to the daughters]? If one forsakes profit and follows duty, can one either take or not take [land from the son]? The amount that Hsiao-hsien is today giving is not enough to damage kind feelings, and the amount the daughters are taking is not enough to damage their probity. If one judges the case in this way, it can be decided at a glance.[56]

The heir was given the harsh sentence of 100 strokes of the bamboo and put in shackles for his impudence, and the daughters were each apportioned their share of the land.

Fan's verdict and rhetoric demonstrate that the ancestral patrimony was popularly thought to belong to daughters as well as to sons. Moreover, he suggests that daughters should get a sizable share of the patrimony. In this example the proportionately small size of the bequest to the daughters renders other considerations such as the validity of the will irrelevant to Fan. He emphasizes that the daughters are born to the father himself and ancestral property is to benefit natural offspring, female or male. It is not exclusively for a male heir who performs sacrifices and carries on the house.

Confucian ideals of agnatic solidarity and patrilineal descent lines had limits. In the course of the judgment, Fan does not hide his disapproval of the father's miserly bequest to his daughters and the heir's greedy actions. He calls the heir stingy (*k'o-po*), and the father's actions obdurate (or perverse, *ku-chih*) and "contrary to what is right in the extreme" (*pu-i chih shen*).[57] His harsh words cannot have shocked his listeners, for Fan was highly praised by his contemporaries for his expert handling of lawsuits. According to them, his uncanny ability to expose the truth cleared up cases in a timely manner and left "even the defeated party willing to submit."[58] The great Learning of the Way advocate Chen Te-hsiu (1178–1235), from Chien-ning, wrote a placard for Fan's courthouse, and Fan's judgments were collected and published.[59]

Two other cases from the *Collected Decisions* indicate that the law on family division that prescribed "equal division among brothers" was meant to apply to sisters, and one of these mentions a one-half rule. This latter comes from Shao-yang county, Ching-hu South circuit (modern Hunan). The ruling was by Hu Ying in the 1240s while he served as

---

56 CMC 8:291.   57 CMC 8:290.   58 *Sung-shih*, 410:12345.

59 *Sung-shih*, 410:12345. The placard read *tui-yüeh*, a reference to the *Shih-ching* (*Book of Odes*), suggesting that Fan deliberated cases with the carefulness and exactitude of the sage ruler Wen Wang. See *Shih-san-ching chu-shu*, 583; Mao #266; Legge trans, *The She King or Book of Poetry* (1871; reprint, Hong Kong: Hong Kong University Press, 1961), 569–70. Fan's published decisions, titled *Tui-yüeh chi*, are no longer extant.

prefect of Shao-chou.[60] In it Hu applied the half-share rule to a daughter's inheritance, even though she had no brothers. A man died leaving two brothers and an unmarried daughter in an undivided household. The daughter married out but subsequently sued to retrieve her father's portion of the estate in family division.[61] Hu Ying rejected the draft verdict of his subordinates that the daughter should be treated as married and thus receive only one-third of her father's property. Instead, he applied a one-half rule, citing Sung inheritance law:

> The dispatch from the Judicial Intendant clearly states that, although the lawsuit was filed after she was married, the household became extinct before she was married. Thus one should treat her as an unmarried daughter and apply the law (*fa*) that "children (*tzu*) receive their father's portion"[62] to give her one half of the property."[63]

The other case, a draft decision by a prefectural law secretary (*ssu-fa*)[64] on behalf of the Fiscal Intendant of Ching-hu North circuit (modern Hupei), makes two references to a daughter receiving dowry property as part of "equal division" and reveals that daughters could sue to receive this "equal" portion. A man from T'ung-ch'eng county died leaving four daughters and an adopted son. The first two daughters married uxorilocally, the third married out, and the fourth remained unmarried. A careful reading reveals that first the youngest daughter sued for a division of the family property, fearing that without dowry she

---

60 Internal evidence from this and other cases tells us the approximate date and Hu's office as prefect, in which capacity he decided this case; see CMC 3:97; 4:124–6. Hu served concurrently as Fiscal Intendant (*t'i-chü ch'ang-p'ing*); *Sung shih*, 416:12478–9; Ch'en Chih-ch'ao, "Chieh-shao," 681. Cf. Bernhardt, "Inheritance," 306 n. 9.

61 CMC 8:280–2. A translation of this case is found in McKnight and Liu, *Enlightened Judgments*. The translation below is my own.

62 Or "sons receive their father's portion" (*tzu ch'eng fu-fen*); SHT 12:197.

63 CMC 8:281–2. Hu Ying also granted her all of her father's assets purchased with "personal funds" (*ssu-fang*), which typically comprised the mother's dowry property and profits from it. See next section, Private Property within Marriage, for discussion of such assets. In this interesting twist, Hu Ying divides the property between a daughter and her uncle and cousin (rather than a brother) and gives the daughter one-half of what a son *would* have received. This would seem to contradict Sung law that gave daughters all the inheritance when no sons survived. Linck argues that a portion of property went to the uncles to "keep the peace"; *Zur Sozialgeschichte*, 118. It is also possible that the complicating factors of the undivided household and her marriage, as well as others not mentioned by Hu, such as a posthumously appointed heir, led to this solution (see interpretation in McKnight and Liu, *Enlightened Judgments*). See my discussion of extinct households in this chapter, and for a different interpretation, see Bernhardt, "Inheritance," 291–3.

64 While in T'ang this officer decided cases, during Sung the law secretary was formally charged only with reviewing the statutes and determining punishments. See Hsu Dau-lin, "Separation," 5–6. Here we see him drafting a verdict for a superior, which may represent an expansion of his usual duties in line with T'ang practice.

would be "sold" into a marriage (i.e., into servile status) or not be married off at all. The written judgment suggests that her coresident siblings (her two older sisters, their husbands, the adopted brother and his wife) were reluctant to partition the land and let her take her portion into another household in marriage, and were thus delaying her betrothal. Both the county court and the law secretary on appeal sided with the unmarried daughter: "County magistrate Chao had a deep understanding of the situation, thus he ruled that the property should be equally divided (*chün fen*) and arrangements made for [the fourth daughter's] marriage."[65] Both judges linked the division of the property to the marriage of the youngest daughter and the apportionment of property to her as dowry. In fact the appeal judge ordered the head of the household to arrange her marriage promptly after the division, before her dowry portion "disappeared" (i.e., got spent by others in the household).[66] In response to this state-ordered division, the older sisters filed a countersuit claiming that the adopted brother was not made a legal heir, and thus the property should all go to the resident daughters as in an extinct household. The judge rejected this claim and noted that as married daughters their claims to further property through family division were weak. His words reconfirm the strong position of unmarried daughters: "[The plaintiffs] have not considered that there is no clear provision for married women to inherit portions, whereas there is a definite law (*ting-fa* 定法) giving unmarried women equal portions [in family division]."[67]

The judge also remarks that the third daughter may not have been properly married out with a dowry, but may have been "sold" into another household as a foster daughter. This is further evidence that the older siblings had illegally appropriated the family wealth by refusing to give the younger sisters their shares.[68]

I can find no surviving statute that indicates any limit on a father's (or mother's) full authority to determine the size of a daughter's dowry if her marriage took place before the parents' death and thus before family division, as it ideally would. This is consistent with the gendered structure of marriage in premodern China. Before family division, no law could dictate the size of a daughter's dowry vis-à-vis the

---

65 CMC 7:217. This entire case is translated in McKnight and Liu, *Enlightened Judgments*.
66 CMC 7:217.   67 CMC 7:217.
68 CMC 7:217. This shows the importance of dowry for a woman to maintain nonservile status. Regarding the fourth daughter, the law secretary writes "[losing her dowry] would be contrary to the Fiscal Intendant's intention of caring for the orphan [girl]"; thus we find genuine concern on the part of judges to endow orphaned daughters with property.

inheritance of other family members, since the family fortunes could change after her marriage or another child could be born. Sung law assumed there would be no family division while the parents were alive, and thus gave parents full discretion in apportioning dowry. But if both parents had died and the house divided before a girl was married, she became a participant in family division; and in this case, we find that late Southern Sung law understood "equality" or "fairness" to mean she should get a portion half the size of a son's, often to be distributed by lot. Participants in family division had to be resident in the household. When women married out, they were no longer resident; thus, like sons who had left the household, they were not party to family division.[69] The concepts of "*chün fen*" or "*chün-p'ing*" ("equality" or "fairness") could not be applied in any absolute way before family division, thus leaving a daughter's share of property when she married at this time only vaguely defined and without guarantee. In family division though, equality and fairness between sons and daughters could be determined. We see from the cases above, from four different circuits (see Map 3), that by the mid-1200s when both parents had died and the courts were called upon to settle family division disputes, a half-share rule applied to unmarried daughters. The concept of "equal division among brothers" had been extended to sisters using the half-share formula.[70]

69 Recall that sons lost eligibility for family division after living separately for more than three years or having run away for more than six years; SHT 12:197.

70 Not all scholars have accepted the existence of a general half-share rule, as I have described it here. Some have accepted the rule for one son only; Linck, *Zur Sozialgeschichte*, 118; Yeh et al., *Min-fa shih*, 417. (Neither of these authors cites the second of Liu K'o-chuang's cases above, where we find the rule applied to a family of two sons and two daughters. Linck's 1986 book is necessarily based on the old edition of the *Ch'ing-ming chi*, which does not include the relevant part of Liu's case.) Others discount it by assuming it applied only when the sons were minors; Nagata Mie, "NanSōki ni okeru josei no zaisanken ni tzuite," *Hokudai shigaku* 31 (1991): 9, 13; Takahashi Yoshio, "Oya o nakushita musumetachi: NanSōki no iwayuru joshi zaisanken ni tsuite," *Tōhoku daigaku: Tōyōshi ronshū* 6 (Jan. 1995). (In the T'ung-ch'eng case above, the son was married and thus not a minor, though granted this case cites an "equitable" share as opposed to a half share per se.) The great Japanese legal scholar Shiga Shūzō, while not denying the half-share rule, argued that daughters' inheritance of land generally was an aberration within Chinese history practiced only by Sung elites; *Genri*, 440, 454 n. 7, 516–17. See also Hsiao-tung Fei, *Peasant Life in China* (London: Routledge and Kegan Paul, 1939), 68. The most radical challenge to the existence of a half-share rule comes from Kathryn Bernhardt, who contends that it did not exist at all or was a local custom that was an anomaly not only within the sweep of Chinese history but even within the Sung itself; "Inheritance" and *Women and Property in China, 960–1949* (Stanford, Calif.: Stanford University Press, 1999), ch. 1. A detailed response will appear in another venue. For a response to Nagata, see Yanagida Setsuko, "Shohō: Nagata Mie, 'NanSōki ni okeru josei no zaisanken ni tzuite,'" *Hōseishi kenkyū* 42 (1993): 300–1.

STATE SUPPORT OF FEMALE INHERITANCE

While I have found no other direct references to the half-share rule in Sung legal texts, a mountain of other evidence confirms a daughter's general rights to a share of family property in the presence of sons. References to "daughters' portions" (*nü-fen* 女分) are numerous; and they are found in different places and across centuries. The frequent mention of laws and lawsuits further confirms that daughters (and their husbands) might have recourse to the state if these portions were not distributed fairly.

An early reference to an unmarried daughter suing her siblings to receive her dowry from family division comes from the Northern Sung statesman Ssu-ma Kuang (1019–1086). In a warning about the dangers of children who covet property, he tells of a man who kept his household undivided and did not marry out his daughter. When the man died, his sons fought over the property, and "even his virgin daughter veiled her head and clutching documents went to the prefectural court to sue for her dowry property."[71] These examples confirm that daughters had certain inheritance rights based on the laws of "equal division." According to these laws, an orphaned daughter could sue to receive her fair share of family property.

A passage from the famous advice book by Yüan Ts'ai (fl. 1140–1195) published in 1178 suggests the existence of explicit laws protecting an orphaned daughter's share in an extended family. Yüan Ts'ai was from Ch'ü-chou in Liang-che East, but served in office in the capital and around the Southeast.[72] He writes:

> When an orphaned daughter is due a share (*fen*) of family property, marry her with as generous a portion as you can. If she ought to receive land, you must apportion it to her in accordance with the statutes (*t'iao*). If you are stingy in the present, you will surely be sued after the marriage.[73]

We find a similar example in the *Collected Decisions.* In a case from Chien-yang county, Fukien, dating to the early 1230s, then magistrate

---

71 *Chieh-tzu t'ung-lu* (SKCS ed.), 5:18a–b.

72 Yüan's important book, *Yüan-shih shih-fan*, has been translated by Patricia Ebrey under the title *Family and Property in Sung China: Yüan Ts'ai's Precepts for Social Life* (Princeton, N.J.: Princeton University Press, 1984). References to the text are given by *chüan* and page number in the original Chinese (TSCC ed.), followed by a citation of Ebrey's translation given by chapter and item number. Translations follow Ebrey unless indicated otherwise. For Yüan Ts'ai's career and background, see Ebrey, *Family and Property*, 18ff.

73 *Yüan-shih shih-fan* (TSCC ed.), 1:6; translation modified slightly from Ebrey, *Family and Property*, 1:17 (p. 218).

Liu K'o-chuang orders an uncle in an undivided household to give an orphaned niece the landed property that is due her as dowry:

I admonish Wei Ching-mo to think of his [deceased] brother and feel sympathy for his brother's daughter. He should take the property of the clan group and after discussion [with others in the household] should apportion some to make up her dowry. This will soothe the concerns of the deceased.[74]

Judge Liu shows further concern for a fair distribution of property between the orphaned girl and her brother when previously in the judgment he warns that land her brother has illegally mortgaged rightfully belongs to her as dowry:

[The deceased] Wei Ching-hsüan's portion of the family estate has mostly been mortgaged by Wei Ju-chi. Jung-chieh is the unmarried daughter [of Wei Ching-hsüan]. The land that has already been divided out [and mortgaged] should go to make up her dowry.[75]

Other cases from the *Collected Decisions* similarly reveal a conceptual similarity between sons' and daughters' inheritance, which contradicts the ideology of Confucian patrilineality. Two judgments are similar to Fan Ying-ling's above in stating a daughter's unequivocal right to some inheritance. Both are by Wu Ko, who was originally from Szechwan (Lu-shan county, Ya-chou) but served in office in Kiangsi, Fukien, and at the capital of Hangchow (Lin-an fu) around the midthirteenth century. His senior from Fukien, Liu K'o-chuang, was a friend and wrote a colophon for a collection of his poetry.[76] Wu's first case was similar in both circumstance and outcome to Fan's. A man had two daughters and no sons, but adopted an agnatic relative to be heir. His will, duly sealed by the county authorities, stated that land taxed at 800 strings should "be apportioned" to the two girls. After he died, the natal father of the adopted son, Tseng Wen-ming, claimed that the will was a forgery and the seal not official, and tried to keep all the land for himself and his son. Judge Wu strongly objected, saying the suit "went against human feelings." He further criticized Wen-ming, saying, "No doubt Wen-ming wants to take care of his son, but he prevents Ch'ien-chün from taking care of his daughters.[77] Where is the principle (*li* 理) in that?" And, "[For the heir] to claim that the will is a forgery is not to act like a brother to his older sisters. This amounts to being unfilial to his father!"[78] Disin-

---

74 CMC 9:356. For dating and location of the case, see CMC 9:349–51.
75 CMC 9:355.
76 Ch'ang Pi-teh et al. *Sung-jen chuan-chi tzu-liao so-yin* (Taipei: Ting-wen shu-chü, 1973), II, 1097; Ch'en, "Chieh-shao," 683.
77 Literally "treating his son as a son," "treating his daughters as daughters."
78 CMC 7:237–8.

heriting daughters went against both principle (*li*) and human feelings, and was unfilial besides.

In the second case, a Mr. Kao Wu-i died leaving his bondsmaid (*pi*) Ah Shen and an infant daughter born to her. Ah Shen's claims to the land were mitigated by Kao's brother, who got his son to be made a posthumous heir and was granted three-fourths of the land. Meanwhile Ah Shen remarried, taking the little girl with her, and the Kaos tried to keep all the land for themselves. Nine years later, in 1241, when Ah Shen filed a suit, Judge Wu Ko upheld the daughter's claim to her one fourth.[79] He considered the portion to be small, and as in his other verdict he accused the brother of "going against human feelings" and acting "very much counter to humaneness (*pu-jen chih shen* 不仁之甚)."[80] In both these cases, vocabulary that we associate with Confucian father–son values, "principle, humaneness, filiality" (*li, jen, hsiao* 理仁孝), is applied to the father–daughter relation with regard to property.

Other concepts and vocabulary in the *Collected Decisions* further under-score the similarity of a daughter's inheritance to that of a son. Two subsections address women's property, with the headings: "Women Inheriting Portions" (*Nü ch'eng-fen* 女承分), and "Women Receiving Portions" (*Nü shou-fen* 女受分).[81] Even Shiga Shūzō, who argues strongly against women's inheritance, notes that the language of the documents in the *Collected Decisions* evokes the concept of inheritance of a family portion as expected for sons. Shiga cites seven cases from the incom-plete Sung edition of the *Collected Decisions* that use the term "appor-tionment" (*po* 撥 or *piao-po* 標撥) applied to women, which he translates into Japanese as "to divide and take out a share" (*torinoke wakachidasu*).[82] More examples can be found in the complete Ming edition.[83]

A strong statement about daughters participating in family division comes from the late Northern Sung, long before the lawsuits recorded in the *Collected Decisions*, in a complaint about practices in Chien-ning (then Chien-chou), Fukien, the prefecture where the *Collected Decisions* was published. In a memorial of 1109, the Fukien official Ts'ai Hsiang complained of infanticide in Chien-chou, which he attributed to premortem inheritance by sons *and* daughters:

In Fukien, while the parents are still living, the sons and daughters confer with each other and calculate the size of the family estate. They divide it among them-selves, giving the parents an equal share. After the division, if another successor

79 I will show in the next section (Inheritance by Daughters without Surviving Brothers) that this was a small proportion. It is explained perhaps because the girl was by a maid.
80 CMC 7:238–9.   81 CMC 8:287–9 (one case) and 7:237–9 (two cases).
82 Shiga, *Genri*, 440 and 453 n. 2.   83 E.g., CMC 6:198; 7:237; 7:217.

is born, the infant is not raised but killed by drowning (locally this is called "weeding out children"), because of worries about further dividing the property. The problem is worst in Chien-chou. So far there is no prohibition, I respectfully request that a law be enacted and enforced.[84]

Whether or not families in some areas practiced illegal division of estates before the death of the parents, the tradition of daughters receiving inheritance through family division was strong throughout the Southeast, as evidenced in cases that cover nearly the entire area of the Southern Sung state.

DAUGHTERS' INHERITANCE BY TESTAMENT AND LEGAL PROTECTION OF THE PROPERTY OF MINORS

Beyond family division, daughters could receive additional inheritance on top of their dowry after they were married, even in the presence of sons. As we saw in the T'ang and before, parents might give additional property to their married daughters, by testament or otherwise, even in the presence of sons who would otherwise inherit such property. In the Sung these gifts included land. A dramatic example comes from the family instructions of Chao Ting (1085–1147), which he wrote in 1144 while in exile. Chao, a northerner who had to flee the Jurchen invasion, wanted his descendants to maintain an undivided estate where family members would be supported by equal distributions of the produce of their communal land (rather like the *tsung* ideal of ancient times, and a model anticipating the communal estates of later times). To this end, the thirty items of his instructions repeatedly forbid his sons and grandsons to divide the family estate. In a postscript, Chao further states that keeping the land undivided is the primary goal of his admonitions. And yet, in seeming contradiction to this goal, in item 27 Chao orders his sons to apportion a sizable piece of land to one of his daughters after his death:

I particularly love my daughter the Thirty-sixth maiden. After I die, apportion her property producing two-hundred piculs of grain from the rental lands in Shao-hsing prefecture, to add to her dowry property. Submit documents to the county office to change the registration to her name.[85]

---

84 SHY hsing-fa 2:49b (p. 6520). See also Niida, *Hōseishi* III, 389; and Niida, *Mibunhō*, 817.

85 *Chia-hsün pi-lu* (TSCC ed.), 3–4. A picul was approximately 133 lb. For more on Chao's communal family, see Joseph McDermott, "Equality and Inequality in Sung Family Organization: Some Observations on Chao Ting's *Family Instructions*," in *Yanagida Setsuko sensei koki kinen: Chūgoku no dentō shakai to kazoku*, ed. Ihara Hiroshi (Tokyo: Kyūko shoin, 1993), 1–21.

In an example a century later, a man willed his land to his daughter and son-in-law, even though he was survived by his wife and a son. When the son-in-law established a grave for his own mother on the land, the son sued, claiming the will was a fake. Judges at both the county and prefectural level rejected the case, saying the man had a right to give the land to his daughter and noting that the wife and son had not contested the will at the time of the bequest.[86]

We saw above that fathers could give their daughters less dowry than custom might dictate, but they could also give more, and they could will additional land to daughters after marriage. Sons in the family, who would expect to succeed to such property, could not object, though the law protected sons from being completely disinherited. Throughout the Sung, daughters were customarily understood to have a right to a portion of family property, and as time went by, Sung law came more and more to support this customary right.

When girls received property as part of family division, they were normally orphaned and not yet married. (Married daughters had already received dowry and left the household, and were thus not participants in family division). Such girls could become substantial holders of property in their own right. Sung law provided for the preservation of property for both male and female orphans:

> The government will audit or take an inventory of properties, estimate the needs of the orphans, and entrust a reliable relative to care for them and to return to them all their property when they come of age.[87]

Money for year-to-year upkeep was paid out to the trustee, and the remainder was returned to the orphan upon his or her majority. In the case of girls in particular, the property was to return to them when they "came of age" as opposed to when they married.[88] Such property constituted their inheritance, which could be taken into their marriage as dowry, but which could exist separate from and prior to dowry. Yanagida Setsuko has argued that references in the sources to "female households" (*nü-hu*) often referred to such unmarried girls and their estates.[89]

State involvement in preserving assets for underage girls reveals state support for women's property rights and official concern for the endowment of daughters in their own right (as well as distrust of relatives).

---

86 CMC 6:197–8.
87 CMC 7:228, as translated by McKnight and Liu, *Enlightened Judgments*, 254. The punishment for stealing audited property was two years of penal servitude; CMC 8:281.
88 See CMC 7:232–3; McKnight and Liu, *Enlightened Judgments*, 259.
89 Yanagida, "Sōdai no joko."

Surviving examples from the Northern Sung usually involve daughters of high officials or those from the imperial family. In 997, the Right Grand Master of Remonstrance, Wang Tzu-yü, died leaving a widow, a son, and three young daughters. The emperor ordered an audit (*chien-chiao*) of his home estate in Ch'u-chou to be preserved for his children (suggesting concern that the widow could or would not preserve it herself). Subsequently the son died and the widow returned to her natal parents. Five years later, a male relative petitioned the emperor to be allowed to return Tzu-yü's body to Ch'u-chou and sell his mansion in the capital, with the proceeds to be "sent to the government treasury in Ch'u-chou to augment the dowry of the three girls."[90] Undoubtedly, the relative kept some commission, but the involvement of the local authorities in auditing and keeping the estate for the girls is noteworthy. When the Lü-kuo-ch'ang princess died, she left her husband with two daughters and no sons. When her husband, a wealthy official at the end of his life, offered to donate his estate to the government, emperor Jen-tsung (r. 998–1023) would not let him, and instead ordered an audit. He assigned two executors to verify any needed expenditures (for the funeral presumably) and put the remaining property under state management for the two girls.[91]

Examples from the *Collected Decisions* in the Southern Sung show that when it came to girls who were not related to the emperor or to high officials, the state also tried to preserve inheritance that was due them and protect them from scheming relatives. In one case, a concubine successfully petitioned the government to gain control of the large inheritance due her two daughters that had been appropriated by a male agnate of her deceased husband.[92] In another, the government intervened to give a daughter back her inheritance after she was sold as a foster daughter and her inheritance taken over by a clansman (and partly by her mother).[93] In other cases, judges ordered audits to prevent guardians (often the mother) from squandering a girl's inheritance or to preserve property that was being disputed.[94]

The cases in the *Collected Decisions* reveal the abuses to which orphaned girls with property were subject. As seen in the cases cited, a girl's relatives or even her guardian might steal the property. In one example, the

90 *Hsü tzu-chih t'ung-chien ch'ang-pien* (Shanghai: Ku-chi, 1986) [hereafter cited as HCP], 51:430.
91 SHY ti-hsi 8:49; *Sung shih*, 463:13556. See also Yüan Li, "Sung-tai nü-hsing," 175.
92 CMC 7:232–3.   93 CMC 7:230–2.
94 CMC 8:253. In the T'ung-ch'eng case discussed above, the judge ordered that a daughter be married off and her inheritance given to her, before it "disappeared," i.e., was squandered by her family; CMC 7:217.

concubine mother of a ten-year-old heiress stole some of her daughter's assets for her own dowry and remarriage, then let her daughter get sold into a minor marriage.[95] Or sometimes relatives called on the government to audit property that was not subject to an audit merely to gain control of it themselves.[96] In other cases, the officials themselves audited property unnecessarily as a means of illegal confiscation.[97] It is unclear to what extent the Sung government was effective in correcting such abuses and protecting the property of underage girls, but it is significant that it made the attempt.

Inheritance by Daughters without Surviving Brothers

A family line, or household, was said to be "cut off" (*hu-chüeh* 戶絕) when no sons survived and both parents were deceased, that is, when no direct male descendant remained to carry on the ancestral sacrifices. Such circumstances where only daughters, or no one, survived may have prevailed in over 20 percent of households in Sung times.[98] These were of much concern to the state, which did not want property to disappear from the tax registers or get appropriated illegally by other families. Local officials were required to report cut-off households within three days, make an audit of the property, and determine who if anyone was entitled to receive it. Those in office who appropriated such property for themselves or concealed its actual extent were to be punished.[99]

Daughters traditionally inherited property in cut-off households, and the Sung was no exception. The Sung court issued regulations in unprecedented detail that clarified and improved a daughter's position. But the Sung state also placed new limits on inheritance by both males and females, as it sought to take a larger share of property for itself. The results of these legal developments parallel developments in other property law: taken together, they worked to the detriment of the agnatic patriline and instead were directed toward the material benefit of

---

95 CMC 7:230–2. See also CMC 7:232–3; 8:280–2.
96 E.g., CMC 7:228.   97 CMC 11:413.
98 Historical demography tells us that significant numbers of women probably had no brothers. Rough statistics from genealogies between 1050 and 1400 show that 22% of men had no surviving sons; Wolfram Eberhard, *Settlement and Social Change in Asia* (Hong Kong: University Press, 1967), 39. Modern data from Kwangtung shows one-third of men having no sons; Wolfram Eberhard, *Social Mobility in Traditional China* (Leiden: E. J. Brill, 1962), 153. These figures agree with European data and demographic models; see Anthony Wrigley and Roger Schofield, *Population History of England* (Cambridge: Cambridge University Press, 1989).
99 SHY shih-huo 61:38b–39a; Wei T'ien-an, "Sung-tai 'hu-chüeh t'iao-kuan' k'ao," *Chung-kuo ching-chi shih yen-chiu*, no. 3 (Sept. 1988): 31–2.

daughters and other nonagnates. Those who benefited included residents in the household with whom parents had relations of affection and dependence while alive. Close agnatic relatives lost their previous claims to family property through laws that contradicted Confucian notions of patrilineality.

NEW PROVISIONS FOR DAUGHTERS IN CUT-OFF HOUSEHOLDS

The T'ang statute of 737 that granted daughters without brothers their father's estate, after funeral expenses were paid, was copied verbatim into the *Sung Penal Laws* (*Sung hsing-t'ung*). No distinction was made between married and unmarried daughters in the text, though it is likely that the law was understood to apply only to unmarried daughters resident in the household:[100]

In all cases when a person dies and the household is cut off, close agnatic relatives are ordered to take all of the bondservants, maids, unfree dependents, buildings, and movable property and sell them. After deducting funeral expenses, they are to give the remaining property to the daughters.

(*Commentary*: If the household register is still the same, but the property has already been divided, also follow this rule.)

If no daughters survive, the property is to go to agnatic relatives (*chin-ch'in*) in order of closeness. If no relatives (*ch'in-ch'i*) survive, the government is to audit [and confiscate the property]. If the deceased left a testament as to the disposition of the property that is clear and verifiable, disregard this statute.[101]

We find the same rule, identified still as a statute (*ling*), quoted in the *Collected Decisions*, where it was explicitly applied only to unmarried daughters: "In all cases where the family line has been cut off (*hu-chüeh*), the property should all be given to the unmarried daughters."[102]

The T'ang commentary regarding household registers indicates that the law applied only when the family had already divided. If the deceased had lived in a joint household, his line was not considered cut off. In other words, before family division, an orphaned daughter's paternal uncles could carry on the family line of her father, thus depriving her of her father's estate. This had changed by Southern Sung times and possibly well before.

---

100 Niida, *Hōseishi* III, 381.
101 SHT 12:198. The T'ang law is found in Niida, *Tōryō*, 835; Niida, *Hōseishi* III, 381; Niida, *Mibunhō*, 478–9; Shiga, *Genri*, 396. See Shiga on the meaning of *chin-ch'in* 近親 and *ch'in-ch'i* 親戚; *Genri*, 409 n. 2. He suggests that the latter may include both agnates and affines, but I believe that in this context they both refer to agnates.
102 CMC 8:251.

We find in the *Collected Decisions* an expanded definition of a cut-off household that resulted in daughters inheriting more often. The law on cut-off households (*hu-chüeh fa*) was now applied to each conjugal unit within a joint family.[103] If any man failed to produce sons, his line was cut off, whether or not he lived with brothers or nephews who could continue sacrifices. Each nuclear family unit (*fang*) within a joint household had its own family line and rights of inheritance. An unmarried daughter inherited her father's portion even if she still lived in a joint household with paternal uncles surviving. Her father's share of the communal property was held in reserve for her and passed to her at the time of family division, which could be well after her father and mother had died. We also find in the *Collected Decisions* that a daughter could redeem lands that her father had mortgaged.[104]

While daughters may have benefited from these new regulations, they also represent the Sung state's unprecedented intervention in the transmission of family property. Other laws, discussed below, claimed a larger share of *hu-chüeh* property for the state, and these could now be applied more often. Of note is that agnatic kin lost out. Even when they lived in a joint household with the deceased, they could not keep the property but had to let it pass to daughters, who would take it out of the patriline. This was one more way in which a daughter in the Sung approached the status of a bonafide portion holder or coparcener. When she had no brothers, she virtually took her father's place in the line of property transmission.[105] This circumstance matches the words of Kao K'ang in the twelfth century (cited above), "a daughter inherits her father's portion" (*nü ch'eng fu fen*), and indeed the broader definition of *hu-chüeh* may have been part of the law to which Kao referred.[106]

Married daughters also inherited under Sung *hu-chüeh* laws, but in contrast to their unmarried sisters, married daughters lost out somewhat, as the Sung state sought to take a larger share for itself. An edict of 836 (copied into the *Sung Penal Laws*) stated that married daughters received the property if there were no unmarried daughters (as long as they had not been covetous or unfilial and had not schemed with their husbands to get the property).[107] But the *Sung Penal Laws*, compiled in 963, broke with this precedent and decreed that married daughters

103 CMC 7:217; 8: 251; 8:280. See also Niida, *Hōseishi* III, 383; Shiga, *Genri*, 402; Yüan Li, "Sung-tai nü-hsing," 176.
104 CMC 9:315–16.   105 See also argument in Niida, *Hōseishi* III, 382.
106 Note that the CMC cites this as a "statute" (*ling*), CMC 8:251, which is what Niida conjectures that Kao was citing; Niida, *Hōseishi* III, 382–3, 388.
107 SHT 12:198; Shiga, *Genri*, 401; Niida, *Mibunhō*, 478; Yüan Li, "Sung-tai nü-hsing," 179.

could inherit only one-third of the estate, with the remaining two-thirds to be confiscated by the government:

From now on, in households that have been cut off where there are [only] married daughters, apart from the funeral expenses, all of the buildings, domestic animals, and movable property should be divided into three. One-third should go to the married daughters and the remainder should be confiscated by the government.

If there are estate lands [among those confiscated] they can be rented to relatives.[108]

The Sung government revised this rule further and went on to issue numerous regulations on married women's inheritance. A modification in 1026 backed away from government confiscation. It gave the remaining two-thirds to relatives and nonrelatives who had resided in the household for at least three years and who had helped manage the estate. The nonrelatives included uxorilocal sons-in-law, foster sons, or children the wife brought from another marriage. Only if none of these existed could the government confiscate the property. The 1026 rule also stated that if there were no married daughters, the one-third portion could go to married sisters, aunts, or their children.[109] Significantly, the property did not go to nonresident agnates, though in the absence of coresidents, confiscated lands could go to "agnates, tenants, or sharecroppers," who would assume the tax burden on them.[110]

In early Sung law, married daughters could inherit only if there were no unmarried daughters in the household.[111] But a revision of this rule in 1098 by the Ministry of Revenue decreed that if the estate was over 1,000 strings, married daughters should also share a portion.[112] The decree went on to micromanage inheritance by married women, when only married daughters survived in a family. If the estate was worth less

---

108 SHT 12:198. Note that in the list of heritable property the different categories of unfree dependents are replaced by domestic animals.

109 SHY shih-huo 61:58a (p. 5902). Married daughters could petition for more than one-third, especially if the estate was large. See for instance HCP 106:947. See also Yüan Li, "Sung-tai nü-hsing," 179–80; Wei, "Sung-tai hu-chüeh," 33.

110 SHY shih-huo 61: 58a–b (p. 5902). Giving away land to those who could assume the tax burden no doubt reflects the Sung state's difficulty in gaining income from confiscated lands. On this subject generally, see Umehara Kaoru, "NanSō Kainan no tochi seido shitan," *Tōyōshi kenkyū* 21:4 (1963); and Itabashi Shin'ichi, "Sōdai no kosetsu zaisan to joshi no zaisanken o megutte," in *Yanagida Setsuko sensei koki kinen Chūgoku no dentō shakai to kazoku*, ed. Ihara Hiroshi (Tokyo: Kyūko shoen, 1993).

111 SHY shih-huo 61:58a (p. 5902).

112 HCP 501:4688. Yüan Li, "Sung-tai nü-hsing," 180, 183, claims this portion was one-third, but the decree does not specify. One-third is unlikely because that would give unmarried, married, and returned daughters equal portions, contrary to other laws.

than 300 strings they got 100 strings; if it was worth less than 100, they got all of it. For estates over 300 strings, the married daughters received one-third, up to a maximum of 2,000 strings. When the estate was over 20,000 strings, the official in charge was to notify the court to determine if more than the the 2,000 string limit could be given out.[113] In 1132 the Ministry of Revenue approved a proposal from the Judicial Intendant of Chiang-nan East that in these cases the limit be raised to 3,000 strings.[114]

Sung law also made provisions for women who were divorced or widowed and had returned to their natal homes. According to the *Sung Penal Laws*, they were to be treated like unmarried daughters and inherit the entire estate, as long as they had not come into property from their husbands. The provision of 963 reads:

> If a married daughter has been divorced or is widowed without children, and has returned to her parents' house, and if moreover she has not obtained any portion of her husband's property for herself, then in the case of a cut-off household, she should be treated the same as an unmarried daughter and the appropriate statutes and edicts applied.[115]

The "appropriate statutes and edicts" were presumably the T'ang statute of 737 and the edict of 836, printed just before in the *Sung Penal Laws*, that gave unspecified daughters (now interpreted to be unmarried or returned) all of a father's estate after funeral expenses were paid.

As with married daughters, the Sung state further regulated inheritance of those daughters who had returned to the household and assigned them portions vis-à-vis other daughters. A ruling of 1098 by the Ministry of Revenue upheld the equal treatment of unmarried and returned daughters: they were to divide the entire estate equally. But it went on to give returned daughters only two-thirds of the estate when no unmarried sisters were left. Of the remaining one-third, half of it, or one-sixth of the total, could go to married daughters. (Presumably the other one-sixth was confiscated.) The married daughter's share was further elaborated on: if the remaining one-third portion was less than 200 strings, she got a full 100, and if less than 100, she got it all.[116] By the midthirteenth century, a returned daughter's share had been cut back further. A statute cited in the *Collected Decisions* gave her just half of

---

113 HCP 501:4688.
114 SHY shih-huo 61:64 (p. 5905). In an example of 1133, the emperor Kao-tsung gave the married daughter of a deceased favorite minister one-third of his imperial grants, an amount that must have surpassed 3,000 strings. *Chien-yen i-lai hsi-nien yao-lu* (Wen-yüan ko SKCS ed.), 63:2b–3a (325–818); Yüan Li, "Sung-tai nü-hsing," 181.
115 SHT 12:198; Shiga, *Genri*, 402.
116 HCP 501:4688; cf. Yüan Li, "Sung-tai nü-hsing," 183.

Table 1. *Changes in Regulations Affecting Married and Returned Daughters (in Households with No Sons)*

Year	Regulation	Source
	Married daughters	
836	Married daughters receive all the property but only if no unmarried daughters survive	SHT
963	Married daughters get only 1/3 of property, remaining 2/3 confiscated	SHT
1026	Remaining 2/3 not confiscated but given to coresident relatives and other males (including uxorilocal sons-in-law, foster sons, children from wife's previous marriage)	SHY
1026	If no married daughters survive, 1/3 of property (i.e., married daughters' portion) given to other married female relatives	SHY
1098	Married daughters can get property in the presence of unmarried daughters if estate worth over 1,000 strings (prob. 1/3:2/3 division)	HCP
1098	2,000 string limit on married daughters' inheritance, plus other details for estates less than 300 strings	HCP
1098	If married and returned daughters both survive, returned daughters get 2/3 of property, married get 1/6, 1/6 confiscated	HCP
1132	Limit on married daughters' inheritance raised to 3,000 strings in cases of large estates	SHY
	Returned daughters	
963	Treated same as unmarried daughters	SHT
1098	Divide all of estate equally with unmarried daughters (consistent with equal treatment of unmarried and returned daughters in A.D. 963 rule)	HCP

Table 1. *(cont.)*

Year	Regulation	Source
1098	Get only 2/3 of estate if no unmarried daughters survive	HCP
1240s	Get half of unmarried daughters' share (interpreted to mean if no other daughters survive, get 1/2 the estate)	CMC

N.B. Married daughters lost property to the Sung state, but over time the state backed away from confiscation, giving remaining property to unrelated coresidents (as opposed to nonresident agnates). A returned daughter's portion gradually got reduced.

what an unmarried sister received.[117] These evolving limits on married and returned daughters' inheritance are summarized in Table 1.

As seen above, Sung law made a distinction between three kinds of daughters: unmarried (*tsai shih*), married (*ch'u chia*), and returned (*kuei chia*) (that is returned to their parents' home after being divorced or widowed). These three conditions determined whether they were resident in the household, living with a husband in a different household, or whether a dowry portion had previously been given to them. These issues had a bearing on how much of the communal family property they could receive at the time of division. As when sons survived in a family, residence was still the key factor in determining a daughter's inheritance at the time of family division. Nevertheless, the residence rule did not operate absolutely for women. Reflecting continuing economic bonds after marriage, married daughters, and in the absence of these, other female relatives who had married out, could still receive shares of family property when no sons survived.

An exception to the three kinds of daughters mentioned in the laws of cut-off households was a woman who married uxorilocally. In such cases, a daughter was considered to be "married" although she lived in the home of her natal parents (and had thus not "married out"). An uxorilocal husband brought "dowry" from his natal family into the household, and this became the private property of the couple in undivided households. (This further confirms the symmetry between a

117 CMC 7:217; 9:316. The law can also be read to mean that if only returned daughters survived, they divided half the estate.

daughter's and son's inheritance. When a son left the household before family division, he too received a premortem inheritance as "dowry.") In most cases, a daughter with brothers whose husband married into the household was treated as an unmarried daughter in family division.[118] We saw in cases above how daughters with uxorilocal husbands received a half share just as daughters who would expect to marry out. Nevertheless when no sons survived, the law of 1026 granted uxorilocal sons-in-law the remainder of the estate after the married daughters got their one-third, and such grants to live-in sons-in-law are found in Southern Sung case law.[119] In this way the residence test operated informally in a range of situations: Those residents in the household who helped manage the estate and care for the aged owners were favored to inherit over those who may have had more abstract claims of patrilineal connections.

INTERVENTION OF THE STATE

The succession of laws and regulations that affected a daughter's inheritance when a household was cut off reveal the Sung state's concern about family inheritance matters and its willingness to intervene. The early Sung state tried to assert latent claims on the land of the realm, and new laws often resulted in more land and other property going to the state compared to T'ang, despite the ideals of the equal field system. We saw how married daughters and others lost property to the state, but the group most affected was agnatic male kin.

In a series of measures that we can surmise were aimed at preventing land aggrandizement by powerful families, as well as securing more revenues for the state, the government staked out a larger share of *hu-chüeh* property for itself at the expense of agnatic male relatives. Amid much debate, some *hu-chüeh* laws that disadvantaged agnates were relaxed over time or not rigorously applied, but the pattern overall followed that of other Sung property law: women and other house-

---

118 But note the T'ung-ch'eng case above, where the judge argues that since the elder daughters are already "married" (albeit uxorilocally), they have weaker claims to family property than their unmarried sister.

119 Kawamura Yasushi, "Sōdai zeisei shōkō," in *Yanagida Setsuko sensei koki kinen*, ed. Ihara Hiroshi, 347–63; and Patricia Ebrey, "Property Law and Uxorilocal Marriage in the Sung Period," in *Family Process and Political Process in Modern Chinese History* (Taipei: Institute of Modern History, Academia Sinica, 1992). Kawamura stresses that the son-in-law was not recognized as an inheritor, rather his wife was; whereas Ebrey states that judges do not seem to have systematically differentiated between property going to the wife as opposed to the husband. Both agree that the wife and husband were expected to manage the property together.

hold residents benefited from new legal guarantees to property while the interests of the Confucian patriline (represented by nonresident agnates) suffered.

The T'ang law on cut-off households of 737, which was copied into the *Sung Penal Laws,* granted all of the estate to close agnatic relatives when no daughters survived. Only in the absence of daughters or agnatic relatives did the state confiscate the property.[120] In an edict of 1015 however, the Sung emperor made a radical break from this long tradition and declared that *hu-chüeh* land would no longer go to agnatic relatives but instead would be taken over by the government to be sold off. Lands that were not sold would be rented out.[121] The policy was likely aimed at rich families, for in 1023 the official Ch'i Sung requested that exceptions be made for poorer families and at the least their relatives be allowed to assume the tenancy of confiscated lands. Other officials complained that rents on the confiscated lands were set too high to the detriment of the people, or recommended that the lands be sold to tenants.[122]

Members of the Sung bureaucracy were of mixed opinion about appropriating private lands, and the issue of how to treat *hu-chüeh* property in the absence of daughters continued to be debated. The ruling of 1026 on married women's property backed away from confiscation and gave the previously confiscated portion of an estate to those resident in the household for at least three years. These might include agnatic relatives, but also included uxorilocal sons-in-law, foster sons, children of the wife from a previous marriage, and even tenants. Only if none of these survived did the government confiscate the property. Nonresident agnates still did not get property directly, but the 1026 law specified that confiscated lands could be awarded to them, or to tenants or sharecroppers, to assume the tax burden. When an earthquake hit Hsin-chou (modern Shansi) in 1038 and twenty-five families died out, the government in lieu of confiscation allowed nonresident agnates to purchase the lands at a 30 percent discount.[123] When a monk died, relatives (nonresident in the case of a monk) were allowed to arrange his

---

120 SHT 12:198; Niida, *Tōryō,* 835. The law is translated on page 98.
121 SHY shih-huo 1:21a (p. 4812), 63:171b (p. 6072); Niida, *Tōryō,* 837–8. It is clear from the context that this was only in the absence of daughters.
122 SHY shih-huo 1:21a (p. 4812), 63:171b–172a (p. 6072); 63:174b (p. 6073). I am grateful to Brian McKnight for showing me these and other relevant texts and for discussing them with me. For more on *hu-chüeh* land laws, see Brian McKnight, "Who Gets It When You Go: The Legal Consequences of the Ending of Family Lines (*juehu*) in the Song Dynasty (960–1279)," *Journal of the Economic and Social History of the Orient* 43:3 (2000), 314–63.
123 HCP 122:1104.

funeral, and the government awarded them property from the estate for that purpose.[124]

At the end of the dynasty, laws on confiscation that denied property to agnates and others were still on the books, but some judges chose to forgo such appropriation. In a case dating to about 1244, a judge awarded family property to a faithful servant and her husband, asking them to manage the funeral of the deceased.[125] In another example, the same judge declared his reluctance to confiscate property, and gave property that by law could have been confiscated to agnates.[126]

After the 1015 law that deprived close agnatic kin of property from families that had died out, the only way they could obtain such property was to set up an heir for the deceased head of household to reestablish the family line. Such an heir had to be an agnatic male relative of the proper generation to act as a son of the deceased, and he had to renounce any inheritance from his natal father. No one person could be the heir for two separate lines in Sung law.

It is likely that agnatic relatives resorted to posthumous adoptions with increasing frequency after the policy changes of the early Sung, for less than a century later we find the issue hotly debated in the context that government revenues from cut-off households were decreasing. In 1092 agnates were forbidden to establish posthumous heirs, the government taking over the task; but by 1094 the policy was reversed and they were allowed to again.[127] Then in 1113 a debate ensued over whether such heirs should be permitted at all. Some argued that they were condoned by Confucius and were a necessary part of the people's lives. Others countered that allowing them would prevent any household from being considered cut off and would eliminate this already diminishing source of revenue for the state. At this juncture the emperor decided to continue to allow posthumous heirs.[128]

Two decades later, in 1132, however, a compromise policy was enacted. Henceforth, posthumous heirs would be treated the same as married daughters and receive only one-third of the family property, the other two-thirds going to the state.[129] On top of this, caps were placed on how much such heirs could receive at all. They could only receive

---

124 *Ch'ing-yüan t'iao-fa shih-lei*, 51:487; Niida, *Tōryō*, 838. The regulation dates to the Ch'ing-yüan period, 1195–1200.
125 CMC 10:377–8.
126 CMC 8:281–2; Itabashi, "Sōdai no kosetsu zaisan," 377–8.
127 SHY li 36:16a (p. 1316).
128 SHY li 36:16a–b (p. 1316). See also Nagata, "NanSōki," 5.
129 SHY shih-huo 61:64a (p. 5905). Niida and Nagata following him argue that the wording of this new law suggests that posthumous heirs were receiving nothing for a period prior to this. See Niida, *Mibunhō*, 484–5, 487 n. 25; Nagata, "NanSōki," 5.

property worth a maximum of 3,000 strings of cash, but if the estate was over 20,000 strings in value, they could petition for more.[130] In 1179, emperor Hsiao-tsung, known for personally correcting laws, ordered that this provision be eliminated, along with several others that garnered more revenue for the state.[131] Nevertheless, we find it back on the books in the thirteenth century, with the limit automatically raised to 5,000 for estates over 20,000 strings.[132]

The one-third limit on the inheritance of posthumous heirs, in the absence of daughters, is cited frequently in the *Collected Decisions*.[133] Nevertheless, by this time some judges were openly critical of aggressive policies of state confiscation. A judge in Chien-yang county, Chien-ning, for instance rejected confiscation, arguing that there in Chu Hsi's place of residence, officials should follow principle (*li*) and not seek profit.[134] When daughters survived in addition to the posthumous heir, the law established firm rights vis-à-vis the heir, as will be discussed in the next section.

The twelfth century laws that capped inheritance make no direct reference to daughters, but evidence from the thirteenth century shows that the caps were also applied to daughters, or anyone receiving property from a family with no male heir. Judge Fan Ying-ling can be understood to have been referring both to daughters and posthumous heirs, when he wrote: "The total [inheritance] must not exceed 3,000 strings. But if [the entire estate] exceeds 20,000 strings, an additional 2,000 strings may be inherited."[135] He applied the limits even more explicitly to daughters in another case,[136] but in the final analysis he did not confiscate any property in either case. This law, like others, provided the judge with a threat to coerce the parties into complying with his ruling, but Fan and others seem to have applied it only rarely.

130 SHY shih-huo 61:64a; Burns, *Private Law*, 270.
131 *Hsü tzu-chih t'ung-chien* (Peking: Ku-chi ch'u-pan she, 1957), 147:3922; *Sung shih*, 200:4993–4. Niida finds a reference to this incident in *Yü Hai*, ch. 66 dated 1177; Niida, *Tōryō*, 838.
132 CMC 8:288. See also Niida, *Hōseishi* IV, 411–12.
133 CMC 4:107, 110; 8:251, 258, 266, 287.
134 CMC 8:258.
135 CMC 8:288. Shiga, *Genri*, 404; Niida, *Mibunhō*, 484–5; Yanagida, "Joshōbun," 235; Burns, *Private Law*, 267. This case can be read to apply the limit only to the posthumous heir; see Shiga's comments (*Genri*, 411 n. 15). But Yanagida ("Joshōbun," 235) and Niida (*Mibunhō*, 484–5) take it to limit a daughter's inheritance as well, and I agree.
136 CMC 4:110. This gives the limit as 300, which Shiga thinks is a misprint for 3,000; Shiga, *Genri*, 402–3; Burns, *Private Law*, 270. The judge says that since the value of the estate did not exceed "300 (or 3,000) strings," it could all be inherited by the daughter. He might have just been stating that an inheritance of 300 strings did not exceed the limit. (I translate this case in full in the next section.)

Testamentary succession was another area where the state imposed limits and stepped in to claim any property over them. In the T'ang, a man could will his property to anyone he wanted if he had no sons. (If sons survived, a father could not disinherit them.) The statute of 737 (included in the *Sung Penal Laws*) on inheritance by daughters when the family line was cut off says at the end:

If the deceased while still living made a testament that is clear and verifiable, then this statute [about daughters' inheritance] should be disregarded.[137]

This right to will property was severely reduced during the Northern Sung. The change in the law came sometime between 1064 and 1086, which suggests that it might have been part of Wang An-shih's New Laws aimed at garnering more income for the state. We know of the law from a memorial of 1086 criticizing the change, the date of which suggests that the memorial was part of the Yüan-yu (1086–1093) opposition to the New Laws. The memorial reads:

The left policy critic, Wang Yen-sou said, "I humbly feel that in this world nothing is more grievous than to be old and have no sons or grandsons. The ancient kings displayed their humanity in their giving succor and their generosity in what they bestowed. Thus in the ancient system of testamentary succession there were no limitations on the amounts. All could be given, whether to those of their own clan or to relatives of a different surname. . . . But thereafter officials concerned with profits were unwilling to perpetuate their intent, and have set up laws limiting [the amounts that can be given]. This offends against normal human feelings. Estates amounting to less than 300 strings of cash can be given away. For estates of less than 1,000 strings, 300 can be given away. For 1,000 or more, one-third can be given and that is all. Our state possesses the vastness that is within the four seas and the riches of the Nine Provinces. How can we act in this way? . . . I humbly hope that the emperor will especially issue an order reviving the old law on testamentary succession of the Chia-yu period (1056–1063) in order to soothe the hearts of the solitary and old, encourage the intentions of those who care for the solitary and old, and improve the customs of the people.[138]

Limits on testamentary succession were relaxed a little in 1162, when emperor Hsiao-tsung first took the throne. Five hundred strings could be given for estates of 1,000 to 1,500 strings, and one-third of estates

---

137 Niida, *Tōryō*, 835; SHT 12:198. This of course gives fathers the right to disinherit daughters, but we have seen how late Sung judges, in view of the half-share rule, were reluctant to uphold wills that left too little to daughters.

138 HCP 383:3609. Niida, *Mibunhō*, 480–1; Shiga, *Genri*, 399; McKnight, "Chinese Law and Legal Systems," 45–6; Burns, "Private Law," 271. Translation is modified from McKnight. Shiga also conjectures that the law had something to do with Wang An-shih's reforms; *Genri*, 411 n. 9.

over 1,500 up to a limit of 3,000. Moreover, the new ruling allowed the remainder to go to foster sons rather than be confiscated; and it specified the division of an estate between foster sons and uxorilocal sons-in-law if these existed.[139] In this way, the Sung state acquiesced to the 1086 memorial and rewarded "those who care for the solitary and old," but it dictated much of the distribution instead of leaving it up to the "solitary and old" themselves.

Even within these limits, property could be willed only to agnatic or affinal relatives within the mourning grade of *ssu-ma* (cousins of the fourth generation). A statute to this effect is cited in the *Collected Decisions* in two cases by Weng Fu, one of which was written sometime after 1242.[140]

DAUGHTERS AND POSTHUMOUS HEIRS

If a couple had no sons, they could adopt an heir from their agnatic kinsmen, who would be treated by law as a natural son with full rights of inheritance and succession. The person (and process) was called an "established heir" (*li-chi* 立繼), and the wife could appoint such an heir after her husband's death.[141] A household was not technically cut off as long as the wife lived, since she could always make such a same-surname adoption to continue the family line. When both the husband and wife had died, however, it was still possible to rescue the family line from extinction if an heir was designated on behalf of the deceased couple. Such a postmortem adoptee could be appointed by senior agnatic relatives (*tsu-chang*) or by the state. Such an heir was labeled a "mandated heir" (*ming-chi* 命繼), that is, a posthumous heir.[142]

The Confucian concept of a ritual patriline dictated the need for a male heir who could carry on the family sacrifices. (Recall that Mencius described the most unfilial of all acts as having no progeny.[143]) T'ang law is unclear and may have made no distinction between premortem

---

139 SHY shih-huo 61:66b (p. 5906). Niida, *Mibunhō*, 749–50.

140 CMC 5:141–2; 9:304. Shiga, *Genri*, 399, 410 n. 8.

141 By law, the boy had to be of the same surname, but children of different surnames could be adopted under some conditions if they were under 3 *sui* at the time of adoption. In line with my argument that patrilineal principles were largely disregarded in Sung law, the state was frequently willing to recognize nonagnatic adoption. Wives frequently adopted boys of tenuous eligibility from among their own natal relatives. See McKnight, "Chinese Law and Legal Systems."

142 CMC 8:265–7.

143 *Mencius* 4A:26. For evidence of how this played out in both elite and popular culture, see Ann Waltner, *Getting an Heir: Adoption and the Construction of Kinship in Late Imperial China* (Honolulu: University of Hawaii Press, 1990).

and postmortem adoption.[144] Sung law on the other hand clearly distinguished between a posthumous heir and a regular adoptee.[145] By the thirteenth century, in the face of frequent conflicts between posthumous heirs and the natal daughters of a household, the law provided new protections for daughters' inheritance in the presence of a posthumous heir. As seen in the *Collected Decisions*, daughters lost some property to these posthumous heirs, but still received the major part of the family estate.

The rules of division between a posthumous heir and the surviving daughters can be discerned from a body of verdicts that quote laws covering all sorts of contingencies in these property disputes. These rules are presented below and in Table 2.[146] (The table covers all scenarios, including those with surviving sons.) The cases where the information is found are listed in the footnotes together with the location of the trial if known. Where the relevant law is cited in more than one verdict, I have found the wording to be identical or nearly so. The presiding judge sometimes chose not to divide the property exactly as specified in the law, because of unusual circumstances. This was especially true, as with other laws described in this chapter, when the judge decided to forgo confiscation and instead distributed the property among the parties to the suit.[147] Over all, the citation of statutes and application of law is remarkably consistent between different judges in different prefectures.

RULES OF DIVISION BETWEEN DAUGHTERS AND POSTHUMOUS HEIRS

1. If only *unmarried* daughters survive and a posthumous heir is set up, the heir gets one-quarter of the estate and the daughters divide the remaining three-quarters. (For example, if there is only one daughter, she gets three times as much as the heir. If there are three, the heir and the daughters each get the same amount.)[148]

2. If only *married* daughters survive and a posthumous heir is set up, the heir gets one-third of the property, the married daughters get one-third, and the state

---

144 Niida, *Hōseishi* III, 383; Burns, *Private Law*, 268. Niida, *Tōryō*, 234, quotes a statute that says a posthumously adopted son must be over 18 to receive his portion. Niida, *Mibunhō*, 786, points to the lack of clarity on this issue in T'ang.
145 See, for instance, CMC 8:265–7. This judgment and the appeal are titled: "The difference between a posthumous heir (*ming-chi*) and an established heir (*li-chi*)."
146 There is much reference to these rules in the literature; e.g., Niida, *Hōseishi* III, 383–6; IV, 410–12; Shiga, *Genri*, 401–5; Yanagida, "Joshōbun," 234–8; Linck, *Zur Sozialgeschichte*, 117–19, 130; Yüan Li, "Sung-tai nü-hsing," 184.
147 See, for instance, CMC 8:251–3, 8:258; 7:205–6.
148 CMC 8:251 Chien-ch'ang (Kiangsi); 8:266 Chien-ning (Fukien); 8:287 Yüan-chou (Hunan); 4:100 (proportions not clear); 4:110; 7:215a; 7:238 (last two modified).

Table 2. *Distribution of Inheritance among Daughters, Sons, Posthumous Heirs, and the State by Midthirteenth Century (after Death of Both Parents When Division Carried out by the State)*

	Daughters	Posthumous Heir	State
	Sons and Daughters		
1. Natural sons & daughters	Each daughter 1/2 son's share	—	—
2. Adopted son (*li-chi*) & daughters	Same as 1	—	—
3. Sons & adopted daughters	Same as 1	—	—
	Daughters Only		
4. Unmarried daughters only	All (up to 5,000 strings)	—	—
5. Married daughters only	1/3	—	2/3
6. Returned daughter only	2/3 or 1/2	—	1/3 or 1/2
7. Unmarried and married daughter	All to unmarried (unless over 1,000 strings)	—	—
8. Unmarried and returned daughter	2/3 to unmarried 1/3 to returned	—	—
9. Married and returned daughter	2/3 to returned 1/6 to married	—	1/6
	Daughters and Posthumous Heir		
10. Posthumous heir & unmarried daughter	3/4	1/4	—
11. Posthumous heir & married daughter	1/3	1/3	1/3
12. Posthumous heir & returned daughter	1/2	1/4	1/4
13. Posthumous heir & unmarried and returned daughter (Unmarried daughter 8/15 Returned daughter 4/15)	4/5	1/5	—
14. Posthumous heir & unmarried and married daughter	?	?	—
15. Posthumous heir only	—	1/3	2/3

N.B. Rules 1–3 apply only to unmarried daughters. When both sons and daughters survive in a family, a married daughter gets no additional inheritance beyond the dowry she has already received.

gets the remaining one-third.[149] (Note that this is the same amount married daughters received without a posthumous heir and that a posthumous heir received in the absence of daughters.)

3. If *unmarried* daughters survive together with daughters who have *returned* to the family after marriage (by virtue of widowhood or divorce), and a posthumous heir is adopted, the heir gets only one-fifth of the property, and the daughters divide the remaining four-fifths.[150]

4. If only *returned* daughters remain, and a posthumous heir is adopted, the situation is unclear, but probably one-half goes to the returned daughters, one-fourth to the heir, and one-fourth to the state.[151]

Rule 1, which gives unmarried daughters three-quarters of the property when an heir was adopted posthumously is applied the most often in the sources. Of seven judgments citing this rule in the *Collected Decisions*, two modified it. In one modification, the daughter of a maid, who was less than a year old when her father died and went with her mother into a remarriage, was given one-quarter of her father's property and the nine years of back income from it that the posthumous heir and his agnatic relatives had stolen (in collusion with a tenant on the land).[152] In another, two daughters aged nine and under were given two-thirds of their father's land instead of three-fourths after a posthumous heir was established.[153] In a modification of Rule 2, a judge split the property of each of two brothers between their married daughters and posthumous heirs without confiscating any. The judge was influenced by the fact that the daughters had uxorilocal husbands and thus lived at home.[154]

149 CMC 8:287 Yüan-chou (Hunan); CMC 7:205–6 (latter modified). Diagrams of the former case are printed in Shiga, *Genri*, 404–5, and Yanagida, "Joshōbun," 235. I have found no verdicts that address the case of married *and* unmarried daughters. Perhaps married daughters were disinherited, as when no heir was appointed.

150 CMC 8:266–7 Chien-ning (Fukien); 8:287 Yüan-chou (Hunan). See also Burns, *Private Law*, 267–8, 270. We can conjecture that unmarried daughters would get twice what returned ones would, as in the absence of an heir; see CMC 7:217 T'ung-ch'eng (Hupei); 9:315 (probably the capital Lin-an fu, modern Hangchow, Chekiang; see Ch'en, "Chieh-shao," 682).

151 CMC 8:266–7 Chien-ning (Fukien); 8:287–9 Yüan-chou (Hunan). The statute cited in these is unclear, saying only that returned daughters get property "according to the law of cut-off households." A law that says returned daughters receive half of unmarried daughters can be interpreted to mean that returned daughters alone get half the estate; CMC 7:217 T'ung-ch'eng (Hupei); 9:316 (probably Lin-an fu, Chekiang). See Shiga, *Genri*, 404; Yüan Li, "Sung-tai nü-hsing," 184; Nagata, "NanSōki," 3; and Bernhardt, "Inheritance," 274. Yanagida states that the amount cannot be determined; "Joshōbun," 235.

152 CMC 7:238.

153 CMC 7:215a. The judge in this case does not cite any statute.

154 CMC 7:205–6.

Women's Property within Marriage

When a woman married, she took all of her property, whether apportioned to her at the time of her wedding or inherited previous to her
marriage through family division, into the household of her husband as
"dowry." The tax liability on cultivable lands was transferred to her
husband's household, but government registers and legal contracts
clearly identified the land as the wife's own and distinguished it from
other property of the household.[155] Land thus attached to a woman
received special legal treatment both during the woman's lifetime and
after her death.

Sung discourse characterized a woman's land as "private," in contrast
to the "public" lands held communally by males in a household. This
gendering of property was part of the structure of the Chinese communal family, and it had important consequences for individual family
members. Sung law followed T'ang precedent and upheld the ideal of
"communal living, common property" (*t'ung-chü kung-ts'ai*), where property was held in common under the control of the household head. The
punishment for dividing the family before the father had died was three
years of penal servitude, and a father could not disinherit his sons or
pass the family estate to outsiders if he had living sons. Sons were strictly
forbidden to dispose of any family property.[156] Whereas some private
assets could be held by men and could result in considerable inequality
between brothers, a male's assets were never unequivocally recognized
as separate from the family's common estate.[157] Only one kind of property was allowed absolutely by law and custom to be held and disposed
of privately by an individual within the household: property that
belonged to women who married in. A woman's property then could be
more freely disposed of and had fewer strings attached to it than a man's.

---

155 Sung shih 178:4334; *Wen-hsien t'ung-k'ao* (Kuo-hsüeh chi-pen ts'ung-shu ed., 1959),
13:138–9; CMC Appendix 2:607; Shiga, *Genri*, 522; Yanagida, "Joshōbun," 239; Hsing
T'ieh, "Sung-tai te lien-t'ien ho mu-t'ien" *Chung-kuo she-hui ching-chi shih yen-chiu*, no.
1 (1993): 36–53. Hansen has shown how private contracts superseded the perennially out-of-date government land registers as legal proof of ownership in Sung; Valerie
Hansen, *Negotiating Daily Life in Traditional China: How Ordinary People Used Contracts,
600–1400* (New Haven, Conn.: Yale University Press, 1995).
156 SHT 12:192, 196–7.
157 Male private funds could come from officeholding or from personal enterprises generated without using family capital. Yüan Ts'ai (fl. 1140–1195) provides these three
sources of private property: wife's property, officeholding, and personal entre-
preneurial business. Disparities arising from them seem to have been common in the
Sung. See *Yüan-shih shih-fan*, 1:8–9, 1:9, 3:60; Ebrey, *Family and Property*, 1.25, 1.26,
3.56; and Shiga, *Genri*, 507–11. See also Lau Nap-yin, "Sung-tai t'ung-chü chih-tu hsia
te suo-wei 'kung-ts'ai'," *Chung-yang yen-chiu yüan, li-shih yü-yen yen-chiu so chi-k'an* 65:2
(1994) for an excellent discussion of this issue.

The special terms used to refer to a wife's property distinguished it from other property in the household. These tended to associate dowry with a woman's own body and adornment and minimize its economic significance. The resulting discourse helped obscure the contradiction between women's private property and Confucian patrilineality. By Sung times, elite dowries were substantial and often included land, and new terms appeared to indicate a woman's real property, while retaining allusions to the body and her person. Sung Chinese no doubt failed to notice any oxymoron in expressions like *lien-t'ien* 奩田, literally "cosmetic-case lands," or *tzu-sui t'ien* 自隨田, literally "lands that accompanied [the bride into marriage]." At a time when a wife's dowry could equal the entire estate of her husband's family, such terms served less to obscure its significance than to reinforce the special nature of the assets and guarantee the protections that separated them from male, communal property.

In contrast to much of the premodern West, where a wife's property was combined with her husband's and where she could not enter into a contract on her own, a Chinese wife's assets were never legally combined with her husband's family estate and her ability to conclude separate contracts was a feature of the socioeconomic dynamic of Sung family life. Moreover, additional inheritance obtained by the wife after marriage, or land or goods purchased by the wife or her husband with the wife's money, plus income and interest on these personal assets, were all lumped together and labeled as "dowry." The legal benefits that accompanied such labeling created enclaves where individual interests could be indulged and where anticommunal and antipublic forces operated within the theoretically communal family.

Once property was attached to a married woman, by whatever method, it stayed with her permanently. Sung law allowed all of this property, even if obtained after the marriage, to be taken out of the household and into a remarriage in case of divorce or widowhood. The special legal treatment given women's property was aimed at providing material support and class status in her lifetime and ritual support through sacrifices after her death. It thus transcended marriage and family structure. Since Sung widows or divorcées could control considerable assets, and since remarriages between adults could be arranged by the parties themselves, previously married women became attractive marriage partners. (The demographic reality of early death no doubt also contributed to the prevalence of widow remarriage.) By encouraging remarriage, developments in Sung law once again worked counter to the agnatic principles of Confucian doctrine and against the material interests of the male patriline.

Taking Property out of a Marriage after the Husband's Death

The special nature of married women's property and the rather broad definition of it that included assets acquired after marriage are best illustrated by the ability of a wife to take her property into a remarriage after her husband died. The law was aimed at keeping a wife's property out of family division, but it had the effect of distinguishing a wife's property from her husband's even in households already divided.

Legal protections of a widow's private property are well demonstrated in the *Collected Decisions* by a case entitled "Son and Stepmother Quarrel over Property." The author, styled T'ien-shui (Heavenly Water), has five cases in the *Collected Decisions* but cannot be otherwise identified.[158] This judgment demonstrates the tension between Confucian ideals like widow chastity and the clear position of Sung law, which protected a wife's private property and encouraged remarriage. In the following case, Judge T'ien-shui personally disapproves of the practice of separately registering lands purchased after marriage under a wife's name, and of a wife's remarrying and breaking up her husband's estate, but he is helpless to enforce his views in the face of unambiguous law. Since his wording and commentary reveal much about legal thinking on this issue at the time, I translate the case in full:

Son and Stepmother Dispute Property[159]

Ever since the cypress boat poems[160] stopped being written, widows have not been able to preserve their integrity to keep peace in their homes. And ever since south wind poems[161] were disregarded, sons have not been able to exhaust filiality to serve their mothers. I record these old poems and sigh three times over them.

Wu Ho-chung was a prefectural graduate[162] who passed away some time ago, so we cannot know what sort of a person he was. But today an examination of

158 Ch'en Chih-ch'ao, "Shu-lüeh," 152; Ch'en Chih-ch'ao, "Chieh-shao," 685. T'ien-shui is a county and commandery (*chün*) alternately in Ch'in-feng and Li-chou circuits (near the modern border area of Shensi, Kansu, and Szechwan). For convenience I refer to this author as Judge T'ien-shui.
159 CMC 10:365–6. See also Yanagida, "Joshōbun," 231–3.
160 See *Shih-ching* Mao #45; Legge, *The She King or Book of Poetry* (Oxford University Press) Bk. 4, Pt. 1, p. 73. The "Little Preface" took this poem to be about the faithful widow Kung Chiang, wife of Kung Po, Prince of Wei. Chu Hsi accepted this interpretation, and the poem was cited by Sung Confucians to support the doctrine of widow chastity. See, for instance, Liu K'o-chuang's words in CMC 9:354. For a different interpretation, see Arthur Waley, *Book of Songs* (New York: Grove Press, 1937; reprint 1960), 53 n. 53.
161 *Shih-ching* Mao #32; Legge, *She King*, 3:1:7, 50. Chu Hsi interpreted this poem to be a lament by a woman's sons that they were not filial enough to prevent their mother from remarrying. (Cf. Waley, *Book of Songs*, 73 no. 78.)
162 A *kung-shih*, literally "tribute scholar" (same as *chü-jen*) was someone who passed the prefectural examination, the first of two basic levels in the Sung civil service

the court record shows that in his household were stored several thousand volumes of books, so he must have been a fine gentleman. His first wife had died leaving him with a seven-year-old son when he married Madam Wang. They [no doubt] expected to care for each other for a hundred years.

Had Madam Wang been a virtuous woman, she would have known that to serve her husband with reverence and to care for her son with kindness is the proper way of a woman. After she married and came to live with her husband, how could her heart change so easily? They bought land after the marriage, and on the contract that was drawn up, all the land was listed as Madam Wang's dowry (*chuang-lien*). The intent of the law is to avoid the misfortune of future lawsuits over family division when brothers live together and buy property with their wives' money. Yet when Madam Wang served Scholar Wu [as his wife], there was no father- or mother-in-law above to care for, and no older or younger brother below with whom to divide the property. Within the household, from the smallest hair on up, everything was the property of Madam Wang and her husband. Why did they need to set up boundaries between their fields and purchase private property separately? What was their intention in doing this?

Scholar Wu was infatuated, and would agree to anything his wife wanted. But he was mistaken about her. Even at that time, she probably had no intention of keeping the "oath of eternal fidelity."[163] Scholar Wu died in the twelfth month of the ninth year of the Chia-ting reign (1216), and the family fortunes were [still] quite good. If Madam Wang had been able to keep her oath and preserve her chastity, support her household and educate her son to get him established, then not only would she have been a virtuous wife, but Scholar Wu would have had descendants.[164] Her thinking was one-sided, however, and went only as far as herself. She gave no more thought to her husband and young son.

As for the son, Wu Ju-ch'iu, he was willful and licentious, profligate and unrestrained. In the older generation Madam Wang gathered up her belongings,[165] while in the younger Wu Ju-ch'iu destroyed the estate. The affection between mother and son was lost, and the patrimony of Scholar Wu was ruined. Before long, Madam Wang took her personal property (*nang-t'o*) and remarried. Wu Ju-ch'iu subverted the family assets by wanton spending; [soon] he was impoverished and unable to support himself. Thus he came and filed a lawsuit. Does he know the way of filiality; can he intone the poem of the filial brothers?[166]

recruitment exams. Such "graduates" gained legal privileges and important status in the community. See Chaffee, *Thorny Gates*, 31–2; and Hymes, *Statesmen*, 29–62, esp. 48, and 280 n. 93.

163 *Shih-ching* Mao #45, the same poem cited in the first line.

164 The implication is that without resources his household will not continue and no sacrifices will be performed to him by descendants.

165 Literally, "rolled up the mats." These words allude to *Shih-ching* Mao #26, Legge, *She King*, 38; Waley #75, another poem titled "cypress boat," but not the one quoted in the first line. The whole line reads, "My heart is not a mat, It cannot be rolled up."

166 *Shih-ching* Mao #32, Legge, *She King*, 50; Waley, #78. This poem is the one about filial sons cited at the beginning of the judgment.

Since the matter has come before the court, it must be investigated. Before Scholar Wu became ill, he had one house, 130 *mou* of land, movable property, and various goods all intact. But just three years after he died, his wife and his son had squandered it all and nothing was left. Is this the way for a man's wife or a man's son to act?

The 23 *chung*[167] of land that Madam Wang originally brought with her in marriage, the 47 *chung* of fields purchased with her dowry (*chuang-lien*), and the chests of goods from her trousseau (*nang-ch'ieh*) in the Wu household were all taken away by Madam Wang when she remarried. After Wu Ju-ch'iu had wasted away his late father's estate, why should he further make trouble with his stepmother and bring a lawsuit?

Today, according to the [son's] plea, the 47 *chung* of land that Madam Wang obtained [after her marriage] were purchased with the personal wealth of her late husband; and moreover money and valuables that had been pawned to them were all taken by Madam Wang. Nevertheless, a magistrate must rely on written documents, and when the contract of sale was brought forth and examined, the contract was made in Madam Wang's name. What more can be said?

When Wu Ju-ch'iu's father died, Ju-ch'iu was not young and ignorant. Had there been money and valuables from the pawn business, why wouldn't he have dealt with the matter himself? Then when he had sold all his property and wantonly spent the money, why wouldn't he have retrieved the pawnshop money and valuables to use? Only now, after his stepmother has remarried, is there a complaint. Can one not recognize that he [should have] acted sooner? As for the silver vessels and other movable property that were taken away over time, the receipts should be investigated to see if they still exist. These two complaints [regarding pawned goods and land purchased] are hard to resolve.

Nevertheless, Madam Wang was the wife of scholar Wu, and Wu Ju-ch'iu was the son of scholar Wu. If she has not forgotten the duty between a man and a wife, can there be no affection between mother and son? When Madam Wang remarried, she obtained a new home, while Wu Ju-ch'iu is by himself with no place to live. He is to be pitied. I request that Madam Wang think of her former husband, and take the house of Mr. Liu Hsien-wei that she purchased and give it to Wu Ju-ch'iu to live in. Wu Ju-ch'iu is not to be allowed to mortgage it. May there thus be no break in relations between husbands and wives and mothers and sons; and may those alive have peace, and those who have died find comfort down below. The complaints and documents should all be entered into the file, and the contracts should be examined and returned.

This case deserves discussion. Like most cases, it has three parts: the first is a general statement of moral and ethical principles, the second lays out the facts of the case, and the third states the judge's decision.

---

167 A *chung* is a unit of land of uncertain value. One possible meaning of the word is an area that can be sown with seed (*chung*) in a given period of time; Umehara, *Seimeishū*, 17 n. 3. Another possibility is land with a certain yield measured in seed. A similar unit of land, *pa* ("handful"), also appears in the CMC; see note 179 below.

The first two parts were usually worded so as to offer justification for the final verdict, with the losing party often painted in dark tones to show fault and general lack of virtue.

To recap briefly, in the first part of the case, T'ien-shui cites two poems from the *Book of Odes*, which proclaim the principles of widow chastity and filial piety respectively. Chu Hsi and other Sung Confucians celebrated the first poem as sanctioning widow fidelity, and by citing these poems Judge T'ien-shui demonstrates his sympathies for such Learning of the Way ideals.

In the second part, the judge describes the facts of the case. An educated and fairly well-off man, referred to as Scholar Wu, married once and had a son, Wu Ju-ch'iu. When Ju-ch'iu was seven, his mother died and Scholar Wu married again to Madam Wang. Madam Wang brought considerable land with her as dowry, 23 *chung*; but in addition, after the marriage another 47 *chung* were purchased and registered in her name. Some years later, Scholar Wu died. Soon afterwards, as her stepson dissipated the estate, Madam Wang remarried, taking all she could of the movable and immovable property with her. This included the 47 *chung* of land that she and Scholar Wu had purchased after their marriage plus most of the household articles. The son then brought a lawsuit arguing that some of this property was his father's, to which he was entitled.

In part three, his final decision, the judge takes a striking stand completely in favor of Madam Wang. He rejects all claims of the son, despite the fact that Wu Ju-ch'iu is destitute "with no place to live." In asking at the end that Madam Wang provide her stepson a home, the judge uses the unusual term "request" (*ch'ing* 請). He does not even issue an order with the force of law. The law rests entirely on the side of Madam Wang and places no obligation on her toward her stepson. This is all the more striking because the judge bemoans at the beginning of the case the very behavior that he sanctions legally at the end. Contrary to the standard form of written judgments, the verdict T'ien-shui finally delivered did not support his own general principles of widow chastity.

This case vividly illustrates four aspects of Sung law that granted elite women significant financial protection.

First, the law presented no obstacles to widow remarriage. On the contrary, the statutes gave widows economic protection and considerable incentive to remarry. Judge T'ien-shui found himself in a quandary. He wished to promote the values of widow chastity and filial piety, which could have mitigated the tragedy of Scholar Wu's premature death. But he had to admit that widow chastity was rarely practiced: not since the days of the ancient poems had widows remained chaste; and he saw nothing in the law to enforce chastity or compel a woman to maintain her husband's patrimony and ensure posthumous sacrifices to him. Despite his disagreements with Madam Wang's actions, he had no hesitation about her legal right to them. Sung law was out of step with what he saw as Confucian ideals, and the magistrate had no choice but to follow the law.

Second, the law recognized separate property of a husband and wife within marriage. The property of the two individuals was not merged after their marriage. Rather, the law provided a clear distinction between land that belonged to the wife, labeled "dowry land," and land that belonged to the husband or to his family. Moreover, land that was newly purchased after marriage, land that she could not have brought as part of her trousseau, could also be identified as the wife's own, personal property. Once again Judge T'ien-shui found the law to be at odds with his own values. He demonstrates the wish and expectation that land be held in common within marriage: "Why did they need to set up boundaries between their fields and separately purchase private property?" Indeed, the demarcation of the lands set the stage for the wife's ultimate remarriage. Nevertheless, the judge was bound to uphold the privilege: "The contract was made in Madam Wang's name; what more can be said?"

Third, while the protection of a married woman's property was intended for wives in joint households, it continued to apply after family division to wives within a conjugal unit. Judge T'ien-shui cited the statute in the *Sung Penal Laws* (copied from the T'ang statutes of 719 and 737) which was the basis for the separation of married women's property: "Property from the wife's family is not included in family division."[168] He went on to explain that this law was to prevent inheritance disputes between married brothers at the time of family division. But Scholar Wu had no brothers and neither of his parents were living. There was no question of family division, for there was no one "with whom to divide the property." Everything from "the smallest hair on up" belonged to Scholar Wu and his wife, with no other claimants to the property. Rather than benefiting a conjugal unit (*fang*), the law was being used to benefit an individual woman against the interests of her husband's offspring.

Judge T'ien-shui lamented that the law could be abused to support the selfish interests of a scheming woman. As he saw it, Madam Wang had no commitment to chastity when she married and thought "only as far as herself." She took advantage of her husband's "infatuation" and got him to purchase land in her own name. This gave her the utmost

168 SHT 12:197. Niida, *Tōryō*, 245; Shiga, *Genri*, 245.

independence in the event of widowhood or divorce, and protected her from any future encroachment by her stepson.

Fourth and last, the law allowed Madam Wang to break up the family estate and leave her husband's son destitute. She "gathered up her belongings," which included land, chests of goods, silver vessels, cash, and other items from the pawn business, and took them all away. Judge T'ien-shui would have preferred that she stay in the household and support her stepson with the wealth. But far from legally compelling her to leave some property behind for her first husband's son, he chastises the son for pursuing the mother after her remarriage: "Only now after his stepmother has remarried, is there a complaint." The judgment is all the more striking when one notes that the amount of land purchased after the marriage, 47 *chung,* was more than twice the 23 *chung* brought by Madam Wang initially as dowry. The suit claimed that the land was bought with the husband's money, and such a claim seems possible given the size of the purchase; but Madam Wang's story was documented and the law protected her. In addition, the judge dismissed claims that movable property was taken illegally by Madam Wang. She had the authority to take away her legitimate possessions and there was no way to know if she had acted improperly. Sung property law was ostensibly based on the Confucian values of communal ownership within a household and mutual support within a patriline. In practice, however, it could be exploited in such a way as to undermine these values. Faced with clear statutes, the judge felt unable to stop this.

The dilemmas raised by married women's separate property were of concern to people other than judges. One of these was Yüan Ts'ai (fl. 1140–1195), whose book *Precepts for Social Living* was admired by his contemporaries. Yüan saw property as a major source of disputes between brothers who lived together. He repeatedly admonished his readers to practice strict equality when distributing communal funds within the household and when actually dividing the family estate.[169] A wife's dowry was the primary source of personal property within the household, and thus a primary source of discord. He specifically warned against machinations like those of Madam Wang and Scholar Wu seen above:

The laws established by the government relating to division of family property are nothing if not complicated in regard to circumstances and exhaustive in detail. Nevertheless, some people in fact embezzle common family property to operate a private business; *they may claim on the bill of sale or mortgage that the prop-*

169 *Yüan-shih shih-fan,* 1:1, 6, 8, 9–10, 21; Ebrey, *Family and Property,* 1.1, 1.15, 1.22, 1.27, 1.62.

erty was bought with their wives' assets or register it under a false name. The courts find it difficult to get to the bottom of such cases.[170] (emphasis mine)

And:

Another person will buy land in the name of his wife's family or other families related through marriage and all too often end up losing it. *Yet another will place land in his wife's name. Frequently what happens then is that, after he dies, his wife remarries and takes the property with her.* Superior men should give careful thought to these problems and keep them in mind.[171] (emphasis mine)

Yüan's account is uncannily similar to the case of Madam Wang and Scholar Wu.

We see in another Sung lawsuit exactly the problems Yüan Ts'ai predicted. In a case adjudicated by Liu K'o-chuang in the 1220s while he was magistrate of Chien-yang, a man named Wei Ching-mo illegally established a separate household under the name of his brother's widow, née Chao, in order to purchase land and other property privately. Judge Liu determined that the assets used were from the common estate of the undivided household in which Wei lived with his brothers and mother, and should therefore be under the control of the mother. Moreover he found that a shipping business controlled by the widow Chao had in fact belonged to her husband's first wife and could not be taken over by her.[172] Had these properties come from widow Chao's dowry, the extensive personal entrepreneurship described would have been legal.

Other verdicts in the *Collected Decisions* further demonstrate legal support for taking property out of a marriage. In one case an elderly widow, née Chang, whose son had died, took her ten *chung* of land and returned to her natal family, where two nephews could help care for her (and presumably manage her lands). A relative of her husband's, Wu Chen, and his son filed a lawsuit accusing her of stealing Wu family property. The suit was dismissed. Soon afterward widow Chang died, and Wu Chen renewed his suit, this time requesting that his grandson be made heir to widow Chang and her late husband. To support his suit, he claimed to have the approval of a lineage elder for this posthumous adoption. The judge determined that all of the property involved was dowry and that the supposed lineage elder was none other than Wu Chen himself! In his final verdict, the judge followed the advice of a real lineage elder and ordered that some of widow Chang's land be sold to

---

170 *Yüan-shih shih-fan*, 1:8–9; Ebrey, *Family and Property*, 1.25.
171 *Yüan-shih shih-fan*, 1:9; Ebrey, *Family and Property*, 1.26. See also Burns, *Private Law*, 175–6.
172 CMC 9:353–6.

pay for her and her son's burial, and that a proper heir be set up and given the rest of the land to provide sacrifices for the family. Wu Chen and his family were forbidden to interfere any further, and Wu Chen's son was beaten eighty strokes for trying to steal widow Chang's land.[173]

This example shows how a woman's dowry was for her personal upkeep and benefit during her lifetime and was to continue to serve her after death. In the first part of the case, the judge makes clear that the widow can do what she wants with her dowry land, including giving it to nephews in her own natal family to manage. Quoting the testimony of the lineage elder, he writes "the land is land Madam Chang brought with her (*tzu-sui t'ien*), it is not property of the Wu family." Widow Chang gets full rights to these lands even though they constitute all that is left of her and her husband's conjugal estate. After her death, the property is still to be used for her (and her husband's) benefit, in the endowment of sacrifices. Wu Chen's offspring are not considered suitable heirs because they have shown themselves to be greedy for profit without regard to widow Chang's welfare. After the death of both the husband and wife, the dowry is seen to be part of the couple's conjugal estate to be inherited by their joint heir. But this aspect of patrilineality did not prevent widow Chang from taking the property out of her husband's household during her lifetime.[174]

Further evidence that land owned by a woman went with her into a remarriage comes from a curious source. One of the more gruesome but intriguing cases in the *Collected Decisions* is about a family of outlaws who amassed a large enough party of followers and bribed enough clerks to be able to terrorize "a region of ten thousand households" in the counties of Chien-yang (Chien-ning) and Shun-ch'ang (in neighboring Nan-chien prefecture). Their reputed crimes included salt smuggling, illegal levies on merchants, taking over fields and houses, killing draft animals, and kidnapping girls to become slaves. The tortures they inflicted (such as pouring red hot sand into a victim's ear) are described in vivid detail. At the end of the list of outrages comes the following: "They kidnapped people's wives and forced them to remarry their own henchmen, thereby obtaining the [women's] property."[175] It seems that a wife's property stayed with her even if she was kidnapped and forced to remarry against her will. By controlling her, the bandits expected to

---

173 CMC 8:258–9. No place is given for this case, but the same magistrate has a judgment from Chien-yang, Chien-ning, just before this one, and this is probably from there as well.
174 Shiga interprets this differently, emphasizing the right of the husband's family to establish an heir for a woman's dowry; see *Genri*, 525.
175 CMC 11:471–2.

reap the profits from her lands, leaving the first husband without any claim to the property. (This example suggests too that an unscrupulous husband who physically controlled his wife could manage to use her lands for himself.)

The legal practice that attached a wife's dowry to her physical body could extend even to her corpse after death. In a remarkable case from Kiangsi adjudicated by Huang Kan in the 1210s, a woman née Chou married and divorced twice. She then married a third time to a Mr. Ching Hsüan-i. When after less than a year he took his concubine and left her behind to serve in office elsewhere, she assumed he had abandoned her for the concubine and fled back to the household of her first husband, where she died four years later. Ching Hsüan-i then sued to retrieve her body for burial and her dowry property with it. Huang Kan rejected Ching's suit saying that since he had left her in the other household for more than four years, they could understand to have divorced. Her body and her dowry property with it were to stay with the first husband's family.[176]

Even after the death of both parents, the mother's private property was treated separately from the father's property in determining the disposition of the estate. In a judgment by Hu Ying from Shao-yang (modern Hunan), three brothers lived together. One died together with his wife, leaving an only daughter. She was married off (presumably with dowry), but later when the household was divided she demanded further property from her parents' portion of the estate, as their only surviving child. Judge Hu sided with the daughter, giving her all of her mother's dowry property (identified as "privately purchased assets" *ssu-fang chih-tao wu-yeh* 私房置到物業) and half of her father's portion of the communal estate. Even after the death of both parents and the marriage of an only daughter, the wife's dowry property could be identified and excluded from family division by the judge.[177]

In an even more dramatic case, we see again that property of a wife could never be treated the same way as property held by males, even if the wife left the household to remarry *without* taking her property with her. In a judgment from Kiangsi by Fan Ying-ling, a woman laid claim retroactively to dowry from her first marriage some time after entering into a second marriage. As recorded in the *Collected Decisions*, the widow Ah Kan left her own and her deceased husband's property to a young daughter and remarried. Then, when the daughter died, she tried to get some of the property back based on a dowry claim. A full translation of the judgment follows:

176 CMC Appendix 2:602–3.   177 CMC 8:280–2.

Hsiung Pang and His Brother Dispute Property
with [the widow] Ah Kan[178]

Mr. Hsiung Chen-yüan had three sons. The eldest was Pang, the next was Hsien, and the last was Tzu. Hsiung Tzu passed away, and his wife, Ah Kan, went and remarried, leaving behind an only daughter. [Tzu's portion of] the estate had 350 *pa* of land[179]; since its value at the time was not more than 300 strings of cash,[180] in accordance with the statutes (*t'iao*) it was all given to the daughter as her inherited portion (*ch'eng-fen*). [But] before she was even betrothed, the daughter also died. Today, the two older brothers are each arguing to have their own son established as heir, and Ah Kan is saying that of the lands in question, 100 *pa* are lands she purchased herself, and she wants her portion.

As to establishing an heir, though in name this would be for the sake of the younger brother, the intent is to obtain the land. And lands that were purchased after the marriage cannot be taken away by Ah Kan. If we apply the articles (*lü*) of the law, all the property should be confiscated. And even if an heir is established, since it will not have been done in the father's lifetime, the household is cut off, and only one-fourth of the property should go to the heir.[181] But it is not the desire of this official to follow the rules [blindly] and confiscate everything. Let 10 strings of cash be taken out for the burial of the daughter, and let the remainder of the land be divided into three equal parts to be given to each of the three parties. This is not the intent of the law, but this official is inclined to be generous. It is permitted for them to cast lots [for the portions]. If there is any dispute, however, [confiscation] should be carried out according to the articles of the law.

In this case, widow Ah Kan wished to retrieve her dowry land from her husband's household, even after she had left it behind and remarried, and even though she had no documentary evidence to support her claim that some of the land was her own. The judge's mention of casting lots indicates that no particular parcels of the land were identified as Ah Kan's. Nevertheless, the judge countenanced her claim that 100 *pa* of

---

178 CMC 4:110. See also Yanagida, "Joshōbun," 234; Shiga, *Genri*, 402; Burns, *Private Law*, 272. Fan Ying-ling's cases stretch between 1206 and 1227, but this one is undated. Most of his cases are sited in Ch'ung-jen county, Kiangsi. For other possible sites of his cases, see Ch'en, "Chieh-shao," 682.

179 *Pa* is a unit of land of unclear measurement. Shiga comments that the term is found in prewar North China and seems to mean the approximate area that could be sown by scattering seeds from one place; *Genri*, 202.

180 This is presumably a reference to the 3,000 string limit on inheritance in cut-off households. In the previous section I followed Shiga in suggesting that 300 is a mistake for 3,000, but here I translate as the text reads. See Shiga, *Genri*, 402–3.

181 According to the laws of inheritance, discussed in the previous section, a posthumous heir in a cut-off household with no daughters would get one-third of the property (rather than one-fourth), with the rest confiscated by the state. Fan Ying-ling seems to be applying the rule as if the unmarried daughter were still alive. Perhaps he simply wants to emphasize that he is being generous with the plaintiffs.

land were purchased with her own assets and thus could be considered part of her trousseau. Note that he states a general principle that a wife cannot take away land purchased after her marriage ("lands purchased after the marriage cannot be taken away by Ah Kan"). In fact, wives routinely did just this, as in the case of Scholar Wu and Madam Wang, and as Yüan Ts'ai testifies. Moreover, Fan contradicts himself and gives Ah Kan one-third of the 350 *pa* (minus 10 strings) estate, even though by her own words the lands she claimed as dowry were purchased by her after the marriage. Fan wants to emphasize the generosity of his verdict by first challenging the claims of each party. His generalization is correct in that lands not purchased in the wife's name, which cannot be proven to belong to her, cannot legally be taken away. And yet it was so routine for wives to take their dowries into a remarriage that Fan felt obliged to let Ah Kan draw lots for a share, which depending on the price of the land may have amounted to even more than her original request of 100 *pa*. Fan's verdict shows how women's property always had strings attached to it that exerted a constant pull on it away from the husband's patriline, even after the wife herself seemed to have left her claims behind.[182]

REMARRIAGE AND THE LAW

Sung law sanctioned remarriage when a widow was too impoverished to support herself and if at least 100 days had passed since the death of her husband.[183] In practice, however, no limits were placed on remarriage. Even serial remarriages were not uncommon or shocking, if we are to judge by their frequent mention in Sung sources. Indeed, contrary to the intent of the statutes and to Confucian notions of virtue, Sung property law made remarriage easy and attractive, especially for the elite. A widow could keep her property and could choose her next partner herself. This was frustrating to many judges whose verdicts are found in the *Collected Decisions*, but these same judges felt compelled to uphold property law and allow women freedom to remarry and keep their assets.

182 For a contrasting view of married woman's property from that presented here, see esp. Shiga Shūzō, who argues that all personal property held by the conjugal unit (*fang*) essentially belonged to the husband and that a wife had to leave behind even her dowry for his children to inherit if she remarried; *Genri*, 520–2. For Shiga's reading of the case presented here, see *Genri*, 422; 402–3. Hsing T'ieh makes a similar argument that dowry is essentially owned by the husband; "Sung-tai te lien-t'ien," esp. 38–9. See also Yüan Li, "Sung-tai nü-hsing," 192–4. Yanagida raises objections to Shiga similar to mine; "Joshōbun," 233.
183 CMC 10:378.

Judges like T'ien-shui denounced widow remarriage in their pro-nouncements but felt compelled to uphold a woman's legal right to it. Huang Kan, Chu Hsi's son in-law, maintained that dowry stay with an heirless woman, who had entered and exited three different marriages, even after her death.[184] Another example is Hu Ying, who repeatedly expressed strong disapproval of remarriage in his written judgments,[185] but who in contradiction to his expressed views protected the right of a woman to choose whether to remarry or not. In support of a woman who went through three husbands and was being sued by her brother-in-law to prevent the latest remarriage, Hu Ying wrote:

Ah Ch'ü is a woman who changed husbands three times. She certainly has lost her chastity! But Li Hsiao-te is her brother-in-law; how can he presume to control her destiny? . . . After [her husband] Li Ts'ung-lung has died, whether to remarry or not to remarry is the decision of Ah Ch'ü alone. How can Li Hsiao-te interfere with it?[186]

The brother-in-law got a verbal thrashing and physical beating of 100 strokes, even though his frustration with his sister-in-law's remarriage mirrored Hu's own attitude.

Hu Ying's opposition to remarriage comes through in the case of another woman who married three times, whom he describes as "chang-ing husbands like changing inns."[187] Ah Ch'ang abandoned the mother of her second husband, Military Inspector Hsü, and married her third husband, Military Inspector Chang. When she learned of the mother's death two years later, she sued for the household property (showing again that a wife might make dowry claims even some time after remar-rying). Hu Ying refused the request as too far fetched and granted the property to a maidservant and her husband who had cared for the mother (confirming Sung law that gave coresidents certain rights to property). He blamed Ah Ch'ang's lack of chastity and Military Inspec-tor Hsü's having married a widow for causing the end of the Hsü family line and its property going into a different surname: "Heaven will not enrich a family without morals (*pu tao chih chia*)!"[188] For Hu, the Con-fucian precept of widow chastity could have saved these families from ruin, but Sung law worked against this precept.

Sung property law also provided incentives not to remarry. This was especially true when the household was already divided, for then the widow became head of the household in place of her husband and could control both his property and her own. Widows were expected to pre-

184 But see Chapter 3 for his very different treatment of a woman with children.
185 CMC 377–8, 379, 379–80.   186 CMC 344–5.   187 CMC 10:377.
188 CMC 10:378.

serve the first husband's patrimony for his heirs, and widows were thus forbidden to sell off lands if they had minor children.[189] In practice, however, widows with children bought and sold lands quite freely with little interference from the law.[190] Moreover, when the sons reached their majority (over 16) they needed their mother's signature on any contract of sale of family property. Contracts could later be invalidated if they lacked this.

The strong authority widows had over household property is best illustrated by a peculiar provision found in Northern Sung law that allowed a widow with minor children or no children to invite in a second husband (or quasi-husband, *chieh-chiao-fu*) to live with her without forfeiting control of the first husband's estate. Such a widow continued to be the legal head of her first husband's household and could manage its assets with her new husband, but was not allowed to re-register them in his name. When she died, or if she "remarried" outside the household, the household was declared extinct (*hu-chüeh*) and the property disposed of accordingly. (Or if she and her first husband had heirs, the property went to them.)[191] Southern Sung law tried to stem the abuses allowed by this regulation by requiring that the first husband's property be audited by the state and that only 5,000 strings worth be given to the widow and her quasi-husband, but it is not clear how well this was enforced.[192] The law of both Northern and Southern Sung was meant to keep the first husband's property within his patriline, but the evidence suggests that when the deceased husband had no relatives nearby, it was not difficult for his widow in collusion with a second husband to take his property into another patriline.[193]

Separate Property within Marriage While the Husband Was Alive

The issue of a woman's actual power of disposal of her property within her marriage when her husband was living is a difficult one. In the

---

189 CMC 5:141.   190 Yüan Li, "Sung-tai nü-hsing," 201.

191 SHY shih-huo 61:58. If the first husband's children were grown, these quasi-husbands (literally "heel-following husbands," *chieh-chiao-fu*) were not legal, but abuses were common; see for instance CMC 9:296–7.

192 CMC 8:272. In the Southern Sung, we find many complaints by literati of the abuses of these "heel-following husbands." For more on these, see Kawamura, "Sōdai zeisei shōkō."

193 For a discussion of changes in widow authority from Sung to Ming, see Bettine Birge, "Women and Confucianism from Song to Ming," in *The Song-Yuan-Ming Transition in Chinese History*, ed. Paul Smith and Richard von Glahn (Berkeley: University of California Press, 2001); and Bernhardt, *Women and Property*, ch. 2. On widow control of property in the Sung generally, see Yüan Li, "Sung-tai nü-hsing," 200–12; and Shiga, *Genri*, 415–37.

Confucian family system the husband and wife were considered to be "one body," and the law assumed they would act together. Nevertheless, the rules of married women's separate property allowed the wife considerable autonomy. Wives could purchase land and enter into contracts on their own. But while we find many instances in the sources of married women selling jewelry and other movable property themselves, landed property is usually described as being purchased or managed by the husband on his wife's behalf. There are instances in the *Judicial Decisions* of husbands and wives suing each other (usually ending in divorce),[194] but I have found no case of either a wife or a husband suing the other specifically for misusing dowry property. The law did not intend to allow a wife, in the expectation of being widowed or divorced, to secretly hoard her wealth beyond the reach of her husband. Nor did it sanction the husband taking action without his wife's permission. As if to prevent either situation, judges often reiterated that dowry lands were to be managed by the husband and wife "together."[195]

A judgment by Weng Fu of Chien-ning (c.s. 1226), a conservative judge generally hostile to women's property rights, reveals how the laws on married women's separate property operated when both husband and wife were living. A Mr. Ch'en Kuei filed a lawsuit against his son Ch'en Chung-lung and the son's wife, née Ts'ai, accusing them of illegally mortgaging common estate property to the wife's brother Ts'ai Jen. When questioned, Ts'ai Jen was able to produce documents that showed the property in question had been purchased with Madam Ts'ai's personal assets. The judge concluded that the land was thus dowry property and not subject to any interference by the head of the household. He cited two articles of the law (*fa*) to support his verdict:

According to the law, "property from the wife's family is not to be part of the division;"[196] and "the wife's assets are controlled by her together with her husband." Now Ch'en Chung-lung has himself mortgaged his wife's dowry lands (*chuang-lien t'ien*); this is a legitimate transaction.[197]

Because Ts'ai Jen was the brother of the wife, and because of a suspicion that the son was coerced into mortgaging the land against back rents he owed to Ts'ai Jen, the judge insisted that the land be returned even though the three-year limit for redemption had passed. In an inter-

194 E.g., CMC 10:380–1.
195 E.g., CMC 5:140; 9:315. Shiga Shūzō uses modern data to argue that the husband needed the wife's consent to dispose of her dowry property, and that her natal family might intervene to protect it; *Genri*, 521–2. This would seem to be the case in the Sung, but the evidence is inconclusive. See also Burns, *Private Law*, 186.
196 Exact quote from the T'ang and Sung codes; Niida, *Tōryō*, 245; SHT 12:197.
197 CMC 5:140.

esting move, however, he offered two possibilities: either the land could be returned outright to Madam Ts'ai and remain her personal property; or the father Ch'en Kuei, who was suing to get the land, could pay her the twenty strings of cash for which the land was originally mortgaged, and procure the property for his estate, to go into family division. (In such a case, Madam Ts'ai and her husband could expect to get back a share in future family division, in addition to receiving the money in the present.) The case ends with "If Ch'en Kuei does not pay the money to redeem [the land], it will return to Madam Ts'ai and be subject to the law on dowry lands (*sui-chia t'ien fa* 隨嫁田法)."[198]

This last line tells us that the land (if not redeemed) will go back to Madam Ts'ai to be *her* personal property, even though the mortgage and even the original purchase seem to have been carried out by her husband. The reference to a "law governing dowry land" (*sui-chia-t'ien fa*) further underscores the existence of legal sanction protecting the wife's property within marriage. Shiga and others have interpreted the line "The wife's assets are controlled by her together with her husband" to mean that primary authority rested with the husband.[199] But I would argue that the judge is here citing this law to legitimize *the husband's* involvement in the transaction, not to limit the wife's own rights of disposal. Her husband's involvement with management of assets did not reduce Madam Ts'ai's rights of ownership, and throughout the various transactions (including the original purchase from a Madam Hu) the land was identified as Madam Ts'ai's trousseau land.

A second case from the *Collected Decisions* reveals the lengths to which one husband thought he had to go to gain custody over his wife's dowry assets. Chiang Pin-yü, a man from Shao-wu (the commandery just west of Chien-ning, Fukien) accused his wife, née Yü, of theft and adultery in an attempt to divorce her and obtain her property for himself. Judge Hu Ying found no proof of adultery and ruled that the vessels and dishes Madam Yü was supposed to have stolen (with the aid of a concubine) were already her private property (*tzu-sui chih wu*). Hu ordered the husband to be beaten eighty blows for bringing false accusations, and he allowed the couple to divorce. Though no offense was committed, he reasoned, he could not see forcing the pair to continue living as husband and wife. Madam Yü returned home with her belongings.[200]

198 CMC 5:140. This case is translated in McKnight and Liu, *Enlightened Judgments*; see also Shiga, *Genri*, 517; Burns, *Private Law*, 180–1. My reading differs slightly from each of these.
199 *Genri*, 521–2; Burns, *Private Law*, 186; see also Yüan Li, "Sung-tai nü-hsing," 195.
200 CMC 10:380–1.

Legal protection of dowry had its limits. An unscrupulous husband could take advantage of his wife and use her dowry to his own ends. We saw above how bandits in Fukien were accused of kidnapping women to obtain their dowry property.[201] A story in the Sung dynastic history mentions how a husband squandered all of his wife's property, forcing her to return to her natal family with her children for support.[202] The sources implicitly condemn such actions, but wives were protected in such instances more by social pressure and the influence of their natal families than by any firm legal position or the willingness of the state to intervene.

Divorce

Both the T'ang and Sung codes allowed for "amicable divorce," or "peaceful separation" (*ho-li* 和離): "If the husband and wife are not compatible and peacefully separate, there is no sanction."[203] For a divorce to be legally recognized, a formal divorce document had to be drawn up, signed, and presented to the wife. The husband's parents had to condone the divorce; and, like a land sale contract, a divorce agreement needed to be approved by the authorities.[204] The document was of great importance to the wife, for it allowed her to leave and remarry without being accused of abandonment, for which she could be sentenced to two years' penal servitude.[205]

Divorce was supposed to be initiated only by the husband. Liu K'o-chuang wrote in one of his judgments: "There is the principle (*li*) whereby the husband can expel his wife; but there is no law (*t'iao*) that says a wife can discard her husband."[206] Modern scholars have understood this rule to apply in all periods of Chinese history.[207] Nevertheless, we find examples in the *Collected Decisions* where the wife initiated a successful suit for divorce, or where the husband was coerced into signing divorce papers so that his wife could follow her desires and remarry. In one case a wife sued for divorce, charging her husband with having an incurable disease and her father-in-law of adulterous intentions toward her. Judge Hu Ying sentenced her to a sixty-stroke beating, calling her

201 CMC 11:471–2.
202 *Sung shih*, 460:13485. For other examples, see also *I-chien chih*, chih-wu 10:1131; Yüan Li, "Sung-tai nü-hsing," 195.
203 *T'ang-lü shu-i*, 14:268 (Art. 190); SHT 14:224. Niida, *Hōseishi* IV, 398.
204 CMC 9:352; 10:380–1. The signature was often a handprint.
205 Niida, *Hōseishi* IV, 399–400. CMC 9:345–6, 349–51, 353.
206 CMC 9:345. Niida, *Hōseishi* IV, 399. Note that the husband's rights are associated with higher "principle," while the wife's are associated with mere "law."
207 Tai Yen-hui, "Divorce in Traditional Chinese Law," 105.

accusations false, but he granted the divorce on the grounds that her suit had destroyed the harmony of the household.[208] In another case, a woman's brother sought to end her marriage and seek a better one after he passed the civil service examinations. The woman's husband, in contrast, had faired poorly at business. Though the divorce was clearly initiated on the wife's side, Judge Liu K'o-chuang allowed the divorce to stand after ascertaining that the husband had signed the divorce papers and had sent his wife back to her natal home with their five daughters.[209]

In cases of amicable divorce, a wife kept her dowry, and the husband could expect to retrieve the betrothal gifts paid, so that each had resources to remarry.[210] In cases where the wife was legally expelled for misdeeds, the evidence suggests that she also kept her dowry in Sung as in earlier times. Pre-Sung law states clearly that women kept their dowry when expelled. The *Record of Rites* (*Li-chi*) says that a woman's private property was to be returned to her in the event that she was expelled from her husband's house.[211] Han dynasty law also specified that if a wife were expelled, she could keep the slaves and property she had brought into her marriage.[212] Sung law probably followed this, though no specific statute survives.[213]

More importantly, the line between expulsion and amicable divorce was blurred in law and practice. The Sung code, like earlier ones, specified as grounds for expulsion the "Seven Conditions for Divorce" (*ch'i ch'u*), which included such vague offences as jealousy, disobeying parents in-law, and talking too much.[214] The Seven Conditions

208 CMC 10:379.
209 CMC 9:345–6. See CMC 9:352 for a case where the wife may have colluded in being sold (illegally) into a new marriage. For more discussion and examples, see Chang Pang-wei, "Sung-tai fu-nü tsai-chia wen-t'i," in *Sung-shih yen-chiu lun-wen chi*, ed. Teng Kuang-ming and Hsü Kuei (Hang-chou: Che-chiang jen-min ch'u-pan she, 1987), 591–2; and T'ao Chin-sheng, "Pei-Sung fu-nü te tsai-chia yü kai-chia," *Hsin-shih hsüeh* 6:3 (1995).
210 CMC 9:353, 345–6; 12:453–4. This was the practice in other periods as well; see Niida, *Bunsho*, 498–9.
211 *Li-chi*, "Tsa-chi" Pt. II, 7:239; Legge, *Li Chi* II, 170–1. The text also suggests that women could seek divorce on their own initiative. See also Niida, *Bunsho*, 498–9.
212 Yüan Li, "Sung-tai nü-hsing," 199; Tai, "Divorce and Traditional Chinese Law," 105. Tai adds that dowry had to be returned in cases of compulsory divorce as well. (Compulsory divorce resulted from illegal marriages, same surname, etc., and from "violation of duty.")
213 My argument below disagrees with Niida, who suggests that dowry might not always be returned in cases of expulsion; *Bunsho*, 498. Niida notes the lack of evidence for the Sung and uses Yüan law, which I show in Chapter 4 represented a major break from the Sung.
214 SHT 14:223; *T'ang-lü shu-i*, 14:267 (Article 189). Expulsion without one of these reasons was punished by one and a half years of penal servitude. The Seven Conditions also included having no children, adultery, theft, and having an incurable

131

were rarely cited as the legal basis for divorce, however, in Sung or in other periods.[215] Instead both judges and litigants invariably cited incompatibility as the ultimate reason for separation, even when the wife was charged with one of the Seven Conditions. In this context, it is clear that divorced women kept their dowry, no matter what the reason for the divorce.

In the divorce suit mentioned at the end of the last section, the husband Chiang Pin-yü accused his wife Madam Yü of adultery, the most serious of the "Seven Conditions." Moreover, according to the plea, Madam Yü had offended her mother-in-law, as attested by the older woman: another cause for repudiation. In his judgment Hu Ying cited the "Seven Conditions for Divorce," and the locus classicus on divorce, the *Record of Rites*, to establish that the legal conditions for expulsion were more than fulfilled. Nevertheless, Mr. Chiang felt it necessary to accuse his wife of stealing dishes and kitchen utensils in order to keep any of his wife's property after the divorce. In the end, Hu Ying allowed the divorce to go through but concluded that the wife was falsely accused.[216] Madam Yü retained her property, and it seems clear from the text that she would also have kept her property had she been expelled for adultery. Only had the accusation been true that she had stolen articles from the husband's estate would she have had to leave these behind when she left the household.

In one respect at least, women in the Sung were given greater freedom than before to separate from their husbands. In the T'ang a woman had to follow her husband into exile or penal servitude. But in the Sung if a man was sentenced to exile (*i-hsiang*) or penal servitude (*pien-kuan*), his wife was allowed to divorce him. She could also leave and remarry if her husband disappeared and did not make contact for three years.[217] In one case in the *Collected Decisions* a wife remarried after her husband had been away for six years in penal servitude. Her father registered the divorce and sealed a contract promising to return the betrothal gift of

---

disease. Divorce was mandated by law in cases of "Violation of Duty" (*i-chüeh*), a term that was vaguely defined but included violent crimes by the husband or wife against the other's family, such as beating or killing.

215 McKnight, "Chinese Law and Legal Systems"; Hansen, *Negotiating Daily Life*, 101–3. For pre-Sung, see Dull, "Marriage and Divorce," 52–7. There were also "Three Limitations" on divorce under which a wife could not be expelled, but these were also largely ignored in legal proceedings.

216 CMC 10:380–1.

217 CMC 9:353; Niida, *Hōseishi* IV, 398–9; Brian McKnight, "Divorce in Sung China," in *Proceedings of the Second Symposium on Sung History* (Taipei: Chung-kuo wen-hua ta-hsüeh, 1996), 112–13.

45 strings worth of paper money. The husband returned and sued to get his wife back, but he had to be satisfied with the cash alone. His wife was allowed to stay in her second marriage.[218] In a case by Huang Kan, discussed above, a woman née Chou fled back to a previous husband's household after her third husband went off to serve in office with a concubine. Even though the woman had fled on her own initiative, Huang ruled that the husband had no marital rights over her (in this case he wanted the return of her corpse) for he had not attempted to contact her for more than three years.[219] In both these cases, the dowry stayed with the wife (or in the latter with her corpse).

When a woman was divorced, for whatever reason, she could easily contract a remarriage. Divorce cases described in the *Collected Decisions* show women quickly remarrying. It has been noted that judges were reluctant to deny divorces when either party had already remarried, and this may account for fast remarriage.[220] In any case, divorcées, like widows, seem to have had no trouble finding new husbands. With their dowries in tow, such women might offer lucrative matches. Madam Chou was divorced for "Violation of Duty" (*i-chüeh*) from her first husband, and yet seems to have suffered no stigma. She was able to marry twice more (with dowry), and to officials no less.[221] In a society where marriage was universal for laypersons, it is not surprising that we find evidence of strong social pressure against divorce in general. By the same token though, Sung people assumed that a divorcée should be able to remarry easily. In arguing for expulsion of unworthy wives, Ch'eng I nevertheless objected to making public accusations that could prevent their remarriage:

Someone commented, "There is an old saying, 'In divorcing a wife, make it so she can remarry; in severing a friendship, make it so he can make new friends.' Is this the idea?"
[Ch'eng I] said, "Yes."[222]

Widows and divorced women returned to their natal families, and their parents were responsible for contracting remarriages. Women without families could contract remarriages themselves, though if they had no relatives to support them (and help protect their dowries) they might also be left destitute.[223] It was important in Sung law that remarriages were contracted by the natal family, for if the husband or his

218 CMC 9:353. 219 CMC Appendix 2:602–3.
220 Hansen, *Negotiating Daily Life*, 103. 221 CMC Appendix 2:602–3.
222 *Ho-nan Ch'eng-shih i-shu*, 18:243; as translated in Ebrey, *Inner Quarters*, 258.
223 E.g., *I-chien-chih*, chih-ting 9:1036; Ebrey, *Inner Quarters*, 258.

family received the betrothal gifts it would look like wife selling, which was strictly illegal.[224] In the case of a man who tried to sell his wife to a drinking companion, the court returned her to her mother to arrange a legal remarriage.[225] In a similar case where the wife had no family, the court put her in the custody of a matchmaker to arrange the remarriage.[226]

Sung marriage and property law made divorce and remarriage easy. As with widow remarriage, virtually no obstacles were raised to remarriage of divorcées by the courts, popular attitudes, or social practice. By taking her property with her, a divorced woman acted against the interests of her husband's patriline, and the law supported her in this.

Disposition of Dowry When a Wife Died without Heirs

When a wife died, her assets passed to her children or to an adopted heir for her and her husband. If her husband was still living, he controlled the deceased wife's property as part of their conjugal fund. When the husband had died and a woman had no heirs, however, her property entered a sort of limbo with no clear owner. Members of the husband's family could not automatically take over such property; strings were still attached to it.

Both judges and litigants expected a woman's property to be used to provide for her in death as it had in life. This meant that, short of outright repossession, the wife's natal family could raise objections if the property was not used to this purpose. In a lawsuit handled by the Fukienese judge Wang Po-ta (ca. 1184–1253) and most likely brought to trial in Chien-ning,[227] a deceased wife's father sued to prevent her father-in-law from taking over her lands himself. The judgment begins:

It has been learned that while Yü Ai was still alive, he married Madam Ch'en, and obtained 120 *chung* of land that was apportioned to her from her family and came with her in marriage. Sadly, Madam Ch'en and Yü Ai died one after another. Yü Ai's father, Vice Magistrate Yü, however, did not manage to set up

224 SHT 14:223; *T'ang-lü shu-i*, 14:266 (Article 187). The punishment was two years of penal servitude.
225 CMC 10:382–3; Hansen, *Negotiating Daily Life*, 103.
226 CMC 9:352–3. All involved were given beatings (rather than penal servitude); the first husband's parents were spared only because of their age.
227 Wang Po-ta was from Fu-chou, Fukien. He passed his *chin-shih* in 1214 and held office in the capital and several localities. He became prefect of Chien-ning in 1248 and died in 1253; this case probably from that time. He is the author of only this one case in the CMC. *Sung shih*, 420:12567–70. Ch'en Chih-ch'ao, "Chieh-shao," 152; Ch'en Chih-ch'ao, "Shu-lüeh," 684.

an heir for them, leading Assistant Ch'en [Madam Ch'en's father][228] to bring a lawsuit. Only when Fiscal Commissioner Ch'iao rendered a verdict ordering an heir to be established, did Vice Magistrate Yü confer and select from the agnates (*tsu*) Yü Chi, the son of Yü Sheng-fu, to be the heir of Yü Ai. This shows that Vice Magistrate Yü's original intent was not good.[229]

We see here that Madam Ch'en's father had the right to object to the way that Vice Magistrate Yü was handling his daughter's dowry lands. Ch'en was allowed to insist that an heir be established to perform ancestral sacrifices for his daughter and her husband. The property could not just stay with Madam Ch'en's father-in-law.

This incident seems to contradict the commentary of the 737 T'ang statute on inheritance copied into the Sung code. The statute (translated in Chapter 1) specified that a wife's personal assets stayed outside of the family division, but the commentary went on to state that a wife's family was not to interfere with the disposition of her dowry after her death: "If the wife has died, her family may not seek to dispose of any of her assets or slaves."[230] Neither the T'ang nor the Sung legal code specified further what was to happen to the wife's assets in case of her death, and the question seems to have remained an unresolved problem in legal doctrine. Based on this case and others, Burns conjectures that the statute, which would seem to forbid interference and certainly requisition by the wife's family, applied only while there still existed a possibility of adoption. In other words, in the absence of a posthumously adopted heir, the wife's family, *may* have been able to reclaim her property.[231] This suggests that Assistant Ch'en in the case above might have been trying to take back the dowry he had given his daughter.[232]

The uncertain status of a deceased wife's property and the problem this presented to the legal system is seen in the words of Judge Wang further on in the case. Regarding the intentions of the father-in-law, Vice Magistrate Yü, Wang writes:

Originally, the establishment of Yü Chi as heir was not the prime intention of Vice Magistrate Yü. It was simply that his son, Yü Ai, had received his wife's dowry lands, and when she died the property had nowhere to go. Then when the

---

228 Their titles tell us that both men were low-ranking officials: Mr. Yü's position was just under a county magistrate, and Mr. Ch'en's was in an unranked clerical post (lower than Mr. Yü's).
229 CMC 5:248. Cf. Ebrey, "Kinship," 118; Burns, *Private Law*, 183.
230 Niida, *Tōryō*, 245–6; SHT 12:197.
231 Burns, *Private Law*, 183.
232 Note that he could not have done that before she died. In a judgment by Hu Ying, Hu makes it clear that once a daughter's property has been "divided out," it cannot be contested or retrieved by her natal family; CMC 9:322.

lawsuit was filed by Assistant Ch'en, [Yü] began to "feel anxious about gaining and losing,"[233] and he felt this more keenly each day. Thus he followed the verdict of Commissioner Ch'iao, and for the time being acted [to set up the heir] in order to resolve the immediate complication.[234]

This passage strongly suggests that the wife's marital property under certain circumstances might indeed have gone back to her natal family. The line "the property had nowhere to go," and Vice Magistrate Yü's anxiety about "losing" the land indicate that it could have left the Yü household entirely and returned to the Ch'ens. Such property did not belong unequivocally to the husband's family, even after both husband and wife had died.

So far I have found no explicit cases from the Sung where a woman's dowry was actually returned to her natal family. It may be worth noting, however, that such examples can be found in the twentieth century from both North and South China. A government survey published in 1930 describes the procedures for registering land to daughters at the time of their marriage in northern Fukien (the same area as the above case). A contract on special paper had to be drawn up by the parents, specifying the name of the girl as owner, the location and amount of land, and other particulars. Then it explains that if the daughter died without heirs, some of this dowry land could be returned to the natal parents as "sustenance land" (*yang-shan t'ien* 養膳田).[235] The same survey describes similar regulations drawn up in counties in Anhwei and Shensi provinces that stated simply that after the daughter died, her dowry "went back to her natal family." These documents added that the husband's family could not intervene in any way.[236] A Western scholar observed similar practices in northern Kwangtung in the early twentieth century. He writes that once the title deed for land was transferred to a daughter as dowry, "upon her death the land is inherited by her posterity only; otherwise, it *reverts to the family of her father*" (emphasis mine).[237]

Unfortunately, we do not have such explicit evidence for the Sung, but another verdict in the *Collected Decisions*, from the county of Ou-ning in Chien-ning, shows that even in the absence of claims by the natal

233 *Analects* 17:15. The whole passage reads: "When they have not obtained it, they are anxious about how to get it. When they have obtained it, they are anxious that they will lose it. When they are anxious that they will lose it, they will stop at nothing" (my translation).
234 CMC 8:248.
235 *Min shang-shih hsi-kuan tiao-ch'a pao-kao lu* (n.p.: Chung-hua min-kuo ssu-fa hsing-cheng pu, 1930), Vol. 3, chap. 12, sec. 9; as quoted in Shiga, *Genri*, 526, 546 n. 34.
236 Cited in Shiga, *Genri*, 526, 646 n. 35, 36.
237 Daniel Kulp, *Country Life in South China: The Sociology of Familism* (New York: Teacher's College, Columbia University, 1925), 175.

family, dowry property had to be treated differently from other property in the household. This judgment makes no mention of the wife's relatives, and the resolution of the suit seems to have represented the limit to which a wife's dowry lands could be incorporated into the husband's family estate after her death.

In a joint household, with both parents living, there were four sons. The eldest married and had a son, but he, his wife and their son all died, leaving his branch line cut off. The judge wrote: "From the standpoint of Principle (*li*), an heir should be established." But the parents did not set up an heir for the son's future portion. His property remained undivided in the common estate, while his wife's property was used for sacrificial lands (*cheng-ch'ang t'ien* 丞嘗田) that would be rotated between the three remaining brothers to provide sacrifices for the couple. The arrangement applied only to the "land and other [assets] acquired from the wife's dowry" (*ch'i chuang-lien chih-tao t'ien-yeh teng*), and in 1228 it was recorded in the land registers (*chen-chi pu*). The rest of the property (the husband's portion) belonged to the common estate, and would be distributed equally to the three remaining brothers at the time of division. As explained in the verdict, the parents did not want to set up a grandson as heir, since such an heir would inherit the total estate of the eldest son, leaving a single brother (the heir's father) in control of half the common estate property while the other two sons had just one-quarter each. Instead, the parents wanted their three sons to have equal portions of the joint estate. Nevertheless, by not appointing an heir, the question of the wife's property became a problem. As in the case of Vice Magistrate Yü and Madam Ch'en, above, such property "had nowhere to go."[238]

The expedient adopted by the parents was praised by the judge, since it left the brothers with three equal parts of the estate and still ensured sacrifices to the couple so that their ghosts would not go hungry. But fifteen years after the arrangement and eight years after the family division, when both parents and the second brother had all died, the third brother tried to establish his son as heir and take over both the dowry lands and the eldest son's portion of the joint estate. The widow of the second son took him to court. The judge ruled on the side of the widow and upheld the earlier arrangement. He reaffirmed that dowry lands, now converted to common sacrificial lands, were in a separate category from the other divided property and should continue to be shared by all three family branches.[239] Even long after the wife's death, and in the

238 CMC 8:260–2.
239 CMC 8:260–2. See also Burns, *Private Law*, 183; Ebrey, "Kinship," 118.

absence of claims by the wife's natal family, the special status of dowry property was preserved.

Conclusion: Property, Gender, and the Law

The formal law codes of the T'ang and Sung, following Confucian doctrine, were designed to support a patriarchal, patrilineal family system where property was held communally under the control of a male household head and where assets passed down along the male agnatic line. Women's property created contradictions within this system from earliest times, and these reached a peak in the Sung. At a time of increasing commercialization, unstable financial conditions, and state activism, the government and its local magistrates on one hand and people at all levels of society on the other adopted practices that suited immediate needs and which undermined the ideals of patrilineality. The result was a complicated property regime that transmitted unprecedented assets through daughters and gave women unforeseen economic independence and mobility within marriage and beyond. By late Southern Sung, this gender-property regime presented a stark challenge to patrilineal Confucian ideals.

A qualitative change in gender and property relations distinguished the Sung from previous eras. While parents in earlier periods routinely transmitted a portion of the family estate to their daughters, unconcerned that it would be alienated from the patriline, new interpretations of old concepts in the Sung gave unprecedented legal weight and moral justification to such transmission. Southern Sung judges reinterpreted the age-old concept of "equal division among brothers" (*hsiung-ti chün-fen*), the backbone of Chinese inheritance law, to mean "equitable division among children," and an "equitable" portion for a daughter was defined as a share half the size of a son's. Daughters participated in drawing lots for these shares together with their brothers, to further ensure equitable division. Similarly, the legal phrase "sons inherit their father's portion" (*tzu ch'eng fu fen*) was interpreted to mean "sons and daughters inherit their father's portion." A daughter's dowry had become such an important part of the social fabric in Sung China that traditional inheritance law, which ostensibly kept property within the male patriline, was now cited to alienate substantial assets away from the patriline and into the hands of women.

The characteristics of the patrilineal, patrilocal family system, whereby women married out, assured a different dynamic of property transmission to sons and daughters that can obscure the conceptual similarity between a son's inheritance and a daughter's that pervaded Sung legal

138

thinking. The use of labels like "dowry" to distinguish a daughter's inheritance, moreover, diminished its importance and helped mask the contradictions between actual inheritance practices and Confucian patriline principles. The half-share rule could only apply to daughters who still lived at home and were thus eligible to participate in family division. And it operated only if the state was called upon to carry out the division after the parents' death. (Theoretically, family division always took place after the parents' death, but it could be mediated by other relatives without recourse to the state.) While alive, parents had full discretion to determine the size of a daughter's dowry (i.e., her inheritance). Nevertheless, evidence of large dowries in the Sung suggests that in practice many men did indeed give their daughters property commensurate with half of what their sons might later receive in family division.

A plethora of new laws affecting inheritance in households without sons, called cut-off households, also worked against the agnatic patriline in numerous respects. In T'ang and earlier, daughters in these households received the estate, but Sung made this more frequent by expanding the definition of "cut-off" to include each conjugal unit within a joint family. The share of communal property to which a deceased father had rights, which previously went back into the pool for later division among male agnates, was now to be held in trust for any surviving daughters, according to the rule that daughters, like sons, "receive their father's portion."

The Sung state placed limits on inheritance in cut-off households starting early in the dynasty. These reduced the total amounts that daughters received, but they affected agnatic male relatives even more. When no children survived, agnates were deprived of property they had previously received, and amounts that could go to a posthumously appointed male heir were reduced. In disputes between daughters and posthumous heirs, a detailed set of rules awarded daughters the lion's share of family property. The Sung state also claimed more property in cut-off households for itself, but as the dynasty progressed, laws on confiscation were relaxed or ignored, and judges used them more to threaten recalcitrant litigants than to garner income for the state.

Another striking legal development in the Sung was the awarding of property, beginning in 1026, to residents in the household with no blood ties to the owner, who were understood to have contributed to the estate and "aided the old and solitary." These included foster sons, children from a wife's previous marriage, uxorilocal sons-in-law, and even faithful servants. In addition, if no daughters (married or unmarried) survived, a portion of the estate could go to married sisters, aunts, or other female relatives. These changes in how property was legally distributed amount to the recognition of the material needs of family members while alive, and a willingness to reward a network of support for those without sons, at the expense of more abstract demands of perpetuating the agnatic descent line.

The development of charitable estates and corporate kinship groups that accelerated in the Southern Sung can be seen as a way to bring back into confluence the demands of perpetuating the patrilineal descent line after someone's death with the material needs of families in life. Government support for these nascent lineages and their increasing intervention into family inheritance disputes had the effect of redirecting property transmission back to the agnatic patriline and away from daughters. By the end of the Sung, therefore, daughters' strong rights to property were beginning to erode. On balance though, for most of the dynasty property law favored daughters and unrelated coresidents, while nonresident agnates lost out.

When a bride entered her new household, her assets, both movable and immovable, were enumerated in detailed lists and labeled with various terms translated as "dowry." This labeling gave a married woman's property special status that distinguished it from the property of males and bestowed on it legal protections and separate treatment during the woman's lifetime and after her death. Dowry property was not combined with the communal estate and was not subject to control by the household head. It was "private" property, in contrast to the "public" (or communal) property attached to the males in the household. As such, dowry represented a sort of free capital that the wife and her husband could dispose of on their own, not subject to the controls of the patrilineal inheritance system. It carved out for the woman and her husband a sphere of economic independence that undermined the principles of patriarchal control and communal consciousness. It also provided a safety valve that may have been precisely what allowed the patriarchal, patrilineal Confucian system to endure.

Being free of controls, a woman's assets could easily be invested outside the home. In the cases described above we find women augmenting their assets through activities such as a pawn business or a shipping enterprise. Women could also, on their own initiative, repair temples or build dams.

In a joint household, it was to a man's personal advantage to try to get as much property as possible transferred into the legal category of dowry, or wife's private property, so as to gain personal control over it. Some husbands tried to funnel communal property to their wives by entering contracts that labeled the assets as dowry property. This was possible in Sung law, for no matter how many times a woman's property was exchanged, whether jewelry was sold to buy land or profits made from business, the resulting assets kept the label "dowry" with all its legal protections. Land registers and formal contracts clearly distinguished dowry property, female property, from nondowry property, male property, precisely because of the special legal treatment dowry property enjoyed.[240]

Even after family division and the establishment of a conjugal household, dowry property retained its special nature. Despite the hope and even expectation of Confucian officials that the fund of the two partners be merged once the husband had title to property of his own, the property of the wife remained clearly demarcated from the husband's. When a woman left her marriage, in cases of widowhood or divorce, her property went with her. It was meant for the material benefit of the woman as an individual, both within a marriage and outside it in case her marriage ended. Dowry endowed a woman with financial status that was independent of her marital status. Moreover, dowry benefited a woman even after her death. We find Sung judges insisting that a woman's dowry be used to endow sacrifices to her if she died without heirs, and special legal treatment continued to be afforded such property in inheritance disputes many years after a woman's death.

The implications of Sung women's property law for remarriage were especially detrimental to the Confucian order. According to the Confucian tradition, husband and wife were united at marriage to form the next link in the patrilineal chain of descendants. Their property ensured the continuation of the house and the material resources to maintain ancestral sacrifices, ideally in an unending chain. While either the wife or husband still lived, there remained the potential for continuing the family line, through adoption if necessary, and accordingly, either widow or widower remained in control of the conjugal fund. Nevertheless, a widow was in a very different position from a widower. A man represented the family line in a way that a woman did not. A childless widower could remarry and produce or adopt an heir to inherit the conjugal fund, thus keeping it intact. When a widow was left without children, the continuation of the line and the inheritance of her own and her husband's property came into question. Confucian values dictated that

---

240 Of course dowry could also improve a wife's position in her marital household. Eulogy writers considered a mother-in-law worthy of praise if she did not treat her daughters-in-law differently based on the size of their dowries, and Confucian philosophers warned that women with large dowries would be insubordinate; Ebrey, *Inner Quarters*, 102. Wives could also use their dowry to gain prestige and influence in the household; see e.g. *Nan-chien chia-i kao*, 22:22b.

the widow stay chaste and raise her children or adopt an heir for herself and her husband to whom the conjugal fund would pass. But Sung property law gave her the different option of subverting Confucian norms by remarrying and taking her property with her. Remarriage broke up the conjugal fund, and if a couple had no children or if the wife took the children with her (as often happened), it left the husband's line without an heir.

Sung law encouraged remarriage. As seen in the *Collected Decisions*, Confucian judges in the Sung promoted widow chastity in their pronouncements but had to lament that they had no power to enforce it. Even judges who felt that remarriage was detrimental in a particular instance felt bound to support it. While some wealthy or older women stood to gain by staying chaste and keeping control of their husband's estate, for many others remarriage was more attractive.

Even as women in the Southern Sung enjoyed stronger property rights than they ever had, a movement had begun that aimed at stripping these rights away. Learning of the Way philosophers began to promote Confucian ideals more seriously, and an emphasis on keeping property within the agnatic patriline was eroding the strong position enjoyed by Sung women. These developments will be explored in the next chapter.

3

Women's Property
and Confucian Reaction
in the Sung

The legal protections and social customs governing women's property that developed in the Sung had social consequences. Daughters' inheritance syphoned assets away from the patriline and, when taken into marriage as dowry, strengthened the standing of affines at the expense of agnates. Large dowries rendered wives in elite households into independent economic entities, who to some extent were buffered from the fortunes of the house. Possession of personal property (by men or women) undermined the authority of the household head, who ostensibly regulated the daily life of family members through the power of the purse. The very concept of communal living and shared property was fundamentally incompatible with personal property. A wife's personal assets also gave her power vis-à-vis her husband and threatened the ideal of obedience and submission to him. Worst of all, the property rights of widows made remarriage especially easy and very attractive. While Chinese for centuries had lived with these contradictions between Confucian ideals and legal practice, Sung thinkers who sought to reinvigorate Confucianism confronted them head on, and not surprisingly, raised objections to women's property rights.

The Confucian reaction to women's property came from those who associated themselves with the new interpretation of Confucianism called the Learning of the Way (*tao-hsüeh*). These influential thinkers sought to reaffirm classical Confucian gender roles, and in the process could not help but challenge the laws and customs that supported women's property rights. They questioned inheritance by daughters and instead encouraged agnatic adoption to carry on family lines. They whittled away at the barrier between a wife's property and that of her husband by encouraging women to donate all or part of their dowry to their husband's household. Toward the end of the dynasty, judges challenged property laws more directly and sought to prevent women from leaving marriages with their personal property. At the same time, Learning of the Way Confucians gave women a prominent role in controlling property in the area of household management. They promoted an image of women undertaking aggressive management of family finances to release husbands for study and public affairs. Examining each of these areas of the Confucian reaction in more detail, we can trace a hardening of attitudes toward women's property over the centuries of the Sung dynasty.

Patrilineality and Daughters' Inheritance

Learning of the Way adherents promoted a radical form of patrilineality called the "descent-line system" (*tsung-fa*). As discussed in Chapter 1, this was the extended family organization prescribed in the Confucian classics, that was supposed to have existed in early Chou times (but probably never did). According to this ideal, agnatic relatives within the mourning circle, those with a common great great grandfather, shared income and ritual obligations. The eldest son of the main line, called the descent-line heir (*tsung-tzu*) presided over the ritual functions of the lineage and administered the lineage property. In the Northern Sung, Ch'eng I (1033–1107) articulated the need to revive the descent-line system as the basis of social and political order: "In order to control the minds of the people, unify one's kin, and enrich social customs so that people will not forget their origin, it is necessary to clarify genealogy, gather members of the clan together, and institute a system of descent-line heirs."[1] Ancestral sacrifices carried out according to descent-line organization would teach moral principles and the individual's place in the family and society. Fundamental to these principles was the subordination of juniors to seniors and women to men.

One component of the descent-line system was shared property. Ch'eng I wrote, "ancestral property must not be divided but must be put in charge of one person."[2] We saw in Chapter 2 how a little later Kao K'ang (1097–1153) opposed equal division among brothers and inheritance by women, which he believed threatened the family altar and continuance of the house. Chang Tsai (1020–1077), another leader of the

---

1 Found in *I-shu*, by Ch'eng I, quoted in *Chin-ssu lu* (Kuo-hsüeh tsung-shu ed.), 9:254. Translation slightly modified from Wing-tsit Chan, *Reflections on Things at Hand: The Neo-Confucian Anthology Compiled by Chu Hsi and Lü Tsu-ch'ien* (New York: Columbia University Press, 1967), 227–8.
2 *Chin-ssu lu*, 9:254; Chan, *Reflections on Things at Hand*, 229.

Northern Sung Confucian revival, complained similarly that equal inheritance by brothers destroyed patrimonies, and that without the descent-line system great families could only decline: "Nowadays those who accumulate wealth and honor can only plan for thirty or forty years . . . when they die their sons will divide and separate and soon be bankrupt, so that the family (*chia*) does not survive. If, in this way, they cannot preserve their family, how can they preserve the state?"[3] These remarks point to the political aspects of descent-line organization. Ch'eng I also saw it as a means to strengthen the position of the emperor and foster loyalty to the state.[4] Both Ch'eng I and Chang Tsai recommended implementing the descent-line system only in limited or modified form. Ch'eng I suggested that it be tried by "one or two families of high officials," and Chang Tsai wanted the descent-line heir to be chosen by official rank not by hereditary seniority.[5] They both recognized some of the impracticalities of the the ancient ideal, but they strongly promoted certain aspects of it and the values it represented.

Chu Hsi and Lü Tsu-ch'ien, the two most influential leaders of the Learning of the Way movement, further advocated descent-line practices and values. They highlighted Ch'eng I's remarks on reviving the descent-line system by including them in their influential anthology *Reflections on Things at Hand (Chin-ssu lu)*, published in 1173. Most important was the performance of family rituals, which were seen to embody moral principles and teach social and familial hierarchy. The quotes from Ch'eng I in the *Reflections* covered some aspects of these rituals, and Ch'eng I's collected works included others. Chu Hsi carried these much further when he compiled a complete text, based largely on ritual prescriptions of Ch'eng I and Ssu-ma Kuang, that updated the ancient rituals and adapted them for use in the present. This work, called *Chu Hsi's Family Rituals (Chu-tzu chia-li)*, became extremely influential from the time of its publication just after Chu Hsi's death in 1200, and numerous commentaries and updates were produced over the centuries.[6]

3 *Chang-tzu ch'üan-shu*, 4:9a–b, as quoted with slight modification in Ebrey, "Conceptions," 230.
4 Ch'eng I went so far as to suggest that positions at court be passed down in great families through the descent-line heirs, as they were thought to have been in Chou times; Chan, *Reflections on Things at Hand*, 231.
5 Chan, *Reflections on Things at Hand*, 229; Ebrey, "Conceptions," 230–1.
6 The work has been translated by Patricia Ebrey as *Chu Hsi's Family Rituals: A Twelfth-Century Chinese Manual for the Performance of Cappings, Weddings, Funerals, and Ancestral Rites*. For its influence, see Ebrey, *Chu Hsi's Family Rituals*, xxvi–ix, and Ebrey, *Confucianism and Family Rituals*, 146–66. For a discussion of when the text was produced and the issue of Chu Hsi's authorship, see Ebrey, *Confucianism and Family Rituals*, 102–44.

Chu Hsi in his *Family Rituals* promoted the descent-line system in its ritual aspects, without advocating any radical pooling of assets. He prescribed setting aside common lands to support sacrifices and supply the offering hall. These lands would be managed by the descent-line heir, while other property would still be divided equally among brothers.[7] The descent-line was meant to be the focus of family rituals. Cappings (for coming of age), weddings, funerals, and ancestral rites all centered on the descent-line heir, and each family member participated according to his or her gender, age, and position within the descent-line scheme. Chu Hsi's intent in his own words was to "preserve status responsibilities (*ming-fen* 名分) and give concrete form to love and respect."[8] This would enhance descent-line consciousness, and promote group values that supported agnatic kinship relations.

Chu Hsi's ritual prescriptions focusing on the descent-line heir were nearly all modified in later editions and rewrites; and the descent-line system was never put into practice in the Sung or after. Nevertheless, the agnatic ideals that went with it provided an ideological basis for the development of corporate lineages. While the original idea of the corporate lineage, as formulated by Fan Chung-yen (989–1052), was to combine all property into a charitable estate (*i-chuang*), the plan quickly changed to include only a portion of land to be held and administered by the lineage as a group. Fan's model did, however, make the lineage into a semireligious entity and a "perpetual corporate cult group."[9] Essential to this model was the continuation of the male line and avoidance of a break in the household (*hu-chüeh*) at all costs. Fan's own attempt to establish an agnatic corporation failed repeatedly, as did the attempts of others. As a result, then and even in later times lineage members often had to call on their affines to bail them out financially, thus contradicting pure agnatic principles.[10] But eventually, by Southern Sung times, corporate descent groups began to develop, and agnatic solidarity began to change social consciousness. We saw in the last chapter how lineages in the late Sung were beginning to affect women's inheritance rights. The social development of lineages and the philosophical ideal of the descent line intersected in a set of values and practices. As articulated by Chu Hsi, these included keeping property within the patri-

---

7 Ebrey, *Chu Hsi's Family Rituals*, 10–11.   8 Ebrey, *Chu Hsi's Family Rituals*, 3.
9 Twitchett, "The Fan Clan's Charitable Estate," 101.
10 See, for instance, Linda Walton, "Kinship, Marriage and Status in Sung China." For later examples, see Keith Hazelton, "Patrilines and the Development of Localized Lineages"; Robert Hymes, "Marriage, Descent Groups, and the Localist Strategy"; Jerry Dennerline, "Marriage, Adoption, and Charity in the Development of Lineages," all in *Kinship Organization in Late Imperial China, 1000–1940*, ed. Patricia Ebrey and James Watson (Berkeley: University of California Press, 1986).

line (as opposed to going to women), opposition to private property within the household, objection to nonagnatic adoption, regarding nephews to be as important as sons, and great emphasis on ancestral sacrifices and the continuation of the ritual patriline through male heirs. These affected the attitudes of many Sung men toward women's property and women's roles in the household.

Chu Hsi's many philosophic treatises nowhere directly address the issue of women's property; nevertheless, he expressed a firm opinion on the matter. His views on the subject are found in his more occasional writings, particularly funerary inscriptions, where he turned his attention to the individual and the family and spoke of wives and mothers in his vision of social order. His remarks reveal both his own ideals and the contemporary Sung practices that differed from them. Chu's Confucian agenda was in conflict with many social customs of his time. In keeping with his emphasis on personal moral transformation, he presented models for ethical behavior that went against current practices. He was not looking for government intervention or legal reform. That would only come later.

Chu Hsi's emphasis on patrilineality is demonstrated in his opposition to daughters' inheriting their parents' estate when they had no brothers. Chu praised men in his funerary inscriptions for refusing (or getting their wives to refuse) inheritance that came from the wife's parents. One example is Chu Hsi's early teacher, who became his father-in-law, Liu Mien-chih (1091–1149). In 1198, "fifty years" after he died, Chu Hsi wrote in an inscription for him:

Mr. Liu would not take even a single straw inappropriately.[11] His wife's family was wealthy, but they had no sons. They planned to give all of their property to their daughter. Mr. Liu refused to take it. Moreover, he chose a worthy member of their lineage and conferred the property on him, making him carry out sacrifices to them.[12]

This passage demonstrates Sung practice whereby a daughter with no brothers could inherit her parents' estate. This inheritance often occurred, as in this case, after a woman was married, and was not affected in practice (if not in law) by her having previously received a dowry. Chu Hsi, by choosing to include these words in his father-in-law's funerary inscription, shows he was opposed to this kind of inheritance by women. He disapproved of property devolving to daughters who

---

11 *Mencius* 5A:7. "If it were contrary to what is right (*i*), . . . even a single straw he would not give to or take away from other people."
12 *Chu-tzu ta-ch'üan*, 97:21a.

took it into a different patriline. Such property was obtained "inappropriately."[13] Instead, he wanted to preserve the male line and sacrifices to agnatic ancestors, even when these were fictively established through adoption.

Chu Hsi's inscription was meant to promote the adoption of male heirs to carry on patrilineal sacrifices, and to discourage property going exclusively to women. His words were cut in stone and copied into later books. In particular, this passage within the inscription was reprinted almost *verbatim* in the *Sung Dynastic History (Sung shih)*,[14] and it gained additional prominence in the Ming when it was included in Liu Mien-chih's biography in the Neo-Confucian anthology *Case Studies of Sung and Yüan Confucians (Sung-Yüan hsüeh-an)* by Huang Tsung-hsi (1610–1695) et al.[15]

In the same inscription, Chu Hsi praised Liu for setting up agnatic male heirs in two more instances. Liu and his wife themselves had two daughters and no sons, but Liu adopted the "son of one of his agnatic cousins, Liu Ssu-wen, to be his heir."[16] His older daughter married Chu Hsi (and had children of both sexes) while his younger daughter married one Fan Nien-te. It seems that both daughters had children, but the adopted son Ssu-wen had none. Accordingly, another agnatic cousin was adopted to be Liu Mien-chih's grandson and heir.[17] Though Liu's two daughters must have received some dowry, Chu Hsi implies that Liu's estate was never passed down to females (and that Chu Hsi himself did not benefit from it).

For a man to obtain considerable wealth through his wife was not uncommon in the Sung.[18] But it also was grounds for criticism by moralizing officials and political enemies. Ironically, in a famous memorial of 1196 impeaching Chu Hsi, Chu was criticized for arranging just such a profitable marriage. The memorial was presented to the throne in the tenth month by Shen Chi-tsu (*chin-shih* 1169), as part of the mounting

13 Note that Chu Hsi leads us to understand that Liu had complete control over his wife's inheritance. Elsewhere, as we will see, he acknowledges women's authority over their own property precisely by celebrating their conscious surrender of it.
14 *Sung shih*, 459:13463.
15 *Sung-Yüan hsüeh-an* (Beijing: Chung-hua shu chü, 1986), 43:1395; hereafter cited as SYHA. For the significance of this anthology and others in the later development of the Confucian tradition, see Thomas Wilson, *Genealogy of the Way: The Construction and Uses of the Confucian Tradition in Late Imperial China* (Stanford, Calif.: Stanford University Press, 1995). For more on Chu Hsi's ideas about adoption and their influence beyond China, see James I. McMullen, "Non-Agnatic Adoption: A Confucian Controversy in Seventeenth and Eighteenth Century Japan," *Harvard Journal of Asiatic Studies* 35 (1975): 130–89.
16 *Chu-tzu ta-ch'üan*, 97:21b.   17 *Chu-tzu ta-ch'üan*, 97:21b.
18 For examples, see Ebrey, "Shifts," 102–6.

attack on *tao-hsüeh.*[19] Despite their trumped-up and almost comical nature, the charges are revealing. Shen accused Chu Hsi of six major crimes, from being unfilial to his mother to mismanaging affairs as an official, then buttressed these with a host of lesser improper acts. These included his having arranged a profitable marriage for the son of his colleague Chao Ju-Yü and his trying to marry his children into rich families generally.[20]

The memorial charged that in return for favors from the great statesman Chao Ju-yü, Chu Hsi sponsored the marriage of his son Chao Ch'ung-hsien to the daughter of Liu Kung (styled Kung-fu, 1122–1178), and that Chao Ch'ung-hsien subsequently came to possess "property in the tens of thousands after her death."[21] We know from an inscription by Chen Te-hsiu that Chao Ch'ung-hsien indeed married Liu Kung's daughter as arranged by Chu Hsi.[22] She was Ch'ung-hsien's second wife, after his first wife died young. Liu Kung before he died entrusted his daughter to Chu Hsi to find a husband. She died nineteen years before her husband Ch'ung-hsien, so he could indeed have obtained her considerable dowry property for himself.

On Chu's marrying his own children to rich spouses, Shen Chi-tsu wrote: "As to the marriage of his sons and daughters, he always chose rich families in order to profit from the large dowry or betrothal gifts."[23] Mercenary marriages were generally condemned, and the problem of large dowries was much discussed by Sung literati.[24] At the same time dowry had become an expected source of wealth in elite families, leaving many open to charges like those brought against Chu Hsi.[25]

Interestingly, it was just two years after Shen Chi-tsu's memorial that Chu Hsi wrote the inscription cited above, in which he praised Liu Mien-chih for declining his wife's inheritance. The inscription hints that Chu Hsi himself inherited little from his wife since his father-in-law adopted a son. Modern scholarship presents evidence that Chu Hsi received a

19 Conrad Schirokauer, "Neo-Confucians under Attack: The Condemnation of *Wei-hsüeh*," in *Crisis and Prosperity in Sung China*, ed. John Winthrop Haeger (University of Arizona, 1975), 163–98.
20 *Tao-ming lu* (Chih-pu-tsu chi ts'ung-shu), 7A:17a–23b. I thank Kinugawa Tsuyoshi for drawing my attention to this source. See also Wing-tsit Chan, *Chu Hsi Life and Thought* (Hong Kong: The Chinese University Press, 1987), 12–14.
21 *Tao-ming lu,* 7A:19b.
22 *Hsi-shan chi* (SPTK ed.), 44:13b. I thank John Chaffee for drawing my attention to this inscription.
23 *Tao-ming lu,* 7A:20b.   24 See for instance Ebrey, "Women, Money, and Class."
25 If Ebrey is correct that dowries were larger than betrothal gifts for the Sung elite ("Shifts"), then Chu Hsi and others were less likely to profit from the marriage of their daughters. Evidently Shen Chi-tsu held that both dowry and betrothal gifts were negotiable and either could outweigh the other.

comfortable official stipend but that he was not particularly wealthy by elite standards.[26]

In a funerary inscription written for a woman, Chu Hsi reiterated the stance against female inheritance that he had taken in the inscription for his father-in-law, Liu Mien-chih. But this time Chu Hsi portrays the wife herself, not the husband, as the one who rejected her inheritance. The inscription was for a woman from his home prefecture of Chienning, whose sons were childhood friends of his.[27] This remarkable woman, Madam Yü, had complete control of a large estate during forty years as a widow. She took care of her husband's parents and siblings together with her own children, and also cared for her aging stepfather. This man had no other surviving children, and when he died, she stood to inherit his property. But instead, she used her authority as the owner of the property to act as Liu Mien-chih had done: "[After her father died] she selected on his behalf someone from the lineage to carry on the sacrifices, and she returned the property to [this heir]."[28]

This inscription describes a woman who had considerable authority over property, both what she had inherited from her parents and what belonged to her husband's family. This authority gave women responsibility to work toward a property regime that was consistent with classical Confucian ideals. Chu Hsi wanted both women and men to preserve patrilines by adopting heirs and renouncing women's inheritance.

Opposition to Private Property within Marriage

Another aspect of women's property that contradicted Confucian ideals was women's private property within marriage. Men in the Sung who were concerned with reviving the Confucian Way (*tao*) commented on this. Most often they praised women for surrendering this property to the husband's family or for using it to bail out the family in a time of need. Chu Hsi adopted this stance. His funerary inscriptions for women reveal his assumption that women held personal property within mar-

---

26 See Wing-tsit Chan, "Chu Hsi's Poverty," in *Chu Hsi New Studies* (Honolulu: University of Hawaii Press, 1989); and more complete information in Chan Wing-tsit [Ch'en Jung-chieh], "Chu-tzu ku ch'iung," in *Shu-mu chi-k'an* 15:2 (1981), reprinted in *Chu-hsüeh lun-chi* (Taipei: Hsüeh-sheng shu-chü, 1982), 205–32. See also Kinugawa Tsuyoshi, "Shūshi shōden" Pt. 1, 10; Kinugawa, "Sōdai no hōkyū," and Kinugawa, "Kanryō to hōkyū."

27 *Chu Wen-kung wen-chi* (SPTK ed.), 92:12b. Chu Hsi also wrote an inscription for her son Chiang Ming, with whom he studied as a youth. *Chu Wen-kung wen-chi*, 93:1a.

28 *Chu Wen-kung wen-chi*, 92:13b. Madam Yü was already married when her father died; it seems that all the property went to her and then to the newly adopted heir without any going to the state. For more information on her, see Birge, "Chu Hsi and Women's Education," 346ff.

riage, over which they had exclusive control, but they also reveal his disapproval. He sought change in this Sung practice, by encouraging women to surrender their property to the husband's family. His writings, and those of others, presented dowry donation as an important aspect of wifely virtue.

Chu's Hsi's Encouragement of Dowry Donation

Chu Hsi spoke explicitly of women's private property in six of his seventeen inscriptions for women. He did not assume women would customarily give up their property; rather, he lauded them for this act, treating it as unusual and exemplary. Moreover, even Chu Hsi's model women usually donated funds for a particular need, rather than unconditionally surrendering their property.

In one case, a young wife, née Luo, contributed her own dowry to provide a dowry for her husband's younger sister:

[Her husband] Mr. Chang was very poor. When he first became an official, he planned to marry off his younger sister, but he had no property [for her dowry]. Madam Luo took all the contents of her trousseau and presented them to him, without any hint of regret.[29]

In another case, a woman paid for her father-in-law's funeral. This was especially praiseworthy for it showed filial piety:[30]

When her father-in-law passed away, her husband was very poor. The elder and younger brothers looked at each other and planned to sell some fields to pay for the funeral. Madam Yü said, "Do not destroy the patrimony of your ancestors." She then withdrew and sold the contents of her trousseau to meet the expenses of the funeral. Because of this, Mr. Huang was able to arrange the funeral without troubling the rest of the family.[31]

In another example, a wife was left behind with four children while her husband was in exile in the South. The household became increasingly impoverished, so the woman, née Kuan, sold her jewelry to support the family, never telling her husband about the desperate straits they were in.[32] Along the same lines, Chu Hsi described a woman from Ming-

---

29 *Chu Wen-kung wen-chi*, 90:15a.
30 Filial piety, especially to one's in-laws, was the most important virtue of a wife; Birge, "Chu Hsi and Women's Education," 335–8. Mark Elvin notes that Confucians in the Ming and Ch'ing considered it virtuous for daughters to sell even themselves to pay for the burial of parents and relatives. "Female Virtue and the State in China," in *Past and Present*, no. 104 (Aug. 1984), 148 n. 172.
31 *Chu Wen-kung wen-chi*, 91:14a.   32 *Chu Wen-kung wen-chi*, 92:8b.

chou (Ningpo area) as having a huge dowry. Her husband was a Northern official who fled the Jurchen invasion, and she "contributed all [of her dowry] to help pay for the daily needs [of the household]."[33] In these cases, Chu implies that the women did contribute their entire dowries to the general operating fund of the household.

Finally, we can see Chu Hsi's attitude toward individual property in the household in an inscription written in 1185 for the mother of two of his contemporaries, students of Lü Tsu-ch'ien: Shih Hao and Shih Ch'i.[34] This woman, née Shao, died in 1183 at the age of 71 *sui* after a long period of widowhood during which she was active in community relief work and estate management. Chu Hsi described her strict regulation of the household in some detail as it was told to him in a letter from her son. She insisted that all income and expenditure of the sons and daughters be reported to the family head (herself), as well as any acquisition of concubines or bondservants. In particular she had a regulation that stated: "In all cases the wives of the various sons are forbidden to accumulate private property."[35] Her (or Chu Hsi's) use of the word "accumulate" (*hsü* 畜) suggests the profits made on the investment of capital. It is possible that Madam Shao was not going so far as to abolish the wives' private property in itself (since that was an accepted fact of Sung society), but that she opposed accumulation of profits on such property that generated excessive inequality between married brothers in a family.[36]

To sum up, Chu Hsi (and ostensibly women like Madam Shao) found problems with the independent wealth of women within marriage. He advocated the complete sharing of resources within a joint household. Women's personal property upset family hierarchies and social relations and undermined the key virtue of unselfishness and publicspiritedness. It threatened the authority of the household head, whether male or female. Chu Hsi's inscriptions posited an ideal aimed at undermining the institution of individual property within the household. This ideal was not new to Chu Hsi, but it steadily gained acceptance among his followers in the late Southern Sung.

---

33 *Chu Wen-kung wen-chi*, 92:3b.
34 *Chu Wen-kung wen-chi*, 90:12a. For information on the sons, see *Chu Wen-kung wen-chi*, 79:9b.
35 *Chu Wen-kung wen-chi*, 90:13a.
36 Personal labor applied to private property in the household to generate profits was a major issue in joint households. Yüan Ts'ai spoke of "personal fortunes" and business enterprises separate from the common estate; Ebrey, *Family and Property* 1.25, 1.26 (pp. 198–200). See also Lau Nap-yin, "Sung-tai t'ung-chü chih-tu." Modern-day anthropologists have observed related phenomena, though nothing to the extent that Yüan Ts'ai described in the Sung. Cohen, *House*, 179; Goody, *Oriental*, 38.

Dowry Donation and the Learning of the Way Fellowship

We do not find much emphasis on dowry in the works of the Ch'eng brothers, the progenitors of the Learning of the Way movement, because almost no funerary inscriptions for women by them survive. The one extant inscription by Ch'eng Hao (1032–1085) was written for the daughter of Ch'eng I who died in childhood. Of two by the longer lived Ch'eng I (1033–1107) in his collected works, one is for his niece who died before getting married and the other is for his mother. Ch'eng I does not emphasize that his mother donated her dowry to the household (which was large and had many servants). He says only that when she once took in an abandoned merchant boy, the many relatives in the household were displeased, so she "purchased food with her own funds to feed him."[37] Ch'eng I praises his mother for generously helping a needy child, but his words also underscore his mother's ability to use her private money for her own personal concerns.

We find more comments on women's dowry toward the middle of the Sung dynasty and among men who were somehow associated with Chu Hsi or the area he came from. One of Chu's predecessors in the burgeoning Learning of the Way fellowship wrote inscriptions similar to his in their emphasis on dowry. This was the famous scholar-official Hu Yin.

Hu Yin (1098–1156) was from Ch'ung-an county in Chien-ning, Fukien. He was adopted by his father's older brother, the literatus Hu An-kuo (1074–1138), after nearly falling victim to infanticide.[38] Hu An-kuo moved around in office, but eventually settled in Heng-chou (Hunan province) in 1129, where he went to escape civil disturbances. Hu Yin and An-kuo's other sons went there with him, and together they founded the Hunan school of Confucianism, of which Hu Yin and his adoptive brother Hu Hung (1106–1161) were the most prominent representatives.[39]

Hu Yin was a staunch proponent of the Ch'eng brothers' school of Confucianism, and was known for his uncompromising opposition

---

37 *I-ch'uan chi*, 8:6a, in *Erh-Ch'eng ch'üan-shu* (SPPY ed.). The other inscriptions are found in *I-ch'uan chi*, 7:8a, and *Ming-tao chi*, 4:9a, both in *Erh-Ch'eng ch'üan-shu*. Most of the inscription for Ch'eng I's mother is translated by Ebrey, *Inner Quarters*, 183–4.

38 The standard histories report that Hu's own mother tried to drown him, because she felt she had "too many sons," and that he was saved by Hu An-kuo's wife; *Sung shih*, 435:12,916 (Vol. 37); SYHA 41:1341 (Vol. 2). Sources of gossip closer to the event give a concubine as the birth mother who tried to drown him, a rather unlikely occurrence; e.g., *Ch'i-tung yeh-yü* by Chou Mi (1232–1308) (Shanghai: Shanghai shu-tien, 1990), 6:7b. Cf. Ebrey, *Inner Quarters*, 181–2.

39 For his brother Hu Hung's thought and his contribution to Learning of the Way Confucianism, see Tillman, *Confucian Discourse*, esp. 29–36. Unfortunately, no women's funerary inscriptions by Hu Hung survive.

to Buddhism.[40] His writings are filled with diatribes against Buddhism and exhortations to study hard for moral rejuvenation rather than for personal gain and official advancement. He found the typical profit-seeking activities of literati elites around him intolerable. He glorified poverty and considered his family to be poor, despite his own officeholding.[41]

Six funerary inscriptions for women are included in Hu Yin's collected works. Three of them describe women who donated their dowry to the household, and their reasons reflect his own concerns with poverty and learning. The first example was Hu Yin's own wife, Chang Hsiu-lan, who was from Nan-chien chou, the prefecture neighboring Hu Yin's native Chien-ning. Hu Yin married her in 1122 when she was only fifteen, and she went with the family to Heng-chou, Hunan. There Hu left her to take care of his father while he went away to serve in office. Hu Yin writes:

I, Yin, got my first appointment by lot[42] to the Western Capital (Loyang). My social circle was broad, but my salary was irregular. To pay expenses, my wife provided her entire dowry without giving it a thought. Later, when troubles broke out,[43] the family was even more impoverished. They ate only coarse grain and vegetable broth, and sometimes even lacked salt and oil. But my wife was able to take it all calmly.[44]

We find here a description of using the dowry in its entirety for household expenses. Hu Yin describes his family as being in dire straits, but it is interesting to speculate about young Madam Chang's personal wealth. Her father, Chang K'o (1046–1128) was a high official at court, serving as the Director of the Bureau of Military Appointments in the Ministry of War (*Ping-pu lang-chung*, rank 6a) when Hu Yin married

---

40 He wrote the famous essay "Ch'ung-cheng pien," one of the harshest attacks on Buddhism by a Neo-Confucian, but highly praised by Chu Hsi; SYHA 435:1342. See also Conrad Schirokauer, "Chu Hsi and Hu Hung," in *Chu Hsi and Neo-Confucianism*, ed. Wing-tsit Chan (Honolulu: University of Hawaii Press, 1986), 482.

41 Hu Yin may have been especially hostile to merchant activity because his own family had been merchants just two generations before. Moreover his father, Hu An-kuo, had relied on the support of a rich merchant and local powerbroker named Li Ming to settle in Heng-shan county, Heng-chou. Hu Yin became a friend of his, but in a letter to Li Ming in 1145, Hu Yin reprimanded him for "monopolizing markets," "buying titles," and "privately settling lawsuits" (including meting out punishments); *Fei-jan chi*, 17:28b; Watanabe Hiroshi, "Local *Shih-ta-fu* in the Sung," in *Acta Asiatica*, no. 50 (1986): 54–72.

42 "Appointment by lot" was a common term for one's first posting. It may derive from the perceived chance nature of the assignment.

43 This is probably a reference to the Jurchen invasion in 1126, four years after Hu Yin was married.

44 *Fei-jan chi*, 26:15b.

her.[45] Their marriage represented the ideal elite strategy of combining high-powered capital connections with local place influence.[46] When Hu Yin passed his *chin-shih* exam in 1121, he was immediately approached by the Vice Director of the Secretariat (rank 3b), also named Chang, to be his son-in-law. Hu Yin refused this extremely prestigious match because, as he said himself, "At that time I despised the high officials of our times."[47] This unusual move caught the attention of Bureau Director Chang K'o (no relation to the other Chang), and Hu Yin made a match with *his* daughter, who was 15 *sui* at the time.[48] Hu Yin had previously established a relationship with Chang K'o: his future father-in-law had been one of Hu Yin's examiners, and Hu had made a personal visit to thank him for the high marks he had received.[49] Chang K'o's daughter may well have been a better match for him, because she was from Hu Yin's home area in Fukien, and because her father was less vulnerable to the factional struggles at court in which Hu Yin himself was later caught up.[50] All of this suggests that Hu Yin's wife would not have been left to go hungry, despite Hu Yin's protestations of being poor.[51]

In a funerary inscription for another woman, Hu Yin commended her for helping monetarily with the education of her sons:

[Madam Li] bore four sons. Her husband invited in a teacher and strove to educate them. Madam Li used all her energy to help him. She would supple-

---

45 *Fei-jan chi*, 26:15a; *Kuei-shan chi*, 37:1b. For Sung bureaucratic ranks, I follow Miyazaki Ichisada, "Sōdai kansei josetsu: Sōshi shokkan shi o ika ni yomubeki ka," in Saeki Tomi, ed., *Sōshi shokkanshi sakuin* (Kyoto: Society of Oriental Research, 1963), 1–57. A convenient chart with ranks appears on p. 44. English translations mostly follow Charles O. Hucker, *A Dictionary of Official Titles in Imperial China* (Stanford, Calif.: Stanford University Press, 1985).
46 This strategy is detailed in Hartwell, "Demographic, Political, and Social Transformations of China"; Hymes, *Statesmen*, ch. 3; and Hymes, "Marriage, Descent Groups, and the Localist Strategy." See also Bossler, *Powerful Relations*.
47 *Fei-jan chi*, 26:15a. Patricia Ebrey describes how new *chin-shih* (civil service exam graduates) were sometimes bribed to be sons-in-law; "Shifts," 104–6.
48 Fifteen was young for marriage of women. The average and median age of marriage in both the Northern and Southern Sung was 19 or 20 *sui*. On a sample of 160, I found both the mean and median age of marriage to be 20 *sui*; Bettine Birge, "Age at Marriage of Sung Women," (M.A. thesis, Columbia University, 1985). Patricia Ebrey found the mean to be 19 on a sample of 65; *Inner Quarters*, 74–7.
49 *Fei-jan chi*, 26:15a; 27:1b.
50 Hu Yin was a staunch revanchist and thus eventually collided with Ch'in Kuei. He was exiled to Hsin-chou in Kwangtung; *Sung shih*, 435:12916ff (Vol. 37). On factionalism see Robert Hartwell, "New Approaches to the Study of Bureaucratic Factionalism in Sung China: A Hypothesis," *Bulletin of Sung and Yüan Studies* 18 (1986): 33–40.
51 In a touching elegy to her, and in his funerary inscription, he lamented that the family had not been able to afford better medicine and medical attention for her before she died at the young age of 30; *Fei-jan chi*, 27:3a; 26:15b.

ment the salary of the teacher, even if she had to pawn her own clothes and jewelry. She never complained of being poor. Her son Ch'i passed the examinations and was appointed to office.[52]

Madam Li's sons subsequently became rich, making up for her sacrifice. Although Hu Yin describes Madam Li as being poor and fatherless, she had no brothers and thus may well have had significant inheritance.[53]

In another inscription, Hu Yin again praises a woman for helping with education. This woman, Madam Chieh, married a widower, and although she gave birth to three sons, she took care of the first wife's two boys and saw to their education: "When [her stepsons] Hsien and I went out to study, she personally saw to their teacher's provisions and clothes." We can infer from the words "personally saw to" that Madam Chieh was using her own assets. Moreover, Hu Yin describes the household as extremely wealthy, with the finances under the aggressive management of Madam Chieh's mother-in-law, who commended Madam Chieh for personally caring for her stepsons. It does not seem likely that Chieh was merely distributing common estate funds to the teachers or that she had the authority to do so.[54]

A Confucian born twenty years later, associated closely with the Learning of the Way fellowship, Han Yüan-chi (1118–1187), provides similar examples. Han was the father-in-law of the Learning of the Way leader Lü Tsu-ch'ien (1137–1181) and a friend of the younger Chu Hsi. He grew up in Shao-wu prefecture, just west of Chu Hsi's home of Chienning, and served as prefect of Chien-ning. Three of his seven inscriptions for women discuss dowry donations. A Madam Li (d. 1177) gave all of her dowry to help buy land and build a new house for her husband's family.[55] Lady Mao sold her hairpins and earrings to supply sacrifices for her deceased husband.[56]

The most detailed inscription is that for Great Lady Shang-kuan (1094–1178), who was born into a wealthy Shao-wu family of scholars

52 *Fei-jan chi*, 26:66b. (I make no distinction between dowry in the form of land and of movable property in this discussion, for reasons discussed in the introduction.)
53 *Fei-jan chi*, 26:66a.
54 *Fei-jan chi*, 26:36b–37a. We see her zeal for education in the treatment of her own two sons. Her older son Hsün was beaten by his teacher and ran away, but his mother insisted he return. Her younger son struggled to become a scholar, but died young; *Fei-jan chi*, 26:36b.
55 *Nan-chien chia-i kao* (Wu-ying tien Chü-pen pan-shu ed, 1828), 22:25a (SKCS chen-pen, 22:28a). (All page numbers refer to the Wu-ying-tien edition unless otherwise specified. For the convenience of scholars who may not have it available, I also give page numbers in the SKCS chen-pen edition, but it should be noted that this latter contains errors.)
56 *Nan-chien chia-i kao*, 22:31a (SKCS chen-pen, 22:34b).

and office holders.[57] After "long consideration" (a common euphemism for late marriage), her father arranged her betrothal to Mr. Chi Ling (1081–1135) of Ch'u-chou in the neighboring circuit of Liang-che (modern Chekiang). Han Yüan-chi describes Chi Ling as "poor," because his father had died when he was young, but he was already a student in the Superior College (*shang-she*) of the Imperial University (*t'ai hsüeh*) when he married, and was well on his way to high office in the capital.[58]

Any problem of poverty was probably due more to the scheming of Chi Ling's relatives. Han Yüan-chi tells the story as follows:

There were some in the Chi clan who were not of good character. They secretly sold their ancestral burial lands in Ch'ing-p'ing hamlet to a monastery.

Vice Director Chi Ling requested leave to return home, feeling he had to redeem the lands. But his salary was meager and he had no savings, so he planned to borrow from someone.

His wife wept and said, "My father and mother's property was given to me in order to help my husband's family. If my husband cannot preserve the trees of the family graves himself, how else should I use [the assets]?" Then she took out her entire dowry to redeem the graves. Moreover she used the leftover [funds] to expand the lands greatly, and she set up a cloister to protect them.[59] She said, "Let later generations know that these lands came from you, so others won't dare to interfere [again]." Thereafter the members of the Chi lineage (*tsu*), whether young or old, all praised her worthiness and submitted to her wisdom. To this day, when people collect firewood, they do not dare approach the trees on the tomb lands, saying, "This land was given by Lady Shang-kuan."[60]

Madam Shang-kuan was seen to have done a noble deed that gave her high standing in her husband's family and among his more distant relatives. Her magnanimity even imbues the lands with a sort of divine protection from woodcutters or scheming relatives. The wealth she brought

57 Her father, Shang-kuan Hui, was a noted Confucian scholar who obtained the prestige title (*san-kuan*) of Left Grand Master of the Palace (Rank 4b). Han Yüan-chi records that he was the first to bring prestige to his family, but in fact he was the nephew of the great scholar and official Shang-kuan Chün. Thus the family was already among the highest elite; *Nan-chien chia-i kao*, 22:22a (SKCS chen-pen, 22:24b); SYHA, 19:804.

58 *Nan-chien chia-i kao*, 22:22a. *Sung shih*, 377:11646 (Vol. 33). Chi Ling held several high offices at court and was commended for rescuing the imperial ancestral tablets and personally carrying them when the court fled to the South. Despite a brief demotion to magistrate of Shu-ch'eng county (Lu prefecture, Huai-nan W. circuit) in 1128, Chi Ling became a Vice Director in the Department of State Affairs and Vice Minister of the Court of Imperial Sacrifices.

59 On these grave cloisters (and their frequent connection with White Lotus groups), see Chikusa Masaaki, "SōGen Bukkyō ni okeru an dō," in *Tōyōshi kenkyū* 46:1 (1987): 1–28. See esp. p. 23, which discusses a White Lotus grave cloister for a man's mother in this same prefecture of Shao-wu, Fukien.

60 *Nan-chien chia-i kao*, 22:22b. Cf. Ebrey, *Inner Quarters*, 15.

into her marriage gave her prestige when it was applied in this fashion to the cult of the ancestors. Han Yüan-chi was also promoting dowry contributions when he quoted Lady Shang-kuan to say that her dowry property was primarily meant to "help her husband's family."

This same inscription incidentally reveals the freedom to return home that personal property gave to a widow. When Chi Ling died in 1135, Shang-kuan was 41 and had four small sons. Saying that she "had no one to depend on in the Chi family" and ought to "depend on her own mother and father," she took her children and returned to her natal family. There she worked hard to educate her sons so they could "join the ranks of the scholarly class," and she cared for her own aging parents, whose other children had all died. As the only living child of an elderly official, Shang-kuan was in charge of a large, wealthy estate. Her funerary inscription recounts how she built a house in the prefectural capital of Shao-wu and collected together her father's many relatives. Her nephews and grand nephews, together with her own offspring, gained offices in large numbers. And her parents lived into their nineties.[61]

Han Yüan-chi felt it necessary to declare a reason, in Shang-kuan's own words, for her return to her parents: "so as not to burden her in-laws." But it was common for widows of the upper class to return home.[62] In this case, Shang-kuan surely gained financial power by returning to her parents. She was likely to inherit her father and mother's estate, since there is no mention of any other heir to her father. Han Yüan-chi did not object to the widow Shang-kuan's returning to her natal family, and he praised the good works she performed there. Nevertheless, his wording suggests that he had heard the voices of stauncher Learning of the Way proponents (like his younger friend Chu Hsi and his son-in-law Lü Tsu-ch'ien), who wished to transform accepted practices and discourage widows from leaving their husband's household.

When we look at leaders of the Learning of the Way movement who were contemporaries of Chu Hsi, or who came after him, we find further emphasis on dowry donation. Lü Tsu-ch'ien was the preeminent leader of the Learning of the Way movement until his premature death in 1181.[63] Lü emphasizes dowry donations in five of the eleven inscriptions

61 *Nan-chien chia-i kao*, 22:23a–b.
62 Jennifer Holmgren argues that rich, upper-class women returned home with their property while poor widows were more likely to stay and be supported by their in-laws. "Economic Foundations of Virtue: Widow Remarriage in Early and Modern China," 7–9. See also Ebrey, "Kinship"; Ann Waltner, "Widows and Remarriage in Ming and Early Qing China," both in *Women in China*, ed. Guisso and Johannesen; and Chang Pang-wei, "Sung-tai fu-nü tsai-chia."
63 On this point. see Tillman, *Confucian Discourse*, esp. 82, 90–2.

he wrote for women. Three of these went toward the education of the sons. Lü quotes one son saying of his mother, "Whenever I went away to study, my clothes and food, grain, salt and other expenditures all came from my mother's hand."[64] Another mother sold her hairpins and earrings "worth several hundred thousand [cash]" to obtain books for her sons. Her sacrifice gave her sons extra incentive to study, for as Lü recorded: "She told them . . . 'when you see these books in the future, I want you to remember my intentions.' After she died, whenever her sons repeated this to me, they always cried without stopping."[65] A third woman hired a tutor for her sons and helped the man raise his two daughters, even contributing toward their marriages.[66] The two other women whom Lü praises gave out relief to sick or poor relatives or gifts to visitors. One of them is said to have "unfastened her earrings and taken off her clothes [to give away] without begrudging them," whenever she heard a relative was sick.[67] The theme of generosity and not clinging to material goods was important in the doctrine of the Learning of the Way. We see here and elsewhere that it applied to women as well as to men.

A prominent advocate of the Learning of the Way in the next generation was Wei Liao-weng (1178–1237). Four of his eleven inscriptions praise women for relinquishing their dowry or other personal possessions. One woman, while still a child, sold her own hair to support her parents. Another helped out a friend of her husband who had been demoted and joined her husband in supplying the dowries for a local widow's two daughters. A third helped out needy relatives and villagers, and shared anything she received with her sisters-in-law. The fourth woman, Madam Li, who was her husband's second wife, used her dowry to help rebuild her husband's ancestral residence on the model of his forebears and make further improvements. The remodeling lasted fifteen years.[68] In inscriptions where Wei failed to mention dowry, the woman usually died young or was not well known to him.

Even more prominent as a Learning of the Way leader was Wei's friend and contemporary from Chien-ning, Chen Te-hsiu (1178–1235). Chen mentions dowry in both of the inscriptions he wrote for women. The first woman gave away her dowry to her husband's sisters for their marriages, "without any stinginess." The second used her own funds to make up the dowry of her husband's daughter by a previous marriage.[69]

---

64 *Lü Tung-lai wen-chi*, 8:199.   65 *Lü Tung-lai wen-chi*, 8:201.
66 *Lü Tung-lai wen-chi*, 8:198.   67 *Lü Tung-lai wen-chi*, 8:161.
68 *Ho-shan chi* (SPTK ed.), 73:3b (592); 80:18a (665); 81:8b (669); 70:6b (565).
69 *Hsi-shan chi*, 45:15b, 28b.

Not everyone who wrote of dowry donations was associated closely with the Learning of the Way movement. Yüan Shuo-yu (1140–1204) was not included in the original Ming compilation of Sung Confucians (*Sung-Yüan hsüeh-an*), but he hailed from Chu Hsi's home of Chien-ning and his writings on women reflect concerns similar to those of Chu Hsi and others associated with him.[70] Yüan was born in Chien-an county but later moved his residence to Hu-chou (in modern Chekiang), after attaining high office. He passed the *chin-shih* exam in 1163 and went on to hold many important posts both in the capital and the provinces, reaching the position of a Vice Grand Councilor (*ts'an-chih cheng-shih*) and Administrator of the Bureau of Military Affairs (*chih shu-mi yüan*).[71]

Yüan wrote three inscriptions for women, all long and intimate in tone. Two of them recount in some detail how the women contributed their dowry to the household of their husband. The third was for his own wife, who died when she was only 31.

Of the two inscriptions that mention dowry, the first is unusual for its length and completeness.[72] With a total of 15 ½ pages and 2,552 characters, the inscription is one of the longest for women in the entire literature. It was written for the first cousin of Yüan Shuo-yu's mother on the maternal side, who grew up in Chien-an with Yüan's mother and became like a sister to her. Yüan refers to her as "like a mother" to himself. She married an official, and her sons held office; it seems that Yüan had continuing family and professional ties to her and her family.

The woman's name was Yeh Miao-hui (giving her full name is also unusual), and she lived from 1104 to 1185. She married a widower with several children named Tan Hsin (dates unknown) who was from an official family in the capital district of Hangchow. He died when she was just 30 *sui*, leaving her in charge of a large family: nine children from two mothers plus her in-laws. Despite their official standing, Yüan Shuo-yu writes that the family was in financial straits when she married into it, in part because her mother-in-law was preoccupied with Buddhism and ignored household affairs.[73] Yeh Miao-hui, he writes, "secretly" took the hairpins and ear ornaments as well as the clothes and embroidery of her trousseau and sold them to help out with the household. More-

---

70 Yüan does not appear in the SYHA, but he was added into the later supplement *Sung-Yüan hsüeh-an pu-i* (Ssu-ming ts'ung-shu ed.), 35:186. His views were friendly to Buddhism, which may explain why he was not embraced by members of the Learning of the Way fellowship during his lifetime.

71 *Tung-t'ang chi* (SKCS chen-pen ed.), 20:33b–34b; *Sung-Yüan hsüeh-an pu-i*, 35:65 (186).

72 *Tung-t'ang chi*, 20:22b–30a.   73 *Tung-t'ang chi*, 20:23a.

over, she allowed herself only simple food to eat to save money. Her parents-in-law were so pleased with this behavior that they delegated complete control of the household finances to her.[74]

In his other example, a young wife "pawned her clothes and hairpins each day to supplement her mother-in-law's food and clothing."[75] Later she used her own assets to pay for fine teachers for her sons, spending whatever was needed for provisions during the day and lamps to study by at night, without begrudging the cost.[76]

These acts were very much in keeping with Chu Hsi's ideals of women donating their own money for their in-laws' needs or for educating their sons: activities that supported the family into which a woman had married. The high praise given to women for using their private property in this way proves that it was not normally required, or even expected, of them. We have seen that wives could gain considerable prestige and influence in the family in return for their financial contribution. As time went by, it is possible that women experienced increasing pressure to surrender their dowry and their financial independence. Ch'eng I described his mother in the early Sung as taking in an abandoned child on her own initiative – that is, using her dowry for her own personal projects. In contrast, Ch'eng I's later followers describe women using all of their possessions to fulfill the needs and aspirations of their husband and his relatives.

The Growing Concern over Dowry during the Sung

During the three hundred years of the Sung dynasty, as the Learning of the Way movement gained popularity, there seems to have been a growing concern about the disposition of a wife's dowry. Although legal guarantees still protected a woman's private property no matter how much she had, the discourse in funerary inscriptions suggests that greater pressure was being put on women to surrender their dowry for use by the whole household. The fact that funerary inscriptions throughout the Sung continued to praise wives for giving away their property shows that such charity was not taken for granted; dowries were still by law and custom the private property of wives. Nevertheless, an increase in references to dowry donation over the course of the Sung shows that sacrificing personal wealth was becoming an important virtue for women. Moreover, those who promoted this model were frequently associated with the Learning of the Way movement.

74 *Tung-t'ang chi*, 20:23b.   75 *Tung-t'ang chi*, 20:19b.   76 *Tung-t'ang chi*, 20:20b.

Examples of such sacrifice are found in Northern Sung tomb inscriptions, as in Southern. But a survey of more than 400 inscriptions by over 40 authors from Northern and Southern Sung reveals increasing frequency of references to dowry in the Southern Sung. Out of 171 inscriptions from the Northern Sung, just 17, or 10 percent, mention dowry donations. In the Southern Sung, the proportion almost triples to 27 percent (65 of 240).[77] Learning of the Way leaders Lü Tsu-ch'ien and Wei Liao-weng are among those with high percentages. Ch'en Liang (1143–1194), who was antagonistic to the Learning of the Way movement, is noteworthy for making no mention of dowry in any of his 18, detailed inscriptions. It was clearly not an important issue for him. While those associated with the Learning of the Way fellowship did not have a monopoly on the issue of dowry donation, as a group they generally included it as an aspect of wifely virtue in a high proportion of their inscriptions.[78] These results are presented in Tables 3 and 4, which give the author and the title of each collection checked, the number of surviving inscriptions for women by that author, the number that mention dowry donation, and the percentage these represent of the total.

If we examine the extant inscriptions by men from Chien-ning prefecture (a stronghold of the Learning of the Way, in Northern Fukien), we find that of 31 by Southern Sung authors, 39 percent make explicit reference to women contributing their personal property to household expenses. I could find only one inscription for a woman written by a Chien-ning author in Northern Sung and it does not mention dowry. Two others, by Liao Kang (1071–1143) from the neighboring prefecture of Nan-chien, written for women from Chien-ning and Nan-chien, also make no mention of dowry. Of the inscriptions from Southern Sung Chien-ning, ten of the twelve mentioning dowry are by men who were closely associated with the Learning of the Way: Hu Yin, Chu Hsi, and Chen Te-hsiu. See Table 5.

Looking at the circuit of Fukien, excluding Chien-ning prefecture, we find that of 18 inscriptions in the Northern Sung, only two (or 11%) mention dowry. One was by the prime minister and scientist Su Sung (1020–1101), whom Chu Hsi admired and for whom Chu wrote a shrine inscription. The other was by Yang Shih (1053–

---

77 Patricia Ebrey found that in a random sample of 161 inscriptions for women in the Northern and Southern Sung, 15% mentioned the woman's dowry. She contrasts this with the absence of any reference to dowry in 42 random inscriptions from the T'ang; "Shifts," 109 n. 12, 13. My overall average for Northern and Southern Sung based on 411 inscriptions is 20%.

78 I could find no surviving inscriptions for women by important Learning of the Way philosophers Chang Tsai (1020–1077), Chou Tun-i (1017–1073), Shao Yung (1011–1077), and Chang Shih (1133–1180).

Table 3. *Funerary Inscriptions Referring to Women Giving Away Their Private Property (Northern Sung)*[a]

Author and Title[b]	Total Inscriptions for Women	No. Mentioning Dowry	%
Chang Fang-p'ing (1007–1091) *Le-ch'üan chi*	17	0	0
Ch'eng I (1033–1107) *I-ch'uan chi*	2	0	0
Fan Chung-yen (989–1052) *Fan Wen-cheng Kung chi*	2	0	0
Hsü Hsüan (916–991) *Hsü-kung chi*	7	0	0
Li Kang (1083–1140) *Liang-ch'i chi*	1	0	0
Li Kou (1009–1059) *Chih-chiang chi*	9	2	22
Liao Kang (1071–1143) *Kao-feng chi*	2	0	0
Lu Tien (1042–1102) *T'ao-shan chi*	20	5	25
Liu Yen (1048–1102) *Lung-yün chi*	3	0	0
Ou-yang Hsiu (1007–1072) *Ou-yang chi*	21	0	0

Table 3. *(cont.)*

Author and Title[b]	Total Inscriptions for Women	No. Mentioning Dowry	%
Ssu-ma Kuang (1019–1086) *Ssu-ma chi*	4	1	25
Su Shih (1036–1101) *Su Tung-p'o chi*	5	0	0
Su Sung (1020–1101) *Su-wei chi*	7	1	14
Ts'ai Hsiang (1012–1067) *Tuan-ming chi*	4	0	0
Tseng Kung (1019–1083) *Yüan-feng kao*	25	3	12
Wang An-shih (1021–1086) *Wang Lin-ch'uan chi*	31	4	13
Yang Chieh (late 11th cent.) *Wu-wei chi*	5	0	0
Yang I (974–1020) *Wu-i chi*	1	0	0
Yang Shih (1053–1135) *Kuei-shan chi*	5	1	20
Totals	**171**	**17**	**10**

[a] Authors in alphabetical order.
[b] For the edition used, see bibliography under the short title given here.

Table 4. *Funerary Inscriptions Referring to Women Giving Away Their Private Property (Southern Sung)*[a]

Author and title	Total Inscriptions for Women	No. Mentioning Dowry	%
Chen Te-hsiu (1178–1235) *Hsi-shan chi*	2	2	100
Ch'en Liang (1143–1194) *Ch'en Liang chi*	18	0	0
Chu Hsi (1030–1200) *Chu-tzu wen-chi*	17	5	29
Chou Pi-ta (1126–1204) *Wen-chung chi*	15	2	13
Fang Ta-ts'ung (1183–1247) *T'ieh-an chi*	5	2	40
Han Yüan-chi (1118–1187) *Nan-chien chia-i kao*	7	3	37
Hsü Yüan-chieh (1194–1245) *Mu-yeh chi*	1	0	0
Hu Yin (1098–1156) *Fei-jan chi*	6	3	50
Huang Kan (1152–1221) *Mien-chai chi*	6	0	0
Lin Hsi-i (ca. 1210–1273) *Chu-hsi chüan-chai chi*	4	0	0
Lin Kuang-ch'ao (1114–1178) *Ai-hsüan chi*	1	0	0

Table 4. (cont.)

Author and title	Total Inscriptions for Women	No. Mentioning Dowry	%
Liu K'o-chuang (1187–1269) Hou-ts'un chi	35	8	23
Liu Tsai (1166–1239) Man-t'ang chi	22	7	32
Liu Tzu-hui (1101–1147) P'ing-shan chi	2	0	0
Lou Yüeh (1137–1213) Kung-k'uei chi	10	4	40
Lu Chiu-yüan (1139–1193) Lu Chiu-yüan chi	2	0	0
Lu Yu (1125–1210) Wei-nan wen-chi	14	4	28
Lü Tsu-ch'ien (1137–1181) Lü Tung-lai chi	11	5	45
Wei Liao-weng (1178–1237) Ho-shan chi	11	4	36
Yang Wan-li (1127–1206) Ch'eng-chai chi	22	12	54
Yeh Shih (1150–1223) Yeh Shih chi	26	2	7.7
Yüan Shuo-yu (1140–1204) Tung-t'ang chi	3	2	67
Totals	**240**	**65**	**27**

^a Authors in alphabetical order.

Table 5. *Funerary Inscriptions Referring to Women Giving Away Their Private Property (Northern and Southern Sung, Chien-ning)*[a]

Author and Title	Total Inscriptions for Women	No. Mentioning Dowry	%
Northern Sung			
Yang I (974–1020) *Wu-i chi*	1	0	0
Totals N. Sung	**1**	**0**	**0**
Southern Sung			
Hu Yin (1098–1156) *Fei-jan chi*	6	3	50
Liu Tzu-hui (1101–1147) *P'ing-shan chi*	2	0	0
Chu Hsi (1030–1200) *Chu-tzu wen-chi*	17	5	29
Yüan Shuo-yu (1140–1204) *Tung-t'ang chi*	3	2	67
Chen Te-hsiu (1178–1235) *Hsi-shan chi*	2	2	100
Hsü Yüan-chieh (1194–1245) *Mu-yeh chi*	1	0	0
Totals S. Sung	**31**	**12**	**39**

[a] Inscriptions are included here if the author is either from Chien-ning or spent most of his life there.

1135), the disciple of the Ch'eng brothers who introduced the Learning of the Way into Fukien. For the Southern Sung, the proportion doubles to 22 percent, or 13 of 58, with authors associated with the Learning of the Way accounting for all of them. These results are presented in Table 6.

Table 6. *Funerary Inscriptions Referring to Women Giving Away Their Private Property (Northern and Southern Sung, Fukien Circuit)*[a]

Author and Title	Total Inscriptions for Women	No. Mentioning Dowry	%
Northern Sung			
Su Sung (1020–1101) *Su-wei chi*	7	1	14
Yang Shih (1053–1135) *Kuei-shan chi*	5	1	20
Liao Kang (1071–1143) *Kao-feng chi*	2	0	0
Ts'ai Hsiang (1012–1067) *Tuan-ming chi*	4	0	0
Totals	**18**	**2**	**11**
Southern Sung			
Lin Kuang-ch'ao (1114–1178) *Ai-hsüan chi*	1	0	0
Han Yüan-chi (1118–1187) *Nan-chien chia-i kao*	7	3	37
Huang Kan (1152–1221) *Mien-chai chi*	6	0	0
Fang Ta-ts'ung (1183–1247) *T'ieh-an chi*	5	2	40
Liu K'o-chuang (1187–1269) *Hou-ts'un chi*	35	8	23
Lin Hsi-i (ca. 1210–1273) *Chu-hsi chüan-chai chi*	4	0	0
Totals	**58**	**13**	**22**

[a] These do not include Chien-ning. As in Table 5, inscriptions are included in this count if the author is either from Fukien or spent most of his life there.

In conclusion, the evidence suggests that among followers of the Learning of the Way, in areas where it was taking hold, and as the Sung dynasty progressed, there was an increased interest in the disposition of a wife's property, and a willingness to present the relinquishing of one's dowry as an aspect of womanly virtue. It was becoming less acceptable, in some eyes, for a wife to use her private property solely for her own needs.

Learning of the Way Ideals and Women as Household Bursars

Those who promoted Learning of the Way ideals objected to women keeping private property for themselves. But it does not follow that they saw women as helpless dependents within the communal family with no control over its assets. They viewed the family as a collectivist corporation where individual freedoms, male and female, were sacrificed for the well-being of the entire entity. Each family member had a role to play that contributed to the larger group. Women also had a crucial role to play, depending on their life-cycle stage. Although brides, as daughters-in-law, may have been urged to give up their personal assets and thereby forfeit their financial independence, more senior women in the household had responsibilities that could include considerable control over property.

As described in the Introduction, the philosophy of the Learning of the Way emphasized a clarification of gender roles. As articulated in the Confucian classics, women were given responsibility for the inner, domestic sphere and were confined to that arena. Chu Hsi and others elaborated on this function by valorizing women's management of the household, including financial management. By contrast, men were urged not to pay undue attention to daily economic issues and instead to concentrate on higher pursuits of study, self-cultivation, and public service. The trials and tribulations of quotidian life were best left to a competent wife to deal with. When women were able to respond fully to the demands of domestic management, they could release their husbands and sons for higher, "outside" pursuits. For Chu Hsi and his followers, womanly virtue included far-reaching and aggressive estate management activities. In this role, women were given control over money and property that could blur the boundary between inner and outer.

Northern Sung Discourse on Women as Household Managers

The portrayal of wives as financial managers was not invented by Learning of the Way philosophers. The theme can be found only rarely in

169

inscriptions before the Sung,[79] but it begins to emerge more definitely during the Northern Sung. The appearance of a discourse that praises women for managing the household economy has been linked to the development of the new literati elite in the Sung. Elites in the Sung could no longer rely on their ancestry and prestigious pedigree to ensure success and high government office. Instead, a larger group came to participate in government that maintained itself through education and personal achievement. The language of funerary inscriptions gradually came to reflect this change. Sung inscriptions most often emphasized the virtue and accomplishments of individuals that helped them to struggle up from humble origins. Such effort and perseverance was a sign of moral quality. T'ang inscriptions by contrast assigned moral superiority to those with illustrious ancestors, and this ancestry, not the individual, was most often praised in eulogies.[80]

Specific references to women managing property are still fairly rare in the Northern Sung. Influential men like Ou-yang Hsiu (1007–1072) and Wang An-shih (1021–1086), who wrote large numbers of inscriptions for women, sometimes commend wives in general terms for their service in the household and for managing the family. Frugality and making do with scant resources is a recurrent theme, and they clearly attach some importance to the woman's role in maintaining a household.[81] Nevertheless, they make no reference to actual control over family property and resources. This is especially striking in inscriptions by Wang An-shih for five women who were widowed and had to raise small children by themselves. They must have had to supervise the finances, but Wang is silent on the issue. He only praises them for their seclusion and chastity.[82] In one inscription, Wang does raise a theme that becomes central to Chu Hsi's thought in the next century. Wang comments that the wife's handling of domestic affairs allowed her husband to devote himself to his work as a high official "without worrying about the

---

79 In a scan of two dozen T'ang inscriptions for women, I found no references to household management. In a survey of 63 T'ang inscriptions, Bossler found only one reference (in a funerary inscription for a T'ang woman dating to 832; *Powerful Relations*, 20). A brief reference is found in an inscription for a Madam Li of the N. Wei dynasty (386–534), cited in Patricia Ebrey, *The Aristocratic Families of Early Imperial China* (Cambridge: Cambridge University Press, 1978), 57.

80 This point is well illustrated by Bossler, *Powerful Relations*, esp. 12–24.

81 For example, *Wang Lin-ch'uan chi*, 100:633, 634–5. *Ou-yang chi* (reprint in *Ch'üan Sung wen*), 95:377–8, 384–5. Wang wrote 31 inscriptions for 30 women, a number second only to Liu K'o-chuang of the S. Sung (who wrote 35) in the entire corpus of surviving Sung inscriptions for women. Ou-yang wrote 23. These large numbers compared to other writers makes the lack of detail on household management especially noteworthy.

82 *Wang Lin-ch'uan chi*, 99:627–8, 628–9; 100:634–5, 636, 637.

family."[83] Ssu-ma Kuang makes a similar comment about the mother of Su Shih, saying that her contribution to the family, both financial and managerial, allowed her husband, Su Hsün, and sons to devote themselves to study. His four other eulogies for women fail to mention financial responsibilities.[84] In the case of the Ch'eng brothers, who had the most direct influence on the Learning of the Way, again the only inscription between the two that describes a woman who lived to maturity is that for Ch'eng I's mother. Ch'eng I speaks of her ability to handle servants and her frugality and contentment with limited resources, but he does not mention any role as household bursar.[85] Other progenitors of the Learning of the Way have no surviving inscriptions for women.[86]

Detailed praise of women managing the household, while unusual in the Northern Sung, was not absent. An excellent example is by the famous Kiangsi scholar Li Kou (1009–1059) in an inscription for his mother. Unlike Ch'eng I's mother, who lived in a large household with many servants (despite Ch'eng's protestations of limited resources) where others had primary responsibility for the household economy, Li's mother was widowed at forty and left to raise her fourteen-year-old son alone with only "two or three *mou* of irrigated land." Li Kou describes how she saved the family from cold and hunger: "She hired young laborers to burn off the fields and plough and weed them, and she shared the profits with them. By day she supervised the farming; by night she attended to woman's work. She sold what she produced to help with [household] expenditures."[87] Li Kou places these comments within the crucial framework of his mother having enabled him to study and establish himself:

[Because of my mother's efforts] I was able to leave home to study, to find teachers and make friends. I did not on account of family affairs have to give up my heart's intentions, and thus was able to finish my studies and establish myself. Had it not been like this, [I would have become] a pitiable fellow, working as a hired servant [tutor] or a pedlar, still unable to support [the family]. How would I have had the leisure for diligent pursuit of study?[88]

83 *Wang Lin-ch'uan chi*, 100:633.
84 *Ssu-ma ch'uan-chia chi* (Kuo-hsüeh chi-pen ts'ung-shu ed.), 78:967–8. (SPTK ed. 76:11b–12b). In his family advice book, Ssu-ma emphasizes the need for husbands not wives to keep control of the household; *Chia-fan* (Chung-kuo tzu-hsüeh ming-chu chi-ch'eng ed.), esp. 7:650–8; 8:659ff.
85 *I-ch'uan chi*, 8:6a, in *Erh Ch'eng ch'üan-shu*. See also translation in Ebrey, *Inner Quarters*, 183–4.
86 As already noted, these include Chang Tsai (1020–1077), Chou Tun-i (1017–1073), Shao Yung (1011–1077), and Chang Shih (1133–1180).
87 *Chih-chiang chi* (SPTK ed.), 31:7b.
88 *Chih-chiang chi*, 31:7b. See also Liu Ching-chen, "Nü wu wai-shih? Mu-chih-pei-ming chung suo-chien chih Pei-Sung shih-ta-fu she-hui chih-hsü li-nien," *Fu nü yü liang-hsing hsüeh-k'an*, no. 4 (March 1993): 31.

We cannot know if Li Kou really started from such humble origins, but he studied with Fan Chung-yen and became a renowned scholar and authority on ritual who held high office. He used his study time well, for he wrote some of his most influential works while still in his twenties.[89] Undoubtedly his difficult family situation contributed to his appreciation of women as household managers, and we see this in some of his other inscriptions.[90]

The theme of a woman's efforts releasing her son or husband for study or other pursuits is central in the writings of another Northern Sung scholar-official, Lu Tien (1042–1102). Like Li Kou, Lu Tien was an accomplished scholar and an expert on ritual. He was from Yüeh-chou (in modern Chekiang) and held high office at court, punctuated by demotions to the provinces due to the factional struggles of the eleventh century.[91] In several of his twenty inscriptions for women, Lu Tien tells us that a wife took over household management and relieved her husband of this burden. In one case he writes that when a Madam Chiang's father- and mother-in-law died, her husband relied on her to supervise the household (*ching-li ch'i chia*). She organized the outdoor bondservants to do spring planting and the indoor maids to weave cloth, all in a timely manner. Another woman relieved her husband of any concerns about the family after he retired, so he could concentrate on "outside affairs" (*wai-shih*).[92] Lu Tien writes of his mother's sister that she similarly saved her husband from worries about the household after he retired, by taking over "all big and small matters of the family." These included arranging marriages and buying tomb lands (some with her

89 From 1032 to 1044, between the ages of 23 and 35, Li wrote several works on the *Chou-li* that sought to use ancient institutions and rituals to improve state finances and strengthen the army. For this reason he is sometimes seen as an influence on Wang An-shih, and thus in Wang's "school," but his thought is hard to place. He shared the concerns of later Learning of the Way reformers in his opposition to Buddhism (which he thought undermined human relations and the authority of the state), his desire to realize the ancient *tao* in the present world, and his emphasis on morality and social duty. See S. Ueda, "Li Kou," in *Sung Biographies*, ed. Herbert Franke, 574–5; SYHA 3:155ff; *Sung shih*, 432:12839–42. See also discussion in Bol, "*This Culture of Ours*," 185–6, 370 n. 133.

90 *Chih-chiang chi*, 30:9b–10b, 14b–15b; 31:1a–2a. Four of Li Kou's seven inscriptions for women make explicit reference to them managing the family enterprise. Two of these were for widows.

91 Helmolt Vittinghoff, "Lu Tien," in *Sung Biographies*, ed. Herbert Franke, II, 687–91; SYHA 98:3258; *Sung shih*, 343:10917. He was associated with Wang An-shih's reform party and insisted on sacrificing to Wang after his death and giving him proper credit for his achievements, but his stance toward the reforms was neutral at best. He is included in the *Case Studies of Sung and Yüan Confucians (Sung-Yüan hsüeh-an)* as a disciple of Wang An-shih. Wang An-shih was much criticized by the Ch'eng-Chu school, but Lu Tien escaped this censure.

92 *T'ao-shan chi* (TSCC ed.), 16:180; 15:174.

own money). Lu records, "She handled the family very strictly and managed affairs with utmost principle. Even her husband had to submit [to her judgment]. She was indeed an unusual woman."[93]

In another dramatic example of a woman freeing up men from estate management, Lu eulogizes a Miss Chou, from his home county of Shan-yin in Yüeh-chou (modern Chekiang), who was taken into the Fu family as a concubine when she was twenty-six years old. Lu Tien writes that her hard work, frugality, and decorum eventually won over the principal wife (whom a concubine was supposed to serve), then tells us of the vital part she played in increasing the wealth of the family:

In the K'ang-ting period (1040–1041) the members of the Fu kin group were growing more numerous every day, and Mr. Fu [her master] worried that he did not have adequate resources to support them. He went out of the city to East Lake and there procured 100 *ch'ing* of vacant mountainous land and several hundred *mou* of unused marsh pond land. He exchanged 1,000 pieces of gold for the lands saying, "The fields will be used to cultivate glutinous and non-glutinous rice, and the marshes will be used to grow reeds and rushes." He saw that his sons were still young, and he wanted to encourage them to study to continue the family line for generations, so he asked who could take charge of the lands. His mind settled on Miss Chou, and she agreed with his idea. He was pleased and said, "With your talent, I can indeed entrust this matter to you." Thereafter he often went to the area, but he only handled the essential matters while delegating the details to her. Of all the projects that were newly undertaken or modified, three or four out of ten were her ideas. After she had lived there for some time, the enterprise proceeded in due order. Year by year there was surplus income, and Mr. Fu did not have to worry about caring for his household. It was indeed because of Miss Chou's assistance. In the Ch'ing-li period (1041–1048) the principal wife passed away, and during Huang-yu (1049–1053) so did her husband. Miss Chou continued to live in the mountains for another ten or more years. When the clan members (*tsu-jen*) divided the property, Miss Chou was an old woman with white hair, and she finally returned to the [main] household. She [now] dismissed financial matters and recited Buddhist sutras for the rest of her days.[94]

The inscription goes on to describe how she encouraged the two sons born to her to study to be gentlemen highly regarded in the local community, rather than to pass the exams, and how she gave them the contents of her trousseau for this purpose.[95]

---

93 *T'ao-shan chi*, 16:182.   94 *T'ao-shan chi*, 16:185–6.

95 It is noteworthy that a secondary wife (concubine) had a "trousseau." Evidently she came into the household with a few belongings of her own, which suggests that the difference in property holding between the first wife and the secondary wives was primarily a matter of degree. Cf. Patricia Ebrey, "Concubines in Sung China," *Journal of Family History* 11 (1986): 1–24.

We find scattered references to this theme of women taking over the financial affairs of a household to release husbands and sons for outside pursuits in inscriptions of the Northern Sung,[96] but the theme becomes far more common in the Southern Sung. In particular, Chu Hsi and his followers adopted it and popularized it for the generations after them.

Chu Hsi and Women's Roles in the Household

Chu Hsi's writings on women stress the importance of household management. In almost every one of the seventeen funerary inscriptions he wrote for women, he made some mention of their handling of household affairs. The only exceptions were for two women who died young.[97] As a bride, a young woman was called on foremost to serve her mother- and father-in-law and participate in ancestral sacrifices. Service to the living and the dead was a new wife's principal responsibility, and Chu Hsi makes this clear in his eulogies for women and his promotion of family rituals.[98] Maintaining the ancestral cult lasted for a woman's married life, but as she got older and her mother-in-law aged or died, a wife moved into the position of inner manager, which gave her authority over the family property.

Following Northern Sung models, Chu Hsi praised women for making do with limited resources. Chu raised the concept of frugality to a near obsession, to avoid the hint of any pursuit of profit.[99] Men were forbid-

96 In a comprehensive survey of Northern Sung funerary inscriptions for women, Liu Ching-chen found 560 by 76 authors (compared with 1,467 for men by 95 authors). In addition to some of the examples I have discussed here, Liu cites single examples of women freeing men for study in works by Hsieh I (d. 1113), Chao Ting-ch'en (b. 1070, c.s. 1091), Li Hsin (d. after 1123), Ch'ao Yüeh-chih (1059–1129), and Huang T'ing-chien (1045–1105). Liu independently identifies the examples of Li Kou and Lu Tien that I have singled out here to be the most compelling. (My own survey of Northern Sung chose 19 prominent authors and covered 171 inscriptions.) In an examination of 65 Northern Sung inscriptions for men and women, Bossler found 4 examples of women freeing men for study or careers; *Powerful Relations*, 245 n. 42.

97 *Chu Wen-kung wen-chi*, 93:1a, 92:28a. The first was Chu Hsi's daughter, who died unmarried at age 15 *sui*. The other died at 27 *sui*, before being in a position to take over the household.

98 All of Chu's eulogies speak of performing sacrifices, sometimes under difficult circumstances; e.g., *Chu Wen-kung wen-chi*, 90:13b, 92:14a. Chu praised women for catering to the strictest and most finicky mothers-in-law; e.g., *Chu Wen-kung wen-chi*, 92:13a–b. For more discussion, see Birge, "Chu Hsi and Women's Education," 335–48.

99 The condemnation of profit seeking was part of the doctrine of the Confucian revival from its very beginnings in the T'ang. In the Sung, it was inherent in the idea that one needed to study for self-perfection, not for success in the examinations or pursuit of office. See for instance Wm. Theodore de Bary, "A Reappraisal of Neo-Confucianism," in *Studies in Chinese Thought*, ed. Arthur Wright (Chicago: University of Chicago Press, 1953), 85–6.

den to think of seeking increased income, so that household needs could only be met by reducing expenses. The burden fell on women, and Chu Hsi illustrated this duty by examples of self deprivation. It was especially commendable for a woman to continue to live with spartan simplicity after a household had become wealthy. For example, the wife of an official, née Kuan, entered her husband's house when he had been demoted and lived in "extreme poverty," with virtually no possessions. Later her husband reached highest office at court and was showered with titles, but: "What she allowed herself to eat, drink, and live on was no different from former days."[100] Another woman was commended for wearing the same simple, ceremonial robes that came in her trousseau for her whole life, even after her husband's rank would have allowed her to wear more extravagant costume.[101]

Going beyond mere frugality, Chu Hsi makes clear that household management included acting as family bursar. In his portrayal of model women described in funerary inscriptions, Chu shows us that some women assisted their husbands in supervising the home. But even better was for wives to take on total responsibility for household finances to relieve their husbands of the burden. Best of all, they would spare their husbands any worry over money by keeping them in the dark about the true financial status of the household. One woman named Hsü had to scrounge to cover her husband's entertaining expenses, while he supposedly remained unaware of the difficult situation:

Mr. Chang's family previously had abundant wealth, and he loved to entertain guests. In his middle years, when the family became in want and constrained, he was not the least bit troubled. When old friends came to the door, he always ordered the kitchen to prepare delicacies, and together with his guests would enjoy drinking as in former times. When he housed guests in his home, he did not mind if they stayed ten days or a month. His wife [Madam Hsü] economized with her clothes and food in order to provide the [needed] money, and never expressed any difficulty. She did not let Mr. Chang know that things were different from before.[102]

In another example, a woman's husband was said to be "genial and easy-going"; and "did not consider matters of the family and the property to be his business." His wife took care of the household, sparing him any worries.[103] One wife's efforts allowed her husband to devote himself to duties of office without worrying about income, while another talked her husband out of accepting questionable payments and later

---

100 *Chu Wen-kung wen-chi*, 92:8a–b.   101 *Chu Wen-kung wen-chi*, 90:15b.
102 *Chu Wen-kung wen-chi*, 91:26a. It should be noted that entertaining guests generously was thought to be required of a gentleman.
103 *Chu Wen-kung wen-chi*, 93:25a.

convinced him to refuse office entirely, both times reassuring him that the family had no financial need.[104]

These examples show how women managed the household while their husbands were living. The need for competent financial management was even stronger when a woman was widowed and herself became the formal head of the household. In such cases women had direct control of the household purse strings. In contrast to Wang An-shih or Ssu-ma Kuang, Chu Hsi does not linger over widows' seclusion, but calls on them to support the family by exercising authority over all aspects of the household enterprise.[105] One good example is Madam Shao (1113–1183), who was married to Shih Ju-i (1110–1174), a strict disciplinarian who established detailed rules of behavior for family members and servants. When he died, she copied out the rules on a screen and insisted that they be followed to the letter. The first rule admonished all children not to disobey the family rules. The second commanded that at the sound of a wooden gong at dawn everyone line up in the main hall in order of age, and bow. The third stated:

> The comings and goings of men and women, all income and expenditure of money and property, all procurement and dismissal of servants and maids must be reported to the head of the family [i.e., Madam Shao].[106]

In the fourth rule, Madam Shao forbade wives from accumulating private property; she was clearly mistress of the household economy.[107]

A second example is a Madam Lü (1122–1177), from Chu Hsi's home county of Chien-yang. As a girl she had had to care for her younger siblings when her mother died. After her marriage she was widowed with three sons. Her mother-in-law had died previously and soon afterward both her father and her father-in-law died, leaving her alone to take care of her own children and her husband's younger siblings. Chu Hsi describes how she vowed to stay a chaste widow with unbreakable determination. Chu also tells in unusual detail how she jealously guarded the money in the household:

---

104 *Chu Wen-kung wen-chi*, 90:19b–21a; 92:3a–4b. The woman in the former example was married to the son of the famous statesman Fan Tsu-yü; Chu Hsi implies that the family suffered hardship after his death because he had not thought to accumulate wealth in office, thanks to his wife.

105 Compare this with the writing of Yüan Ts'ai, who lamented that few widows are competent to handle the family finances and that if they don't have a kinsman to trust matters to, "the usual result is the ruin of the family"; Ebrey, *Family and Property*, 221.

106 *Chu Wen-kung wen-chi*, 90:13a.

107 The fifth and final rule was that maids could not go out of the middle gate without permission, and male servants could not improperly enter the main hall or go into the kitchen. *Chu Wen-kung wen-chi*, 90:12a–13a.

She was careful with income and expenditures, and did not keep even one copper penny for herself. The records and accounts were all in order. No amount large or small ever disappeared. Nevertheless, if anything was missing she would fret about it and not relax for many days.[108]

The reference to records and accounts suggests the household enterprise was large and complex. Chu Hsi further mentions her taking in relatives who were widows and orphans.

Chu Hsi's examples of women managing property extend to activity beyond what one might consider the "domestic domain." He describes some women getting involved in community charity, as in the case of a widow née Shao (1113–1183):

Of the farming households of southeast Ch'ing-chiang (modern Kiangsi), several hundred lived in thatched huts along the river. Periodically the river flooded over them. The people scrambled up buildings and trees to save themselves, but some would be swept away. Madam Shao began to order boats and rice porridge to save them and she came to do it every year. She would store up coffins in advance and dress the bodies of those who died in epidemics. People cherished her kindness.[109]

Chu Hsi's praise of women who exercised authority over property and ruled the household with meticulous attention takes on even greater significance when compared to some of his comments about men. We saw above how in women's inscriptions he praised men who were oblivious to financial circumstances in the household. In inscriptions for men, he commended them for never inquiring about income nor building up the family estate.[110] Moreover, when he did make reference in inscriptions to men managing the household, the context is significant. He sees the responsibilities of running a large household as precluding the work of a scholar.

In a telling example, Chu Hsi describes the predicament of his father-in-law's older brother, who was unable to study because of his duties as head of the household:

Mr. Liu was the oldest of all the brothers. Thus from an early age he had responsibility for the affairs of the household, and because of this, he was not able to study. Nevertheless, his filiality, reverence, trustworthiness, and generosity of themselves surpassed those of other people. The family was honest and poor. In the time of Mr. Liu Shih-chiu, the mouths to feed were multiplying more and

---

108 *Chu Wen-kung wen-chi*, 91:9a.
109 *Chu Wen-kung wen-chi*, 90:13a. Other examples of women giving away money, to relatives or others, are found in *Chu Wen-kung wen-chi*, 92:13b, 14b; 93:27a.
110 See for instance *Chu-tzu wen-chi* (TSCC ed.), 16:546; 17:570, 582, and discussion in Ebrey, *Family and Property*, 46ff.

more. Mr. Liu oversaw the family in every detail, but he never lost the essence [of morality].[111]

Chu Hsi goes on to explain that Liu stayed home all his life to take care of the family, thus allowing his younger brothers "to travel to the four corners" to study. Later in his life, as Chu Hsi tells it, Mr. Liu never stepped beyond the village gate.[112] The burden of managing the family detracted from the higher pursuit of learning in Chu's eyes. Not only does he offer it as the explicit reason why Mr. Liu could not become a scholar like his brothers, but he feels the need to explain that Mr. Liu maintained moral principles even though he was not able to plumb them in deep study of the classics. Here his language is reminiscent of funerary inscriptions for women, whom he describes as moral despite their lack of book learning.

In another case, a Mr. Huang Ch'ung of Shao-wu was a promising student as a child, but again was unable to pursue a scholarly career because of the burden of domestic management:

From when he was a child he studied hard. Each day he memorized 1,000 words, and people said he would bring greatness to his family. But when he grew older, he inherited responsibility for the family's affairs, and from then on could no longer pursue his interests.[113]

Chu Hsi notes that having been stuck at home, Mr. Huang could not attain an official position, contrary to expectation. Only later in his life on account of his sons did he receive a government title.[114] Chu takes pains to tell his readers that Mr. Huang was not preoccupied with money, despite his headship of the family. He writes that Huang entrusted large amounts of money to a neighbor to manage and invest for him, "without asking any questions," and furthermore gave away all his deceased brother's property to his widow.[115]

We can conclude from these examples that Chu Hsi regarded the day-to-day organization of a household as a burden that prevented men from pursuing the ultimate moral path of self-cultivation and scholarship. Ideally, a man needed a strong and intelligent wife who could shoulder the burden of household finances and release him for higher pursuits. Chu Hsi gave high praise to women who showed such ability, even if it was only to allow their husbands to enjoy something as unexalted as drinking with friends without worrying where the money would come from. Not all men had the luxury of such a wife, and such men could be kept from the higher life of scholarship by the burden of domestic duties. Chu Hsi's scenario of honoring women for their property

111 *Chu-tzu wen-chi*, 17:576. 112 *Chu-tzu wen-chi*, 17:576.
113 *Chu-tzu wen-chi*, 17:592. 114 *Chu-tzu wen-chi*, 17:593.
115 *Chu-tzu wen-chi*, 17:592.

management contains the implication that the household was a realm of material concerns and mundane desires that was beneath the true calling of a man. It was best for women to take over the daily concerns of household survival so men could be liberated from the limits these placed on their moral and scholarly development.

The important role of the wife in maintaining the family economy made Chu Hsi and his followers especially concerned about the remarriage of widows. When a man died, his widow was left alone to save the household from disaster. At this juncture, her financial management was vital. She was also left to educate her sons and establish the next generation. Her labor and authority were needed to perpetuate the sacred patrilineal line. Furthermore, a widow had to continue to serve her mother- and father-in-law and carry on sacrifices to the dead. The emphasis in Ch'eng-Chu philosophy on the loyalty of widows had both a material and religious dimension. Remarriage seriously damaged a household by virtue of losing the wife's labor, financial management, and dowry property. Moreover, it upset family relations, destroyed filial piety, and threatened the very existence of the patriline.

Chu Hsi's Contemporaries and Followers

Chu Hsi was not alone in telling of detailed financial management by the women he eulogized. His contemporaries and followers wrote similar anecdotes into their inscriptions for women, some even fuller and more dramatic than Chu's. As with Chu Hsi, themes integral to the larger Confucian agenda appear with great frequency. Frugality was an essential quality for anyone deserving a funerary inscription, and women were nearly always praised for helping educate their sons. Serving one's mother- and father-in-law was universally stressed. These issues will come up in the passages I discuss below, but my sharper focus will be on explicit discussions of the management of money.

Many of the same authors who praised wives for forfeiting their dowries also commended them for skilled financial management to preserve the estate of their husband's family. We saw above how Han Yüan-chi (1118–1187) praised women for their dowry donations. These same women are described by Han as having considerable control over resources in the household. Lady Shang-kuan (1094–1178) entered her husband's family after the death of his parents. Han writes, "she would take stock of the possessions of the household and always prepare [the sacrifices] nobly."[116] As mentioned previously, she purchased tomb lands

---

116 *Nan-chien chia-i kao*, 22:22a (SKCS chen-pen, 22:25a).

for her parents-in-law and built a cloister on them. After the death of her own parents, she built a large house in the prefectural capital of Shao-wu for relatives in her natal family, whom she collected together to live there. Another woman, née Mao, was widowed at twenty-seven and left with seven children – three born to her and four born to the first wife.[117] Han writes: "She remained chaste and no one could dissuade her. She herself managed the lands and buildings in order to preserve the [family] livelihood."[118] Her sons and grandsons subsequently passed the civil service examinations and reached office. Recall that Madam Mao sold her hairpins and earrings to pay for sacrifices to her husband. A wife was to combine her own assets with those of the house, not just manage other people's money. (Han's separate mention of the dowry contribution, however, shows that it was still unusual and worthy of special praise.)

Han Yüan-chi joined Chu Hsi in promoting the image of wives securing financial security for the family while men remained in the dark about daily operations. One example is Madam Li (1104–1177), whose second marriage was to a cousin of Han's father Han Ch'iu (d. 1150), a dedicated official. Han writes:

Her husband had a famous reputation both in the capital and out in the prefectures. He devoted himself to affairs of office and never asked about the resources of the household. Madam Li said, "Managing the household is my occupation." She took what she'd accumulated [from household funds] as well as her own personal dowry property, and used these to buy good land and build a house in Lin-ch'uan, fulfilling the family's intention of establishing a residence there.

One day someone came carrying a sack of rice to deliver to the house. Her husband was surprised and asked her about it. She laughed and said, "This is rent for our household." He thereupon thanked her for being a true help to the family.

Han goes on to say:

Madam Li was skilled at managing the family. She had rules for governing all household matters, large or small. With money and grain she knew when to economize. She relieved relatives, both agnates and affines, according to their needs and relation to the family.[119]

---

117 *Nan-chien chia-i kao*, 22:30b (SKCS chen-pen, 22:34b). She had four stepchildren from the previous wife, two sons and two daughters, and two sons and a daughter of her own. (The SKCS chen-pen edition mistakenly writes that the first wife had "two sons" instead of "sons and daughters two each.")
118 *Nan-chien chia-i kao*, 22:31a (SKCS chen-pen, 22:34b).
119 *Nan-chien chia-i kao*, 22:25a–28a. See also, Ebrey, *Inner Quarters*, 118. It is interesting that Han Yüan-chi tells us that Madam Li was previously married. He names her first husband, Ch'ien Tuan-i, an official, and tells of the marriage of Madam Li's daughter fathered by this man.

Madam Li managed the entire estate herself, collecting rents and handling expenditures. Her multifarious activities included distributing relief to poor relatives and buying and selling land. When her husband died, she bought land for his grave and set up a cloister with three monks to do services for him and his previously deceased mother.[120]

The great Learning of the Way scholar and Chu Hsi collaborator, Lü Tsu-ch'ien (1137–1181), who was also Han Yüan-chi's son-in-law, adopted the same themes in his funerary inscriptions for women. A Madam P'an managed the family according to rules and ritual, serving her blind mother-in-law and aggressively encouraging her sons to study. An impoverished widow née Chou raised her four young sons on only a few dozen *mou* of land and managed to send them to school, never letting them worry about food or fuel.[121] Others helped their husbands, one never tiring of household management even after turning grey.[122]

In keeping with the motif that a woman's efforts released men from household burdens, Lü Tsu-ch'ien quotes a letter from a friend telling how his wife had handled every kind of domestic affair: "I never once asked her about any of it. When I was hungry, I had food to eat; when I was cold, I had clothes to wear; when guests came, I could serve them food and wine. . . . From the time my wife came, I stood by with my hands in my sleeves and only commented when there were problems with the household supervision." When his wife died, he told Lü, he had to retire to tend to the household. Only then did he realize how hard the job was, and he thought of how his wife had toiled at it on his behalf for forty years.[123] Another woman took over household management when her father-in-law died and her mother-in-law was old. Whenever she spoke to her husband she would say, "While father-in-law was still well, how were eminent guests hosted, how were the children educated? You take care of outside affairs and I will handle the inside. We mustn't let anything be diminished from how it was before."[124] Lü Tsu-ch'ien himself married three times, as each of his wives died young.[125] His repeated remarriages may reflect the importance he

---

120 *Nan-chien chia-i kao*, 15:10b ff; 22:25a–28a.   121 *Lü Tung-lai chi*, 7:161, 7:175–6.
122 *Lü Tung-lai chi*, 7:180, 8:198.   123 *Lü Tung-lai chi*, 7:167–8.
124 *Lü Tung-lai chi*, 8: 200–201. Recall that this same woman, née Ch'en, used her dowry "worth several hundred thousand [cash]" to buy books for her sons.
125 *Lü Tung-lai chi*, 7:166–7, 8:193. See also discussion in Tillman, *Confucian Discourse*, 90. Lü was married to two daughters of Han Yüan-chi and to a daughter of Jui Yeh (1114–1172). Both fathers were prominent officials from outside his home area. By Western counting, Lü enjoyed only eight years of matrimony between his three wives.

placed on having a principal wife around to act as the female head of household.

Later followers of Chu Hsi carried on the same tradition of encomiastic discourse. The inscriptions of Wei Liao-weng (1178–1237) provide an example. One woman he eulogized took care of the household while her husband was away studying, keeping up his prohibition on family members accumulating private property.[126] More impressive are his descriptions of women who were widowed. Madam Chiang (1169–1235) was the wife of Chu Hsi's student Li Hsiu-chi (fl. late twelfth century), but was widowed with young children. Through difficult times she raised her own children and those from a first marriage and educated them together with nephews. Wei tells us that when a famine struck in 1229–1230, she ordered the servants to calculate the number of people in the village, and then she sold grain to them at the same price as harvest time, even while the price had more than doubled in neighboring areas. Into old age, she personally supervised every aspect of the household.[127]

Wei Liao-weng's grandmother, Madam Kao, similarly carried out famine relief. While her husband was alive, she lent grain to farmers and helped bereaved villagers. Her greatest challenge came after she was widowed at 51, when famine and unrest struck her home of P'u-chiang, in Szechwan. Wei writes:

In the Spring of 1171 there was a famine. The price of grain rose to 12,000 [cash] per picul. The bodies of the starving lay everywhere, and fighting broke out between the government and the common people. My grandmother fearlessly called together her sons and told them, "People have become desperate. We are fortunate to have food and clothing to last us. How can we bear to sit by watching day and night and not pity these people?" Thereupon she opened the storehouses and gave out the grain. Those who received it came in throngs with their children strapped to their backs. Thus she saved many lives and prevented people from joining the unrest.[128]

As Wei Liao-weng describes to us, managing the household meant preserving the family estate against all kinds of threats, by confronting the dangers of society at that time. The boundary of the "household" was indeed a concept that varied with context. Wei speaks of his grandmother as "closing the door" and living in seclusion after she was widowed, but her seclusion did not prevent her from being a major force in the family and community, with control of substantial resources. Three of Wei's eleven inscriptions are written for women who were second principal wives, married after the death of the first wife. This

126 *Ho-shan chi*, 81:8a–b.   127 *Ho-shan chi*, 87:12a–14b.   128 *Ho-shan chi*, 88:1a–b.

may indicate again how important a wife was in the household. Widows were not to remarry, but widowers were almost required to.

The image created in these inscriptions is one of an authoritative female head of household who managed the finances of even large estates and protected the family from society's dangers. This was coupled with the model of these same wives sacrificing their own personal property and contributing it to these estates, thereby forfeiting the financial independence that their dowries provided them within the family.

A tension existed between the activist role of the female head of household and the subservient role assigned to women by Confucian doctrine in general and the Learning of the Way in particular. This tension did not go unnoticed by Learning of the Way thinkers themselves. Some revealing comments are provided by one of the foremost Learning of the Way interpreters after Chu Hsi, Chen Te-hsiu (1178–1235).

Chen Te-hsiu was from Chien-ning, the home prefecture of Chu Hsi. His precocious talent for learning launched him into an official career early in life (he passed his *chin-shih* at age 21). He gave distinguished service at court and, when periodically out of favor, in his home province of Fukien. Though he was not a direct disciple of Chu Hsi, Chen was recognized in his time as the foremost successor to Chu. He was active in getting the ban on the Ch'eng-Chu school lifted, and he worked tirelessly to promote Chu Hsi's philosophy in the prefectures and at court. Like Chu Hsi, he held the position of "lecturer from the classics mat" and instructed the emperor on the *Great Learning* (*Ta-hsüeh*) in which he "took up where Chu had left off."[129]

During his productive career as a scholar, teacher, and official, Chen Te-hsiu wrote only two funerary inscriptions for women, both toward the end of his life.[130] Both are long and detailed, and he praises both women for contributing their dowries. Chen's second inscription portrays a woman who comes to wield considerable power in the household and community. Chen did not know the woman personally; he claims to have agreed to write her inscription only after being impressed by the biographical essay (*hsing-chuang*) written for her by his older colleague Liu

---

129 de Bary, *Neo-Confucian Orthodoxy*, 86. For more on Chen, see *Sung shih* 437:12957–64; SYHA 81:2695; and Julia Ching, "Chen Te-hsiu," in *Sung Biographies*, ed. Herbert Franke, I, 88. His biographical essay (*hsing-chuang*) was written by fellow Fukienese Liu K'o-chuang; *Hou-ts'un chi*, 168:1a–40b. For the content and significance of his work, see *Neo-Confucian Orthodoxy*, esp. 83–91, 98–126; and Chu Ron-guey, "Chen Te-hsiu and the Classic on Governance," (Ph.D. dissertation, Columbia University, 1988).
130 *Hsi-shan chi*, 45:15a–16b and 45:27a–31b.

Tsai (1166–1239).[131] Liu's essay is extant and provides a valuable comparison.[132] Chen's comments are all the more interesting when we consider that he is creating her image from secondhand accounts. We can see what he chose to include from Liu Tsai's biography (and how he rewords direct quotations), and how he shaped his additional commentary.

Chen's subject, née Ts'ai (1154–1223), became the second wife of Wang Wan-shu (1143–1205) at the age of twenty-six, after the death of his first wife the previous year. Her husband's parents had already passed away at the time, and Madam Ts'ai came to be the powerhouse of a large family, especially after her husband died in 1205. She took in poor, orphaned, and widowed relatives of all ages. She raised and educated her sons and nephews, paying for teachers, presiding over cappings, and arranging marriages. She provided dowries for girls in the family (using her personal funds for her stepdaughter), and even outfitted with dowry a government sing-song girl originally from an official family who had fallen into servitude, so the girl could marry back into an established household. Madam Ts'ai's efforts extended to combatting heterodox cults in the local community and exposing a charlatan midwife who practiced questionable magic.[133]

Before concluding the prose section of the inscription, Chen Te-hsiu felt compelled to comment on the contradiction between Madam Ts'ai's tough-minded initiative (as described by Liu Tsai) and the classical virtues of submission and obedience that were emphasized in Confucian doctrine:

The *Book of Changes (I-ching)* takes the female principle (*k'un*) as the way of a woman, [but] people are only aware of yielding (*jou*) and obedience (*shun*) and that is all. Previous Confucians elaborated on this, saying, "If a woman is not resolute (*chien*), she will not be able to complement (*p'ei*) the male principle

---

131 The woman's son requested the inscription during Chen's second period of impeachment in Ch'üan-chou, before he was recalled to the capital in 1232; *Hsi-shan chi*, 45:27a. Biographical essays were detailed accounts of a person's life usually written soon after death by someone who had been close to the deceased. For men, these usually narrated one's official career, but they were common for women as well, providing in both cases a record from which the more public funerary inscription could be written later.

132 *Man-t'ang chi*, 34:13b–21a.

133 *Hsi-shan chi*, 45:27a–31b. See also *Man-t'ang chi*, 34:13b–21a; 28:1a–5a. Chen Te-hsiu mistakenly gives the husband's surname as Liu. Madam Ts'ai's grandfather was the younger brother of the great Northern Sung statesman and calligrapher Ts'ai Hsiang (1012–1067) from Fukien. Her father died in office in Kwangtung when she was six. Her husband, Wang Wan-shu, came from a family of officials, and by virtue of his father obtained a number of local offices. His highest assignment was prefect of Chi-chou (Kiangsi), but he died before taking up the post; *Man-t'ang chi*, 28:1a–4b. See also Ch'ang Pi-te et al., *Sung-jen chuan-chi tzu-liao so-yin* I, 356.

(*ch'ien*)." Therefore even though the worthy women of old took complaisance, yielding, purity, and kindness (*wan, i, shu, hui*) as fundamental, when it came to their accomplishments, there are some things that even heroic men cannot do. Who can have done these without strength (*kang*) and intelligence (*ming*)? Can one say that women like Madam Ts'ai are not strong and intelligent?[134]

Chen had to explain how women could fit into the classical Confucian model and still take on the challenging roles that he and others of his day endorsed. Chen wanted to temper exhortations of obedience with a call for women to act with courage and strength. In the verse section of the inscription (the *ming*), Chen again juxtaposes terms associated typically with women (obedience, submission, *jou, shun*) with those one might use to describe men (strength and intelligence *kang, ming*):

Use obedience and submission to establish the foundation, use strength and intelligence when extending to action. Only then will a woman's virtue be complete.[135]

Chen found it necessary to explain the apparent contradiction between submission and initiative seen in the life of Madam Ts'ai and others of her kind. Submission to husbands and fathers-in-law was essential, but within their assigned sphere, aggressive and unyielding behavior by women was admired. A woman's relation to property according to Learning of the Way ideals reflected this contradiction. Wives were called on to relinquish their personal assets and thereby lose independence and insurance against mistreatment, but at the same time they were entreated to take on powerful managerial roles that left them mistresses of considerable family assets.

Huang Kan's Enforcement of Learning of the Way Ideals

Chu Hsi and his followers promoted a model of womanly virtue that included a wife's combining her personal property with the communal estate of her marital family and applying herself to enhance that estate. Yet the evidence suggests that Chu Hsi and others still took for granted certain features of Sung law and custom that kept a woman financially separate from her husband's household. For instance, Chu assumed that women had private property and that not all wives, even among his exemplary subjects, would give up their property. In some contexts he also took remarriage for granted or tolerated it as a necessary expedient. In a funerary inscription for one woman, he mentions quite matter-of-factly that she married twice, and he includes in his great anthology

134 *Hsi-shan chi*, 45:30b.   135 *Hsi-shan chi*, 45:31a.

Reflections on Things at Hand a funerary inscription by Ch'eng I where Ch'eng praises his father for arranging the remarriage of his grand niece.[136] While Chu Hsi encouraged behavior that was different from popular custom, as a magistrate he did not intervene with traditional practices and did not press for changes in the law.

Learning of the Way followers in the generation after Chu Hsi, however, took a more aggressive approach to issues of women and property, and began attacking the legal foundation of women's property rights. The most striking example is Chu Hsi's disciple and son-in-law Huang Kan (1152–1221). Huang's attitudes are of importance because, of all of the Learning of the Way philosophers, he was to have the greatest influence in the Yüan dynasty. The Confucianism that came to dominate at court and among officials of the Yüan was Huang Kan's interpretation of the Learning of the Way.[137]

Huang was from Fu-chou, Fukien, but spent time studying at Chu Hsi's academy in Chien-yang. He served in office in various parts of Fukien, and a number of his judicial decisions survive. Huang promoted patriarchal authority and strict patrilineality in both his public and private life. Like other Learning of the Way followers, he was concerned with shoring up agnatic solidarity within the descent group. We do not find him promoting the archaic and idealistic descent-line system; rather, we find Huang concerned with practical issues of how to strengthen his own descent group with realistic methods suitable to the present. One issue of special concern was that of grave sites and grave rites. He believed in graveside sacrifices as an important part of Confucian ritual, and in his own family he worked to preserve a communal graveyard and promote group rites, for which he set up an endowment. He saw women's access to property as a threat to the agnatic descent group. A dispute in his own family over his ancestors' gravelands drove home to him the threat that women's access to property presented to the agnate group, and this may have made him especially critical of laws and practices that protected women's dowry.

---

136 *Chu Wen-kung wen-chi*, 92:9b; Chan, *Reflections on Things at Hand*, 179. When asked about arranging this remarriage, Chu Hsi responded, as recorded in the *Classified Conversations*, "Generally speaking, [widow chastity] should be the case. But people cannot follow that absolutely"; *Chu-tzu yü-lei* (Beijing: Chung-hua shu-chü, 1986), 96:2473 (Vol. 6). In a letter to a friend Chu Hsi again contrasted practicality with principle: "If you look at it from the point of view of custom, it truly seems impracticable, but if you look at it from the point of view of one who knows the classics and understands principle (*li*), then you know one cannot deviate from this [precept of widow chastity]"; *Chu Wen-kung wen-chi*, 26:29a. For more discussion see Birge, "Chu Hsi and Women's Education," 339–40.

137 Chan, "Chu Hsi and Yüan Neo-Confucianism."

The graveyard dispute lasted more than twenty years and involved several lawsuits and appeals to local headmen and lineage elders. In the early thirteenth century, Huang described the prolonged and nasty battle in a final appeal to the authorities.[138] Huang's ancestors, going back three hundred years, he claimed, had founded the graveyard outside the East gate of Fu-chou city and had built a Buddhist shrine on it. Huang's father had converted part of the shrine into a study, but at the behest of his aunt (or possibly his sister, Huang Kan's paternal aunt), had allowed a female cousin to live there with her husband, Chao Kung-heng. They subsequently had twelve children and took over the whole shrine as their living quarters, then began grazing horses on the tomb lands and blocking the path to the sacrifices. Despite court orders against them, the sons even violated the eighteen paces of "sacred space" around the tombs. Confrontations ensued, becoming violent at times. Things got worse when the Chao grandsons knocked down repairs made to the earthen tomb mounds and cut down a bamboo grove shading the graveyard.[139] Reading between the lines, it seems that the Chaos could flout the rulings against them, either because of the influence of low-level officials in the Chao family (which may have been related to the imperial clan), or general squatters' rights.

In his complaint, Huang Kan lamented that affinal ties could not guarantee good relations or respect for ritual:

The sons of Chao Chang-kuan [Kung-heng] were born of a woman of the Huang family herself [i.e., not a concubine]. Thus the tombs are those of their own mother's ancestors. Even if they cannot treat their maternal uncles in a moral way, can they not think of their own mother? If they cannot think of their own mother, what would they not stoop to? They do not respect the laws of the dynasty, they do not obey the injunctions of the lineage head, they do not give consideration to their mother's own relatives. Can this be human?[140]

We do not know the exact outcome of the case, but it seems that Huang's intervention resulted in some redress, for it was after this that he endowed lands to support the communal graveside sacrifices. Significantly, however, Huang was afraid the court might divide the land between the male and female lines. He argued explicitly against this, saying there was already too little space for proper sacrifices, and lamented, "If the area is divided, how could I face my ancestors below?"[141] This would suggest that the female cousin, originally granted use of the study, may have had some inheritance claim to the land it was on.

138 Patricia Ebrey, "Early Stages in the Development of Descent Group Organization," in *Kinship Organization in Late Imperial China*, ed. Ebrey and Watson, 26–7.
139 *Mien-chai chi* (SKCS chen pen ed.), 28:31b–34b.
140 *Mien-chai chi*, 28:34a.   141 *Mien-chai chi*, 28:34b.

Huang's attitudes toward women's property are not revealed in his funerary inscriptions. He wrote six for women, but they are all impersonal and lack detail of dowry or household management (except to praise mothers for educating sons).[142] Huang used the medium to expound on key Learning of the Way issues of filiality, education, and anti-Buddhism. It is likely that Huang Kan did not know any of the women well enough to comment on an issue like dowry donation, but it is also possible that none of his subjects donated her dowry. (Given that Huang's contemporaries continued to note incidents of dowry donations in their inscriptions, it is unlikely that Huang considered it to be routine and therefore omitted it from his eulogies.)

Nevertheless, any lack of expressed opinion about women's property in Huang's funerary inscriptions is more than made up for by a body of written judgments that survives in Huang Kan's collected works. In his legal decisions Huang Kan aggressively applied Learning of the Way ideals, even if this meant reversing decisions by other judges. He minced no words in his harsh opinions and showed little tolerance of traditional practices. He went against established custom and law by insisting that women with children did not have private property rights within marriage.[143] He tried to take away the financial independence that had made remarriage an attractive option for Sung widows and their second husbands.

The following case best illustrates Huang's thinking on women's property and is cited in full. The lawsuit was filed in Lin-chiang prefecture, Kiangsi, in the 1210s, and was being appealed to the Circuit Intendant at Chi-chou prefectural seat (see Map 2 in the Introduction).[144] Huang Kan, who was magistrate of Hsin-kan county in Lin-chiang prefecture, was probably rendering a decision on the Intendant's behalf, which did not have the force of law until confirmed by him.[145]

---

142 See *Mien-chai chi*, 37:20a, 28a; 38:4a, 6b, 35a, 48a.

143 But note that in the case described in Chapter 2 of a woman with no children, whose husband had abandoned her, he ruled that her property stay with her corpse, both in the possession of a previous husband's family.

144 CMC Appendix 2:603–4. *Mien-chai chi*, 33:30b–32a. For dating, see also *Lin-chiang fu chih* (1871 ed.), 16:6b; and *Hsin-kan hsien-chih* (1873 ed.), 6:7b. The cases before and after this one in his collected works are also from Lin-chiang, and several are appeals from Chi-chou; *Mien-chai chi* 33:25b–34b.

145 When a case was appealed to the Judicial Intendant, he would routinely choose some lower level magistrate to render a decision. This lower judge could be outside the prefecture in question, and Huang Kan received several cases from the Judicial Intendant of Kiangsi, located in neighboring Chi-chou prefecture. Huang prefixes his verdict in this case with "*yü*," "I wish" or "I suggest," to indicate the advisory nature of his decision. For a general discussion of these procedures, see Miyazaki Ichisada, "SōGen jidai no hōsei to saiban kikō," in *Ajiashi kenkyū*, Vol. 4 (Kyoto: Dōhōsha, 1975), esp. 194–214. Cf. Gudula Linck, *Zur Sozialgeschichte*, 55–9, esp. 57–8.

The first part of the case, which as usual in written judgments sets out the moral framework of his argument, is a forceful articulation of the orthodox Confucian concept of marriage. The subsequent facts of the case, however, also reveal how these ideal concepts could clash with established practice in the Sung of widows returning to their natal homes. The written judgment is as follows:

> The Hsü family accuses the Ch'en family of taking their
> daughter-in-law and her fields and property.[146]
>
> by Huang Kan

I

When a daughter is born, you want to find her a family. That is to say, you take her husband's family and make it her family. When a woman gets married, you call it "going home" (*kuei*). This means that when she obtains a family to marry into she is obtaining a home to go home to. No one is more important than her husband. No one is more venerable than her mother-in-law. No one is more beloved than her son. These relationships are all alike and cannot be changed. Can feelings change just because a person has died?

II

Madam Ch'en is the wife of Hsü Meng-i. Therefore Hsü Meng-i's home is her home, and she has obtained a place to "go home to." Unfortunately her husband has died. She must take his place to fulfill the purpose of his life, and serve her mother-in-law for the rest of her life. Even if she had no children, she still could not go home her parents. Since she has three daughters and one son, she may still less be permitted to pick them up and return to her father's house. And even less may she abandon them and leave, thereby not serving her mother-in-law herself, and additionally burdening her mother-in-law with her children. Can this be the way of a human being?

Her father gave her lands when he gave her in marriage. This became land of the Hsü family. When her husband bought land and called it her "dowry" (*chuang-lien*), it was also land of the Hsü family. How can the Ch'ens get it into their possession?

If Mr. Hsü had no children, then Madam Ch'en could take her land and claim it to be her own. But since she has four children, she should divide her land among them. How can she take away her land and abandon her children? If indeed Madam Ch'en had such an intention, her father Ch'en Wen-ming and her brother Ch'en Po-hung should have exerted themselves to warn her against such action. How could they allow her to return home and even assist her in being undutiful (*pu i*)?

When I investigated the circumstances of this case, I found that it did not necessarily arise from the ideas of Madam Ch'en. Rather, Ch'en Wen-ming and his

---

146 CMC Appendix 2:603–4. *Mien-chai chi*, 33:30b–32a. I have added roman numerals I, II, III, to indicate the three sections of the case.

son Ch'en Po-hung actually brought the matter up on her behalf. But does not Ch'en Wen-ming have a son and daughter-in-law? If Ch'en Po-hung died and his wife also abandoned her children, burdening his father and mother with them, and taking her property returned home, would not Ch'en Wen-ming file a lawsuit? Madam Ch'en is just a simple wife, and Ch'en Wen-ming is already old. Thus Ch'en Po-hung is surely the guilty party.

III

The prefect Wu Ssu-pu did not investigate the significance of this case. On the contrary, he ruled against Hsü Meng-i's younger brother Hsü Shan-ying, saying that he should not have told his mother to file a suit. This amounts to indulging the undutiful actions of Madam Ch'en. I wish to rule that Ch'en Po-hung be given 60 strokes of the bamboo, and that Madam Ch'en be escorted in custody back to the Hsü household. Furthermore, as for the two *ch'ing*[147] of land, the Hsü family should be allowed to take over its management for their benefit. [Madam Ch'en should] teach her son and marry off her daughters so that they all fulfill their life stations.

Report this to the office of the Judicial Intendant and have the court receive the orders from him. Have the concerned parties submit bonds [to be sure they do not flee while waiting for the verdict].

This case warrants considerable comment. In the introduction Huang Kan uses the double meaning of the word *kuei*, "to marry" or "to go home," to argue that a girl's family was not the one into which she was born but the one into which she married. In this view a woman did not properly belong, even temporarily, to her natal family. Rather, marriage bestowed on a woman her first true home, and her husband's family was her only true family. (Note how this perspective contrasts with Han Yüan-ch'i's (1118–1187) praise for the Lady Shang-kuan, who when widowed took her children back to her own parents and administered their estate.) For Huang Kan, a woman's attachment to her husband's lineage was to be permanent and final.

In Part II of the judgment, Huang peppers his description of the events of the case with his own opinion of how the principals should have behaved. Instead of remarrying, Madam Ch'en should have acted in the place of her deceased husband to "fulfill the purpose" of his life (*tang-t'i ch'i fu chih i*).[148] This was to be done by serving her mother-in-

---

147 The text reads *hsiang* 項, which I take to be a mistake for *ch'ing* 頃. A *ch'ing* was a common unit of land equal to 100 *mou*, or about 33 acres. The term appears frequently in court records.

148 Shiga emphasizes this point. He sees the role of a woman in the family as being to "take the place" of her husband in a legal sense. She preserved the inheritance of her children by acting as a sort of place holder until her sons (natural or adopted) were grown. *Genri*, 415ff.

law, relinquishing her dowry to the household, and providing her husband's family with heirs.

Huang then describes three unacceptable scenarios for widows, and by including them reveals that they must have been quite usual. One was for a widow without children to return to her natal family. Another was for a widow with children to take these back with her to her father's house. The third was for a woman to leave her children behind, "to abandon" them, and return home, thereby forcing her mother-in-law to take care of them. (Ironically, Huang Kan uses the verb *kuei* "to go home" in these three instances to mean "go home to one's natal family," thus contradicting his semantic argument in Part I.) The third offense (that of Madam Ch'en) was the worst, since a daughter-in-law had a duty to raise heirs for her in-laws and to relieve her mother-in-law of any burden in the household. He disregarded the possibility – indeed likelihood – that the in-laws would rather have the children than let them be taken away.

The lines quoted speak to the ritual and reproductive obligations of a wife: to serve her mother-in-law and create progeny to ensure no break in the line of descendants who would perform ancestral sacrifices.[149] The next paragraph, however, speaks to the material patrimony. Here Huang Kan's views were in even more conflict with Sung practice.

Huang Kan states categorically that the dowry a father provided to his daughter belonged to her husband's family ("this land became land of the Hsü family"). Moreover, he describes the situation warned against by Yüan Ts'ai and witnessed by T'ien Shui and other judges, in which a husband purchased land and registered it as an addition to his wife's "dowry." He states that such land also belonged to the husband's common estate and not to the wife *even if it were registered in her name as "dowry."* This line specifically contradicts the statutes in the T'ang and Sung codes, which state that a wife's dowry was *not* part of her husband's estate. Moreover it was precisely these laws that had forced judges like T'ien-shui to allow an "unfaithful" widow to take away property from her husband's son and caused Yüan Ts'ai to warn that a man who purchased land and registered it in his wife's name was liable to lose it. Huang Kan was acting contrary to previous law and custom and was changing the rules of female property rights.

Nevertheless, in the next breath, Huang Kan had to qualify his statement, obviously to accord with the law that was plainly in force. Thus he wrote, "if Mr. Hsü [the husband] had no children, then Madam Ch'en

---

149 Actually, from this perspective, Huang's implication that leaving the children behind is the worst offence seems inconsistent. At least in that case, the husband and in-laws would have heirs, contrary to his first two scenarios.

could take her land and claim it to be her own." In other words, Huang had to acknowledge that a woman's property was legally her own and *could* be taken out of a marriage. It was not "land of the Hsü family" under all circumstances. But he imposed a new condition, namely that it was only her own if she had no children. If she did have children, her property had to be left for them to inherit. Moreover, "her children" were those fathered by her husband, not necessarily those born to her. Even if he had children from another marriage or by a concubine, since the principal wife was technically speaking their "mother," she had to leave them her property. This view was a radical imposition of the same Confucian ideals that T'ien-shui could only lament had rarely been followed in modern times.

With regard to inheritance for children, it is interesting to note that Huang Kan meant girls as well as boys. He ordered Madam Ch'en not to take her fields with her but to leave them to be "divided among her several children" (*fen ch'i chu-tzu*).[150] He tells us in an earlier passage that these "several children" were one son and three daughters.[151] Huang Kan was thinking of inheritance by Madam Ch'en's daughters, and firmly included them in references to family division. The wording of the text also suggests that a wife's dowry could be an important source of endowment for children.

Huang Kan thus supported the basic Sung practices of female inheritance (described in Chapter 2), but he clearly saw women only as conduits for inheritance by others. Rather than holding independent rights to property from her parents, a woman merely conveyed property into a marriage for her husband or *his* children to enjoy. When her husband died, she was to hold her property in trust for his children rather than take it back home or into a second marriage (the way many Sung women did).

Part III of the judgment, the final verdict, further reveals Huang Kan's belief that women were mere conduits of property that was rightly controlled only by males. It also shows his opinion that women were incapable of financial initiative (in this he differed from Chu Hsi). He scolded Madam Ch'en's father and brother for her actions and concluded that she had been put up to taking her property from the Hsü household by her two male relatives. It follows that Huang also placed the blame on the man most likely to benefit from the deal – Madam Ch'en's brother Ch'en Po-hung. Accordingly, this unlucky fellow was given the harshest sentence, sixty blows of the

150 CMC Appendix 2:604.
151 Note that here, as we saw elsewhere, the word *tzu*, "son" or "child," specifically includes girls.

bamboo.[152] The father escaped punishment on account of being old, and Madam Ch'en was ordered back to the Hsü household to live as a model Confucian wife. This meant "teaching her [one] son" and "marrying off her daughters" (presumably complete with dowry). It also meant giving over the management and profits of her land to her in-laws. Note that ownership itself is not mentioned, since the land would have continued to be registered as Madam Ch'en's dowry property. Moreover Madam Ch'en herself was forced to go back to the Hsü household (in custody even). She was *not* being separated from her property or being forced to leave it behind. In the Sung, even Huang Kan maintained some connection between a woman and her property. This was to change in the Yüan.

The last striking point of this case is that Huang was reversing an earlier decision that had gone against the Hsü family in favor of the Ch'ens. County Magistrate Wu Ssu-pu had already ruled that Madam Ch'en had the right to take away her dowry lands and leave her children behind with their father's relatives. He placed blame for the trouble on the Hsü brother for urging his mother to sue (again attributing the initiative to a man). Magistrate Wu's approach was in keeping with many judgments in the *Collected Decisions* and was in accord with contemporary Sung practice. But Huang Kan chose to go against customary practice and accused Magistrate Wu of disregarding deeper principles.[153] Huang wanted to use the legal process to enforce Confucian doctrine that had previously been mostly ignored.

Huang Kan was not entirely alone in his radical approach. Weng Fu (c.s. 1226), a judge from Chien-an county in Chien-ning, took a position similar to Huang's, arguing in a case in the *Collected Decisions* that a woman's dowry was given by her parents to her husband's family and could not be taken away by her if her husband had other heirs.[154] This is in keeping with Huang Kan's ideas but ran counter to other verdicts. It is interesting to note that the judge was from Chien-an, Chu Hsi's hometown and the cradle of Learning of the Way Confucianism. Moreover, the case did not involve dowry per se, but was about a widow who sold some of her husband's land and diverted some of the remainder to her own daughter (by another husband), rather than preserving it all for her stepson. Weng Fu's wording implies that he expected the

---

152 These punishments were routinely reduced in the Sung; 60 blows becoming 13; McKnight, *Law and Order in Sung China*, 335.

153 It should be noted that Huang's cases do not appear in the *Collected Decisions* (they are merely appended to the 1987 edition by the modern editors).

154 CMC 5:141–2. Shiga, *Genri*, 431; Burns, "Private Law," 187. A similar sentiment is expressed in CMC 5:140 by Weng Fu.

husband and wife to merge their property, which should then go to the husband's children, not the wife's.

In another of his written judgments also from Hsin-kan, Kiangsi, Huang Kan seconded the point that a woman's property was conjugal property and should be inherited by her *husband's* children. In this second case, the wife had already died, and Huang wanted all of her husband's children to inherit her dowry, not just the son she bore herself.[155]

A man named Liu Hsia-pang was married to Madam Kuo. He had one son by her, Liu Kung-ch'en, and two others by a concubine, Kung-li and Kung-wu. He owned land taxed at six strings of cash, and his wife had dowry lands that she brought with her (*tzu-sui t'ien*) that were also enough to be taxed at six strings.[156] Liu Hsia-pang and his wife both died, and in 1185 a division was arranged by the eldest brother, Madam Kuo's son Liu Kung-ch'en. He divided his father's estate into three equal portions for himself and his half-brothers, but he kept his mother's dowry lands for himself.[157] (Consistent with the picture I present in Chapter 2, the mother's dowry lands were maintained separately and identified as hers even after her death.) The settlement lasted sixteen years, until the eldest brother died. At that point, in 1201, the widow of one of the younger brothers, Miss Kuo (not to be confused with the mother also named Kuo) and the remaining brother Liu Kung-li sued the eldest brother's two surviving sons for a share of the dowry land. Huang Kan conjectures that the younger siblings had refrained from suing earlier out of fear of their older half-brother, but the results of the suit show that not everyone thought the younger brothers had been wronged.

Over the next few years, the case came to trial *six* times before it reached Huang Kan. It started with a magistrate previous to Huang in Hsin-kan, Kiangsi, and then was repeatedly appealed to judicial offices at the prefectural and circuit level.[158] The six offices that tried the case

---

155 CMC Appendix 2:606; *Mien-chai chi*, 33:34b.
156 Note that the wife's property was equal to the entire estate of the husband.
157 My wording reflects Huang Kan's version that the eldest son was responsible for the division. It is possible, and indeed more probable, that other people were involved, and that the terms were agreed to by all three brothers. Huang Kan suggests later that the younger brothers were intimidated by the eldest into accepting this unequal division.
158 Some of the appeals were heard by judges in Chi-chou, the seat of the neighboring prefecture, where the Judicial Intendant for Kiangsi resided. The case was presumably appealed to the circuit, assigned to a judge in Chi-chou, but eventually tried again in the local county by Huang Kan. This case presents a classic example of the Sung procedure whereby civil cases could be retried virtually ad infinitum. Such cases could not be appealed to the central government, and no court in the provinces had final jurisdiction over them.

came up with three different solutions: two judges for each solution. Two judges said that the sons of the eldest brother, Liu Kung-ch'en, should be able to keep all of the dowry land, not sharing it with the other brothers (according to the original division). Two said that the land should have been divided equally between the three brothers, and that accordingly the two sons had to give up two-thirds of the dowry land to the two plaintiffs. Two more judges opted for a compromise and ruled that the dowry land be divided in half, half being kept by Liu Kung-ch'en's sons and half being shared by their two uncles, the plaintiffs.

The last of the six verdicts (corresponding to the third just described) was delivered by the Military Intendant of the circuit, Mr. Chao.[159] His orders had come down to the county, but not surprisingly the younger Liu brothers had refused to give up any of the property. Under these circumstances, the case came again before the county magistrate, who at this time was Huang Kan. Huang was appalled at the history of the case, and wrote a careful brief that detailed, with his usual eloquence, his views on dowry.

First he spoke "from the legal (*fa*) perspective," arguing that the law on equal division between brothers nowhere stated that the wife's property went only to children she bore herself. He said it could not be used "to set up a separate woman's household" (*pu te li nü-hu*) but rather "should go with the husband's property and thus be treated as his property."[160] As the husband's property, it would be inherited equally by all of the husband's sons.

Second, he argued from the perspective of "principle" (*li*). Since Madam Kuo was the principal wife of Liu Hsia-pang, his sons were her sons.[161] They had to give her filial care while she was alive and mourn her after her death. Thus they were just like her own sons. He noted that even if from the mother's perspective the sons were not from the same womb, from the father's view, they all had his "material essence" (*ch'i*).[162] Thus Huang Kan ruled that the land should be divided equally

159 This judge must be Chao Hsi-i, who was the Military Intendant of Kiangsi circuit from 1209 to 1210, during which time he must have delivered this verdict. See Wu T'ing-hsieh, *Nan-Sung chih-fu nien-piao* (Beijing: Chung-hua shu-chü, 1984), 457; and *Hsi-shan chi*, 45:1a, 4b.
160 CMC Appendix 2:607. This line has been cited to show that women did not separately own property within marriage; see Shiga, *Genri*, 527; Burns, "Private Law," 133ff.
161 There was a legal basis for this perspective. The children of concubines and maids were legally the offspring of the principal wife. Lists of "children" in funerary inscriptions routinely include sons of concubines. For more discussion, see Ebrey, "Concubines in Sung China," esp. 4–5.
162 CMC Appendix 2:607. See Shiga's discussion of the concept of the father providing *ch'i* to his offspring; "Family Property and the Law of Inheritance," 122–4.

among the brothers, just as the father's land was divided. He reiterated the position he took in the case above, that a woman's dowry belonged to the children of her husband, whether or not she had borne them herself. He accused the two judges who had allowed the eldest brother to keep all the property of having the narrow vision of "selfishness" (*ssu*) instead of the broad vision of "public-mindedness" (*kung*). Arming himself with classic Confucian precepts, he said they had failed to promote filial piety and brotherly love and instead were encouraging people to disregard cardinal moral principles. Then came his most telling statement:

When judicial officials decide a case, their job is to change customs by educating people for the good. How can they lead people to be unfilial and unloving, and themselves consider this to be correct?[163]

Here Huang Kan makes his intent explicit. Other judges based their decisions on custom, law, and human feelings. But to Huang Kan, they had followed "the selfish desires of worldly custom" (*shih-su chih ssu-ch'ing*) rather than "the public principles of all under heaven" (*t'ien-hsia chih kung-li*). By doing this, judges had taught people to hold widows and orphans in contempt and disregard the law to their own advantage, as the young Liu brothers had done. Huang was determined to *change* vulgar customs to accord more with the idealistic principles of Confucian teaching. Judges must not follow behind the wishes of the people but must lead them forward on a new path of good. In this way Huang was tacitly acknowledging that he advocated something new with which not all judges would agree. His actions went against general Sung practice and common expectation.

Nevertheless, in the final analysis, Huang made a major concession to previous views and practices. Despite his rhetoric, in his final verdict he did not insist that the dowry land be parceled evenly into three, but only that the last ruling of Military Intendant Chao be carried out. According to this compromise, the dowry land was to be divided into two, half for the eldest brother's heirs and half to be split between the other two brothers or their survivors. He thus still maintained a separate status for the dowry and did not divide it evenly between the three brothers. The plaintiffs had sued to have this order carried out, and Huang Kan dared not push his principles any farther than this. Even though two of six judges had sided with Huang's fundamentalist Confucian opinion, in the end, he too had to make some concessions to the vulgar customs of the Sung.

163 CMC Appendix 2:608.

Conclusion

The Confucian reaction to women's property, as seen in the philosophy of the Learning of the Way, was part of an overall social vision. In the face of unstable economic conditions, men like Ch'eng I and Chu Hsi wanted to reinvigorate patrilineal principles to regenerate morals and reduce financial insecurity. Through lineage-based corporate activities of an economic and ritual nature, Learning of the Way adherents hoped to generate agnatic kin-group solidarity, encourage mutual aid, revive Confucian religious practice, and reinforce gender, age, and social hierarchies. Each individual was called on to contribute his or her part to this system to support the family and contribute to a more moral society in general.

Within this system of strict subordination, women had a vital role in the family, and their sphere of responsibility could extend far beyond the "inner quarters." By taking on the financial management of even large estates, and by thus freeing men to engage in the higher pursuit of learning and social action, women contributed both directly and indirectly to the well-being of the family and the community. We have seen above how accepted activities included keeping accounts, buying or reclaiming land, hiring fieldhands, distributing community and lineage relief, arranging marriages, and educating sons. Within a household, a few women in particular positions could wield considerable power, and this was sanctioned in the writings of Learning of the Way philosophers.

The Sung institutions of women's inheritance and private property in marriage went against the ideals of Learning of the Way Confucianism. Daughters' inheritance took assets away from the patriline and strengthened affinal rather than agnatic ties. Individual property of any kind undermined the Confucian concept of the communal family, where all authority and economic power resided with the family head and where members worked unselfishly for the common good. Sung laws protecting women's property within marriage gave women of the upper classes considerable financial independence and ample incentive to remarry. In Chapter 2 we saw how a judge styled T'ien-shui enforced these laws to the point where a woman's stepson was left destitute and homeless, while she enjoyed her not inconsiderable holdings with a new husband. In contrast, Learning of the Way Confucianism stressed lifelong devotion of a wife to her parents-in-law, children, and stepchildren and loyalty to her husband, before and after his death.

Accordingly, Chu Hsi was opposed to many of the practices of his day. He praised men and women for rejecting property that passed to them from cut-off households and who instead returned it to the agnatic line through posthumously adopted heirs. He and his followers wrote funerary inscriptions lauding wives for donating their dowry property to help their marital families. A virtuous woman would selflessly contribute to funerals, her stepsons' education, her sister-in-law's trousseau, or simply the daily household expenses. Such a wife might also be called on to take over considerable management responsibilities in the household. Widows had an especially important role in supporting and maintaining the family. Widow remarriage posed a threat to the well-being of the lineage: it upset all of the religious, economic, communal, and moral structures of the enterprise.

Nevertheless, even while they promoted these ideals, Chu Hsi and the men of his generation accepted that contemporary practices frequently contradicted them. They took for granted that a wife might receive considerable inheritance from her parents and would enter a marriage with personal property. The fact that they praised women for giving their dowry away shows that such action still constituted a rare virtue worthy of attention. Moreover, the writings of these men reveal that they tolerated widow remarriage and even assumed a widow would keep her property if she left the home of her husband. Some of this tolerance and acceptance of expediency was to change in the generation after Chu Hsi.

In contrast to their predecessors and most of their contemporaries, men like Huang Kan and Weng Fu wanted to put a stop to practices that contravened Confucian teachings. From within the courtroom, Huang promoted a Learning of the Way ideal that represented the far end of an ideological spectrum in the Sung. In this scenario a woman's only legitimate home was that of her husband. Her property, her labor, and her offspring belonged to his family in perpetuity. A man relied on his principal wife to complete his filial obligations and sacred moral duties. Ideally, she gave devoted service to his mother and father in the home, contributed to the family financially with her dowry, and most of all produced offspring to carry on the ritual patriline, then worked to raise and educate these children.

The death of her husband did not reduce a wife's obligations in the household, rather, it made them more essential. The widow alone now had to complete the ritual and material duties of the couple. She alone had to provide heirs and establish them successfully. She might have to adopt a son on behalf of her husband or raise a child of his by a concubine. She would have to see to the education for these children and ensure proper financial support for them, including passing her dowry to them (whether they were her own or not). Within this scheme, widow remarriage was intolerable. For a widow to abandon her mother-in-law, remove her dowry, take children away from the patriline, or leave children behind but remove herself were all transgressions of the highest order that destroyed the foundations of family, society, and the state.

Huang Kan's model was portrayed by later Confucians as an unchanging standard reinforced by centuries of traditional practice and age-old law. This model, however, was not supported by laws in the Sung and before and differed considerably from customary practice in Huang's time. Only toward the end of the Sung, thanks to the efforts of men like Huang Kan, did thinking begin to change and judges begin to pay more attention to Confucian principles and their practical application. This in turn set the stage for major changes in the century following the Sung.

4
Transformation of Marriage and Property Law in the Yüan

Whereas Huang Kan and other adherents of the Learning of the Way in the Southern Sung objected to the strong rights to property that Sung women enjoyed, it is unlikely that Huang's ideas would have seriously affected women's property rights, had it not been for the upheaval of the Mongol conquest of North and then South China in the thirteenth century. This historic event exposed the Chinese to the very different social practices of Mongols and other non-Han peoples, and challenged fundamental moral and legal principles governing marriage and the family. In the space of a century after Huang Kan's death, from the 1230s to the 1330s, laws and practices concerning women, marriage, and property changed dramatically. Under the Yüan dynasty the confrontation between Mongol and Chinese civilization ironically created the conditions for the adoption of laws supporting many of the ideas of Huang Kan and the Chu Hsi school, that redefined women's places in the family and changed women's relation to property. Huang Kan's three admonitions to widows: (1) to stay chaste; (2) to stay and serve in the husband's household; and (3) to relinquish control of personal property, all gained legal support for the first time. The pages below will demonstrate that this resulted not from direct Mongol influence, but from a complicated interplay between indigenous Chinese controversies, described in the previous chapters, and Mongol efforts to preserve and adapt their laws and customs while effectively governing a multiethnic society. In essence, the Mongol conquest, by challenging fundamental Chinese assumptions governing marriage, property, and personal autonomy, opened up an opportunity for the Learning of the Way school to promote its radical agenda.

Marriage and the Levirate in Mongol and Chinese Society

The clash of cultures between the Chinese and the Mongols was profound. The Mongols were a nomadic people who practiced no fixed agriculture and whose economy operated on the basis of grazing rights rather than any concept of privately owned landed property. Although individual families differed in their wealth and economic well-being, no strict sense of social class divided camps or tribes. Daughters did not receive much dowry when they married. Rather, among both rich and poor a system of brideprice operated, where the prospective groom purchased the bride from her family, often at high cost.[1] If he could not afford the price, he might work for the bride's father in her home for a number of years before returning with his bride to his own camp.[2] Mongol men could have multiple wives, while Chinese men could have concubines but only one legal wife.

This dichotomy between a social structure based on fixed agriculture with a dowry system and a nomadic one dominated by brideprice represents the basic two-part distinction between the Eurasian model of production and the African as described by Jack Goody. Goody has argued that in contrast to Eurasia, which includes China and India, African and nomadic societies dependent on grazing or shifting (rather then fixed) agriculture display minimal class stratification, little or no concept of private land rights, the operation of brideprice, and polygyny. These same societies lack the institution of dowry, since parents have less need to establish their daughter in a particular social class by means of personal property.[3] This great social and conceptual divide separated the

1 See for instance William Rockhill, trans., *The Journey of William of Rubruck to the Eastern Parts of the World, 1253–55, as Narrated by Himself* (Nendeln, Liechtenstein: Kraus Reprint Ltd., 1967 [orig. London, 1900]), 77. Note Jennifer Holmgren's remarks on the relative absence of dowry among the Mongols, "Observations on Marriage and Inheritance Practices in Early Mongol and Yüan Society, with Particular Reference to the Levirate," *Journal of Asian History* 20:2 (1986): 129–31. For the relative "classlessness" of nomadic society, see John M. Smith, "Mongol and Nomadic Taxation," *Harvard Journal of Asiatic Studies* 30 (1970): esp. 78–9, 83–5.

2 Holmgren, "Observations," 129–31. This practice probably explains the phenomenon of the temporary uxorilocal son-in-law, which came to be practiced by Chinese during the Yüan (in contrast to the traditional Chinese practice of permanent uxorilocal marriage), and which was the source of many lawsuits. Holmgren argues convincingly that Chinggis khan had to work for his father-in-law to pay for his first wife Börte; "Observations," 133–4.

3 See, e.g., Goody, *Oriental*, esp. chs. 1 and 16; and Goody, "Inheritance, Property and Women: Some Comparative Considerations," in *Family and Inheritance: Rural Society in Western Europe, 1200–1800*, ed. Jack Goody, Joan Thirsk, and E. P. Thompson (Cambridge: Cambridge University Press, 1976), 10–12.

Map 4. The borders of the Yüan empire superimposed on the provinces of modern China.

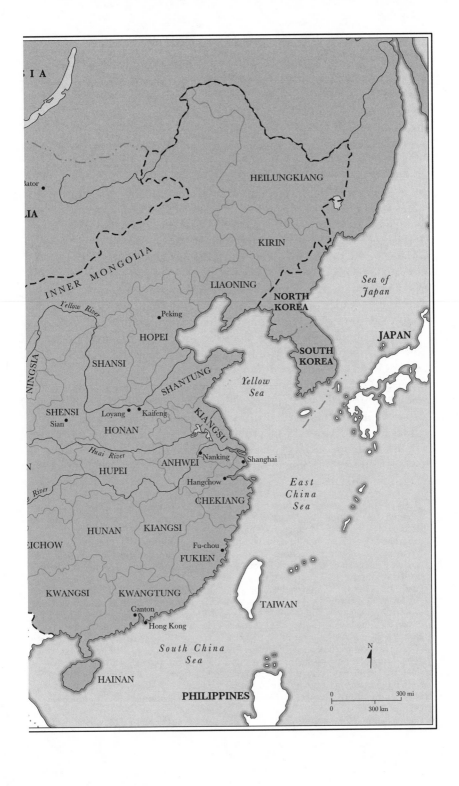

 S I A

Bator

LIA

HEILUNGKIANG

INNER MONGOLIA

KIRIN

LIAONING

NORTH
KOREA

Sea of
Japan

NINGSIA

Yellow River

Peking

HOPEI

SHANSI

SHANTUNG

SOUTH
KOREA

JAPAN

Yellow
Sea

SHENSI

Sian

Loyang   Kaifeng

HONAN

KIANGSU

Huai River

HUPEI

River

ANHWEI   Nanking   Shanghai

Hangchow

CHEKIANG

East
China
Sea

ICHOW

HUNAN   KIANGSI

Fu-chou

FUKIEN

KWANGSI   KWANGTUNG

Canton

Hong Kong

TAIWAN

South China
Sea

N

HAINAN

PHILIPPINES

0   300 mi
0   300 km

Mongols from the Chinese, and it generated a clash of cultures with remarkable consequences for the marriage and property regime of Chinese society.

In addition to being purchased with brideprice, Mongol wives could also be obtained by capture or inheritance, another common characteristic of nomadic societies.[4] The capture of women in battle or through raids was routine among the Mongols. Chinggis khan's own mother Hö'elun was captured from the Merkit man Chiledu as he brought her home as a new bride. In retaliation, the Merkits raided the camp of the young and fatherless Chinggis and captured his new wife, Börte. Chinggis managed to recover Börte later in a major campaign against the Merkits.[5]

Marriage by inheritance entailed a man obtaining the widow of an older male relative. Such practice is called the levirate, and the man the levir. The levirate operated most often in the case of a younger brother inheriting his older brother's widow, but it could also operate across generations: a son could inherit his father's wives (other than his own mother), a nephew his uncle's widow, and so forth. The levirate had an important function in the Mongol household, especially in poorer families. It saved the cost of additional brideprice for the wives of younger males, and it kept the woman herself in the household with her badly needed labor.[6] The woman's productive and reproductive labor were both essential to the survival of most Mongol families. When Chinese argued for the levirate in the Yüan dynasty, they often cited these two benefits. In steppe society it was also beneficial to the woman to stay with her husband's camp. She could not survive on her own, and returning

---

4 Herbert Franke, "Women under the Dynasties of Conquest," in *La Donna Nella Cina Imperiale e Nella Cina Repubblicana*, ed. Lionello Lanciotti (Florence: Leo S. Olschki Editore, 1980), 36–7. Holmgren, "Observations," 144–5. Marriage by abduction and inheritance is typically part of a system of brideprice or bridewealth. For other societies, see for instance Renée Hirschon, "Introduction," in *Women and Property – Women as Property*, ed. Renée Hirschon (New York: St. Martin's Press, 1984), 13–14, and related essays in that volume.

5 Paul Ratchnevsky, Thomas Haining trans., *Genghis Khan: His Life and Legacy* (Oxford: Blackwell, 1991), 15, 34–7. Morris Rossabi, "Khubilai Khan and the Women in His Family," in *Studia Sino-Mongolica: Festschrift für Herbert Franke* (Wiesbaden: Franz Steiner Verlag, 1979), 157. These episodes are all from the *Secret History*, chs. 54–6, 99–102; see Francis Cleaves, trans., *The Secret History of the Mongols* (Cambridge, Mass.: Harvard University Press, 1982), 12–13, 34–6. The evidence suggests that Börte was pregnant by the time she was recaptured. Although this cast a shadow over the paternity of Chinggis's first son Jochi, he and his sons were considered legitimate offspring of Chinggis khan and received domains comparable to the khan's other sons (though Jochi's situation was not without tension); Ratchnevsky, *Genghis*, 34–7.

6 Yang I, "Shuo Yüan-tai te shou-chi hun," *Yüan-shih lun-ts'ung*, no. 5 (1993): 273–4.

to the camp of her natal family was not always feasible.[7] Moreover, purchase from her parents or capture in battle weakened (or even severed) her links to her natal family, and the general absence of property from the wife's family further eroded any lasting cause for intervention on their part.[8]

Marriage by purchase, capture, and inheritance gives the impression that Mongol women were treated like chattel. But the picture is more complex, and by many standards Mongol women enjoyed more freedom and higher status than their Chinese counterparts. The wives of leaders, whether purchased or captured, were highly respected and openly involved in political decisions. Princesses as well as princes and tribal leaders were included in the *khuriltai*, the council of leaders that elected the khan and made major governmental decisions on the steppe. Under nomadic conditions, a woman had to run the family camp and look after the herds while her husband was off on hunting or military expeditions, and a provision for this was included in the *jasagh*, Chinggis khan's early law code.[9] The tradition of a wife acting in her husband's place extended to a widow's position after her husband's death. In the absence of a levir, widows managed the household until the eldest son was in a position to do so, and in the royal family senior widows ruled the empire at times as regents, until the next khaghan could be elected by a *khuriltai*. The most notable of these were Töregene, who ruled from 1241 to 1246 in the name of her deceased husband Ögödei, and Oghul Khaimish, who ruled for Güyüg from 1249 to 1251.[10] Such women did not usually

---

7 Sugiyama Masaaki notes that widows may not always have had conjugal relations with male relatives to whom they were technically married in a levirate union (personal communication, April 1995).

8 Rossabi, "Khubilai and the Women," 153–4; Holmgren, "Observations," esp. 129–31, 151–69, 177–9. As Holmgren explains, Mongol women did sometimes get gifts or other assets from their parents, but in general brideprice greatly outweighed these ("Observations," 129–30).

9 Valentin Riasanovsky, *Fundamental Principles of Mongol Law* (Indiana University Publications, Uralic and Altaic Series, Vol. 43, 1965), 84, 153; Franke, "Women under the Dynasties of Conquest," 36; Rossabi, "Khubilai and the Women," 154. An example of the power of the Chinggisid princesses is seen by a seal issued to the commander-in-chief of Hopei in the early thirteenth century by Chinggis khan's third daughter, Alakha-beki, then acting as "Princess Regent"; see Adam Kessler, *Empires beyond the Great Wall: The Heritage of Genghis Khan* (Los Angeles: Natural History Museum of Los Angeles County, 1993), 156–7 and Figure 99; and Ting Hsüeh-yün, "Chien-kuo kung-chu t'ung-yin yü Wang-ku pu i-tsun," *Nei-Meng-ku wen-wu k'ao-ku* 3 (1984), pp. 103–8.

10 Thomas Allsen, "The Rise of the Mongolian Empire and Mongolian Rule in North China," ch. 4 in *The Cambridge History of China*, Vol. 6, *Alien Regimes and Border States, 907–1368*, ed. Herbert Franke and Denis Twitchett (Cambridge: Cambridge University Press, 1994), 382–4, 389–90; Morris Rossabi, *Khubilai Khan: His Life and Times* (Berkeley: University of California Press, 1988), 17–20; Rossabi, "Khubilai and the Women," 162–6; Franke, "Women under the Dynasties of Conquest," 37.

remarry at all, preferring their freedom as widows. When they did join levirate unions, it was usually for political alliance to solidify a transfer of leadership.[11]

The inconsistent operation of the levirate among elite and nonelite women highlights differences in wealth and status that emerged especially after the rise of Chinggis khan and the tension between control over people and control over property in Mongol society. High-status women seem to have been able to resist levirate marriages. They typically remained celibate and headed independent taxable households, retaining control of their own and their husbands' property. The empress regents represent the pinnacle of this group, but wealthy women generally enjoyed similar options. In very poor families, a widow might be ejected as one more mouth to feed. By contrast, the levirate was most important for middle-level households.

As mentioned above, unlike Chinese women, Mongol women left their natal homes without receiving significant property from their parents. A Mongol wife, however, obtained personal property after her marriage, granted to her from her husband's estate. Like a Chinese bride's dowry, this remained her own for the rest of her lifetime.[12] Adult sons were given a portion of the father's property when they married and established separate residences.[13] The youngest son traditionally remained at home and inherited what was left after both his father and mother had died. When a man died, his widow took over his remaining property and managed it with her own. Since the husband's assets had long been detached from those of his parents, the widow easily controlled them. The widow herself, though, was a legitimate object of inheritance, and control over the widow, in the form of levirate marriage, was considered essential by the majority of Mongol households. The levirate kept the assets of the extended family together and ensured that the youngest son was not disinherited by his mother's remarriage to an outsider. Indeed, remarriage to a man outside of the husband's family, common among Chinese women, seems to have been almost unheard of in Mongol society among any but the poorest families.[14]

11 Holmgren, "Observations," 157–67.
12 Holmgren, "Observations," 130–1 and 152. It is not clear just when a Mongol bride received personal property, probably not until the birth of a son.
13 Separate residence of adult sons was practiced by other steppe peoples as well. The law code of the Jurchen Chin dynasty, the T'ai-ho code, includes a provision allowing for this; Herbert Franke, "The Chin Dynasty," in *The Cambridge History of China*, Vol. 6, 290.
14 Holmgren, "Observations," esp. 151–7. A common explanation for the levirate is that the Mongols believed a husband and wife would be reunited after death. Marriage

The Chinese abhorred the practice of the levirate and considered sexual relations between a widow and any of her husband's relatives to be incest. From early times, Chinese looked on levirate marriage as one of the features that placed the northern nomads outside the boundaries of civilization and distinguished them from the Chinese. Ssu-ma Ch'ien (ca. 145–90 B.C.) described it among the Hsiung-nu, and later histories record the practice among other peoples.[15] The *Secret History of the Mongols* reveals that levirate inheritance by sons and brothers was practiced by the Mongols as much as 200 years before the time of Chinggis khan, and foreign travelers in the twelfth and thirteenth centuries described the practice.[16]

Closely related to the concept of levirate marriage was the idea of a widow remaining in the home of her husband. Though Chinese widows might stay chaste in their husband's household (where they sometimes managed large enterprises) such action was not the rule for any social class in the Sung, despite the admonitions of Huang Kan and other followers of Chu Hsi. Contemporary comments on levirate marriage underscore the fact that most Chinese expected a widow to return to her natal family and found continued residence in the husband's household to be an alien custom linked with the unnatural and immoral act of levirate marriage. A Sung author writing of the Jurchen just after 1138 declared:

It is the custom of the caitiffs (*lu* 虜) to take their wives from another family, but if the husband dies the wife is not ordered to return to her family. Instead, brothers or nephews [of the deceased] are all allowed to become engaged to her. There are even people who have made their stepmother their wife, just like dogs or pigs. With the Chinese this is different because they know that it would be against the law.[17]

outside the family defiled the widow, but levirate marriage did not. See Rossabi, "Khubilai and the Women," 155; Henry Serruys, "Remains of Mongol Customs in China during the Early Ming Period," *Monumenta Serica* 16 (1957): 174. Such a superstition of course coincided well with the economic formation of Mongol families. Keeping with attitudes toward marriage to an outsider, adultery was harshly punished in Mongol society, more so than in Chinese; Rossabi, "Khubilai and the Women," 155; Holmgren, "Observations," 155.

15 *Shih-chi*, 110:2900 (Vol. 9).
16 Hung Chin-fu, "Yüan-tai te shou-chi hun," in *Chung-kuo chin-shih she-hui wen-hua shih lun-wen chi* (Taipei, 1992), 285–8; Christopher Dawson, ed., *The Mongol Mission: Narratives and Letters of the Franciscan Missionaries in Mongolia and China in the Thirteenth and Fourteenth Centuries* (London: Sheed and Ward, 1955), 7; A. C. Moule and Paul Pelliot, trans. and ed., *Marco Polo: The Description of the World* (London, Routledge and Sons, 1938), 170.
17 *Lu-t'ing shih-shih*, in *Shuo-fu* 8:48a (Shanghai, Ku-chi, 1988; p. 173); translated by Franke, in "Jurchen Customary Law and the Chinese Law of the Chin Dynasty," in *State and Law in East Asia: Festschrift Karl Bünger*, ed. Dieter Eikemeier and Herbert Franke

This writer noted that the Mongols practiced exogamy, as did the Chinese, but that it ended with the first marriage. He clearly expected a Chinese widow to return to her natal family (to be "ordered to return to her family"), and considered residence in the husband's household to be inviting immoral sexual relations with the husband's male relatives. Staying in the husband's home and marrying his relatives violated natural principles, was the way of animals, and accordingly was illegal.

More than a century later, one of Khubilai's advisors, Hu Chih-yü (1227–1295) made the same distinction between Mongol culture, where widows stayed in the husband's house to contract a levirate marriage, and Chinese culture, where a widow returned to her natal home. He advocated a dual system where the Mongol "Northerners" followed their own laws and customs and the Chinese followed theirs. He specifically mentioned widow residence and remarriage as an example: "the Northerners [Mongols and other non-Han] should still practice the levirate, the Southerners [Chinese] should still return home [when widowed]."[18] In cases of cross-cultural marriage, he proposed that the ethnic group of the husband take priority.

Levirate marriage vividly illustrates the cultural differences between Mongols and Chinese in the area of marriage, sex, and the family. In the decades of the late thirteenth and early fourteenth centuries these differences came to be reconciled in law and practice, resulting in significant changes in marriage and property law. In particular, widow residence in the husband's home became standard practice for the Chinese, with new property and marriage laws to support it. The sections below document these changes.

Law in the Yüan Dynasty

The major changes in marriage and property law during the Yüan dynasty could almost certainly not have taken place had it not been for the unusual legal situation of that dynasty. Codification of law was undeveloped by the Mongols, and the Yüan dynasty never did adopt a formal law code. This left law open to interpretation in many respects, while the diverse peoples of the Mongol empire borrowed customs from each other. The legal and social conditions of the early Yüan rendered family and marriage law in particular subject to change.

(Wiesbaden: Otto Harrassowitz, 1981), 228; and Franke, "Women under Dynasties of Conquest," 31.

18 *Tzu-shan ta ch'üan-chi* 21:7a–b; as cited in Hung "Yüan-tai," 288.

The development of early Yüan law was closely related to the adoption of a written language for Mongolian. The Mongols had no written language before 1204. When Chinggis khan defeated the Naimans and finally became the undisputed ruler of the Mongolian steppe in 1204, he had a written language developed for Mongolian, based on the Uighur script.[19] His decision was timely, for he soon found it necessary to record his orders and decisions. One reason was the constant quarrels over distribution of rewards after battle. Resentment was especially intense in 1206, when large numbers of subjected peoples were distributed to top generals and the royal family.[20] To prevent further challenges and to govern his widening empire effectively, Chinggis ordered that the distribution of rewards and his other decisions be recorded in a "Blue Register" (Kökö Debter). This collection of precedents and decrees is probably what developed into the body of law and precedent that came to be referred to as the *jasagh*. The extent to which this was a formal code remains in question, but a record of pronouncements by Chinggis khan and other unwritten customary law became the basis for law as it applied to the Mongols in the empire.[21]

When the Mongols invaded north China in the 1230s, they quickly realized that the customary law of the steppe, no matter how augmented by the pronouncements of Chinggis khan, was inadequate to rule the sedentary Chinese. They thus left intact the code of the previous Chin dynasty, the T'ai-ho code (*T'ai-ho lü*), for the Chinese, while keeping Mongol customary law for Mongols and inner Asians. The T'ai-ho code was modeled on the T'ang code and embodied most of the family principles of the T'ang and Sung, though it contained some elements of Jurchen customary law. It was completed in 1201 and formally promulgated in 1202.[22]

---

19 Ratchnevsky, *Genghis Khan*, 94; Allsen, "The Rise of the Mongolian Empire and Mongolian Rule in North China," 345. Some scholars have recently argued that Mongol writing may have developed much earlier than 1204; see Ratchnevsky, *Genghis Khan*, 248 n. 27.

20 His mother Hö'elun is recorded in the *Secret History* as being unhappy with the number of captives she received, and his adopted son Shigi Khutukhu was even more displeased; Ratchnevsky, *Genghis Khan*, 95.

21 The most skeptical view that any written code existed is offered by David Morgan, *The Mongols* (Oxford: Blackwell, 1986), 96–9; for other information, see Valentin Riasanovsky, *Fundamental Principles*, 25–44; Ratchnevsky, *Genghis*, 94–6; Allsen, "The rise of the Mongolian empire," 344–5. The remaining fragments of what was later called the *jasagh* are translated by Riasanovsky, *Fundamental Principles*, 83–91. The so-called *jasagh* addressed military discipline, apportionment of peoples, and criminal punishment for offences like robbery, murder, and adultery.

22 For a complete study of the T'ai-ho code, including comparisons to the T'ang code, see Yeh Ch'ien-chao, *Chin-lü chih yen-chiu* (Taipei: Shang-wu, 1972); (this book is available in Japanese translation by the author, Tokyo, 1980). See also Niida Noboru,

The T'ai-ho code of the Chin operated in China until the end of 1271, when it was abrogated by Khubilai at the same time that he adopted the title Yüan for his dynasty and proclaimed a new era of Chinese-style rule. By declaring the T'ai-ho code invalid, Khubilai caused considerable confusion in the legal realm, for he offered no universal code to replace it. This left his dynasty without any formal law code on which judges could base their decisions. Throughout the Yüan, there was no formal legal code as in other dynasties.

We cannot be certain why Khubilai abolished the T'ai-ho code. The *Yüan shih* (Yüan dynastic history) describes it as being harsh, and implies that the enlightened Mongol rulers were more lenient than their predecessors.[23] There must also have been political considerations. The statesman Hu Chih-yü (1227–1293) articulated this in a memorial when he questioned whether the code of the defeated Chin was appropriate for the new dynasty.[24] By 1271, Khubilai and the khans before him had issued numerous decrees, and it may have been felt that their volume was now sufficient to decide legal cases in future. Wu Ch'eng (1249–1339) stated that Khubilai wanted to set himself as a precedent and abolish previous codes as other new dynasties had done.[25] The change may have been premature, however, for Chinese officials frequently lacked precedents to judge cases and continued to cite the T'ai-ho code.[26] In 1266 Hsü Heng (1209–1281) had advocated the unification of law under a Chinese-style law code but suggested a transition period of thirty years during which Mongol and Chinese law would remain separate. Just four years later Khubilai took the step of unifying the laws by abolishing the Chinese-style Chin code, but he failed to promulgate a new code to replace it.

"Hoppō minzokuhō to Chūgokuhō to no kōshō (1): Kindai keihō kō," in Niida, *Chūgoku hōseishi kenkyū*, Vol. 1: *Keihō*, 453–524. For brief discussions, see Paul Ratchnevsky, *Un Code des Yüan*, Vol. 1 (Paris: Collège de France, Institut des Hautes Etudes Chinoises, 1972–1985), ix–xi; Paul Ch'en, *Chinese Legal Tradition under the Mongols: the Code of 1291 as Reconstructed* (Princeton, N.J.: Princeton University Press, 1979), 11–14; and Franke, "Jurchen Customary Law," 216–17.

23 *Yüan-shih* (Peking: Chung-hua shu-chü, 1976), 102:2603. The text goes on to say that the cutting off of limbs and tatooing of ancient law codes were changed to mere beatings by the Yüan. The Yüan rulers also reduced each grade of beating by three strokes (i.e., 50 to 47, etc.).

24 Ch'en, *Chinese Legal Tradition*, 13.   25 Ch'en, *Chinese Legal Tradition*, 13.

26 In fact, it is only from these later citations that we have any fragments of the T'ai-ho code surviving. See Niida, "Hoppō: Kindai," 459; Yeh Ch'ien-chao, *Chin-lü*, 14–18; Franke, "The Chin Dynasty," 290. See also references to it in the cases cited below.

The absence of a formal code caused considerable concern and consternation on the part of Chinese officials. They issued repeated calls for a definitive code or legal compilation to be issued, on which their decisions could be based.[27] The famous statesman Wang Yün (1227–1304) proposed as early as 1268 that a new code be adopted, and he repeated this proposal in 1292 and 1294.[28] One official, Wei Ch'u, urged that the T'ai-ho code be expunged of Chin customs then updated with decrees and precedents established under Mongol rule to create a new code for the dynasty.[29] A few years later, around 1274, Chao Liang-pi (1217–1286) made a similar request to Khubilai, and in 1283, Ts'ui Yü (d. 1298) made another. A major complaint was that having no code left open the door for bureaucratic corruption and malfeasance, and this concern was intensified during the reign of the finance minister Sangha (1287–1291), who himself blocked regulations against corrupt officials.[30]

In response to these repeated demands, and in recognition of their validity, numerous efforts were made at producing a definitive legal code for the dynasty. Soon after he ascended the throne, Khubilai ordered two top Chinese ministers, Yao Shu (1219–1296) and Shih T'ien-tse (1202–1275), to compile a code. Evidently they made concerted efforts at it, for eleven years later in 1273 we learn that Khubilai read a draft, called the *Ta-Yüan hsin-lü* (New laws of the great Yüan), and submitted it to his Mongolian advisors for revisions.[31] This code was never promulgated (perhaps the Mongolian officials could not yet reconcile themselves to a Chinese-style code), and other attempts at a definitive code proved unsuccessful. Finally, after the purge of Sangha in 1291, the government promulgated a collection of ordinances compiled by Ho Jung-tsu (dates unknown), titled *Chih-yüan hsin-ko* (New statutes of the *chih-yüan* era). This short work in ten sections dealt mainly with administrative matters and official conduct.[32] By imperial command, Ho Jung-tsu made a further attempt at the codification of laws with a work titled *Ta-Yüan lü-ling* (Laws and statutes of the great Yüan), probably submitted to the throne around 1305. Ho's death soon thereafter seems to have prevented it from being promulgated.

---

27 Ch'en, *Chinese Legal Tradition*, xv; Ratchnevsky, *Un Code* I, xi–xii.
28 *Ch'iu-chien wen-chi* (SPTK ed.), 90:3b; Ch'en, *Chinese Legal Tradition*, 8–10.
29 Ch'en, *Chinese Legal Tradition*, 15.　　30 Ch'en, Chinese *Legal Tradition*, 6.
31 Ch'en, *Chinese Legal Tradition*, 14, 15.
32 The 96 remaining fragments of this text are compiled and translated by Paul Ch'en in *Chinese Legal Tradition under the Mongols*; see pp. 16–18 regarding the compilation and promulgation.

By this time, efforts at a formal code were being abandoned. Instead, officials at court turned to compiling imperial decrees and legal precedents, which were the basis for current adjudication. Such a collection of statutes and precedents was issued around the years 1303–1307, titled the *Ta-te tien-chang*.[33] This work does not survive, but one contemporary comment says its punishments were not severe.[34] This collection did not solve the problem, however, for as soon as 1309, ministers in the Secretariat for State Affairs (*Shang-shu sheng*) complained that the law was inconsistent and that rulings were contradictory. They requested that a definitive collection of statutes and precedents be issued:

In our country the lands are vast and the people are many, beyond that of former dynasties. The statutes (*ko*) and precedents (*li*) of previous reigns are inconsistent. Officials who enforce the laws issue light and heavy punishments as they like. We request that the more than 9,000 statutes (*ling*) implemented from the reign of T'ai-tsu [Chinggis khan, i.e., 1206 on] be edited to eliminate the superfluous and render them consistent, and be made into fixed regulations (*ting-chih*).[35]

Earlier, in 1307, there had been a similar request.[36] Emperor Khaishan (Wu-tsung, Külüg khaghan) approved the request of 1309, but died in 1311 before any action was taken. The new emperor, Ayurbarwada (Jen-tsung, Buyantu khaghan), attended to the issue as soon as he acceded to the throne, ordering the Central Secretariat to collect statutes into a unified compilation. He was urged on in this regard by a minister of the Board of Punishments, who complained that the lack of a definitive code allowed official indulgence.[37] These efforts resulted in a text completed in 1316, in three parts: decrees (*chao-chih*), statutes (*t'iao-ko*), and precedents (*tuan-li*), with documents covering the years 1234 to 1316. This was not promulgated until 1321 after further expansion, when it was issued under the title of *Ta-Yüan t'ung-chih* (Comprehensive regulations of the great Yüan).[38] A portion of the statutes section sur-

33 Ch'en, *Chinese Legal Tradition*, 22–3; Uematsu, "Institutions of the Yüan Dynasty and Yüan Society," *Gest Library Journal* 5:1 (Spring 1992): 58. For more discussion of the date of this text and its relation to the later *Yüan tien-chang*, see Niida, *Hōseishi* IV, 189ff.
34 Ch'en, *Chinese Legal Tradition*, 23.
35 *Yüan-shih* 23:516. See also Ch'en, *Chinese Legal Tradition*, 23.
36 *Yüan-shih* 22:492; Ch'en, *Chinese Legal Tradition*, 21–2. Paul Ch'en thinks that this resulted in the compilation of the *Ta-te tien-chang*, and dates the latter to 1307 or after based on this quote. I find no reason to associate these two, and find it more plausible that this request was in response to the inadequacies of the *Ta-te tien-chang*, and together with the 1309 request led to the compilation of the *Ta-Yüan t'ung-chih* or its precursor of 1316. See my discussion below of the *Ta-Yüan t'ung-chih*.
37 Ch'en, *Chinese Legal Tradition*, 23–4.
38 The *Yüan-shih*, 102:2603, states that the *Ta-Yüan t'ung-chih* was based on a text of 1316 called the *Feng-hsien hung-kang*, and most modern scholars have accepted this state-

vives today by the title *T'ung-chih t'iao-ko* (Statutes from the *Comprehensive Regulations*).[39]

At the same time that court sponsored efforts were being made to edit a collection of statutes and precedents, private efforts were getting under way. The result was a voluminous work in 60 *chüan* titled, *Ta-Yüan sheng-cheng kuo-ch'ao tien-chang* [Statutes and precedents of the sacred government of the great Yüan dynasty], or just *Yüan tien-chang* 元典章 (*Statutes and precedents of the Yüan*). The work includes documents from 1260 to 1317, and a supplement includes documents dated as late as 1322.[40] A preface to the supplement says that the *Statutes and Precedents* had circulated for "several years," so it was probably published soon after 1317.[41] A Yüan edition of the work with the supplement appended survives in the Palace Museum of Taipei, and was reprinted in photo-reproduction in 1972.[42]

The production of the *Statutes and Precedents* paralleled efforts at court. A preface to the main work cites a memorial from Kiangsi officials requesting that "statutes and precedents" (*ko li* 格例) be collected and made into a book, to be distributed to local governments.[43] The proliferation of imperial decrees and central government decisions without any systemization was evidently causing hardship for local authorities. We do not know if such a text was ever produced by the central government; the *Ta-te tien-chang* or the *Ta-Yüan t'ung-chih*, mentioned above, may have been in response to such requests. The editors of the *Statutes and Precedents* probably cited this memorial to lend authority to their own efforts. The title was likely modeled on the *Ta-te tien-chang* of ca. 1307, and the content was similar: statutes and precedents collated for ready reference.[44] The terms *tien* 典 and *chang* 章 were more formal terms for

ment. But Paul Ch'en argues that this was probably a separate work, unrelated to the *Ta-Yüan t'ung-chih* and that the *Yüan-shih* is mistaken on this point; *Chinese Legal Tradition*, 24–8.

39 This has been reprinted in punctuated edition, *T'ung-chih t'iao-ko*, ed. and punct. Huang Shih-chien (Hangchou: Che-chiang ku-chi, 1986), and translated into Japanese with full annotation, Kobayashi Takashiro and Okamoto Keiji, eds. *Tsūsei jōkaku no kenkyū yakuchū*, 3 vols. (Tokyo: Kokushohan kōkai, 1964–1976).
40 The supplement is entitled *Ta-Yüan sheng-cheng tien-chang hsin-chi chih-chih t'iao-li* or *Yüan tien-chang hsin-chi* [New collection of statutes and precedents of the Yüan from the *chih-chih* period (1321–1323)], cited hereafter as YTCHC. It must have been issued in 1323, or the very end of 1322.
41 YTCHC kang-mu: 1a.
42 All citations to the *Yüan tien-chang* are to this edition, as reprinted in bound form in 1976 (Taipei: Ku-kung po-wu yüan, 1976). It is cited hereafter as YTC.
43 YTC kang-mu: 1a.
44 Several scholars consider the *Yüan tien-chang* to have been based on the *Ta-te tien-chang*; see for instance Uematsu, "*Institutions of the Yüan*," 58, Ch'en, *Chinese Legal Tradition*, 30. I find no firm evidence for this.

what the Kiangsi officials had asked for in 1303: a collection of "statutes" (*ko*) and "precedents" (*li*).[45]

Many scholars have thought the *Statutes and Precedents* was published under official auspices,[46] but I would suggest this is not the case. The text is a classic commercial production by the printing houses of Chien-yang, Fukien (prefecture of Chien-ning). The pages are crammed with 18 rows to a page, and 28 characters per row. (The supplement raises this to 19 rows of 30 characters each.) The typeface is in a thin, cheap style. The margins display the distinctive black highlights, called *hei-k'ou* (black mouths), seen in Chien-yang commercial productions.[47] (See Figure 5.) The government might have commissioned a work from a commercial publisher in Chien-yang, but the court was separately preparing a similar compilation, the *Ta-Yüan t'ung-chih*. This latter covered the same years (though starting in 1234 rather than 1260), and it seems unlikely that the central government would promulgate two such texts at the same time. Moreover, in 1324, just one year after the *Statutes and Precedents* was republished with its supplement, the new emperor Yesün Temür ordered copies of the *Ta-Yüan t'ung-chih* be distributed to local officials.[48] Had another more up-to-date compilation been produced by the court (namely, the *Statutes and Precedents*), it seems unlikely that the emperor would have overlooked it in this way. The Yüan dynastic history also overlooks the *Statutes and Precedents*: a list of legal compilations of the dynasty found in the dynastic history conspicuously leaves out any mention of the *Statutes and Precedents*.[49]

A comparison of the remaining portions of the *Ta-Yüan t'ung-chih* (now titled the *T'ung-chih t'iao-ko*) with the *Yüan tien-chang* (*Statutes and Precedents*) further confirms the hypothesis that the former was a sort of official version of the latter. The *Ta-Yüan t'ung-chih* entries are heavily edited and always shortened, while the *Statutes and Precedents* appears to

45 Thus my translation of the title as *Statutes and Precedents of the Yüan*, rather than *Institutions of the Yüan*, as has been used by other scholars. In the title of the supplement (*Ta-Yüan sheng-cheng tien-chang, hsin-chi chih-chih t'iao-li*), the term *tien-chang* is parallel to *t'iao-li*, which further suggests the translation "statutes and precedents." (In other contexts, the word *chang* can refer to commentary on the more formal *tien*; or it can mean just a listing of the *tien*.) For the importance of precedents (*li*) as a source of law in the Yüan and their promulgation around the country for this purpose, see Chikusa Masaaki, "Kanseki shihai monjo no kenkyū," *Kyoto daigaku bungakubu kenkyū kuyō* 14 (1973): 30.
46 See, for instance, Ch'en, *Chinese Legal Tradition*, 30–3.
47 I thank Lucille Chia for pointing out many of these features. See Chia, "Printing for Profit."
48 *Yüan-shih*, 29:643; Ch'en, *Chinese Legal Tradition*, 33.
49 *Yüan-shih*, 102:2603. It mentions the *Chih-yüan hsin ko*, the *Feng-hsien hung-kang*, and the *Ta-Yüan t'ung-chih*. The latter, I argue, was an official version of the privately produced *Yüan tien-chang*.

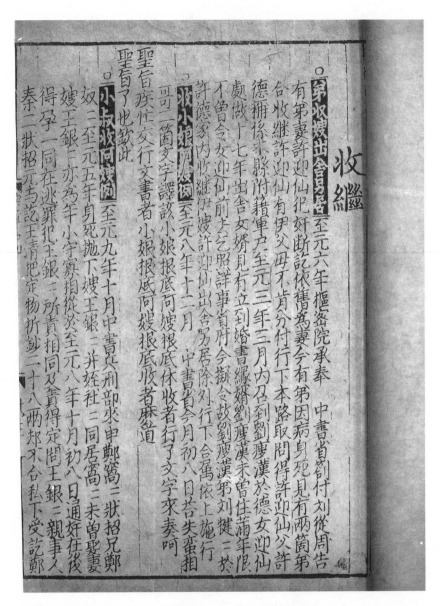

Figure 5. Excerpt from the *Statutes and Precedents of the Yüan*, 1322 edition. The typeface is in a thin, crowded style, typical of Chien-yang commercial productions in the Yüan. (Courtesy of the National Palace Museum, Taipei, Taiwan, Republic of China.)

include complete documents. The *Ta-Yüan t'ung-chih* rulings are more consistent with each other; contradictory rulings by emperors have apparently been cut out. In some cases, the basis of the final verdict is different from that recorded in the *Statutes and Precedents*, evidently to fit more with the agenda of the editors. The *Statutes and Precedents* by contrast reveals changes in policy and inconsistencies over time, suggesting it lacked an official hand in its editing.

If the *Statutes and Precedents* was privately published, where did the documents come from? The contents suggest an answer. The *Statutes and Precedents* appears to consist of a local archive in either Kiangsi or Fukien. Many of the documents are addressed to Yüan-chou circuit (*lu*) in northwest Kiangsi or to local government in Fukien (southern Chiang-che). (See Map 5.) Local yamens kept archives of directives from the court, which served as the precedents for their legal decisions. These were filed according to the ministry that issued them, with the year attached to them for identification.[50] This is in fact the exact format of the *Statutes and Precedents*. The first sections are for decrees (*chao-ling*), sacred government (*sheng-cheng*), court principles (*ch'ao-kang*), and censorate principles (*t'ai-kang*), followed by headings for the six ministries.[51] Within the ministries, the cases are grouped by general topic and chronologically within these topics. Sometimes a case appears under a relevant topic even when it was not judged by the ministry in question. Others might include judgments by more than one ministry. The grouping by subject seems to have taken priority over that of the ministry. Many scholars have assumed that the Kiangsi officials cited in the preface compiled the *Statutes and Precedents*, but it is just as likely that the Fukien publishers included their words only to lend legitimacy to the work.[52] Even the *Ssu-k'u* editors in the Ch'ing dynasty noted that the preface seemed to have little relation to the rest of the work.[53]

An important point about the *Statutes and Precedents* is its general lack of editing or consistent agenda. We find in it contradictory rulings and reversals of policy over time. The complaints in memorials of 1307 and 1309 that the laws were contradictory and inconsistent are well confirmed by the *Statutes and Precedents*. Additionally, the original language of the documents is preserved. This includes three types: documentary Chinese (classical, legal writing), colloquial Chinese, and in places direct

---

50 Uematsu, "*Institutions of the Yüan*" 58.
51 These are Personnel, Revenue, Rites, War, Punishments, and Public Works. For more on these documents, see Tanaka Kenji, "Gentenshō bunsho no kōsei," *Tōyōshi kenkyū* 23:4 (March 1965).
52 I thank Prof. Hung Chin-fu for suggesting this to me.
53 *Ssu-k'u ch'üan-shu ts'ung-mu* (Peking: Chung-hua shu-chü, 1965; reprint 1987), 83:713.

translation from Mongolian, preserving Mongolian syntax. This combination of vulgar and even foreign language incurred the opprobrium of the editors of the *Ssu-k'u ch'üan-shu,* who declined to include it in their great collection.[54] But all of these characteristics make the text especially valuable for us today. The *Statutes and Precedents* was published in the same place as the *Collected Decisions* of the Sung, the main source for my conclusions in Chapter 2. Interestingly, if my hypotheses are correct, they were published under the same conditions and for similar reasons – to satisfy a commercial market. Both may have been collected from a local archive, possibly even the same one. The rest of this chapter explores changes in women's property rights in the Yüan, before marriage and after, as it is revealed in the *Statutes and Precedents* and other texts.

Family Property and Daughters' Inheritance

The financial and military organization of the Yüan state required a reconceptualization of family inheritance that privileged male agnates over daughters. The Yüan government supplied its armies through a system of military households, each of which was required to supply and equip one soldier in perpetuity, and relied on corvée and service obligations, as well as land taxes based on households. Its primary concern was to preserve military households intact to maintain a steady supply of soldiers, but it also needed to preserve civilian households to maintain its tax base. It thus was reluctant to allow households to go extinct, that is, be cut off because of no male heir, and let land go with daughters into other households. To achieve its goals, the Yüan government instituted substantial changes in inheritance law, which coincidentally supported the male patriline to the disadvantage of women. Daughters in cut-off households, married and unmarried, were treated very differently than in the Sung and lost many of the rights they had previously enjoyed. Widowed heads of household who could supply soldiers or other corvée (through payments, etc.), however, retained considerable property rights and household authority.

We do not know how daughters fared in family division vis-à-vis sons. There is no evidence in surviving Yüan records of the half-share rule that operated in the Southern Sung. Evidence for the one-half rule all comes from the South (the only part of China controlled by the Southern Sung), and we do not find it in Chin law in the North. Early Yüan

---

54 *Ssu-k'u ch'üan-shu ts'ung-mu,* 83:713–4. A portion of this entry is translated by Ch'en, 32.

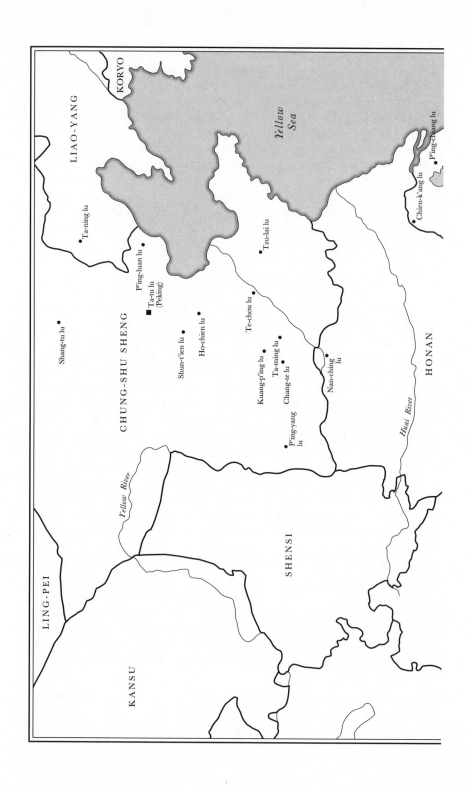

LING-PEI

KANSU

SHENSI

Yellow River

CHUNG-SHU SHENG

LIAO-YANG

KORYO

Yellow Sea

HONAN

Huai River

Ta-ning lu

P'ing-luan lu

Shang-tu lu

Ta-tu lu
(Peking)

Shun-t'ien lu

Ho-chien lu

Tzu-lai lu

Te-chou lu

Kuang-p'ing lu

Ta-ming lu

Chang-te lu

Nan-ching
lu

P'ing-yang
lu

Chien-k'ang lu

P'ing-chang lu

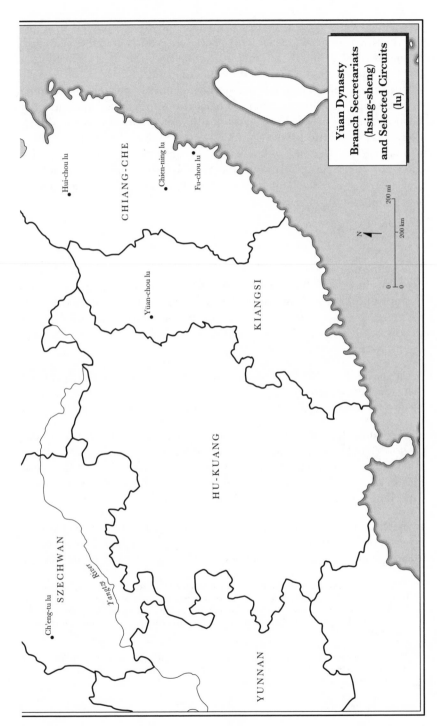

Map 5. Yüan dynasty branch secretariats (*hsing-sheng*) and selected circuits (*lu*).

inheritance law followed that of Chin (except where updated by imperial decree or central government precedent), and since the Yüan government tried to tie inheritance to military service, it is unlikely that
any half-share rule was enforced by the Yüan state.

The sources also lack references to lineage members (*tsu-jen*) stepping
in to establish posthumous heirs. Legislation under the Chin and early
Yüan did not address the issue of posthumous heirs versus daughters'
rights that we saw under the Southern Sung.[55] While daughters in North
China may not have had to battle agnatic relatives for their inheritance,
the tax and military priorities of the Yüan state put them at a disadvantage in other respects and privileged male agnates over daughters, in
sharp contrast to Sung policy.

Inheritance in Cut-off Households

The Yüan state attempted to intervene aggressively in the disposition of
property in cut-off households, even more than the Sung had done.
When Khubilai first came to the throne in 1260 and began to establish
a Chinese-style government, he issued a decree asserting the state's right
to confiscate property if a couple died without heirs. His decree of the
eighth month reads:

In all places, if a person dies [without issue] leaving a cut-off household and
there is no one suitable to inherit, the fields, houses, movable property, servants,
bondsmen, and livestock will all be confiscated by the government.[56]

This edict alone does not tell us what constituted a cut-off household
or how daughters fared in this situation (in fact we only know of this
edict from a quote in a later case), but four years later, in the eighth
month of 1264, Khubilai issued a more detailed decree that stated basic
inheritance rules when no adult heir survived:

PROPERTY OF MINORS AND HOUSEHOLDS WITHOUT HEIRS   In all places, if
a person dies [without issue] leaving a cut-off household, and there is no one
suitable to inherit (namely no children, no brothers' children,[57] or no younger

55 The lack of reference to posthumous heirs in later Yüan sources is more mysterious.
   It is possible that, given the context of other limits on women's property rights in
   Yüan law, described in this chapter, together with an increase in lineage power, daughters were no longer able to fight lineages in court to claim property from posthumous
   male heirs.
56 YTC 19:9a.
57 These two terms are *tzu* and *chih*, sometimes translated as "sons" and "nephews." But
   the text following makes it clear that both males and females are included; thus I have
   translated these as "children" and "brothers' children."

or older brothers), the fields, houses, movable property, servants and bonds-men, and livestock will all be confiscated by the government. The local government will invite in a tenant to rent the land. The harvest and other produce will all be clearly noted and a record submitted to the appropriate higher office, which will in turn report to the Board [of Revenue].

If the deceased leaves behind boys or girls under 10 *sui*, they should be given into the care of trustworthy relatives. Their needs should be calculated and income given to them seasonally. Even if the mother survives, if she invites in a second husband or takes the children and remarries, the extent of the [children's] property should be registered with the authorities. If a son has already married or is 15 or over, all the property should be given to him.[58] If the mother is widowed and the children are young, the mother may not improperly mortgage or sell the fields, houses, or slaves, nor free the bondservants. If there is a legitimate need to sell or mortgage the property, she should report this to the appropriate office, which will investigate and verify the facts and only then approve the transaction.

Respect this.[59]

This edict reveals both similarities and differences from Sung law. First, as in Sung, we see the government attempting to keep land in cultivation and on the tax registers. Khubilai repeats his earlier order to confiscate property with no heir, and he orders that tenants be found to work the land, so it can produce tax revenue for the government. Local authorities in the Yüan, like those in the Sung, were to report the income from such land all the way up to the Board of Revenue in Peking. In the early part of his reign, Khubilai issued repeated orders for imperial relatives and high officials who controlled private appanages to report the taxable households and revenues to the Peking government.[60] The same concern for preventing local appropriation of government income is represented here.

Second, children (especially sons) had to establish a taxable household before they had absolute rights to property. In the Sung, the survival of sons of any age prevented a household from being cut off, and the state did not normally intervene. In a significant change, Khubilai ordered the property of male minors to be put under the management of the state, with only an allowance for maintenance given to the children. If a son married, or when he reached 15, the property would be returned to him, ending the state's use of it. In other words, when no adult or married son

---

58 The line reads *ch'ü* 娶 ("to marry"), a term applied only to men. Other evidence presented below will show that daughters were treated separately. Daughters were included in a reissue of this edict in 1321 (where the line reads *chia-ch'ü*), but with these separate provisions understood; see *Yüan-tai fa-lü tzu-liao chi-ts'un*, ed. Huang Shih-chien (Kiangsu: Chekiang ku-chi ch'u-pan she, 1988), 72.

59 YTC 19:8a.   60 YTC 17:1b–2a.

survived, the household entered a state of being temporarily cut off. Only the presence of an adult or married son (who could support labor obligations), constituted a bonafide household. By the same token, a son might lose rights to property if his mother took him into another marriage or invited in a second husband, thereby eliminating the father's household or combining it with that of another adult male.[61]

Third, the rights of the widow to control property in the name of minor children were similar to those in the Sung. Again, the widow had to maintain a separate tax-paying household to prevent the property from falling into the hands of the authorities. Such households were called "women's households" (*nü-hu*) and owed reduced taxes and corvée, but were not exempt entirely.[62] As in the Sung, a widow could not "improperly" (*fei-li*) sell the land or free the bondservants, but Khubilai's edict allowed some leeway to sell land if local authorities approved.[63]

Fourth and most dramatic, the list of eligible heirs at the beginning includes "younger and older brothers." A ruling of 1278 clarified that brothers could inherit even if the family had divided and they were registered in separate households.[64] In the 1278 case, a man sued his deceased brother's widow and obtained the property from her. Lateral inheritance between brothers, especially after a household had divided, was not allowed in Chinese law of any dynasty.[65] In Confucian doctrine, an heir needed to be of the appropriate generation to perform sacrifices (i.e., one generation below the deceased). The legality of brothers' inheritance under the Yüan no doubt reflected its prevalence in steppe practice.

The policy of allowing brothers to inherit would have kept away from daughters some property that in the Sung they would have received. This may have had the effect of keeping property in the male line, but the

---

61 I follow Yanagida Setsuko in interpreting the reference to registration of the first husband's property to mean virtual confiscation, "Gendai joshi no zaisan shōkei," in *SōGen shakai keizaishi kenkyū* (Tokyo: Sōbunsha, 1995), 266. In Sung law, a household would also be cut off if the mother remarried taking her children with her.

62 Households headed by women were in the reduced-tax category of "auxiliary households" (*hsieh-chi hu*), which included those of the very old, young, or sick; Herbert Schurmann, *Economic Structure of the Yüan Dynasty: Translation of Chapters 93 and 94 of the Yüan shih* (Cambridge, Mass.: Harvard University Press, 1956), 94–5.

63 For more on changes in a widow's control of property, see Bettine Birge, "Women and Confucianism from Song to Ming: the Institutionalization of Patrilineality," in *The Song-Yuan-Ming Transition in Chinese History*, ed. Paul Smith and Richard von Glahn (Berkeley: University of California Press, 2001).

64 YTC 19:9b. The ruling was reissued in 1316; *Yüan-tai fa-lü tzu-liao chi-ts'un*, 71.

65 *T'ang-lü shu-i*, 12:237; SHT 12:193. Exceptions were sometimes made in the Sung (see CMC 8:251–7), but it was never formerly allowed.

reasoning of the Yüan government was to tie property inheritance to military service. This is evident by the fact that even adoption of an agnatic nephew, a routine matter in the Sung, came under government scrutiny and was not automatically allowed from the beginning of the dynasty. A ruling by the Bureau of Military Affairs (*shu-mi yuan*) sometime between 1263 and 1268 allowed a man to make his son the heir to his aging and childless older brother only on the condition that this son take over the military service owed by his uncle. The Board of Revenue[66] under the Central Secretariat extended this to apply to all civilian as well as military households, allowing close agnatic adoption for the purpose of maintaining a tax-paying household, or one providing military service.[67] Another ruling in 1268 cited these earlier decisions to allow a man to inherit the property of his childless uncle.[68] Thus even agnatic adoption revolved around issues of tax revenue and military service. The Confucian, patrilineal principles of Sung law did not automatically apply.

Khubilai's edict of 1264 did not specify what happened if only daughters survived in a cut-off household (except to say that property of daughters under 10, like sons, was administered by the government). Case law over the next few years reveals that the Yüan authorities at both the national and local level struggled with this issue but arrived at a solution whereby a daughter could inherit only if she invited in an uxorilocal husband who could continue the household in her father's name and undertake the military service and other corvée owed. This major break from Sung law and practice is revealed in two cases that generated conflicting rulings and which reveal a lack of clear legal support for daughters' inheritance.

The first case came to court in 1268 and was judged differently by four different offices under repeated reviews. (This is reminiscent of the endless appeals in the Sung, but there the litigants themselves appealed, here the judges sent the case up for review.) Chang Ah-Liu,[69] a woman from Nan-ching circuit (modern Kaifeng) sued to keep her father's property after the death of both her parents. She claimed that in 1242 her late father had invited in Mr. Chang Shih-an to be his "permanent" uxorilocal son-in-law, with whom Ah-Liu had now lived for 28 years [sic]

---

66 At this time the Board of Revenue was part of the Three Ministries of the Left (*tso san-pu*). See David Farquhar, *The Government of China under Mongolian Rule: A Reference Guide* (Stuttgart: Franz Steiner Verlag, 1990), 175.

67 YTC 17:13a; TCTK 3:30.

68 YTC 17:13a.

69 Married women's names in Yüan documents are nearly always in this form, where the first (here, Chang) is her husband's surname, and the second (Liu), following the Ah, is her own family name. I capitalize both since they are both surnames.

as wife. In 1252, the father died, leaving Ah-Liu's mother as head of the household, which was registered in the special category of "woman's household" (*nü-hu*). In 1257 Ah-Liu's mother also died, and in 1263 Ah-Liu was summoned by the authorities for not paying her mother's tax obligation. Matters became even more complicated for Ah-Liu when in 1268 two of her family's bondservants, a man and a woman, filed suit in the same circuit demanding their freedom and claiming also to have rights to her father's land.[70]

The first decision, issued by the Three Ministries of the Left in 1268,[71] went in favor of the bondservants. The Ministries accepted the claim that Ah-Liu's father had intended to free the bondservants and give them his property, and it ordered that except for movable property and Ah-Liu's house, the land and other buildings should all go to the bondservants. (The bondservants would presumably set up a tax-paying household, thus giving the government revenue.) This decision, however, was overturned by the Censorate in a verdict of 1270 or 1271. Without discussing the bondservants, the Censorate came up with a more traditional Chinese solution that kept the property in the family. It noted that though Chang Shih-an was supposed to be a permanent uxorilocal son-in-law to the Lius, in 1252 (the year of his father-in-law's death) Chang was reentered in his own father's household register, and had failed to pay his mother-in-law's taxes after she died in 1257 (recall that Ah-Liu was apprehended for tax evasion in 1263).

Nevertheless, the Censorate accepted that Chang had been living in the Liu household as an uxorilocal son-in-law, despite his registration elsewhere, and thus the household was not technically cut off. Under these conditions, it was not appropriate for the government to "confiscate the property for lack of an heir" or to apply the rule for maintaining orphans (seen in the 1264 edict). The Censorate ordered that the property be divided into three parts. One part would go to Ah-Liu *and* her younger, married sister to be divided evenly between them. The remaining two parts would go to the uxorilocal son-in-law,

---

70 For more on bondservants in the Yüan, see Allsen, "The rise of the Mongolian empire," 326; Elizabeth Endicott-West, "The Yüan Government and Society," in *The Cambridge History of China*, Vol. 6, 613–14; Tetsuo Ebisawa, "Bondservants in the Yüan," *Acta Asiatica* 45 (1983). Bondservants were often captured in battle (or sometimes kidnapped), and the residents of whole areas could fall into this kind of servitude. Chinese bondservants in particular often tilled the land for Mongol soldiers.

71 The Three Ministries of the Left included the Ministry of Revenue, whose personnel presumably issued this verdict. The decision must have been issued during 1268 because the Three Ministries were abolished later that year.

Chang Shih-an, who was to take on the taxes and labor services of the Liu household.[72]

Note that Ah-Liu and Chang Shih-an were married to each other, and yet the Censorate gave her a portion of property separate from his. This implies that the same separation of property within marriage applied here in the Yüan as it had in the Sung. Additionally, Chang was being treated as a son in the household. In the Sung, a natural or adopted son would have received twice the share of each of his sisters: in this case a division of one-half/one-fourth/one-fourth. If the daughters were married (as they both were in this case) the son would get all. In the Sung, an uxorilocal son-in-law would get nothing beyond the dowry his wife had received (though if there were no natal sons, the couple could obtain additional inheritance). The one-third portion to married daughters here in Ah-Liu's case is reminiscent of the Sung law on rights of married daughters, except that the state's portion went to Chang Shih-an.

Nevertheless, no clear law governed cases like these, and when the newly independent Ministry of Revenue reinvestigated the case, it rejected the Censorate's reasoning. In a decision similar to the earlier one in favor of the bondservants, the Ministry reiterated that Chang Shih-an had been registered in his *own* father's household since 1252 and had paid taxes there. According to an edict on uxorilocal husbands (duly quoted), he did not qualify as an uxorilocal son-in-law and the Liu household was cut off. Following Khubilai's edicts of 1260 and 1264 (which they also quoted), there was no suitable heir and all property was to be confiscated. The bondservants were to be released and set up in tax-paying households (they might have become tenants on the land confiscated by the government).

The decision of the Ministry was passed up to the Secretariat for State Affairs (*Shang-shu sheng*), the highest branch of government at that time, and close to the emperor. The Secretariat came up with a fourth and final verdict. It cited new evidence from the original go-between for Ah-Liu's marriage that, contrary to Ah-Liu's claims, her husband had not explicitly contracted to be a permanent uxorilocal son-in-law. Moreover, in 1252, Chang Shih-an had registered his wife and son in his natal father's household register and had filed the required documents for this change. The Secretariat argued that he thus had no claim to the Liu family property and was not responsible for the Liu taxes and corvée. It ordered that one-third of the property go to the two married daugh-

72 YTC 19:8b.

ters, who were to be liable for taxes on it, and two-thirds be confiscated, including the bondservants. Of the one-third to the daughters, two-thirds was for Ah-Liu and just one-third for her younger sister.[73]

This last verdict corresponded largely with Sung law. The two-thirds/one-third division between the state and the married daughters is the same as it would have been in the Sung, according to the Sung rules for cut-off households. The rejection of any claim by Chang Shih-an also reflects Sung rules that prevented a son-in-law from inheriting (except in rare cases, as explained in Chapter 2). It also points again to the distinction between a married woman's property and that of her husband. Property going to Ah-Liu was not the same as that going to her husband Chang Shih-an. The further division between the two daughters is interesting. Ah-Liu was given twice her sister's portion, perhaps in recognition that she had stayed at home in an uxorilocal marriage.[74]

In this case, Ah-Liu sought all of her father's property on the basis that Chang was his "permanent" uxorilocal son-in-law. A ruling a little later, dated 1273, clarifies that a daughter without brothers could inherit only if she invited in an uxorilocal husband to continue her father's household. In the seventh month of 1273, the Ministry of Revenue received a report from the headman of the civilian population of the appanage of Vice Minister Yeh-lü. Chin Ting, the head of a tax-paying household, and his wife both died, leaving behind a sole daughter of 13 *sui*, named Wang-erh. The estate had considerable land of one *ch'ing* 45 *mou*, which had now gone fallow. The local authorities decided to take charge of the land and remove it from the tax registers. They would rent the land and provide a maintenance allowance to the daughter Wang-erh, as described in the 1264 edict on the care of underage orphans. But the ruling went on to say that when Wang-erh was old enough to marry, they would invite in an uxorilocal husband on her behalf to reestablish a tax-paying household. (The mother before she died had already arranged a marriage for Wang-erh, but this was not recognized because a go-between had not been contracted and the betrothal gifts had not yet been paid.) The Ministry of Revenue agreed with this decision, and it became a precedent.[75]

73 YTC 19:8b–9a.
74 Yanagida Setsuko, in arguing for continuity between Sung and Yüan, has conjectured that the division reflects the Sung rules of division between unmarried and married daughters (making Ah-Liu by analogy "unmarried"), but she agrees that the legal basis for this division is obscure. "Gendai joshi no zaisan shōkei," 268. For a slightly different interpretation of this case (and the situation of uxorilocal husbands generally), see Oshima Ritsuko, "Genchō no 'josei' ni tsuite," *Shiron* 43 (1990), 80.
75 YTC 19:9a–b.

This decision of 1273 implies that Wang-erh would get back all of her father's property once an uxorilocal husband were found for her. It suggests that she would not get the property if she did not marry uxorilocally but instead married into another household. The attempts three years earlier by Ah-Liu to pass her husband off as an uxorilocal son-in-law, even when the whole family resided and was registered elsewhere, suggests that she expected the same conditions to apply to her.

Confirmation of this law, which reconciled the Yüan goal of linking inheritance to taxes and military service performed by males with the inheritance rights of daughters, is found in the *Ta-Yüan t'ung-chih* (*Comprehensive Regulations of the Great Yüan*) completed in 1316 and promulgated in 1321. That states:

When a household is cut off and a minor daughter survives, the authorities are to be notified [to take over the estate]. They will wait until the daughter is grown and invite in a husband to continue the household and assume the tax and corvée obligations.[76]

In the Sung, an unmarried daughter without brothers inherited all of her parent's estate. In such a case, her natal household would cease to exist and the daughter would take the property into her marriage as dowry (whether she married uxorilocally or not). In contrast, the Yüan government strove to preserve every household as a taxable entity with its service obligations, and thus placed limits on a daughter's ability to inherit an estate.[77] The encouragement of uxorilocal marriages, at the expense of a daughter's inheritance and dowry, was just one part of a larger government policy. Under the Yüan, the goal of maintaining independent households that could pay taxes and supply male labor for military service and corvée deprived daughters of property that had been theirs up to that time under Chinese dynasties. A daughter without brothers could now enjoy her father's property only through her husband, when her father's patriline was retrieved through an uxorilocal marriage and his tax and service obligations met.

76 *Yüan-tai fa-lü tzu-liao chi-ts'un*, 71. The reissue of Khubilai's 1264 edict later in the same collection was changed to say property was returned to sons *and* daughters when they married (p. 72). We know this meant when a daughter married uxorilocally.

77 Shiga Shūzō has interpreted this policy on uxorilocal marriage to mean that the Yüan government was more concerned than was the Sung with preserving patrilineal family lines. But I agree with Yanagida Setsuko that the Yüan was more likely merely trying to increase tax revenues; Shiga, *Genri*, 614–15; Yanagida, "Gendai joshi no zaisan shōkei," 268.

Women's Separate Property in Marriage

The legal separation between a wife's property and that of her husband's family was carried over in Chin law and reiterated in the early Yüan in a 1281 ruling, which repeated the traditional Chinese exclusion of a wife's property from family division.[78] (We also saw in the case of Ah-Liu how an interim verdict granted inheritance to Ah-Liu that was separate from that to her husband.) Nevertheless, this case reveals that once again the Yüan government was preoccupied with preserving military households rather than with issues of women's property.

Wang Hsing-tsu from T'ang-yin county, Chang-te circuit (area of modern Anyang; see Map 5), married uxorilocally in 1266 and took on his father-in-law's military service. In this connection, he obtained his father-in-law's considerable property of a rural cottage, one *ch'ing* of land, a twelve-room tiled house in the town, five bondservants, and a millstone. Eleven years later (1277) Hsing-tsu's brother was dividing the family property and wanted to include these substantial assets. Wang Hsing-tsu sued to prevent the division. The case went to the Ministry of War (since it involved a military household), which cited a Chin law stating:

Property gained from official employment, or that from military service, plus assets obtained from the wife's family are not included in family division.[79]

Wang's property was clearly from his father-in-law and thus no part of his natal brother's division. But in an interesting twist, the verdict went on to say:

The houses, bondservants, and other property that Wang Hsing-tsu has obtained on account of his military service are all his own according to the old regulations. In addition, the assets in the patrimony of his father and grandfather should be divided evenly between him and his older brother, Wang Fu, according to the law.[80]

The Ministry overlooked the point that the property could be excluded because it was from Wang's wife's family, and instead emphasized that Wang Hsing-tsu had exclusive rights to the estate because he had undertaken the military service attached to it. The verdict made clear that land always carried responsibilities, and that assuming these responsibilities gave a person rights to the land. We also see here the new rules for

78 YTC 19:10b–11a.
79 YTC 19:10b–11a. Note the difference from Sung law, which did not mention military service as a source of personal wealth.
80 YTC 19:10b–11a.

uxorilocal marriage in the Yüan. In the Sung, when a man married uxorilocally, he renounced rights to his own father's patrimony. Here, Wang got a share of his father's property equal to his brother, *and* got to take over all of his father-in-law's holdings.

In conclusion, the military structure of Yüan society resulted in the marginalization of women in matters of family inheritance. The emphasis on military service performed by males and taxes and corvée calculated by household privileged males over females and coincidentally supported the patrilineal line. The steppe practice of lateral inheritance by brothers, which was carried over into Yüan law and applied to the Chinese, did not correspond to the traditional Chinese requirement of preserving every son's patriline, but it nevertheless further privileged nonresident male agnates over women in the household.

These changes in the structure of inheritance, all in place by the middle of Khubilai's reign, represent a dramatic decline in women's inheritance rights. They are overshadowed, however, by an even more dramatic change in a woman's rights over her property and her person after she was married.

Changing Laws on Marriage and Property in the Yüan

The process by which laws on marriage and property changed in the Yüan was complicated. It was marked by general confusion over what laws to enforce, and by frequent reversals of decisions on appeal or review, as judges at different levels of government and different ethnic groups disagreed over what law and practice should be. Local authorities passed cases up for review when they could find no precedent by which to judge them. Fear of recrimination if superiors disagreed with a decision also caused many cases to be passed up.

I have identified five chronological stages in the transformation of marriage law in the Yüan. In stage 1, the T'ai-ho code of the Chin was in effect, and magistrates essentially upheld the freedoms and property rights that women had enjoyed in the Sung. During stage 2, beginning in 1271, judges harshly enforced Mongol customs like levirate marriage among the Chinese population, usually to the disadvantage of women. Stage 3 represented a backing away from this policy and a more lenient application of Mongol laws. During this time the practice of chastity became an acceptable alternative to levirate remarriage. In stage 4, from 1294 to 1320, many ideas of the Chu Hsi school were made into law, considerably depriving women of control over property and freedom of movement. Stage 5, from 1320 on, represents the culmination of the Confucian transformation of marriage and property law: the government exalted widow chastity and once again outlawed the levirate for Chinese. The following presentation of evidence is arranged according to these five stages.

Stage 1: Separation of Mongol and Chinese Law, 1260 to the End of 1271

The first stage, from 1260 to the end of 1271, was characterized by the separation of Chinese and Mongol law. The T'ai-ho code of the Chin dynasty applied to the Chinese, while steppe law and customs applied to Mongols and other non-Han peoples. (This was of course all in North China, before the conquest of the South.) The principle of a dual legal system was already familiar to the Chinese, for it appears in the great T'ang code, Article 48 of which reads:

All cases involving foreigners of the same nationality who have committed crimes against each other will be sentenced following their own customary law.[81]

The Khitan of the Liao dynasty followed this "personality principle" (*ius sanguinus*), where laws applied according to the ethnic group of the offender rather than by territory.[82] Despite some attempts to unify laws for all people under their jurisdiction, the Khitan essentially retained ethnic differentiation of the legal system during their entire rule. The Chin continued this policy in principle; but as they became more sinicized they were forced to address conflicts between Jurchen customary law and Chinese law. In 1202 they introduced the T'ai-ho code, which was intended to apply universally to all their people regardless of nationality. It contained a mixture of traditional Chinese law based on the T'ang and Sung codes and Jurchen customary law. But in some areas, especially marriage and inheritance, separate laws for non-Han people based on indigenous customs continued to apply.[83]

Marriage practices of the horse-riding Jurchen, like those of their nomadic cousins the Mongols, were quite different from the Chinese. Before the conquest of North China, some tribes evidently practiced marriage between people of the same surname or even close family members.[84] Such endogamy was prohibited in 1118, but the levirate con-

---

81 *T'ang-lü shu-i*, 6:133.
82 Karl A. Wittfogel and Feng Chia-sheng, *History of Chinese Society, Liao (907–1125)* (Philadelphia: American Philosophical Society, 1949; reprint 1961), 227, 466–7; Franke, "Jurchen Customary Law," 215; Niida, *Hōseishi* I, 431–3.
83 Franke, "Jurchen Customary Law."   84 Franke, "Jurchen Customary Law," 228.

tinued to be practiced by all Jurchen throughout the period of occupation of North China. In this regard, the Jurchen never assimilated or
adopted Chinese custom. Moreover, it seems that the example of the
Jurchen rulers made the levirate acceptable to some Chinese. In 1169
the Jurchen emperor Shih-tsung issued an order that Chinese and
Po-hai people were not to practice levirate marriage:

> On the day *ping-hsü* [in the first month of 1169], an imperial order declared,
> "the wives of [deceased] brothers of Chinese and Po-hai men are to return to
> their natal families at the end of the mourning period and may remarry in accor-
> dance with the rites."[85]

This order once again makes an ethnic distinction between staying in
the husband's house and returning home after the mourning period,
and it upholds a Chinese widow's right to remarry.

The T'ai-ho code of 1202 again outlawed levirate marriage by the
Chinese and maintained the separation between Jurchen and Chinese
law in this regard:

> Chinese and Po-hai people are not included among those who may inherit a
> wife from relatives within the mourning circle.[86]

The "mourning circle" presumably included all five grades of mourning, that is relatives as distant as third cousins. The statute implies that
remarriage outside this group was acceptable. It also suggests that
despite earlier orders forbidding it, in 1202 Chinese under the Chin
continued to practice levirate marriage.

As mentioned above, when the Mongols invaded North China, they
left the T'ai-ho code in effect. This continued to be the basis of law as
applied to the Chinese until the eleventh month of 1271. Mongols and
other inner Asians went by their own customary law. The Central Secretariat (*chung-shu sheng*), the highest organ of civil government in the
Yüan,[87] explicitly stated the principle of separation of Chinese and
steppe law in a judgment issued in the early months of 1270. In laying
down this principle, the Secretariat quoted the Chin code then in effect,
referring to it as the "old regulations":

---

85 *Chin-shih* 6:144. See also Franke, "Jurchen Customary Law," 228; and Franke, "Women
    under the Dynasties of Conquest," 31; Hung, "Yüan-tai," 283.
86 YTC 18:26a–b; Hung, "Yüan-tai," 283.
87 The Central Secretariat gained its prominence when Khubilai reestablished it in 1260.
    For more on its importance and functioning, see Farquhar, *The Government of China*,
    169–75; Ratchnevsky, *Un Code* I, 117–19; *Yüan-shih* 7:127. For certain periods, notably
    1270–1272 and 1287–1291, the Secretariat for State Affairs (*shang-shu sheng*) existed
    as a body over the Central Secretariat.

According to the old regulations: when people of the same group commit crimes against each other, they should follow their own customary law. Chinese and others may not apply other laws by analogy to settle cases.[88]

The Central Secretariat was citing this principle of separation in support of a ruling by the newly founded Secretariat for State Affairs (*Shang-shu sheng*), which in turn was upholding a decision at the circuit level.[89] These offices were staffed by both Mongols and Chinese,[90] and the fact that all three offices enforced separate Mongol and Chinese law shows that official opinion was unanimous on this subject.

Nevertheless, the question of levirate marriage continued to be the subject of lawsuits, and the central government went on to issue further rulings. Soon after the above decision by the Central Secretariat, the Ministry of Revenue (*hu-pu*) addressed the issue in a ruling of the seventh month of 1270. Sun Wa-ke, a woman in Ho-chien circuit, south of Peking (Map 5), filed a complaint saying that in the tenth month of 1269, after the death of her husband and in-laws, and after observing the mourning period, her husband's nephew Fu T'ien-shou had tried to rape her and take her in levirate marriage. She had sent the nephew away, but her father-in-law's older brother declared that by current law a nephew had the right to marry his deceased uncle's wife.[91] When Sun Wa-ke brought the case, the circuit government passed it up for a decision by the Ministry of Revenue, which agreed with her complaint. The Ministry cited an identical case in which a nephew tried to marry his aunt (*shen-mu*, wife of father's younger brother), for which the same circuit passed up a ruling that expressly forbade such action, based on the Chin code:

Ho-chien circuit reports: "Wang Hei-erh presented betrothal gifts[92] and took his aunt Hsü Liu-nu in a levirate marriage. The old regulations state: 'For a nephew

---

88 YTC 18:26a. For the use of the term "old regulations" to mean the Chin code, see Yeh Ch'ien-chao, *Chin-lü*, 17–18; Ratchnevsky, *Un Code* I, x; Hung, "Yüan-tai," 283 n. 17; Franke, "Jurchen Customary Law," 216.

89 The Secretariat for State Affairs was first established in the first month of 1270. The ruling cannot be later than the seventh month, which is the date of the document in which it is quoted; YTC 18:26a.

90 *Yüan-shih* 7:127 records the establishment of the Secretariat for State Affairs and the staffing of it and the Central Secretariat at that time.

91 YTC 18:26a. The term *po-po*, meaning "father's older brother" can refer here either to the nephew's uncle (the woman's brother-in-law) or the deceased husband's uncle. Hung interprets it as the woman's brother-in-law ("Yüan-tai," 301), but I am inclined to read it as her husband's uncle, as does Paul Ratchnevsky ("The Levirate in the Legislation of the Yüan Dynasty," in *Tamura hakushi shoju tōyōshi ronso* (Tokyo: Dōhōsha, 1968), 55).

92 It is unclear why betrothal gifts would be paid for a levirate marriage (since such marriages were meant to avoid such an expense). I assume that these were token gifts, probably of food, that were meant to make the marriage legal by Chinese law.

to marry his aunt (*shen-mu*) amounts to offending against one's relations. Marriage to one of the older generation is the same as fornication and must be dissolved.' Wang Hei-erh is from a Chinese family [and thus comes under this law]."[93]

This decision was sent up for review to the Secretariat for State Affairs, which in turn passed it on to the Central Secretariat. After repeating its statement of earlier that year on the principle of separation of law the Central Secretariat made a major ruling on levirate marriage:

There is to be no levirate marriage. If the woman in question wishes to stay chaste after the mourning period is over, or wishes to return to her natal family and remarry, she should be allowed to do so. Although the aunt Hsü Liu-nu has already been married to her nephew, the marriage should be dissolved.[94]

We see from this case that Chinese men were practicing levirate marriage, which they understood to be sanctioned by Mongol customary law. But the women involved sometimes resisted, and in response to lawsuits brought by these women,[95] both Mongol and Chinese officials enforced separate laws for the Chinese based on the Chin code.

In the early months of 1270, the central government prohibited levirate marriage between a man and his brother's widow. The rationale was the same as with aunt–nephew marriage: the separation of law by ethnic group. The verdicts cite as a precedent the decision of 1270 from the Central Secretariat forbidding aunt–nephew levirate marriage.

The *Statutes and Precedents* includes two cases addressing the issue. The first took place in Ho-chien circuit, just south of Peking, the same locale as the above two instances of attempted aunt-nephew levirate. A man from a military household, Chao I, complained that his wife's daughter[96] Ch'ing-erh, had observed the full mourning period for her deceased husband Ts'ui Chien-erh, but that her husband's older brother, would not let her return home (to remarry presumably), and instead insisted that she marry his younger brother. The case was sent from the circuit up to the Law Office (*fa-ssu*) in the central

---

93 YTC 18:26a.
94 YTC 18:26a. This ruling is similar to the Chin edict of 1169, but the wording is more explicit. Instead of the ambiguous *hsü-hun* (second marriage) this states *kai-chia* (remarry [to an outsider]).
95 One suit names the woman as the plaintiff; the other is almost certainly brought by the woman (the aunt) as well, though this is not explicitly stated.
96 The wording implies that this is a daughter by a previous marriage.

government,[97] which rendered a decision citing verbatim the 1202 prohibition on levirate marriage for the Chinese from the T'ai-ho code:

The old regulations [from the Chin code] state: Chinese and Po-hai people are not included among those who may inherit a wife from relatives within the mourning circle.[98]

The decision was sent to the Central Secretariat, which approved it and repeated the communiqué that it had issued earlier in 1270 in the case of aunt-nephew levirate. The citation repeats both the general rule of separate laws for Chinese and Mongols and the Secretariat's decision specifically outlawing the levirate:

According to the old regulations: when people of the same group commit crimes against each other, they should follow their own customary law. Chinese and others may not apply other laws by analogy to settle cases. . . .
There is to be no levirate marriage. If the woman in question wishes to stay chaste after the mourning period is over, or wishes to return to her natal family and remarry, she should be allowed to do so.[99]

The second case came from Hsi-chou, in Nan-ching circuit (the circuit that included Kaifeng, the Northern Sung capital). In it the Ministry of Revenue used the first case as a precedent in a decision rendered in the eighth month of 1270 and reported to the Secretariat for State Affairs. The complaint was brought by a man named Ting Sung from a civilian household. In 1260, he and his mother had arranged the marriage of his sister Ting Ting-nu to the son of Shih Hsiao-liu of the same prefecture. In 1267 his brother-in-law died, and his sister observed mourning for four years. Now, after the mourning, her father-in-law Shih Hsiao-liu would not let her return home and instead insisted she marry either her deceased husband's younger brother or a nephew in a levirate union. With the support of her family, she refused to comply. The Ministry of Revenue ruled in favor of the woman Ting Ting-nu and her family, using the precedents already established.[100]

Both of these decisions addressed the question of a widow returning to her natal family. In both, a woman or her relatives brought a suit against the husband's family for preventing her from returning home.

---

97 The Law Office (*fa-ssu*) served as a court of appeals similar to the Ministry of Punishments (*hsing-pu*) until 1271, when the T'ai-ho code was abrogated; Farquhar, *The Government of China*, 199; Miyazaki, "Sōgen jidai no hōsei to saiban kikō," 226–7. See also Tanaka, "Gentenshō bunsho no kōsei," 103–4.
98 YTC 18:26a–b.   99 YTC 18:26b.
100 YTC 18:26a. Cf. French translation by Ratchnevsky, *Un Code* II, 132–3. I disagree with his reading on several points.

Levirate marriage and staying in the husband's home was again contrasted with returning home and remarrying an outsider. The government came down strongly on the side of the women and their freedom to remarry. Four different offices, at the highest levels of government, the Central Secretariat, the Secretariat for State Affairs, the Ministry of Revenue, and the Law Office, all agreed on these points: a Chinese widow should be allowed to return to her natal family and to remarry. In this, they were upholding the laws and customs of the Chin and Sung dynasties before them.

The only time a widow could be forced to stay in her marital family's home was during the 27-month mourning period. In 1268, in the area of Loyang, a man sued to keep Han Chao-nu, the wife of his deceased younger brother, in his household during the mourning period. He complained that the wife's mother, Han Ah-Kung, from a neighboring prefecture refused to let her stay in her husband's house after his death. The circuit authorities sent the case up to the Law Office, which decided in favor of the husband's family. The judge wrote that Han Chao-nu must observe the mourning period in her husband's home, in order to "fulfill her duty as a wife," and to "encourage good customs." The verdict is reminiscent of the words of Huang Kan in the Sung, uttered just twenty years earlier in South China, about inculcating proper Confucian values through law. Nevertheless, the actions of the mother Han Ah-Kung to bring her daughter back home as soon as she was widowed show that Confucian values of chastity were not universally accepted. Moreover, the law of the Sung and Chin protected a widow's right to return home well before the 27 months of the formal mourning period were over. Widow chastity as promoted by the Chu Hsi school had not yet penetrated the laws of either North or South China.

The application of different laws of marriage according to ethnic group applied to Muslims as well. In a document dated 1268, a woman's family sued to save her from a levirate marriage. A man named Mohammed (Ma-he-ma), from the capital circuit of Ta-tu (Peking), arranged the betrothal of his daughter Ah-she to a man named Kou-erh in the first month of 1265. The betrothal gifts were duly paid, but the marriage had not yet been consummated, when in the seventh month of 1268, Kou-erh died. His mother wanted to substitute her 15-year-old younger son in a levirate marriage to the 20-year-old Ah-she. Mohammed refused. The circuit authorities summoned a Muslim cleric (*hui-hui ta-shih*), who explained Muslim law on this issue:

If a young man dies before his marriage is consummated, and the younger brother wants to marry the fiancée in a levirate union, he can only do so if her parents agree. If they do not agree, they must return half of the betrothal gifts that have been paid.[101]

The circuit authorities recommended applying this Muslim solution, (which differed significantly from the Chinese). The Ministry of Revenue agreed, and ordered Mohammed to return half of the jewelry, silk, two sheep, flour, and wine that the go-between attested had been paid to him three years before. The language of the document indicates that the authors of the verdict at both the circuit and Ministry level were Mongolian or other non-Chinese.[102] Thus in this period, in the multi-ethnic society of North China, officials of different ethnic groups attempted to settle disputes according to the varying secular and religious traditions of the peoples involved.

Finally, in the second month of 1271, the emperor himself, Khubilai, issued an edict that set down the principle of different nationalities following their separate marriage customs. This edict comprised the "General Rules for Marriage and Betrothal Gifts," item 6 of which reads:

When people of the various nationalities marry within their ethnic group, they should each follow their own customary laws. Those who marry across ethnic group should follow [the customs of] the husband.[103]

Significantly, Mongols were exempted from these rules.[104] Presumably this meant that a Mongol woman married to a Chinese man would still be under Mongol not Chinese law. Khubilai's rule was very much in line with the decisions of the offices below the emperor. The idea that the husband should take precedence is found in the suggestion of Khubilai's advisor Hu Chih-yü (1227–1295), and he may have influenced this edict.

Khubilai also addressed the issue of widows returning home. Item 5 of the "General Rules for Marriage and Betrothal Gifts," reads:

101 YTC 18:21a.
102 This document is in the style of direct translation from Mongolian. For discussion and explanation of this style, see esp. I-lin-chen, "Yüan-tai ying-i kung-tu wen-t'i," *Yüan-shih lun-ts'ung* Vol. 1 (Peking: Chung-hua shu-chü, 1982), 167–8; and Tanaka Kenji, "Gentenshō ni okeru Mōbun chokuyakutai no bunshō," in Yoshikawa Kōjirō and Tanaka Kenji, *Gentenshō no buntai* (Kyoto: Kyoto Daigaku Jinbun Kagaku Kenkyūjo, 1964), 76, 127–8, 156.
103 YTC 18:2b.
104 The way the YTC is written, it is unclear if the exemption for Mongols applies just to this, the last item, or to all the rules. I believe it applies to all the rules, because at least two of them come from a memorial from the Central Secretariat, which appears in the TCTK, 4:47. Here the Mongol exemption is stated as a separate item that applies to all the rules. The Mongol exemption should probably be read as a separate item in the YTC as well, for a note under the title of the edict in YTC states that it has seven items, when only six are indicated. The Mongol exemption was probably meant to be the seventh.

If a woman [wishes to] stay chaste after the mourning period is over, and wishes to return to her natal family, she should be allowed to do so. Her parents-in-law may not on their own initiative arrange a remarriage for her.[105]

Again, this decree reflects the decisions already being made by Khubilai's subordinate administrators. The intent was to maintain continuity with Sung and Chin marriage law and prevent forced levirate among the Chinese. Khubilai's wording, however, though very close to the two decisions of 1270 translated above, is not exactly the same. Unlike the rulings of the Central Secretariat and the Secretariat for State Affairs, Khubilai does not explicitly mention that a woman has the right to remarry. Instead he forbids the first husband's parents from forcing a widow into a remarriage. This could be a levirate marriage or any marriage; Khubilai does not specify. The possibility that Khubilai had mixed feelings about widows' rights of remarriage will be revealed by his later actions.

Khubilai's edict was cited in a ruling nine months later, in the eleventh month of 1271. A mother-in-law, Hsü Ah-Tu, sued to force her widowed daughter-in-law Ah-Liu to invite in a new husband as an adopted son for the mother. In the plaint, the mother complained that her son had left behind grandchildren and without a man in the house she was destitute and could not meet her corvée obligations. The prefectural government (place not specified) sought a decision from the Ministry of Revenue, which sided with the daughter-in-law. The Ministry invoked Khubilai's edict that a widow could stay chaste or return home, and that the parents-in-law could not force her into a remarriage. Nevertheless, it noted that the "three-year" mourning period, defined as 27 months by the Chin code, was not quite over in Ah-Liu's case. The final verdict stated that after the mourning period ended, the mother-in-law had to respect the wishes of the daughter-in-law and could not invite in a new husband for her son's wife. To relieve Hsü Ah-Tu's hardship, it suggested reevaluating her corvée duty, showing leniency.[106] Here, remarriage to an outsider of sorts was at stake, not levirate marriage, but the result was the same: relative freedom for the widow.

That Mongol and other steppe customs were beginning to exert a creeping influence on the Chinese is seen further in the other items of the "General Rules for Marriage and Betrothal Gifts" in Khubilai's edict of 1271. The first item sets out limits on betrothal gifts by official rank and status, given in cash equivalents. The Mongols were known for the high cost of betrothal gifts, or brideprice. The third prohibited same-

---

105 YTC 18:2b; TCTK 3:40. See also Hung, "Yüan-tai," 294. The edict is also quoted in
   YTC 18:13b–14a and 18:14a.
106 YTC 18:13b–14a.

surname marriage, beginning on the twenty-fifth day of the previous month. Marriages contracted before that time could stand, but any thereafter had to be dissolved. Steppe nomads practiced same-surname marriage at various times; evidently some Chinese were now doing so too. The fourth prohibited a man from taking more than one wife.[107] Mongols could have as many wives as they wished, without having to demote second wives to the status of concubines. As previously mentioned, Mongols were exempt from all of these rules, allowing them to continue the practices prohibited by the edict.

These rules suggest that residents of North China had adopted some of the marriage habits of the non-Chinese peoples who had governed them for much of the thirteenth century (or longer in some areas). Chinese were willing to negotiate the new customs they saw around them and use non-Chinese laws to their advantage. To avoid confusion during this confrontation between cultures, the Yüan government chose to maintain separate legal rules for each nationality, and they prevented Chinese from pleading to Mongol or other non-Han law. This was especially true with issues surrounding marriage and the practice of the levirate. In this early period, the result was general continuity with Sung and Chin law that allowed women the freedom to return to their natal families and remarry when widowed.

Stage 2: Mongolization of the Law and Universal Application of the Levirate, 1271–1276

Continuity with Sung and Chin law came to an abrupt end in late 1271. On the day *i-hai*, in the eleventh month of 1271, Khubilai abolished the T'ai-ho code of the Chin at the same time that he adopted the title Yüan for the dynasty.[108] The abolition of the T'ai-ho code had an immediate effect on levirate marriage and the separation of Chinese and Mongol law. Just one month later, in the twelfth month of 1271, Khubilai issued a blanket decree declaring that a man had the right to take his father's wives or his older sisters-in-law in levirate marriage:

Quickly have this order sent out: One's older sisters-in-law or father's secondary wives should be taken in levirate marriage.[109]

---

107 YTC 18:13b–14a; TCTK 4:47. See the similar prohibition on multiple wives in the T'ang code, Article 177; *T'ang-lü shu-i*, 13:255.
108 *Yüan shih* 7:138; Ratchnevsky, *Un Code* I, x; Ch'en, *Chinese Legal Tradition*, xiv–xv. By the Western calendar, this day would be in early 1272. To avoid confusion and make reference to the Chinese texts easier, I treat the Chinese year as equivalent to the Western and retain the Chinese number for the month.
109 YTC 18:23a.

Khubilai's decree represented a sharp break with the policies of his government up to that time and seems inconsistent with his usual tolerance of indigenous customs.[110] Moreover, the decree was in response to a suggestion from two non-Chinese ministers that the levirate be abolished.[111] It is not clear why Khubilai rejected the advice of his ministers and initiated this sudden change of policy. The order may have been related to the fierce interethnic and personal rivalries that plagued Khubilai's government in this period. The Muslim advisor Ahmad (d. 1282), much hated by the Chinese, was gaining influence. One of his main rivals, the Uighur Confucian Lien Hsi-hsien (1231–1280), who in the 1260s influenced Khubilai to maintain a Chinese-style government, resigned from the Central Secretariat in 1270. One reason given in his biographies is that he wished to protest inconsistencies in Khubilai's edicts.[112] Khubilai may also have felt that the time had come for universal laws applying to Mongols and Chinese. As we have seen, many Chinese men in the North believed they had the right to marry their brothers' wives in levirate unions. The levirate was not universally abhorred by the Chinese. Only when women or their families resisted and brought the issue to court do we learn of these cases. Many levirate marriages must have taken place that we do not know of, and some judges may have been pressured to allow the levirate among Chinese. By this time, intermarriage and cross-cultural influences may also have made the continued separation of law by ethnic group less feasible (Though it should be noted that the Mongol state maintained ethnic distinctions in other areas of its administration, such

110 Some scholars have suggested that this edict was meant only for Mongols (see Serruys, "Remains of Mongol Customs," 181; Rossabi, "Khubilai Khan and the Women," 175 n. 18). Hung Chin-fu argues convincingly, however, that it would make no sense for Khubilai to issue such an order for Mongols since they practiced the levirate already and it was never challenged among Mongols; Hung, "Yüan-tai," 294. Moreover, as I will show below, this edict was forced on the Chinese in subsequent lawsuits. See also Ratchnevsky, "The Levirate," 46; Holmgren, "Observations," 179.

111 YTC 18:23a. The two names given are Dashman (or Dasiman; Chinese, Ta-shih-man) and Sangha (Hsiang-ko). Sangha is the name of one of Khubilai's leading ministers, the Uighurized Tibetan infamous for his corruption and harsh fiscal measures, executed in 1291. Dashman could be the high official of the Kereit tribe who lived from 1248 to 1304 and began serving Khubilai at an early age. The life circumstances of these two men make it possible that they are the authors of the memorial, but both names are common and could refer to other people. See Bettine Birge, "Levirate Marriage and the Revival of Widow Chastity in Yüan China," *Asia Major* 8:2 (1995), 121 n. 40.

112 Competition with Ahmad was almost certainly a factor as well. In the same month as Lien's resignation, Khubilai had established the Secretariat for State Affairs with Ahmad at its head; Igor de Rachewiltz, ed., *In the Service of the Khan: Eminent Personalities of the Early Mongol Yüan Period (1200–1300)* (Wiesbaden: Otto Harassowitz Verlag, 1993), 492–3.

as household registration and official recruitment, to the end of the dynasty.)

Khubilai's edict of 1271 caused immediate confusion, as lower level authorities, and the common people themselves, continued to regard levirate marriage as illegal. At the end of 1272 a case came before the Ministry of War and Punishments.[113] Wang Yin-yin, a young Chinese woman from an unnamed circuit was left widowed in 1268 but continued to live with her son and her husband's younger, unmarried brother Cheng Wo-wo. In 1271 (after the mourning period) they had sexual relations and she became pregnant, leading the two to run off together to escape punishment. The local authorities apprehended them, and put Cheng Wo-wo into a cangue for committing illicit intercourse. Meanwhile, Wang Yin-yin's mother accepted betrothal gifts for her remarriage to someone else. When the Ministry received the case, they overturned the lower authorities. Citing Khubilai's edict of the year before, they ordered that Cheng be released and be given Wang Yin-yin in levirate marriage.[114]

The lower authorities and even the principals themselves considered sex between Wang Yin-yin and her brother-in-law to be illegal. Moreover, the mother went ahead and arranged a remarriage for her daughter, receiving substantial betrothal gifts. Evidently the new laws had not yet filtered down to the populace or local authorities. But while local authorities may even have resisted the changes, some of the people were inadvertently acting in accordance with them. In this instance, the young widow Wang Yin-yin was apparently more than willing to accept a levirate marriage. For other women, this was not the case.

In the years following, there continued to be confusion and disagreement in lower courts over marriage law and harsh enforcement of the 1271 edict at the top. In the fifth month of 1273, a mother named Kuo Ah-Ch'in sued to force the fiancée of her recently deceased son to marry her younger son in a levirate union. The judges at the prefectural level in Ta-tu (Peking) objected to a levirate marriage in this case on four grounds: (1) the original marriage with Kuo Ah-Ch'in's older son had not actually taken place; (2) Kuo Ah-Ch'in had only paid the initial go-between gift and not the actual betrothal gifts; (3) Kuo Ah-Ch'in's younger son was only 12 *sui*, not yet old enough to marry, while the girl was 17; and (4) the girl's father had already received the full complement of betrothal gifts and contracted a legal remarriage to someone

113 These two ministries were combined off and on during the Yüan. See Farquhar, *The Government of China*, 197.
114 YTC 18:23a–b. Hung, "Yüan-tai," 302.

else.[115] These four reasons represent two classic Chinese principles of marriage: the need for payment of proper betrothal gifts and completion of ritual steps, and respect for the appropriate age of the principals. Despite these compelling reasons to forgo a levirate marriage, upon review the Ministry of Revenue sided with Kuo Ah-Ch'in. They declared that "previously issued imperial edicts must be respected," and ordered the girl to marry Ah-Ch'in's twelve-year-old son. Kuo Ah-Ch'in was ordered to pay up the rest of the betrothal gifts as promised and the girl's father was obliged to return the betrothal gifts he had received from the other family.

Another case that tested whether betrothal alone generated levirate rights came to court in the third month of 1273, in Hua-chou (just north of Kaifeng). A man was engaged to be married but died before the marriage could be consummated. The groom's father wanted the fiancée to marry the younger son, but the bride's father refused. The Ministry of Revenue again cited the edict of 1271 and ordered the levirate marriage to go forward over the bride's family's objections.[116]

Enforcement of the mandatory levirate law even took precedence over the prohibition against having two wives. In 1273 a woman, Ah-Kuo, brought a suit against her younger brother-in-law, Liu San. She claimed that Liu had been engaged to someone else since 1270, when, within two weeks of her husband committing suicide by hanging, he forced her into a levirate marriage (i.e., raped her). The local authorities determined that Liu San had arranged an engagement but was not yet married. They also pointed out that it was illegal for Liu San to marry his sister-in-law during the mourning period, and such marriages were to be dissolved. Then they noted that two contradictory laws applied to the case. One stated that a man should take his older brother's wife in a levirate union (Khubilai's edict of 1271, twelfth month); the other said that a man must not take two wives, and that if he did, the second marriage had to be dissolved, even if an amnesty had been declared (quoted from Khubilai's "General Rules for Marriage and Betrothal Gifts," issued in the second month of 1271). Pointing out this contradiction, they requested a judgment by the Ministry of Revenue.

The Ministry had a slightly different version of events. They concluded that at the instigation of her husband's older brother (or cousin), Liu Ts'ung, Ah-Kuo had *willingly* married the younger brother Liu San in the second month of 1273, just under one year after her husband's suicide and within the mourning period. They then

115 YTC 18:24a. Hung, "Yüan-tai," 303–4.
116 YTC 18:24a. Cf. Hung, "Yüan-tai," 303; Ratchnevsky, "The Levirate," 46–7.

declared that levirate marriage, as required by Khubilai's edict, did not count as a man taking two wives. Thus Liu San was to take his sister-in-law in levirate marriage, *and* was additionally to pay the remaining betrothal gifts and marry his original fiancée. Liu San and Liu Ts'ung were to be "punished" for marriage during the mourning period, but the marriage was not dissolved. (In fact, it is not clear what sanction they incurred.)[117]

This ruling established that the levirate took precedence over earlier marriage laws. It swept aside Khubilai's edict of 1271 second month, which had established different laws for the Chinese and reaffirmed traditional Chinese marriage practices that precluded the levirate. Mongol marriage practices were now enforced by Yüan law: a Chinese woman could be forced into a levirate marriage against her will, a marriage during the mourning period could endure, and a man was allowed to have two wives. All three of these practices represented Mongol customary law, which differed considerably from the Chinese. In the case of widow Ah-Kuo, one wonders which wife would be the senior one: the widow Ah-Kuo whose levirate "marriage" to Liu San had been consummated first, or the woman who had earlier been betrothed to him.

In a similarly extreme decision in 1273, a woman was forced to marry her younger brother-in-law even though he was already married to someone else and his own parents did not support the levirate union. The deceased husband's younger brother, Fu Wang-po, sued to force his sister-in-law, Niu Wang-erh, to marry him. She countersued, claiming that he was already legally married, and that she wanted to stay chaste. The local authorities determined that Fu's own parents had agreed that Wang-erh could stay chaste and only wanted her to raise their grandson, but he had waited until they were out of the house, and then raped Wang-erh, forcing her to flee to her parents' house.

As in previous examples, the way the local authorities presented the case implies that they opposed the levirate marriage. Nevertheless, the Ministry of Revenue again imposed a harsh verdict. Their decision reads:

Even though Niu Wang-erh wants to stay chaste and raise her son, Fu Wang-po has already sullied her by rape. Moreover, Fu Wang-po is the younger brother of Niu's deceased husband. We must respect the intention of the previously issued imperial edict [of 1271, twelfth month]. The brother-in-law, who is

117 YTC 18:24a–b. Cf. Ratchnevsky, "The Levirate," 47–8. The text of this case has several corruptions and contradictions. I am grateful for the discussion provided by Prof. Hung Chin-fu and the students in his Yüan documents seminar at Ch'ing-hua University in May 1994 for helping me arrive at what I believe to be a correct reading.

already married, is ordered to take Niu Wang-erh as his wife in levirate marriage. Distribute this order and enforce it according to circumstances.[118]

Allowing a man to have two wives and refusing to let a widow stay chaste, even against the wishes of the husband's parents, represented strict enforcement of Mongol customary law.

By this time, some Chinese had begun to practice levirate marriage freely, but the subtleties of Mongol law sometimes eluded them. For instance, Mongols allowed the levirate to operate only when a younger brother inherited his older brother's wife. An older brother could not take the younger's wife.[119] This was poorly understood by the Chinese, who were used to older men taking young concubines, and for whom traditional law harshly punished sex with the wife or concubine of a man's elder, such as his father or older brother. The former director-general (*tsung-kuan*) of Nan-ching circuit (Kaifeng), a Chinese named T'ien Ta-ch'eng, got caught by this confusing rule in 1275. Finding that he had married his younger brother's widow, the regional surveillance office of Shensi and Szechwan sent the case to the Ministry of War for adjudication. The Ministry determined that he had "destroyed human relations and truly damaged civilized customs," by improperly marrying his brother's widow. He was punished with 87 blows of the bamboo and dismissal from office. His wife got 57 blows and was ordered to separate from T'ien.[120] The central government had gone a long way toward the Mongolization of marriage law to find that a man could rape his sister-in-law and take two wives, but that marrying a younger brother's widow in a levirate union "destroyed human relations" and "damaged civilized customs" and had to be severely punished.

An exception to the harsh enforcement of the levirate was made in the case of uxorilocal marriage when the widow additionally vowed celibacy. In 1273 a woman from P'u-yang county (northeast of Kaifeng) appealed to the authorities to prevent the younger brother of her late uxorilocal son-in-law from marrying into the household. The Ministry of Revenue found that the daughter had been celibate for five years after the mourning period for her husband, and that she wanted to stay chaste and with her children support her mother. It turned down the request from the brother for a levirate marriage but required that the daughter

---

118 YTC 18:23b–24a. Cf. Hung, "Yüan-tai," 302; Ratchnevsky, "The Levirate," 46.
119 Holmgren, "Observations"; *Yüan shih*, 103:2643.
120 YTC 18:26b; Hung, "Yüan-tai," 304. A record of this case in the Yüan dynastic history says that T'ien had already died when the decision came down and that his wife was punished with a beating of 80 strokes; *Yüan-shih* 8:161–2.

register a certificate with the authorities vowing not to remarry.[121] (Below, stage 3 of my analysis shows that such vows became a crucial aspect in exceptions to levirate marriage.) It is noteworthy here that the lower court approved the uxorilocal levirate marriage; much confusion still reigned in the courts over the issue.

Another exception was made in a case where a widow maintained a separate household from the prospective levir and was much older than he. In the sixth month of 1273, Liu Kuei sued to marry his older brother's widow of three years, Liu Ah-Ma, "in accordance with the regulations (*i-li*)." A lower court rejected the suit because the widow lived in a separate household with separate labor service, and moreover she was 50 years old, wanted to stay chaste, and had a 36-year-old son to support her. The Ministry of Revenue at the capital agreed on the basis that Liu Ah-Ma wanted to stay chaste, had an adult son, and paid separate taxes and labor service.[122]

Liu Kuei must have seen economic benefits in marrying widow Ah-Ma. She was well past childbearing age but probably headed a substantial household. Liu thought he could take advantage of the Mongol levirate law and obtain some of her assets or at least reduce his labor service by combining the two tax-bearing households into one. Chinese like Liu Kuei tried to use Mongol law to their advantage, but the government at the same time prevented this when it was to its advantage. The ruling by the Ministry of Revenue in this case is consistent with its rulings on inheritance during this same period, which sought to maintain separate tax-paying households.

We have seen that in stage 2 the central government abruptly changed policy in late 1271 and began to enforce the levirate for all peoples. Mongol customary law prevailed, sweeping aside traditional Chinese prohibitions on levirate marriage, taking two wives, and marrying during the mourning period. Meanwhile, local authorities often opposed forced levirate marriages, and in one example even arrested a levir. But local preferences were overruled on review by the central offices. Chinese who practiced the levirate could get tripped up by provisions such as those against marrying a younger brother's widow. The culture gap between the Mongols and the Chinese could not be bridged merely by imperial edicts or laws made in the capital, and during the early 1270s Mongol laws and Chinese practice came into frequent conflict.

---

121 YTC 18:21b. Cf. Hung, "Yüan-tai," 303, Ratchnevsky, "The Levirate," 49.
122 YTC 18:26b. Cf. Hung, "Yüan-tai," 304, Ratchnevsky, "The Levirate," 48–9.

Stage 3: Reassertion of Chinese Values and Lenient Enforcement of the Levirate, 1276–1294

The harsh enforcement of the levirate among Chinese, brought on by Khubilai's edict of 1271, did not last long. As the conquest of Southern China progressed in the 1270s, a number of Chinese officials were brought north to help administer the newly conquered territories. In 1276 the capital Hangchow fell, and the last remnants of the Sung royal family and their followers were defeated at sea in 1279. Already in the late 1270s Chinese officials brought north seem to have been having an effect on policies toward marriage. After 1276 the sources show a distinct softening of the harsh enforcement of the levirate of the early 1270s. As in stage 2 of my analysis, the local authorities during stage 3 seemed to be out of touch with changes at the top. This time, in a reversal of the trend during stage 2, the local authorities often supported levirate marriages while the central government allowed more and more exceptions.

The change of policy was ushered in by a dramatic turnaround on the part of the Ministry of Revenue in 1276 that allowed all widows to escape levirate marriages by staying chaste. We saw how in 1273 a widow from P'u-yang county was allowed to escape having an uxorilocal husband enter her home in a levirate union if she submitted a written oath of chastity, but that women who lived in their husband's home were denied this opportunity. Then in the third month of 1276, the Ministry of Revenue reversed itself and allowed all women the option of staying chaste instead of entering a levirate marriage.[123]

The suit that precipitated the ruling originated in southern Shantung, P'u-t'ai county, Tzu-lai circuit, where a man sued to force his older brother's widow to marry him "according to the regulations."[124] The widow, Ah-Chuang, told the authorities that she wished to stay celibate and not marry anyone, including her husband's younger brother. Moreover, she dramatically proclaimed that if her actions were "contrary to principle" (*fei-li*), she would willingly undergo a punishment of 107 strokes (the severest punishment for an improper marriage). The county magistrate ruled that since the man inherited his older brother's tax and corvée obligation, he should also inherit widow Ah-Chuang. This was entirely in accord with Khubilai's blanket edict of 1271 and with the general principle that inheritance of "property" went with tax

123 YTC 18:27a.   124 YTC 18:27a.

and labor obligations. Nevertheless, on review, the Ministry of Revenue reversed the lower court.

In its verdict, the Ministry cited verbatim the two contradictory edicts of Khubilai's: one in the second month of 1271, the "General Rules on Marriage" declaring that a woman was allowed to stay chaste and could not be forced into a second marriage by her in-laws, and the other, issued in the twelfth month of the same year, allowing all men to take their father's or older brother's wives in levirate marriages. To reconcile these two orders, the Ministry issued a general directive, "to be distributed widely, with the hope that it will prevent further lawsuits" on this issue. It read:

> From now on it should be as follows: If a widow wishes to stay chaste, the man eligible to take her in levirate marriage may not harass her, but must allow her to preserve her chastity. If however, the woman seeks to remarry, both she and the prospective husband are to be punished, and the eligible levir is to be allowed to marry her.[125]

This ruling defied the policies of the previous five years, which had enforced the edict of 1271 twelfth month and imposed levirate marriages under all kinds of conditions. Indeed, the county court had followed the law correctly when it ordered widow Ah-Chuang to marry her brother-in-law. In a separate ruling, the Ministry of Revenue applied the celibacy rule to a woman with the Arabic name Fatima (Fa-tu-ma), who was probably Muslim. We can infer from this that it was meant for all ethnic groups, not just Chinese.[126]

The ruling of 1276 set the stage for all kinds of other exceptions to levirate marriage, though not its actual revocation nor a return to Chin law that exempted Chinese from it. One new basis for escaping levirate marriage was the levir being underage. In contrast to the early 1270s (stage 2 of my analysis), the age of the levir now became a factor in the enforcement of the levirate.

The ruling that set a new precedent on levirate marriages to young levirs was issued by the Ministry of Revenue in the first month of 1277.

---

125 YTC 18:27a. TCTK 3:40 has a summary of the ruling (with the widow's name incorrectly given as Ah-Tsang instead of Ah-Chuang). See Hung, "Yüan-tai," 305; and cf. Ratchnevsky, "The Levirate," 50–1.
126 YTC 18:27a. The ruling in the Arabic widow's case was issued before the general rule, quoted above, and was the basis of it. In that case, widow Fatima, from Ts'ao-chou (northeast of Kaifeng), sued to avoid a levirate marriage with her deceased husband's younger brother, arguing that she wished to stay chaste and would live with her son and continue to pay the household taxes and corvée (as a woman head of household). The continuation of a separate tax- and corvée-sustaining household may have been a factor in the ruling. (As noted earlier in this chapter, elite Mongol widows already often stayed celibate and avoided levirate marriages that way.)

An official (evidently of Jurchen background) in the Municipal Affairs Office of Shun-t'ien circuit (modern Pao-ting in Hopei) sued to force his widowed daughter-in-law to marry his young son. The official complained that the woman's father had taken her home and refused to allow her to return, but that according to the law, now that the mourning period was over, his son should be allowed to marry her. The Ministry noted that the widow, Ah-Hsü, had nursed her little brother-in-law since he was a baby and was a whole generation older than he. Moreover, her father had no other sons or daughters to care for him. Thus they ruled that no levirate marriage should take place and Ah-Hsü was allowed to stay at home and take care of her father.[127] (As though to satisfy some litmus test, they noted that corvée labor obligations would not be affected by the ruling.)

This decision of 1277 directly contradicted a 1272 ruling by the same Ministry (cited under Stage 2) that forced a woman of 17 to marry her 12-year-old brother-in-law.[128] In that case the local court rejected the levirate, citing the young age of the levir and the fact that the couple were not yet married, but the Ministry of Revenue enforced it. This time the local court had gotten the word that the levirate was to be enforced, but the Ministry reversed itself.

In two more examples, the Ministry of Rites, a stronghold of Confucian scholars, also moved to overturn previous rulings on underage levirate marriages. The first case came to them in 1279, from P'ing-yang circuit (modern Shansi). Lu Hsien, the father of two boys, filed a suit to force the fiancée of his older son, a girl named Ts'ui Sheng-erh, to marry his younger son, Lu Ssu-erh, now that the older son had died. The girl's father Ts'ui Hui refused and went ahead and betrothed her to someone else. The suit was passed up to the Ministry of Rites, which ruled:

Ts'ui Sheng-erh is 18 years old, Lu Ssu-erh is only 9. Their ages are too far apart. It would be difficult for them to marry in a levirate union. Ts'ui Hui is ordered to return the original betrothal gifts that Lu Hsien paid. Lu Hsien is to wait until his son Lu Ssu-erh becomes an adult and then marry him to someone else. Ts'ui Sheng-erh is allowed to become the wife of Li Sun-erh, to whom she has already been engaged in remarriage.[129]

---

127 YTC 18:27a–b; Hung, "Yüan-tai," 306. Ratchnevsky, "The Levirate," 62 n. 27, refers to this case but mistakenly says that the widow returns to her mother, not father. The official's name, Wan-yen Ssu-cheng, suggests he is Jurchen.
128 YTC 18:24a.
129 YTC 18:27b. The same case is recorded in TCTK 3:41, which gives a different reason for rejecting the levirate. See note 134 below.

The second case came before the Ministry of Rites in 1281, and the Ministry cited the 1279 case of Lu Hsien as a precedent. The second suit was filed in Ch'ü-chou county (Kuang-p'ing circuit, northeast of modern Anyang). The girl was 28 and the boy was 12, and on the basis of this age difference, the levirate marriage was rejected.[130]

In addition to the Ministry of Revenue and the Ministry of Rites, the Censorate also issued rulings that supported the new policy to reject levirate marriages when the levir was underage. In support of a ruling of 1290 by the Kuang-p'ing circuit Branch Office (the same circuit as the 1281 case judged by the Ministry of Rites) of the Yen-nan Regional Surveillance Office,[131] the Censorate rejected the suit of a mother-in-law to force her widowed daughter-in-law into a levirate marriage. This time the levir was only 8 and the widow 30. The widow was allowed to return home and remarry an outsider, after the mourning period ended. (In fact, while still in mourning for her first husband, the widow had remarried, been widowed again, and been betrothed a third time! The Branch office and the Censorate lamented the two remarriages while still in mourning but allowed that the last marriage could take place as soon as the mourning period ended.)[132]

Another area where the policies of stage 2 were reversed concerned the issue of a widow having been merely betrothed and not actually married. The Ministry of Rites in two cases rejected the demands of a levir on the grounds that the original marriage had not been consummated. These directly contradicted a 1273 ruling by the Ministry of Revenue (discussed in stage 2).[133] The first decision of the Ministry of Rites was issued in 1279, in a case from P'ing-yang circuit (modern

130 YTC 18:27b. Hung, "Yüan-tai," 307; Ratchnevsky, "The Levirate," 50–1. Note that the age of the levir, 12 *sui*, was the same as that in the case of 1273 where the Ministry of Revenue upheld the levirate; YTC 18:24a.
131 The full name for this office was Yen-nan Ho-pei Regional Surveillance Office (*an-ch'a ssu*). It existed from 1275 until 1291, when the name changed; *Yüan shih*, 86:2180. See also Farquhar, *The Government of China*, 242. The Regional Surveillance Offices were the local arms of the Censorate (*yü-shih t'ai*) at the capital, and below them were the branch offices. It is intriguing to speculate whether the mother-in-law who brought this suit was aware that a similar plaint from the same circuit had been rejected in 1281 by the Ministry of Rites and had intentionally brought her case before a different branch of government.
132 YTC 18:9a.
133 YTC 18:24a. The 1273 ruling forcing a levirate marriage was especially harsh, for not only was the widow only engaged to the first husband, but the levir was only 12 *sui*, the complete betrothal gifts had not been paid, and the widow had already been betrothed to someone else.

Shansi).[134] The second was in 1300, in response to a suit from the Branch Secretariat of Honan.[135]

A final condition under which the levirate was no longer enforced in this period was when the levir was already married or engaged. In three decisions by the Ministry of Rites, marriages were rejected because the levir was married or engaged to someone else. In 1279 a man from Chün-chou, Ta-ming circuit (modern Honan, directly north of Kaifeng), sued to prevent the brother of his temporary uxorilocal son-in-law from taking over the remaining four years of a thirteen-year marriage contract. The Ministry of Rites supported the suit because the brother Li Wu-lü was already serving as an uxorilocal son-in-law in another household.[136] He could not be married to two women at the same time, even if temporarily. In the second case, in the same year from neighboring Chang-te circuit (modern Anyang), the Ministry of Rites again prevented a man from taking two wives. Yang Ah-T'ien arranged for her daughter to marry Chang Yang-erh uxorilocally and had paid the betrothal gifts when Chang's older brother died and he inherited his sister-in-law by the levirate. The Ministry decided that Chang had to cancel his uxorilocal marriage and return the betrothal gifts, and that Yang's daughter had to find someone else to marry.[137] As a third example, in the decision of 1300 passed up from the Branch Secretariat of Honan (cited just above), the Ministry gave a second reason for rejecting the levirate marriage: in addition to the sister-in-law only being engaged, the levir already had a wife.[138]

These three rulings by the Ministry of Rites again reversed the severe pro-levirate policies of the 1270s. Recall that in 1273, the Ministry of Revenue denied a woman's attempt to escape marriage to her younger brother-in-law, even though he was already betrothed to another and she had been forced into the marriage (i.e., raped) during the mourning period. That decision explicitly allowed him to go through with his original marriage as well as keep his sister-in-law as a second wife (though

---

134 TCTK 3:41. This case is the same as YTC 18:27b, the 1279 case of Lu Hsien and his son Su Ssu-erh cited above. The YTC version is more detailed and the reason given for rejecting the levir union is that the levir was underage, while in the TCTK it is that the widow was only betrothed.

135 TCTK 3:40–1. This Branch Secretariat covered an area overlapping modern Honan, Hupei, and Anhwei.

136 TCTK 3:41. Hung, "Yüan-tai," 306.

137 TCTK 3:41–2; cf. Ratchnevsky, "The Levirate," 51. (Ratchnevsky lists this case under "exemptions from the levirate." In fact the levirate marriage takes place and the original betrothal gets cancelled.)

138 TCTK 3:40–1; Ratchnevsky, "The Levirate," 52.

he received some sort of punishment for marrying during the mourning period).[139] The author of the 1273 ruling specifically cited Khubilai's 1271 general edict on marriage, which, quoting the T'ang code, said, "If a man has a wife already and marries another, even if there is an amnesty, the [second] marriage must be dissolved."[140] He then proclaimed that this did not apply to a levirate marriage. When the Ministry of Rites reversed this decision in 1279, it cited the same edict that a man could not have two wives, and asserted that the rule *did* operate against the levirate.[141] Its rulings once again made having two wives illegal.

While officials in the central government were reversing earlier policies on levirate marriage, Chinese continued to be caught applying it in ways that were anathema even to Mongols. In the eighth month of 1277, the Ministry of Rites sent a communication to the Ministry of Punishments asking for a ruling on a man who married his younger brother's widow. Chang Yi claimed he had permission from his mother to take his brother's widow in marriage, but the widow's family, a military household, brought the suit to court. The punishment was severe: 107 strokes for Chang Yi, 97 for his wife (though her family brought the case), 37 for the go-between, and dissolution of the marriage.[142] Regarding the mother who had colluded in the illegal marriage, the judges wrote:

As for [Chang's] mother Ah-Wang, who arranged the marriage, if we do not punish her as a warning to others, the laws and rites will be sullied and disordered. If she is not yet too old, she is to be beaten with 57 strokes of the bamboo.[143]

The language was similar to the condemnation of T'ien Ta-ch'eng, the director-general of Nan-ching circuit, whom the Ministry of War accused in 1275 of "destroying human relations" and "damaging civilized customs."[144] T'ien got a slightly lighter sentence of 87 strokes (perhaps because he was an official), but both cases show that the Mongols had their own ethical standards that were a mystery to the Chinese.

In 1289, a Chinese from P'ing-luan circuit (just east of Peking) tried to get away with taking the widow of his cousin (his father's sister's

---

139 YTC 18:24a–b.
140 YTC 18:24a, YTC 18:2b. *T'ang-lu shu-i*, 13:255, Article 177. The punishment for the man was a year of exile.
141 TCTK 3:42.
142 YTC 18:26b–27a. Cf. YTCHC hun-yin: 4a; Hung "Yüan-tai," 306. (Cf. Ratchnevsky, "The Levirate," 54–5. The Shen Chia-pen edition of YTC that Ratchnevsky used inserts several lines from the previous case into this one.)
143 YTC 18:27a. Elderly people could be excused from corporal punishment.
144 YTC 18:26b.

daughter-in-law) in a levirate union. The widow sued, and the marriage was annulled. Moreover, the court issued a general rule forbidding levirate marriage with someone of a different surname, thus clarifying the principles under which the levirate operated.[145]

The foregoing examples show that by the late 1270s the central government was shifting away from a rigid implementation of Mongol customary law. Many of the decisions (though not all) were made by the Ministry of Rites rather than the Ministry of Revenue, which shows that issues of marriage were no longer handled exclusively as matters of revenue but were seen to be in the realm of rites, an area traditionally dominated by Confucian values. Nevertheless, we do not yet see any distinct influence of the Chu Hsi school in these decisions. This is clear when we consider the judges' attitudes in these cases toward remarriage and the mourning period.

In all the cases where the levirate marriage was rejected, the widow was allowed to remarry an outsider. Decisions by all three offices of the central government, the Ministry of Revenue, the Ministry of Rites, and the Censorate, supported the widow's right to return home and remarry, indicating that it was a normal and acceptable path for a Chinese widow. In the 1290 decision by the Censorate, where it rejected a levir who was only eight years old, the widow Li Hsing-nu remarried twice while still in mourning for her first husband.[146] The Kuang-p'ing Branch Surveillance Office lamented that she had violated duty (*i-chüeh*) both times when she remarried, but it and the central Censorate allowed the remarriages to stand. The Ch'eng-Chu school's aversion to remarriage is not in evidence in these cases. Remarriage per se was not at issue.

The absence of strong Confucian values is also seen in rulings on the mourning period. Sung law technically forbade remarriage during the 27-month mourning period and dictated that such marriages be dissolved, but it allowed that, if a widow were poor, she could remarry after 100 days. A Yüan ruling in 1268 from the area of Loyang (a stronghold of the Ch'eng-Chu school) required that a woman stay in her husband's family during the mourning period and not remarry.[147] But the rule was only laxly enforced through the 1290s. For instance, the Kuang-p'ing Branch Surveillance Office in the 1290 case above tried to use this law to confiscate the substantial betrothal presents received by Li Hsing-nu's father (though they let the marriage stand); but the central office of the

---

145 YTC 18:27b–28a; Hung,"Yüan-tai," 308.   146 YTC 18:9a.
147 YTC 18:24b; YTC 18:22a; TCTK 3:40. The Sung rule allowing remarriage in case of poverty after 100 days is found in CMC 10:378; the Yüan specification of 27 months of mourning is in YTC 18:33b; TCTK 4:60–1.

Censorate overturned the branch office decision to confiscate the betrothal presents and allowed Widow Li Hsing-nu to remarry twice while still in mourning without any penalty at all. In doing so, they cited a precedent from 1275 where a remarriage during the mourning period (in which children were already born) was allowed to stand despite the objections of the husband's family.[148]

Another area where we find an interesting mix of Mongol and Chinese values is in the disposition of the betrothal gifts. When the Ministry of Rites rejected the suit of Lu Hsien from P'ing-yang circuit (Shansi) in 1279, they did so on the grounds that the levir was only nine. But they ordered the widow Ts'ui Sheng-erh's father to return the betrothal gifts he had originally received.[149] In T'ang and Sung law, once the betrothal gifts were paid, they could not be returned even if one of the betrothed died. The acceptance of the gifts constituted the contraction of a legal marriage. When a widow remarried, she took her dowry with her, but the betrothal gifts were not returned. In 1272, the Ministry of Revenue upheld traditional law and ruled in a case from Ho-tung county (modern Shansi) that even if the prospective groom died before the marriage was consummated, the bride's family did not have to return the betrothal gifts.[150] When a similar case arose among Muslims in 1269, the Ministry of Revenue followed Muslim law and allowed just half the betrothal gifts to be returned.[151] The Ministry of Rites therefore in 1279 was changing the rules. By ruling that the betrothal gifts *should* be returned if the widow did not enter a levirate union, they were in a sense compromising with Mongol customs. The 1279 ruling implies that if the betrothal gift were not returned, the widow would have to stay and marry the underage levir. As in Mongol custom, the payment of the betrothal gift "purchased" the bride for life for the husband's family, to be inherited by her husband's relatives. This underscores the economic foundations of the levirate. The Ministry of Rites had to balance the Chinese aversion to the levirate with Mongol ideas of marriage payments.

In stage 3 of my analysis, the period after the conquest of South China, we have seen how the Mongolization of the early 1270s was partly reversed and restrictions were placed on the levirate. Khubilai's attempt to apply the levirate to the Chinese was rolled back, and new laws made the levirate more compatible with traditional Chinese marriage practices. Eligibility for the levirate was limited by age, another marriage, and whether the previous marriage had been consummated. Moreover,

148 YTC 18:9a.   149 YTC 18:27b; TCTK 3:41.   150 YTC 18:21b.
151 YTC 18:21a–b.

if no man in the household was eligible, the widow was free to remarry as before. Nevertheless, the most common form of the levirate, a younger brother taking over his older brother's widow, continued to be practiced legally by Chinese and Mongols alike. A widow (of any nationality) who had an eligible younger brother-in-law had just one way to escape levirate marriage: she could stay chaste. The decree of the Central Secretariat of 1276 protected her from "harassment" by her brother-in-law as long as she vowed not to remarry.

Mongol influences on marriage and property law were countered, but we do not yet see major influences of the Chu Hsi school. In the next period, stage 4, things changed further, and went in the direction of the ideals of Huang Kan and his interpretation of Learning of the Way Confucianism.

Stage 4: The Confucian Transformation of Marriage and Property Law, 1294–1320

In 1294, Khubilai's long reign came to an end and his grandson Temür came to the throne as emperor Ch'eng-tsung (r. 1294–1307). Temür generally continued the policies of Khubilai and retained the top ministers from the end of Khubilai's reign in his administration (such as the grand councillor Oljei). Nevertheless, from early on he paid attention to Confucianism and promoted Confucian scholars, and his reign was marked by the increasing influence of Confucian advisors at court.[152] Two figures were especially influential: the Mongol minister Kharghasun (Ha-la-ha-sun, 1257–1308), who was a strong supporter of Confucianism and became prominent after 1303, and the Khangli statesman Bukhumu (Pu-hu-mu, 1255–1300), who was educated in the School for the Sons of the State (*Kuo-tzu hsüeh*) by none other than the great Chu Hsi follower Hsü Heng (1209–81).[153] Finally, it must be pointed out that the Confucianism that began to influence the Yüan regime more and more at this time was the Confucianism of the Chu Hsi school as interpreted by Huang Kan. All three lineages by which Chu Hsi's thought

---

152 After his accession, Temür issued a decree to respect Confucius, built a new temple to Confucius in the capital, and increased the enrollment of students in the *Kuo-tzu hsüeh* (School for the Sons of the State); Hsiao Ch'i-Ch'ing, "Mid-Yüan politics," in *The Cambridge History of China*, Vol. 6, 496–8.

153 For more on these two figures, see *Yüan shih*, 136:3291ff; 130:3163ff. For the influence of Khanglis and other Turks in Mongol administration during this period, see Igor de Rachewiltz, "Turks in China under the Mongols: A Preliminary Investigation of Turco-Mongol Relations in the 13th and 14th Centuries," in *China among Equals: The Middle Kingdom and Its Neighbors, 10th–14th Centuries*, ed. Morris Rossabi (Berkeley: University of California Press, 1983), esp. pp. 289–92.

entered North China were strongly influenced by the thought of Huang Kan, and his interpretation of the Learning of the Way became the Confucianism of the late Yüan dynasty.[154] In the area of marriage and property law, we find remarkable traces of the influence of Huang Kan's thought.

One aspect of Temür's shift toward Confucianism in his administration was a move away from the obsession with revenue that sometimes dominated in Khubilai's reign. Temür ordered the cancellation of tax debts and put an end to rapacious tax collecting. In 1302 he even issued an order not to collect tax revenues beyond the established quotas for an area.[155] Perhaps as a result of this shift, cases of marriage and inheritance came to be handled almost exclusively by the Ministry of Rites, rather than the Ministry of Revenue as in Khubilai's reign. This meant that marriage was no longer in the realm of revenue (once dominated by Muslim financial advisors who sought income by almost any means), but entered the realm of "rites," a more arcane arena where issues of Confucian ethics and morality dominated.

The new respect for Confucianism had the effect one might anticipate: decisions on marriage and property shifted toward a Chinese Confucian perspective. New legislation in Temür's reign and beyond came to reflect the agenda of Huang Kan and the Chu Hsi school. This legislation addressed four issues: levirate marriage, the mourning period, family property (including women as property), and widow chastity.

LEVIRATE MARRIAGE

During Temür's reign, 1294–1307, there was a steady stream of limits placed on levirate unions, as ruling after ruling by different offices rejected them. In one example, the levir was rejected because he had become a monk. In the third month of 1296, a mother sued to keep her daughter-in-law, Chang Pao-nu, in the household. Her older son had died, and her younger son had become a monk, but her younger son left the monastery to marry his sister-in-law in a levirate union. Pao-nu refused, and in the meantime got remarried to someone else. The Central Secretariat, based on a report from the Censorate, supported Chang Pao-nu, declaring that since the younger brother had left the family and entered a monastery, he was not an eligible levir. Chang's second marriage could stand.[156]

154 Wing-tsit Chan, "Chu Hsi and Yüan Neo-Confucianism," esp. 198–201.
155 Hsiao, "Mid-Yüan politics," 497; *Yüan shih*, 20:440.
156 TCTK 3:41; Ratchnevsky, "The Levirate," 53.

In a second example, in 1298, the claims of a cousin were rejected. A girl from Te-chou (modern Te-chou city in Hopei), Yü Huo-erh, was betrothed, but her fiancé died. She stayed chaste for the mourning period, then returned to her father's house. Subsequently, a cousin of her deceased fiancé tried to take her in a levirate union. Her father protested to the authorities. Based on a report from the Censorate, the Ministry of Rites ruled that since the younger brother of the fiancé had allowed the widow to return home, no other more distant relative could claim her in a levirate marriage.[157]

In a third example in 1301, an old man from Shensi successfully sued to prevent a levirate marriage for his daughter who lived with him. He had no other children and had invited in an uxorilocal son-in-law, who subsequently died. The son-in-law's younger brother wanted to claim the widow as his wife. The Ministry of Rites supported the old man, saying that having no progeny was a terrible misfortune. Since the man had no other children, he had to rely on his daughter for support and "should be allowed to find another uxorilocal son-in-law to care for him in old age and take care of his funeral."[158] Presumably the brother-in-law was not willing to marry uxorilocally, or perhaps the Ministry meant that the old man should be able to choose a son-in-law to his own liking.

In a fourth case, the Ministry of Rites in 1302 rejected a claim of levirate marriage because it had arisen too late. Kuo Wen from P'ing-yang circuit (modern Shansi, northwest of Loyang) arranged a marriage for his daughter with the nephew of Li Chü. The nephew died that same year and Kuo asked the go-between to inquire of Li Chü if he knew of an eligible levir. When no such information came back, he married his daughter to another man and they had offspring. Then after four years Li Chü sued to have his son marry Kuo Wen's daughter in a levirate union. The Ministry rejected the suit because it came too late. The daughter had remarried four years before and even had children by her second husband.[159]

Finally, in 1304, the Ministry of Rites outlawed levirate unions between a widow and her husband's nephew for all Chinese. A Chinese shepherd named Wang was a bondservant captured in war (or "war slave" *chün-ch'ü*) of a Mongolian soldier. He died and his wife stayed chaste for six years. After this, the master tried to force her to marry shepherd Wang's nephew. Based on a report from the Bureau of Military Affairs, the Ministry of Rites forbade the union, saying:

---

157 TCTK 3:41; Ratchnevsky, "The Levirate," 53–4.
158 TCTK 3:42; cf Ratchnevsky, "The Levirate," 52–3.   159 TCTK 3:42.

Even though the man is the war slave of a Mongol soldier, he is a Chinese with a surname. Levirate marriage between a nephew and aunt sullies and confuses human relations. It should be outlawed.[160]

The Central Secretariat approved the order. The reference to shepherd Wang being Chinese suggests that there was a return in some respects to separate laws for Chinese and Mongols.

The Ministry of Rites turned its attention in 1308 to levirate unions between a widow and a relative older than her husband. The language condemning it was similar to that against levirate marriage with the husband's nephew. The test case came from Shang-tu circuit, the area of the northern capital K'ai-p'ing (modern Inner Mongolia), and it presented an interesting situation. In 1298 a man named Liu Ta died, leaving his wife Liu Ah-Wang and two small sons. A younger cousin, Liu San, took Ah-Wang in a levirate union, but in the seventh month of 1307 he died also. Then the mother of the first husband, Liu Ah-Niu, arranged a second levirate marriage to another cousin, Liu Chün-hsiang, claiming that she had to keep Ah-Wang in the house to care for the two small boys, her grandsons. Moreover, Ah-Niu got two low-level Mongol officials to vouch that Chün-hsiang was a relative and an eligible levir. (It is possible that she took this step in anticipation of later challenges to the union, but the sources do not tell us.) The problem was that Liu Chün-hsiang was younger than the first husband, Liu Ta, but *older* than the second husband Liu San. In other words, Liu Chün-hsiang would have been an eligible levir the first time around, but now his position was open to question. The Ministry of Rites decided that this was a case of "older-brother" levirate, and citing the precedent of their earlier ruling in 1277, ordered that the marriage be dissolved. The mother-in-law, Ah-Niu, was excused from punishment because of her age of 73, but the other principals, Ah-Wang and Liu Chün-hsiang, got beatings.[161]

The two rulings of 1277 and 1308 by the Ministry of Rites became precedents for severe punishment of older-brother levirate. In 1321 the Ministry of Punishments cited them as precedents in a case from Yin-chou, in the Yangtze delta (modern Kiangsu, upriver from Shanghai). The location shows that Chinese in the south by this time also practiced levirate marriage. A man named Miu Fu-erh arranged to marry his younger brother's widow, Ah-Ku, in the third month of 1318, while she

---

160 TCTK 3:42. The Chinese slave is described as *huo-ni-ch'ih* (Mongolian *khonichi*), which identifies him as a shepherd; Ratchnevsky, "The Levirate," 56. For more on these "war slaves" or bondservants and their use as shepherds, see Ebisawa, "Bondservants in the Yüan," esp. 39–41.
161 YTCHC hun-yin: 4a–b. Hung, "Yüan-tai," 293, 311–12.

was still in mourning. He got his uncle to be go-between and another senior relative to be the presiding man. Moreover, he had the blessing of his mother. The Ministry of Punishments condemned the arrangement and ordered a beating of 107 strokes for Miu Fu-erh, 97 strokes for the widow Ah-Ku (even though she protested that she had resisted the marriage), and 57 strokes for the mother-in-law and uncle who blessed the marriage. Widow Ah-Ku was allowed to return to her natal family with her daughter.[162]

Except for the 1308 case, we have no examples of older-brother levirate between 1277 and 1318, a gap of 41 years. The 1308 case had unusual circumstances and the mother-in-law went to pains to get the levirate union sanctioned by local officials, perhaps because she knew it was questionable. It seems possible that Chinese in the North had learned of this restriction on the levirate and only after the levirate became more widespread in the South did Chinese once again get caught practicing it incorrectly.

Levirate marriages with a husband's nephew or older relative were now anathema to the central government, but other forms continued to be practiced legally by both Chinese and Mongols. Numerous restrictions placed on the Chinese show that it was becoming less and less acceptable to top officials, but levirate marriage was not to be outlawed completely for Chinese until 1330.

THE MOURNING PERIOD

The second big issue addressed by new legislation in this period was the enforcement of a mourning period after the death of a parent or husband. The Chu Hsi school of Confucianism emphasized proper respect for ancestors through the observance of the mourning period, and it was promoted in texts like *Chu Hsi's Family Rituals* (*Chu-tzu chia-li*), which was reprinted in the early Yüan and rapidly gained popularity.[163] As early as 1268, the Ministry of Revenue approved a suggestion of the Law Office (*fa-ssu*) requiring widows to stay in their husband's home during the mourning period.[164] At the end of 1270, the Ministry of Revenue issued an order outlawing all marriages when in mourning for a parent, and in 1271, a report from the Ministry of Rites urged that marriage rites be adopted from Chu's *Family Rituals*.[165] In 1278 the Branch Secretariat of Hu-kuang punished a woman who cremated her

---

162 YTCHC hun-yin: 4a–b. Hung, "Yüan-tai," 313.
163 For more on this text and a translation, see Ebrey, *Chu Hsi's Family Rituals*.
164 YTC 18:21a.   165 YTC 18:33a; TCTK 3:36–8.

husband and remarried immediately afterward (while still in mourning). The punishment was a beating of 77 strokes and dissolution of
her second marriage, as a "warning" to residents of the newly conquered
South.[166] Nevertheless as we saw in stage 2, in the years before and
after this, central authorities let other laws (such as Khubilai's 1271
edict imposing the levirate on Chinese) override considerations of
the mourning period and declined to dissolve marriages contracted
during it. In 1273, the Ministry of Revenue upheld a forced levirate
union during mourning under questionable conditions. In 1291
(stage 3), one woman remarried twice while still in mourning for her
first husband, and the Censorate declined to dissolve the marriages,
though the second was delayed until mourning was over.[167] Toward the
end of Khubilai's reign, the Ministry of Rites began to reverse these lax
policies.

Considerable confusion existed about marriage during the mourning
period. Many Chinese seem to have thought that it did not affect levirate marriages. Thus in 1288 when a young man in T'ai-yüan died, his
father immediately adopted an agnatic nephew, and, after making obeisance before the corpse of his son, married his daughter-in-law to his
newly adopted son. Despite the solemn and intentional nature of the
quick levirate marriage, the Ministry of Rites had no sympathy for the
man. It dissolved the marriage even though a son had already been born
to the new couple.[168] This ruling was used as a precedent ten years later
in 1298, when an official contracted a marriage during the wake for his
father, while the body still lay in the house. The father of chiliarch[169]
Wang Chi-tsu died in 1295, on the twentieth of the sixth month. Wang
took a new wife and with her knelt before the body to pay obeisance.
He buried his father three days later on the twenty-third. The Ministry
of Rites dissolved the marriage and dismissed Wang from office, saying,
"When his father died, and the body still lay out, Wang Chi-tsu forgot
his grief and contracted a marriage. Nothing confuses norms and
destroys customs more seriously than this."[170] In the 1288 case from
T'ai-yüan, marriage on the night of the wake was similarly criticized for

---

166 YTC 18:33a.   167 YTC 18:24b; YTC 18:9a.
168 YTC 18:33b; Hung, "Yüan-tai," 295, 308. I am following Hung's corrections of two
corruptions in the text.
169 A chiliarch (literally "chief of 1,000 households) was a mid- to low-level official in the
military bureaucracy, who could have a number of different duties, from command-
ing troops (anywhere from 300 to 1,000) to supervising agricultural colonies. The
term originally referred to a feudal chieftain with an appanage of 1,000 households,
but that is not the meaning here. See Farquhar, *The Government of China*, 3, 22, 417.
170 YTC 18:33b. I thank Lau Nap-yin for pointing out to me that Wang's was probably
not a levirate marriage.

"greatly harming civilized customs."[171] The strong language of 1288 evidently did not deter even an official ten years later from intentionally contracting a marriage in the presence of his father's corpse.

The new enforcement of rules on mourning could work in a person's favor. In particular, a woman could resist a levirate marriage or other forced marriage on this basis. In 1304 a goldsmith named Ts'ai died. The superintendent in charge[172] forced his widow Ah-Wu to marry silversmith Wang Ch'ing-ho while she was still in mourning. The Ministry of Rites allowed her to dissolve the marriage, citing the mourning period. The Ministry also noted that she already had a son who could take over her husband's goldsmithing labor service, implying that she could not be forced to remarry even after the mourning period.[173]

In this instance, the widow in mourning did not wish to remarry, but in most cases it was the other way around. During the first two decades of the fourteenth century, the stance on remarriage during the mourning period solidified. In numerous cases, second marriages were dissolved because the wife was still legally in mourning for a previous husband. At first punishments varied between beatings of 57 to as high as 107 strokes. But the Ministry of Punishments in 1320, in response to a case in Chien-k'ang circuit (modern Nanking), where a woman remarried one year after her husband's death, made a definitive ruling that was adopted by the Central Secretariat for the whole country. They noted that a lower court's verdict of 77 strokes was higher than their own earlier ruling of 1308, where the woman got 67 strokes. Following the 1308 precedent, they standardized the punishments at 67 strokes for the woman who remarried, 57 for the man, 47 for the elder who presided over the wedding, and 37 for the go-between who arranged it. The marriage was to be dissolved and any betrothal gifts, engagement gifts, payments to the go-between, and so on were to be confiscated. If the man and others involved did not know the woman was in mourning, the punishments were reduced.[174] Though these did not forbid a

---

171 YTC 18:33b.
172 *t'i-chü.* This was presumably the superintendent for the gold and silver workshops. See Farquahar, *The Government of China,* 178ff.
173 TCTK 4:60–1. Under the Yüan government, certain occupation groups were forced to produce for the court in semiservile status. The case of goldsmith Ts'ai shows that local authorities tried to control even the marriages of these people.
174 YTCHC hun-yin: 3a–b. These punishments are reproduced as general regulations listed at the front of the section on "Marriage in the Mourning Period" in the supplement to the *Yüan tien-chang;* see YTCHC hun-yin: 3a. In the 1320 case, the widow was ordered to "live with her son," and this instruction is repeated in the general regulations.

woman from remarrying entirely, they prevented her from doing so during the first 27 months after her husband had died.

The enforcement of the mourning period did not just apply to a woman in mourning for her husband but also to men in mourning for mothers or grandmothers. In an interesting case in 1321, a year after the above ruling, the government alleged that Ch'ien Chang, an official from P'ing-chiang circuit (modern Suchou), requested a leave of absence, falsely claiming that his mother had died. She was in fact seriously ill, and Ch'ien used his home leave to secure the betrothal of his son. The mother died before the marriage took place, but Ch'ien went ahead with the banquet and final marriage celebrations, even before finishing the funeral arrangements for his mother. The circuit authorities gave Ch'ien a beating of 37 strokes, but the Branch Secretariat of Chiang-che declined to dissolve the marriage, for the reason that the bride and groom were only following their parents' orders in going ahead with the marriage. Nevertheless, they sent the case to the Central Secretariat for a final decision, since it would "set a precedent." The case went to the Ministry of Punishments, which cited the 1298 precedent of the official Wang Chi-tsu, whose marriage was dissolved.[175] With this comment they passed the case on to the Ministry of Rites. It ordered the marriage dissolved but declined to punish Ch'ien beyond the 37-stroke beating he had already received.[176]

That the Ministry of Punishments deferred to the Ministry of Rites in this case indicates further that the Ministry of Rites had by this time taken over policy decisions on mourning and marriage. Moreover we see that they were implementing a Confucian agenda in this area. This had the interesting result that once again separate laws had to be set up for Mongols and Chinese. In 1319 the Ministry of Rites together with the Ministry of Punishments approved the suggestion of a Shantung Investigation Commissioner that brothers be prohibited from dividing the family property and setting up separate residences before their parents' funerals had been completed. (The implication was that brothers were dividing property with none left for a decent funeral.)[177] They added the proviso that Mongols and other non-Chinese (*se-mu*) be excluded, no doubt because Mongol men routinely left home and established their own residences when they married, often long before the death of their parents. As we saw in the case of outlawing some types of

175 YTC 18:33b.
176 YTCHC hun-yin: 3b. (Compare the beating of 47 strokes, prescribed just one year earlier, for the presiding man when a woman married while in mourning for her husband. YTCHC hun-yin: 3a.)
177 YTCHC t'ien-chai: 5a.

levirate marriage, as new legislation reflected more and more a Confucian agenda, the government had to return to different laws for different ethnic groups and make allowances for different customs in matters of family and marriage.

Behind the lawsuits surrounding levirate marriage were often issues of money and property. These included the disposition of the husband's property, the wife's property, and the woman herself as property. As the levirate became more restricted and it once again became easier for Chinese women to return home and remarry after being widowed, social and financial problems surrounding widows' autonomy came to the fore. For instance, in numerous cases the party suing for the levirate marriage argued explicitly that the loss of the widow would be a financial hardship or that she was needed to care for grandchildren. The mother-in-law from Shang-tu circuit who coerced her daughter-in-law Liu Ah-Wang into two levirate unions, where the second in 1307 was to a cousin senior to the previous husband, pleaded that she needed someone to care for her two young grandsons (the sons of the daughter-in-law).[178] In addition to saving the costs of brideprice for a younger son, levirate marriages could be of major benefit to the household economy, and the remarriage of widows could be a disaster.

The government signaled its agreement with this point and reinforced the concept that the wife herself was an economic asset in the household in a decision about military personnel made in 1296. The wife of a deceased soldier from the "newly incorporated" Southern Sung armies (*hsin-fu chün*) married her daughter off to a civilian household. The Ministry of Rites approved a proposed regulation by the Branch Secretariat of Kiangsi declaring that, since a brother, nephew, or son of the soldier had to take over his military service, his womenfolk should remain registered in the same household. Only if an eligible levir were unavailable could the wife or daughter go and marry whom she pleased.[179] The implication was that military duty required property to support it, and this property included wives and daughters. Levirate marriage provided the new soldier with capital to support himself.

Another major concern was that a wife who left the family might take away the husband's assets when she remarried. A man named Li T'ung

---

178 YTCHC hun-yin: 4a.
179 YTC 18:18b; Ratchnevsky, "The Levirate," 57. I am following Ratchnevsky's reading, which seems to be the only plausible interpretation of the corrupted text.

complained that when his older brother Li Jung died while serving as a Paper Currency Commissioner in Kwangtung, his wife immediately remarried and took with her all of Jung's assets. In response to these complaints, most severe in faraway Kwangtung, the Regional Investigation Office (*lien-fang ssu*) of Hai-pei Kuang-tung region (*tao*) submitted a report in 1299:

> Kwangtung is a malaria-infested area. Officials from the North are separated from their families by ten thousand *li*. Those who succumb to the infectious earth and water, and get sick and die, are too many to count. Their wives and concubines are unable to stay chaste and [typically] get remarried. They gather the property and bondservants that rightly belong to their former husband and take them all away. Even before the flesh and bones of the deceased official have grown cold, his family's private assets and attendants already belong to someone else. . . . From now on, when officials who serve in Kwangtung pass away, the household personnel old and young who are left behind must obey the local authorities, and according to the regulations be sent back to the official's family. They may not get remarried on their own initiative. Those who offend against this [and remarry] will be prosecuted by the government accordingly, and the [new] marriage will be dissolved. If the family property of the former husband has already been disposed of and lost, the wife or concubine will be forced to make restitution. Such a provision will cut off the source of lawsuits and will help correct human relations and improve customs.[180]

The Ministry of Rites approved the suggestion and the Central Secretariat made it into law. A related decision by the Ministry of Rites ten years earlier, in 1289, prohibited wives of soldiers who had gone on campaign from remarrying under the assumption that the soldier had died. The ruling was again in response to complaints from the Kwangtung area, this time saying that the parents of soldiers' wives often arranged hasty remarriages when soldiers failed to return promptly from campaigns.[181]

Rather than the loss of the husband's assets, a woman's own personal property became the focus of new legislation just a few years later, when the Yüan government, for the first time in Chinese history, promulgated a law that prevented a woman from taking her dowry into a second marriage. I have argued in previous chapters that from earliest times in China, a woman's property was attached to her for her entire lifetime, to support her in a certain social class. There is no indication that this changed in the Yüan before the fourteenth century. Even Huang Kan,

180 YTC 18:15b–16a. See also TCTK 4:50. Kwangtung was a region (*tao*) in the Yüan, covering approximately the same area as the modern province of that name, but located in the southern part of Kiangsi (Chiang-hsi *hsing-sheng*).
181 YTC 18:18b.

who opposed women holding private property, did not try to separate a wife from her dowry. In the early 1300s this tradition was definitively challenged, and women were stripped of lifelong control of their property.

The new regulation originated in 1303 from a Mongolian (or Uighur) local official. We do not know what lawsuit or observation prompted the new measure, but the author, director-general of Hui-chou circuit named Dorchi (Chin. To-erh-ch'ih), was clear in his own mind that it was a break from the past when he wrote the proposal. His suggestion was reported by the Pacification Office of Che-hsi and passed up to the Central Secretariat, which submitted it to the Ministry of Rites for approval. The measure read:

Regarding dowry lands and other goods that a woman brings into her marriage: from now on if a woman who has once been married wishes to marry again to someone else, whether she is divorced while her [first] husband is alive, or is living as a widow after her husband has died, her dowry property and other assets that she originally brought into her marriage should all be taken over by the family of her former husband. She is absolutely not permitted to take them away with herself, as was formerly done.[182]

When the Ministry of Rites received the report, it approved the decision but with an important modification. The Ministry recognized that this unprecedented separation of a woman from her property left wives vulnerable to expulsion by greedy families who coveted the large dowries elite women held. Thus it added the provision: "If a wife is expelled without proper cause, this regulation does not apply."[183] This protected a woman from being arbitrarily expelled from her husband's home and losing her dowry to them.

This new regulation represented a major break with Chinese tradition. The wording of the measure itself indicates its unprecedented nature. Such phrases as "from now on" and "as was formerly done" show that the Yüan authorities were conscious that previous practice had been different. It is significant that the dissolution of the bonds between women and their property came under a non-Chinese regime, whose rulers, the Mongols, did not have the tradition of women bringing large amounts of property from their natal homes. At the same time, the

182 YTC 18:21b–22a; TCTK 4:49–50. The TCTK version, labeled "sixth month of 1303," is shorter and worded slightly differently than that in the *Yüan tien-chang*. The content, however, is identical.
183 YTC 18:22a. See also Niida, *Bunsho*, 498–9; Shiga, *Genri*, 528, 546 n. 37; Yanagida, "Gendai no joshi," 261–2; Holmgren, "Observations," 182. With the exception of Holmgren, these authors fail to note the newness of this regulation; Yanagida in particular challenges this point.

Ministry of Rites at this time was vigorously promoting the ideals of the Chu Hsi school. The officials who promulgated this new law wished to create a new tradition, and in the manner of Huang Kan, to "transform customs." In the climate of the early 1300s, it was possible for both Chinese and Mongol officials to break from traditional Chinese practice.

NEW LEGISLATION PROMOTING WIDOW CHASTITY

The change in the law of 1303 was of profound significance for women and their relation to property and for the remarriage of widows. But it was only one among several items of new legislation that promoted widow chastity. In the first month of 1304, just seven months after the dowry ruling by the Ministry of Rites, emperor Temür issued a decree ordering local officials to help support impoverished widows:

Wives who stay chaste after the mourning period is over should be allowed to do as they please [and not be forced to remarry]. If their chastity is especially meritorious, and they are unable to support themselves, local officials are to provide grain to relieve them.[184]

There is a suggestion here that some widows may have been getting forced into remarriages.

Soon after this decree, in the eighth month of 1304, the Ministry of Rites spelled out the qualifications for a "meritorious" widow and ordered officials to report such women to the government to receive official door insignia (*ching-piao men-lü*) and exemption from corvée labor in recognition of their merit.[185] In a long order, the Ministry of Rites cited the need "to stimulate the reform of greedy habits and by example promote worthy customs." It addressed both filial piety and widow chastity, two issues that were a hallmark of Learning of the Way Confucianism. The criteria for an exemplary chaste widow were defined for the first time: The woman had to have been widowed before she was 30, to have made a public vow of chastity, and to have stayed chaste until she was over 50 years old. The woman required a local sponsor to present her case to the authorities. Local officials were to question relatives and neighbors to verify the woman's virtuous behavior and then report the case on up to the central government. If false reports were made, both the sponsor and the local authorities were to

184 TCTK 3:40.
185 YTC 33:13a–b. For the evolution of such rewards, see Elvin, "Female Virtue and the State," and Birge, "Levirate Marriage," esp. 107–9 and nn. 2, 3.

be punished.[186] This was the beginning of the systematic state sponsorship of widow chastity that so affected women in later periods. The same criteria for chastity were copied into the codes of the Ming and Ch'ing dynasties, and the memorial arches that dotted the late imperial Chinese countryside originated with the door insignia in this regulation. During the Yüan, from this time on, we frequently find in officials' collected works petitions requesting government recognition of widows in their families.[187]

In 1307 a new emperor ascended the throne, and soon after, in 1309, the Yüan court made a radical break from Chinese tradition when it declared that, from then on a widow's in-laws could arrange her remarriage and keep the betrothal gifts received. The order stripped widows of personal autonomy and their authority to return home or remarry on their own initiative. It eliminated the material incentives to remarry that Chinese widows had traditionally enjoyed and transferred power over remarriage away from the widow and her natal family to her in-laws. The order originated from a proposal submitted by the newly reestablished Secretariat for State Affairs. The authors built their case by first reviewing previous edicts on the subject. They quoted Khubilai's 1271, second month, edict on "General Rules for Marriage and Betrothal Gifts," where it said:

If a woman stays chaste after the mourning period is over and wishes to return to her natal family, she should be allowed to do so. Her parents-in-law may not on their own initiative arrange a remarriage for her.[188]

Next they quoted Khubilai's rather contradictory edict of the twelfth month of that year that a widow could be forced into a union with an eligible levir.[189] Then they argued that families with sons were becoming

---

186 YTC 33:13a–b. The rules for verification suggest that the order was also meant to stem the proliferation of questionable petitions. Indeed the wording of the long ruling reveals concern that the rewards would be abused by the undeserving, especially among the rich, and it thus may have been an attempt to limit rewards. There is evidence that the Ministry of Rites was getting flooded with petitions at this time.

187 See, for instance, *Ch'iu-chien wen-chi*, 85:11b–12a (p. 818). We also find inscriptions commemorating chastity awards; e.g., *Yüan wen-lei* (Shih-chieh shu-chü, ed.), 17: 15b–16a.

188 YTC 18:14a; the original is found in YTC 18:2b, 13b–14a, and TCTK 3:40. The 1309 text gives the date as *chih-yüan* 28 (1291), but the original is *chih-yüan* 8 (1271). It is possible that the edict was reissued in 1291, but it seems more likely that this is just a corruption in the text.

189 Original found in YTC 18:23a.

impoverished when the son died and the widow remarried, and that the woman or her natal parents benefited from the remarriage:

Communiqués from every branch secretariat tell how wives when their husbands have died do not stay chaste in their husbands' households, but return to their natal families. During the mourning period, they accept meat, wine, bolts of cloth, and paper money from others, and on their own initiative remarry. . . . For this reason, the families of the husband's father and mother are gradually becoming impoverished.[190]

They concluded with the proposal:

From now on, if a woman wishes to stay chaste after her husband has died, she should be made to do so in her husband's household. If there is no brother-in-law eligible for a levirate marriage, and she wishes to remarry, she should comply with her father- and mother-in-law, who will receive the betrothal gifts and arrange the remarriage.[191]

Emperor Khaishan (Wu-tsung r. 1307–1311) approved the measure.

This new law upset the property regime that had effectively governed Chinese widows for as long as we find records. It also broke the tradition whereby widows returned to their natal homes. Women of any means in China had traditionally been able to return home when widowed and had typically contracted new marriages themselves or with the help of their natal parents. The new measure shifted the balance of legal power from the woman and her natal family to her in-laws, who could determine whether she remarried or not and could profit from the betrothal gifts. If an eligible levir resided in the household, they could force her to marry him. If she stayed chaste, she still had to reside with her in-laws and contribute her labor to them. The steppe concept of "purchasing" a wife, whose body and assets belonged to the husband's family for life, was now translated into Chinese imperial law.

It is significant that this radical break from Chinese tradition came about under a steppe-oriented Mongol emperor. Emperor Khaishan, who came to the throne in 1307 after a bitter succession battle, was known for his disinterest in Confucian culture. He packed the bureaucracy with his inner-Asian cronies and plunged the state into fiscal crisis. The Secretariat for State Affairs was formed to address this crisis and was filled with his own retainers, mostly non-Chinese.[192] In the 1309 marriage legislation, both the concept of a widow staying in the husband's home and the concept of the husband's family controlling the widow's person betray the influence of Mongol customs.

190 YTC 18:14a–b.   191 YTC 18:14b.
192 For a summary, see Hsiao, "Mid-Yüan politics," 507–12.

At the same time, this radical change in the law generated previously unheard of state support for the patrilineal ideals that Learning of the Way Confucians had long promoted. Once a woman married into her husband's family, she was now bound to them as she had not been before. The 1303 regulation assured that her assets were transferred to them and could not be taken by her out of the marriage; the 1309 law meant that her own person as an asset was also transferred to them. The first husband's family controlled a widow's marriage, her person, and her property. A widow's only option for some independence was to stay chaste, and this she had to do in the home of her in-laws as well. Such measures went beyond even what Huang Kan in the Sung had advocated.[193]

The similarity between the ideals of Huang Kan and the Chu Hsi school and the new legislation of 1303 and 1309 is not coincidental. Toward the end of Khubilai's reign, Learning of the Way scholars were already gaining influence at court. These were followers of Hsü Heng (1209–1281), whose teachings were based on the thought of Huang Kan.[194] By the early 1290s, the Yüan had established the largest network of government schools ever seen in China, which transmitted Chu Hsi's writings and the curriculum he advocated. Earlier, in 1271, the Imperial College (*Kuo-tzu chien*) was reestablished for both Chinese and non-Chinese, again teaching Chu Hsi's thought.[195] After Khubilai's death in 1294, Learning of the Way scholars gained more and more influence at court. The Mongol emperors themselves became more Confucian oriented. The reign of Khaishan (1307–1311) was a hiatus in this development. But by an extraordinary confluence of interests, both the steppe-oriented emperor and his ministers and the Confucian Learning of the Way advocates at court were willing to break with Chinese tradition and enact legislation that deprived widows of personal autonomy and property rights.

After Khaishan, in the reign of Ayurbarwada (Jen-tsung r. 1311–1320), the teachings of the Ch'eng-Chu school (as interpreted by

---

193 The title of the entry for the 1309 ruling in the *Yüan tien-chang* reveals the reversal of earlier policy. It is "The father- and mother-in-law may marry off their son's wife." The title of the ruling applying Khubilai's edict in the eleventh month of 1271 reads the reverse: "The father- and mother-in-law may *not* marry off their son's wife." The wording is identical except for the insertion of the one word "not" (*pu*), and the two rulings appear within a page of each other in the 1322 original Yüan edition. YTC 18:13b–14a.

194 Wing-tsit Chan, "Chu Hsi and Yüan Neo-Confucianism"; de Bary, *Neo-Confucian Orthodoxy*, 1–66; Yao Ta-li, "Chin-mo Yüan-ch'u li-hsüeh tsai pei-fang te ch'uan-po," *Yüan-shih lun-ts'ung* 2 (1983): 217–24.

195 de Bary, *Neo-Confucian Orthodoxy*, 55.

Huang Kan) "had reached a new height of influence."[196] The Central Secretariat and other central bureaus contained many Learning of the Way followers, both Chinese and Mongol. In 1313 the civil service examinations were reinstituted based on the Four Books and Chu Hsi's commentaries. In 1315 the first examinations were held, testing one's knowledge of Chu Hsi's interpretation of Confucianism.[197] Also in 1313 Hsü Heng was enshrined in the Confucian temple alongside Chu Hsi, Lü Tsu-ch'ien, Huang Kan, Chen Te-hsiu, and other Learning of the Way masters of the Southern Sung.[198] During Jen-tsung's reign, Chen Te-hsiu's work *Ta-hsüeh yen-i* (*Extended meaning of the Great Learning*), with abridged Mongolian translation, was presented at court and much praised by the emperor.[199]

As the teachings of the Learning of the Way gained adherents both at court and in the provinces, legal developments that shifted power away from women continued. In 1313 (the same year the examinations were reinstituted), a report came from the Supervisor of Chang-te circuit (modern Anyang in northern Honan) proposing that women be prohibited from bringing lawsuits to court. The report complained that the region was plagued by endless litigation over "land, buildings, movable property, marriage and debts," and that among the litigants were "shameless women who fomented disputes, misrepresented male relatives, and knowingly made false claims." It complained that young widows prolonged cases in order to display their good looks and interact with the crowds. Such women would supposedly visit tea houses and wine taverns and lodge with Buddhist and Taoist monks. To stop this behavior and prevent "damage to the way women should behave," the report said:

From now on, it is not permitted for a woman (*fu-jen*) to file a lawsuit. If there are no males in her entire family (*ch'üan chia*) and the matter cannot be settled through private means, such that it is necessary to bring a suit before the authorities, she is allowed to have a relative from her lineage (*tsung-tsu ch'in-jen*) represent her in the suit.[200]

---

196 de Bary, *Neo-Confucian Orthodoxy*, 55.
197 On the reinstatement of the exams and their content, see Benjamin A. Elman, *A Cultural History of Civil Examinations in Late Imperial China* (Berkeley: University of California Press, 1999); de Bary, *Neo-Confucian Orthodoxy*, esp. 53–60; and Yao Ta-li, "Yüan-ch'ao k'o-chü chih-tu te hsing-fa chi ch'i she-hui pei-ching," *Yüan-shih chi pei-fang min-tzu shih yen-chiu chi-k'an*, no. 6 (1982): 26–59.
198 For a list of the Confucian scholars enshrined in the temple, see Wilson, *Genealogy of the Way*, 254–9.
199 de Bary, *Neo-Confucian Orthodoxy*, 55.
200 YTC 53:19a. A French translation of this passage and much of the rest of the case is found in Ratchnevsky, *Un Code* IV, 226–9. Cf. Ratchnevsky, "Jurisdiction, Penal Code,

The Central Secretariat, a stronghold of Learning of the Way adherents, approved the measure with an important modification suggested by the Ministry of Punishments, that it would not apply to widows without relatives to represent them or widows who had to bring suits on behalf of sons who were incapable of representing themselves. Thus women were not entirely excluded from court.[201] (And they were never excluded from interrogation; see Figure 6.)

The new legislation of 1309 and 1313 seriously constrained women's freedoms and opportunities for redress. But it did not resolve the tensions and contradictions that still surrounded issues of the levirate and widow remarriage. Things were not so simple for widows who resisted levirate marriages, especially since they were required to remain in their husband's household even if they wished to stay chaste. The less than ideal conditions that some women found themselves in are vividly illustrated in a lawsuit filed in 1318. (In seeming contravention of the 1313 law, the suit was brought by the widow herself, T'ien Ah-Tuan.[202])

In the tenth month of 1313, Ah-Tuan's husband died and she returned with her four children to the home of her father Tuan Ts'ung, after refusing to marry her husband's next younger brother, T'ien Ch'ang-i. On the twenty-seventh day of the third month of 1317, nearly four years after her husband had died, Ah-Tuan's mother-in-law, Ah-Ma, went with her youngest son, T'ien Wu-erh, to Tuan Ts'ung's house to ask that Ah-Tuan marry him in a levirate union. The widow's father, Tuan Ts'ung, refused, saying, "My daughter is in mourning and is keeping her chastity; [moreover] she has four children. How can a levirate marriage take place?"[203] In response, the mother-in-law Ah-Ma requested that Ah-Tuan return to her house to cook a meal. This she did, and after the meal was over, Ah-Tuan asked to return home. At this point, the older brother, T'ien Ch'ang-i, seized her and in collusion with his two younger bothers beat and raped her. The court documents detail the incident:

and Cultural Confrontation under Mongol-Yüan Law," *Asia Major* 6:1 (1993): 177. It is interesting that we find here a reference to the lineage, something absent from the earlier decisions on property.

201 In fact, when this provision was included in the 1334 legal compilation, the *Ching-shih ta-tien,* is was considerably watered down, saying only that women could not represent men in court, except for widows representing their sons; *Yüan shih* 105:2671. See also Ratchnevsky, *Un Code* IV, 226. A similarly watered down version is already found in the introduction to a collection of legal petition forms published between 1330 and 1333 for people filing lawsuits; see *Shih-lin kuang-chi, pie-chi* 4:1006; and *Yüan-tai fa-lü tzu-liao chi-tsun,* 228.

202 The character for this name in the YTC looks like *hsia,* but it is a common Yüan variant for *tuan.*

203 YTC 18:24b–25a.

Figure 6. Woman being interrogated in court. From *Yü-chüeh chi* (1581. Reprint, Taipei: T'ien-i ch'u-pan she, 1983).

Her brother-in-law, T'ien Ch'ang-i, grabbed Ah-Tuan and dragged her into the main room in which he lived. He bolted the door and ordered his younger brother T'ien Lu-erh to watch it. Then T'ien Wu-erh grasped Ah-Tuan's hands while his brother Ch'ang-i struck two blows to her shoulder with a cudgel, rendering her immobile. They then tied her hair to the window lattice and ripped

270

off her clothes. T'ien Wu-erh held her hands down so that his brother Ch'ang-i could consummate the levirate marriage.[204]

Judges at every level supported the widow T'ien Ah-Tuan. The Liao-yang Branch Secretariat accused T'ien Ch'ang-i of "raping a woman without a husband" and sentenced him to 97 strokes of the bamboo. The Ministry of Punishments increased the sentence to 107 strokes. It also ordered the Liao-yang authorities to give the younger brothers beatings, according to the extent of their complicity (the mother seems to have escaped punishment). The Central Secretariat reduced T'ien's beating back to 97 strokes but agreed that he had violated the law against rape of a widow. Ah-Tuan was allowed to return to her father's home with her four children, and there remain celibate. If she remarried, she would have to marry her brother-in-law T'ien Ch'ang-i, who had violated her.[205]

We see from this example that chastity was a legitimate way to escape levirate marriage. But the Confucian ideal of a chaste widow living harmoniously in her husband's household conflicted with the continued operation of the levirate. The authorities had to allow that if a potential levir threatened a widow's chastity, she could be allowed to reside with her natal family, instead of in her in-laws home as the law of 1309 demanded. Chastity itself had to be protected by law. The graphic description of the rape of T'ien Ah-Tuan in the *Statutes and Precedents* suggests that the authors may have wished to reinforce the insidiousness of the violation to justify protection of the chaste widow's sexual purity, even at the expense of serving her mother-in-law in the husband's home. In earlier cases in the 1270s (stage 2 of my analysis), where widows were forced into levirate unions, similar rapes had clearly occurred, but the judges were silent about them while ruling that the victim had to marry her erstwhile attacker.[206] A very different attitude had come to prevail in 1318.

We have seen that a woman had to vow lifelong chastity to qualify for exemption from a levirate marriage. Such vows carried great weight and legal importance, and women who successfully sued to escape levirate marriages were usually forced to register a certificate of chastity with the local authorities. If a widow violated her vow, the proposed levir could force her to marry him.

204 YTC 18:25a.
205 YTC 18:24b–25a; Hung, "Yüan-tai," 312–13; cf. Ratchnevsky, "The Levirate," 61 n. 21.
206 See for instance the case of 1273 (YTC 18:24a–b), where even though the woman was suing to escape the marriage, the judges accused her of willingly having intercourse with her brother-in-law whom she claimed had raped her.

Even when a widow had no in-laws and no levir existed, the government restricted remarriage. Widows who were eligible to remarry had to file a petition and gain official approval to do so. Standardized forms were available for such petitions, and these were reproduced and distributed with other types of petitions. An example of such a petition survives from a 1325 collection. It reads:

Sample Petition for a Widow without Children
Requesting a Permit to Remarry

Person Submitting Document: Wang Ah-So-and-so. The above Ah-So-and-so is so many years old, is without disease and is not pregnant. She is registered as a civilian in such-and-such hamlet and such-and-such canton, and is the wife of Wang Ta [fill in actual name], who has died. She humbly submits this petition:

I, Ah-So-and-so, originally of a commoner household in such-and-such hamlet am the wife of Wang Ta. I have not borne or raised any children. On the such day, such month of the year such-and-such, my husband Wang Ta died of natural causes. At this time, I have already observed the mourning period, have completed his funeral, and have laid him peacefully to rest. Currently, my household has no income or property to support me. Truly I am impoverished and suffering great misery. If I do not prepare this petition and obtain a permit to remarry, I will have to continue to live as a widow and will be in extreme distress. [Thus] I respectfully submit this petition to the authorities of such-and-such county. I humbly beg them to read it carefully and act upon it. That to which I have testified is true. I humbly await your decision.

Petition from Wang Ah-So-and-so, of such year, such month, such day.[207]

The contents of the petition reveal the conditions under which the government could sanction remarriage. Poverty was the one acceptable reason for it (despite Ch'eng I's famous dictum that it was better for a widow to starve to death).[208] The widow had to have observed mourning and tended to her husband's funeral. She could not have borne any children. If she had children by her first husband, she was expected to raise them on his behalf to carry on his family line. All of these reflect concerns of Learning of the Way Confucians. We saw above that in 1303 emperor Temür urged local officials to provide sustenance to chaste widows. But it is not likely that many of them received this, and these same officials had to recognize that remarriage was usually a more realistic choice for such women.

---

207 *Shih-lin kuang-chi* (reprint of Yüan ed.: Kyoto: Chūbun, 1988) *pie-chi* 4:1016. It is reprinted in *Yüan-tai fa-lü tzu-liao chi-ts'un*, 236–7. This form is among the "new forms" of the collection and was thus probably produced between 1325 and 1330. I thank Lucille Chia for drawing my attention to another example from a Yüan document in the Palace Museum library, Taipei.

208 *Ho-nan Ch'eng-shih i-shu*, in *Erh Ch'eng ch'üan-shu* 22B:3a; Chan, *Reflections on Things at Hand*, 177.

To conclude, by 1320 laws on women's property and widow chastity had undergone a transformation that severely restricted their property rights and freedom to remarry. Women could no longer take their dowry with them out of a marriage in case of either widowhood or divorce. When a widow did remarry, she had to have permission from her in-laws, and these in-laws could choose her new partner and even keep the betrothal gifts from the new husband. If a widow chose not to remarry, she was required by law to stay chaste in the home of her first husband. Levirate marriage was still legal in the form of a man marrying his older brother's wife or his father's secondary wives. A widow could resist levirate marriage by staying chaste, and imperial rewards encouraged her to do so. While the authorities were likely to sympathize if a woman claimed she'd been raped and forced into a levirate union, women were technically forbidden to bring lawsuits to court, and only loopholes allowed them to appeal to the law for protection of their person or property.

During this same period, the first two decades of the fourteenth century, adherents of Huang Kan and the Chu Hsi school were making significant gains at the Yüan court. In 1313 (the same year that women were forbidden to file lawsuits), the civil service examinations were reinstituted based on the Four Books and Chu Hsi's commentaries. The new legislation around the issues of marriage and women's property was remarkably close to what Huang Kan had advocated in the Sung.

Stage 5: The Exaltation of Chastity in the Late Yüan

As the fourteenth century progressed, issues of remarriage, property, and the levirate were still getting played out. Legally a widow could escape levirate marriage by staying chaste, but if we can believe the dynastic history, women still found themselves forced into levirate unions. Very likely a desire to gain control of a widow's property motivated in-laws to pressure women into such marriages. At the same time, women who resisted them, sometimes unto death, gained fame for their virtue and were immortalized in the *Yüan Dynastic History* (*Yüan shih*).

Madam Wang, wife of Chao Mei from Nei-huang (east of Anyang in modern Honan), is one example. Chao Mei drowned in 1321 and Madam Wang pledged eternal fidelity, but Chao's parents had other ideas. Noting that Madam Wang was still young and had no children, they urged her to remarry. Madam Wang told them, "It is the duty of a wife not to remarry; moreover, while my father- and mother-in-law are still alive, how could I abandon them and leave?" The father- and mother-in-law rejected her services and pressured her into marrying a nephew. When she realized she could not avoid the levirate union, she hanged herself.[209]

A different Madam Wang, this time in Ch'eng-tu (Szechwan), was honored in her lifetime for resisting a levirate marriage. Her husband died when she was nineteen, and when his younger brother tried to marry her, she cut off her hair and then an ear, inflicting other injuries on herself in the process. Impressed with her resolve, her relatives nursed her back to health. Then they memorialized her deeds and received a plaque of imperial recognition.[210] By granting rewards like these, the central government came down strongly on the side of widow chastity as opposed to levirate remarriage. The former was indeed gaining prestige as the latter was quickly losing favor.

Mongol women also gained fame for choosing chastity over levirate marriage. T'o-t'o-ni, an "attractive and talented" Onggirrad woman, was widowed at 26. Her husband was survived by two adult sons by another wife, who expected to marry her in accordance with Mongol tradition. They pressed their claims despite her oath of fidelity unto death. In a rage she scolded them saying, "You behave like birds and beasts. If you married me, your mother, how could you face your father below when you died?" The dynastic history goes on to say, "the two sons were ashamed and begged her forgiveness. Thereupon they divided the household property and lived separately. For thirty more years she was known for her chastity."[211]

The reference to dividing the property gives us a hint of the reality behind the record. T'o-t'o-ni almost certainly retained control of her husband's estate, which the sons could have obtained had they married her. Instead, T'o-t'o-ni's resolve led to a compromise solution of splitting the property and setting up separate households. The Ming compilers of the Yüan dynastic history were evidently willing to overlook this contradiction in their desire to promote widow chastity and discredit the levirate. In fact, as Holmgren has argued, elite Mongol women rarely remarried, because they had far more to lose than to gain. By staying celibate, such women retained control of their own and their late husband's assets.[212] Government rewards for widow chastity gave these women honor and advantage for something they had already long practiced and which was already in their best interests.

209 *Yüan shih*, 200:4495; Hung, "Yüan-tai," 314.
210 *Yüan shih*, 200:4496; Hung, "Yüan-tai," 314.
211 *Yüan shih*, 200:4495–6. See also Hung, "Yüan-tai," 291.
212 Holmgren, "Observations," 167.

The situation of the Mongol aristocrat Sengge Ragi must be seen in this light. She was the half-sister of emperor Wu-tsung (Khaishan, r. 1307–1311), and her daughter married his son, emperor Wen-tsung (Tugh Temür, r. 1328–1329). Her husband was the Onggirad prince Diuabala, and when he died in 1310, he left behind an eight-year-old son from a previous marriage.[213] She declined to remarry and lived with her son, who in 1311 inherited his father's title and fief as Prince of Lü. Sengge herself was enfeoffed in 1306 as "Supreme Princess of Lü" (the usual title given to the emperor's paternal aunts), and had considerable personal holdings. In the twelfth month of 1329, Emperor Wen-tsung noted her twenty years of chastity (by Chinese counting) and ordered that she receive recognition. A short time later she was awarded the splendid title of August Imperial Aunt Virtuous Prosperous Chaste and Long-lived Supreme Princess, with the generous income of 60,000 license loads of salt from the four Salt Distribution Commissions of Huai, Che, Shan-tung, and Ho-chien.[214] In the ninth month of 1330, she further received 500 *ch'ing* of land in the area of P'ing-chiang (modern Suchou), a gift of 10,000 *ting* of paper money (worth 50 ounces of silver each), and the mansion of a Mongol noble.[215] Emperor Wen-tsung could conveniently use the pretext of chastity to shower Sengge with favors.[216]

Whether or not selfish motives led Sengge to remain single, the practice of the levirate was quickly losing legitimacy during the 1320s. Finally, in the ninth month of 1330, emperor Wen-tsung issued an edict outlawing all forms of levirate marriage for the Chinese and other peoples who had not formerly practiced it:

Among those for whom it is not their original custom, it is an offense for a man to take his elder sister-in-law or a son to take his father's secondary wives in a levirate union.[217]

These two forms of the levirate were the only ones still practiced by the Chinese, thus this edict effectively outlawed all forms. The prohibition on the levirate for Chinese was included in the major legal compilation

---

213 Hung points out that Holmgren must be wrong in claiming this son was her own, since he was born four years before Sengge's marriage in 1307, "Yüan-tai," 291 n. 42; Holmgren, "Observations," 166 n. 114.

214 A license load was 400 *chin* (a *chin* being about 600 grams). For an explanation of these commissions, see Farquhar, *The Government of China*, 187, 373; and Schurmann, *Economic Structure of the Yüan Dynasty*, 169, 177.

215 *Yüan shih*, 33:746; 34:767; 118:2916–17.

216 Indeed, her "virtue" was not sufficient to get her a biography in the exemplary women section of the Yüan dynastic history.

217 *Yüan shih*, 34:767; Hung, "Yüan-tai," 294.

ordered by Wen-tsung and completed in 1331, the *Great Compendium of Statecraft* (*Ching-shih ta-tien*). There the prohibition reads:

For Chinese in the North and the South, it is forbidden for a son to marry his father's secondary wives when his father dies, and for a younger brother to marry his older brother's wife when the older brother dies.[218]

The 1331 *Compendium of Statecraft* repeated earlier prohibitions on certain forms of the levirate for all peoples, including Mongols. These were marriages between the older brother and the younger brother's wife, and with the wife of a cousin of a different surname.[219] During the mourning period for either parent, even Mongol men (like all others) were forbidden to contract a levirate union with their father's secondary wives. The punishment was harsh: 107 strokes for both the man and the woman and dissolution of the marriage. An official would lose his office.[220] Mongol women like Sengge Ragi might still have entered into a levirate marriage within the remaining legal limits, but they had ample moral authority (and economic motive) to resist as well. In 1334 Emperor Shun-ti, who was even more steeped in Confucian learning than his predecessors, ordered Mongols and Inner Asians to observe mourning for their parents.[221]

By 1331, laws restricting women's property rights, especially their ability to take their dowry out of a marriage, were firmly in place. Nevertheless, the special character of dowry was not entirely erased. The *Great Compendium of Statecraft* of 1331 included a provision as follows:

If a son is not filial and his father kills him on this account, and in the process kills his son's wife too, the father is punished with 77 strokes of the heavy bamboo. The contents of the wife's original dowry should all be returned to her parents.[222]

218 *Yüan shih*, 103:2644; Ratchnevsky, *Un Code* II, 131–2. See Ratchnevsky, *Un Code* I, xxiff; and Ch'en, *Chinese Legal Tradition*, 33–5 for evidence that this section of the *Yüan shih* is in fact taken from the *Ching-shih ta-tien*. The "Judicial Statutes" section of the *Ching-shih ta-tien* (which is where the prohibition is found) was as close as anything in the Yüan to a legal code.
219 *Yüan shih*, 103:2643–4; Ratchnevsky, *Un Code* II, 130–4 (Articles 401, 404). See YTC 18:26b–27a, YTCHC hun-yin: 4a (decisions of 1275, 1277, and 1321) regarding older brother unions, and YTC 18:27b–28a (decision of 1289) regarding cousin marriage.
220 *Yüan shih*, 103:2643–4; Ratchnevsky, *Un Code* II, 131.
221 *Yüan shih*, 38:823, 41:868, 139:3361; Ch'en, *Chinese Legal Tradition*, 37–8. In 1343 Shun-ti ordered the compilation of the Sung, Liao, and Chin dynastic histories. On the Confucianization of the Yüan court in this later period, see John Dardess, *Conquerors and Confucians: Aspects of Political Change in Late Yüan China* (New York: Columbia University Press, 1973).
222 *Yüan shih*, 105:2676; Ratchnevsky, *Un Code* IV, 270; Yanagida, "Gendai joshi no zaisan shōkei," 265.

If a man murdered his daughter-in-law, he could not expect to obtain her dowry. A married woman enjoyed at least this much protection, and to this extent, her property was not completely merged with that of her husband's family. In a related provision, if a married woman's own father murdered her, "because of some transgression," he received 57 strokes of the light bamboo and had to return the betrothal gifts so that the husband "could find a new wife."[223] The lighter sentence for the natal father shows that he still had more authority over his daughter than her father-in-law did. She was still not fully incorporated into her husband's family, legally or financially.

Parting with her dowry was still seen as a rare virtue for women in the Yüan. A Ming account of such a donation in the early fourteenth century credited it with imbuing magic powers that later saved a Ningbo woman and her husband from a fire.[224]

Post-Yüan Developments

The Ming and Ch'ing codes harshly outlawed the levirate in all its forms. The closer the relation, the harsher the punishment: the punishment for marrying a brother's widow was strangling and for marrying a father's concubine was beheading.[225] Cases of levirate marriage can occasionally be found in the Ming and Ch'ing, especially among illiterate peasants, but it was never again legal or accepted as it had been in the Yüan. But the popularity of chastity and the condemnation of remarriage grew stronger after the Yüan.

In particular, subsequent dynasties adopted the most important of the Yüan legislation that restricted women's property rights and promoted widow chastity. Government rewards for widow chastity continued and were augmented by exemption from corvée duty and other privileges. The original Yüan definition of a chaste widow was copied into Ming and Ch'ing law.[226] Most importantly, the 1303 law that prevented a widow from keeping her dowry was carried over into all later codes in China before the modern era. Both the Ming and Ch'ing codes adopted the pertinent language of the Yüan code where they said:

---

223 *Yüan shih*, 105:2676; Ratchnevsky, *Un Code* IV, 268.
224 Elvin, "Female Virtue and the State," 119–20.
225 *Ming-lü chi-chie fu-li*, 6:20b, 21a; *Ta Ch'ing lü-li*, 10:221 (Regulation #396). See also Ch'ü, *Law and Society*, 97.
226 *Ming hui-tien*, 79:457; Farmer, *Zhu Yuanzhang and Early Ming Legislation* (Leiden: E. J. Brill, 1995), 161; Elvin, "Female Virtue and the State," 123–4.

When a widow remarries, the property of her husband and the dowry that she originally possessed should all be taken over by the family of her former husband.[227]

Written judgments from the Ming and Ch'ing show that this statute was applied in legal decisions. In one case from the early Ch'ing, a widow remarried, taking her property with her. She was subsequently sued by her first husband's nephew, who had become heir to his uncle after the death of the only son. The court ruled that she had to give her 40 *mou* of land and two-room house to this nephew since her property now belonged to her first husband's estate.[228] In the twentieth century, courts continued to uphold the statute. A Supreme Court decision of 1918 denied wives control of their own property.[229]

Nevertheless, changes in the law did not necessarily transform practice. The weight of customary practice that went back to the Sung and before continued to have considerable effect. The Ming and Ch'ing codes no longer included the provision that a wife's property be excluded from family division. But survey data from North China in the early twentieth century shows that land owned by peasant wives was normally excluded from family division, and Shiga Shūzō has even suggested that this was so routine as not to need inclusion in the law code.[230] Regarding widows, interviews with peasants done by both Chinese and Japanese survey teams in North and South China show that practice varied considerably and included stark exceptions to the written law. Differences abounded even within regions. In some examples widows could always take their dowry with them (Chekiang and Heilungkiang) and in others they could only have it with the consent of their in-laws (Heilungkiang again). In other examples, respondents claimed a woman could not take her dowry away, as written in the law (Kiangsu).[231] In Taiwan in the twentieth century, Myron Cohen found that a widow could keep her dowry and even take some of her husband's property

---

227 *Ming hui-tien*, 19:130; *Ta Ch'ing lü-li*, 8:195 (Regulation #318). See also Shiga, *Genri*, 332; Farmer, *Zhu Yuanzhang and Early Ming Legislation*, 160; Pierre Hoang, *Le Mariage Chinois au Point de Vue Legal* (Shanghai: Catholic Mission Press, 1915), 160, 165; Ch'ü, *Law and Society*, 104.

228 Shiga, *Genri*, 422–3.   229 Ch'ü, *Law and Society*, 104.

230 Shiga, *Genri*, 513; Yanagida, "Gendai joshi no zaisan shōkei," 265. The surveys were carried out in Hopei and Shantung in the late 1930s.

231 Shiga, *Genri*, 528–9 and 546–7. It is possible that control of dowry depended partly on what form it was in. Rubie Watson has found that dowry in Hong Kong in the form of jewelry was kept by the woman, while earnings from work and other forms of property were not. "Women's Property in Republican China: Rights and Practices," *Republican China*, no. 10 (1984): 1–12.

into a second marriage.[232] Tai Yen-hui claims that the law on dowry was never upheld and that the statute had to be changed in the late Ch'ing.[233] Other authors have stressed that a wife had no control over property, even dowry, and that this was upheld in twentieth century court decisions.[234]

Shiga, while noting the lack of legal protections for women, concludes that in late imperial China there was no fixed rule in practice governing the property of wives and widows, and that variation was the norm. Indeed, the change of the law in the Yüan would seem to have brought it into contradiction with traditional practice leaving a patchwork of legal and extralegal solutions in the centuries following.

Conclusion

When the Mongols completed their invasions of North and then South China in the thirteenth century, they brought with them new concepts of social control and dynastic administration and a marriage and property regime that was very different from that of the Chinese. While Chinese law and practice purported to uphold principles of patrilineality, it was not until steppe laws and customs were introduced by the Mongols that Chinese marriage and property law became unequivocally patrilineal.

Yüan law tied inheritance to the male line far more than traditional Chinese law had done. The Yüan government's system of military households and their use of corvée performed by males privileged men over women and largely excluded daughters from the line of property transmission. The steppe emphasis on controlling people as opposed to areas of land contributed to tax and revenue policies that were based on maximizing households and preventing family lines from dying out. In sharp contrast to their Sung sisters, daughters without brothers under Yüan

232 Cohen, *House*, 186. See also Bernard and Rita Gallin, "The Chinese Joint Family in Changing Rural Taiwan," in *Social Interaction in Chinese Society*, ed. S. L. Greenblatt, R. W. Wilson, and A. A. Wilson, (New York: Pergamon Press, 1982). Cohen argues that property of the conjugal unit (*fang*, or *fo*, property) including dowry was seen to be held jointly between husband and wife; thus when one died, the other controlled all the property. This was true even though the wife had complete control over her *se-koi* (private money, dowry) before family division.

233 Tai, "Divorce in Traditional Chinese Law," 105 and n. 175. (Tai cites evidence from Taiwan, where we have seen that the law was not enforced.) I cannot find evidence for a change in the law, and it was restated in the last edition of the Ch'ing code in 1877; George Jamieson, *Chinese Family and Commercial Law* (Shanghai: Kelly and Walsh Ltd., 1921), 14.

234 Ch'ü, *Law and Society*, 104. See also Fei, *Peasant Life in China*.

law could only expect to inherit substantially from their fathers by inviting in permanent uxorilocal husbands who could continue their father's patriline and take on his service obligations. The result was a shift in property transmission away from women toward men that coincidentally supported the Confucian patriline.

A transformation of marriage law that privileged the husband's family similarly came about through the Mongol's introduction of the levirate. The Chinese were shocked by the practice of the levirate, which by Chinese law amounted to incest. Nevertheless, over time Chinese in a range of income groups found the levirate attractive. It stripped power from the wife and her natal family in favor of the husband and his family. In particular, it kept a widow's assets, her labor, and her person in the home of her husband and saved the cost of betrothal gifts for younger sons. Many Chinese men and their parents in the thirteenth century attempted to carry out levirate unions, while widows and their parents sued to prevent them.

At first the Mongol-Yüan regime outlawed the levirate for Chinese and maintained separate laws for Chinese and non-Chinese peoples. Then in 1271, Khubilai ordered that all peoples practice the levirate: Chinese and Mongols alike. This switch would seem to have appealed to many, but the contradictions between the levirate and Chinese marriage laws quickly made necessary a retreat from this blanket policy. From the late 1270s on, many exceptions were made to the levirate law (such as when the levir was already married, underage, and so forth), and widow chastity emerged as a means to escape levirate marriage. The levirate continued to operate among the Chinese until 1330, however, and if an eligible levir was available, a widow was forced to marry him or remain chaste in her husband's household. She could no longer return home and remarry an outsider.

These events made possible a change in the marriage and property regime that had dominated Chinese society until that time. A married woman's relation to property changed dramatically. New laws in the early fourteenth century stripped women of their property rights and their freedom to remarry. Now if a woman wished to remarry after widowhood or divorce, she had to leave her dowry property behind, both real and movable, with her in-laws. By law a widow needed the consent of her in-laws to remarry at all, and they, not she or her natal family, would receive the betrothal gifts. In 1313 a new regulation excluded women from court, thus weakening their ability to protect what rights they had left.

These changes in the law in the first decades of the fourteenth century brought it into line with the ideals of the Chu Hsi school. At the end of the Sung, Huang Kan had called on widows to (1) reject remarriage and stay chaste; (2) continue to live in their deceased husband's household to serve his parents and not return to their natal families; and (3) give up personal control over their property and share it with their husband's family. By 1320, barely 100 years after Huang Kan's death, new laws supported all three of these precepts. The laws explicitly compelled compliance with the last two, by prohibiting a woman from returning home when widowed or taking her dowry out of the marriage, and they strongly promoted the first with both rewards and sanctions.

The new legislation went even beyond Huang Kan's ideals. Huang Kan never suggested that a woman be forced to part with her property, even if she returned home or remarried. Like other Chinese of his day, he still saw an unbreakable bond between a woman and her personal dowry property. The encounter with new forms of marriage and property relations broke this legal and psychological link between women and their property and put a wife's property and person under the effective control of her in-laws.

The switch in thinking toward Confucian ideals represented a break from previous Chinese tradition as demonstrated in the change of attitudes toward widows returning home. In the early thirteenth century, the idea that a widow should stay in the home of her husband was quite alien to the Chinese and was linked to what the Chinese considered the incestuous and barbaric practice of the levirate. Contemporary commentators contrasted the Mongol practice of a widow remaining in her husband's home, to remarry in a levirate union, with the Chinese tradition of a widow returning to her natal family and remarrying an outsider. But by the early fourteenth century, both Chinese and Mongols in the government were enacting laws to prevent widows from returning home. The old dichotomy between Chinese and Mongol custom, whereby Chinese widows returned home and Mongol widows did not, had disappeared. Yet widow residence with her in-laws was not without tensions. While the levirate was still legal, widows were vulnerable to rape by the husband's relatives, and both before and after the levirate was outlawed, widows were subject to forced remarriages, now that their in-laws had so much to gain financially from a remarriage.

All of these developments gave impetus to new legal and social sanctions in favor of widow chastity. Until 1330, the laws of levirate marriage eliminated remarriage to an outsider for women with surviving brothers-in-law, and chastity was the only option for widows who rejected levirate marriages. Chastity also provided the only way for a widow to retain control of her personal property and her husband's. Chastity suddenly gained practical as well as purely moral appeal among Chinese, and the Mongol aversion to widow remarriage to an outsider began to take root in popular Chinese culture. In later dynasties, the popularity of chastity and the condemnation of remarriage to an outsider remained in place, even as the practice of the levirate among Chinese that had stimulated these developments was harshly outlawed. As with inheritance law, Chinese administrations in the centuries after Mongol rule adopted new Yüan marriage laws, while claiming that these represented a long tradition of Confucian Chinese practice.

Conclusion:
Gender, Mongols, and
Confucian Ideals

In any society, the construction of gender is a continuous process intimately connected to other historical developments such as in society, government, and foreign relations. The case of women and property in Sung and Yüan China provides an excellent example of these connections. The Mongol invasion together with longer-term historical changes over the Sung and Yüan created a new constellation of property and gender relations in China that brought them closer to patrilineal ideals as defined by Learning of the Way Confucians of the Sung.

Patriline principles were part of Chinese society from earliest times, as seen in Confucian ritual texts, legal codes, and popular practices such as agnatic ancestor worship. Nevertheless, the institutionalization of patrilineality in China was never complete, and especially in the area of property relations severe tensions existed between Confucian ideals, state law, and social practice.

Formal law and Confucian rhetoric tied the transmission of property to the male patriline and accompanying ancestral sacrifices. From at least the Han dynasty, Confucian ritual prescriptions that favored only one descent-line heir had been reinterpreted in the light of popular practices to dictate that every son in a family produce an unending line of male descendants, who could perform ancestral sacrifices in perpetuity. Household property, held communally under the name of the household head, was divided equally among the sons at the death of the parents, to allow each son to establish a new household and a ritual line of succession. A son had to be resident in the household to be eligible for his share in family division (contrary to the descent-line system described in the Confucian classics). Accordingly, sons remained in the household while daughters married out, thus creating a system that further bolstered patriarchal and patrilineal social structures. Centuries later the great T'ang code articulated the practice of "equal division among [coresident] brothers" in the first detailed statutes on inheritance that survive today.

Daughters were excluded from this formal inheritance scheme for both ideological and practical reasons: (1) they could not worship their natal ancestors and thus were not in the ritual line of succession; and (2) they typically left home at marriage, so were not likely to be resident at the time of family division. Nevertheless, in a major exception to the dictates of patrilineality, daughters routinely received significant amounts of family property in the form of dowry.

The institution of dowry represented a complementary property regime that endured throughout Chinese history side by side with the patrilineal, male property regime. The rhetoric of Confucian ideals, found in legal codes and written sources of all periods in China, obscures the extent and significance of this property regime. As discussed in the Introduction, words used to label women's property evoked items of personal adornment and created associations with the inner boudoir. In reality, dowry property could include any of the types of assets transmitted to men, and could be of considerable value vis-à-vis a husband's or brother's eventual inheritance through family division.

Although the T'ang code excluded daughters from the guarantees of "equal division," the transmission of family assets to daughters in the form of dowry was conceptually similar to the transmission of assets to sons as part of family division. The awarding of dowry before family division is consistent with the residence requirement for family division and makes dowry look more like a premortem substitute for participation in family division. When family division took place before a girl's marriage, while she was still resident in the household, she participated in it and received some amount of property. T'ang and Sung documents reveal the expectation that sons *and* daughters would participate in family division, often by drawing lots. Moreover, in the Sung we find daughters suing their siblings and other relatives for their fair share of property in family division. When there were no sons to succeed to the property, daughters in the Sung and before routinely received all of their parents' property. The classical emphasis on agnatic ritual obligations would suggest that male agnates should have had greater claim to an heirless couple's property than their daughters. But contrary to the principles found in the Confucian classics, daughters before the Yüan had a greater claim to inheritance from their parents than more distant agnates, even the father's brothers or nephews.[1] The connection between agnatic principles, ritual function, and property was always tenuous at best; and in the minds of most Chinese in the Sung and before, the difference between transmission to sons in family division and to daughters as dowry may have been more one of quantity than quality.

During the Sung dynasty, the contradictions between women's property rights and Confucian patrilineal ideals reached their peak. At a time of dramatic economic and social change and the emergence of a new elite dependent more on resources, affinity, and personal accomplishment for its preservation, dowry took on new importance and reached unprecedented levels. Most remarkably, the language of the T'ang code that was meant to keep property within the male line, to be divided equally among brothers, was reinterpreted to justify the transmission of wealth to women. The term "equal division" (*chün fen*) came to mean "equitable division," and was applied to daughters in family division suits brought to the state. A rule of thumb emerged early in the Sung that gave daughters half of a son's share, and in the thirteenth century this came to be dictated by statute. Similarly, judges applied the rule that "sons receive their father's share" (*tzu ch'eng fu fen*) to daughters, such that for the first time, when a man in a joint household died without sons, his future portion of the communal estate was held out for his daughters as their share in family division, instead of passing to his brothers. To garner income, the Sung state began to claim for itself a portion of property in cut-off households (those without sons),[2] but daughters continued to fare well vis-à-vis agnates, and case evidence from the thirteenth century shows judges reluctant to confiscate property to the full extent provided by law.

Property passed out of the agnatic line in other ways as well. Starting early in the dynasty, Sung law deprived nonresident agnates of property they once received when couples died childless, and bestowed it on various groups including female relatives, sons by a wife's previous husband, and even unrelated coresidents. In this regard it reflected popular concern for those who supported "the old and solitary," without regard to their connection to the agnatic line. Sung law did not tie property closely to a man's ritual patriline, and compared to the T'ang code it showed a distinct disregard for classic Confucian principles of ancestral worship and patrilineality.

---

1 It is noteworthy that inheritance by daughters in the absence of sons occurred in England historically as in China, but that many European systems gave priority to a more distant male relative at the expense of daughters; Erickson, *Women and Property*, 26–7.

2 In this regard, Sung law did regard inheritance by sons differently from that by daughters. The state never tried to lay claim to a son's inheritance.

The treatment of married women's property within the patriarchal household also presented a stark contradiction to Confucian ideals, which intensified in the Sung. Whereas men in a joint household could not formally hold private property, wives who married in could. As with the provisions of inheritance, women's private property in marriage represented an alternative female property regime that operated alongside the male, communal property regime and had enormous significance for both men and women. The T'ang code provided the legal basis for this separate women's property regime, where right after the statute on "equal division among brothers," it stated that "a wife's property is not to be included in family division." This effectively placed women's property outside of the control of the family head and undermined the ideal of common property. A wife's dowry property constituted a kind of free capital that husbands and wives could together use on their own initiative, and evidence from the Sung shows that such funds were indeed often invested in business ventures, lent out at high interest, or otherwise used for personal gain. Female property represented an enclave of freedom within the patriarchal family and may have been the very safety valve that allowed the otherwise stifling patrilineal system to persist through the centuries. The contraction of dowry rights after the Sung thus represented a contraction in individual rights of men as well as women. Keeping property more within the patriline and more under patriarchal control, whether under the control of a family head or lineage head in the post-Sung period, restricted the rights of men as well as of women.

Dowry property was distinguished from property of the husband even after family division with the husband in place as new head of the household. Detailed lists of dowry items including parcels of land, which were part of marriage negotiations, and the display of dowry before and during the marriage ceremony not only reinforced the status and prestige of the bride and her family but served to identify the property as private assets of the bride within her marital household. The very vocabulary that minimized dowry also distinguished it from property of the husband and ensured its special treatment even after the death of the woman herself. Most important, a woman could take her dowry (whether landed or movable) out of a marriage in case of widowhood or divorce. The bond between a woman and her dowry transcended the marital bond. Thus we saw in Chapter 2 how wives took property into three or more marriages and the previous husband of one woman wanted to reclaim her corpse in order to obtain her property.

Such a system made widow remarriage extremely attractive. Elite widows could return home with substantial wealth and take it into a new marriage. Typically a widow returned to her natal parents, who would arrange a remarriage (often quickly). If her parents were no longer alive, a widow could choose a new husband herself. This freedom was countered, however, by the vulnerability of widows who had no family to protect them.

The custom of widows returning to their natal families was so entrenched in China that we find it cited as a mark of Chinese ethnicity, in contrast to both the Jurchens and the Mongols. A Chinese commentator in the twelfth century and a Chinese advisor to Khubilai in the thirteenth both associated the custom of widows remaining in the husband's home with non-Chinese customs dictated by the practice of levirate marriage. Even Chinese women praised for their chastity in hagiographic texts of the Sung and early Yüan usually stayed chaste in their natal homes. Customs, attitudes, and the law that supported both were to change over the course of the Yüan dynasty.

Widows who chose to stay chaste had certain economic authority that was supported by Sung law, and in this limited way the law encouraged widow chastity. A widow in a nuclear family, without in-laws, could legally control the property of her husband as well as her own. Sung sources describe widows (and sometimes wives not widowed) reclaiming farmland, collecting rents, hiring workers, building dams, supporting temples, and donating large sums for community relief. The intent of the law was for the widow to preserve the estate for the first husband's children, or for an heir she adopted on her late husband's behalf. Sung law prohibited the widow's selling off her husband's property or taking it into a remarriage. Nevertheless, the law was open to abuse, and widows frequently invited in quasi-husbands to whom they were not legally married but with whom they could share the household wealth. Widows' selling land was also routine, and even their adult sons needed their permission to buy or sell property themselves. Once again Sung law and social practice gave certain women considerable authority over property, often at the expense of a first husband's agnates.

The contradictions between Confucian ideals of patrilineality and Sung law and practice did not go unnoticed. In their drive to reform society in the name of a return to ancient values, Learning of the Way philosophers sought to reconnect property with the male patriline and its agnatic rituals. In this effort, they were prepared to abolish long-established practices, and their proposals went against Sung law and custom in many regards. Even the most radical of the Learning of the Way advocates did not oppose dowry altogether, but they found large amounts of property going to women unacceptable. It was especially reprehensible to them for daughters in cut-off households to inherit the family patrimony, and a break in the ritual patriline by having no male heir was to be avoided at all costs. Accordingly, Chu Hsi praised women who rejected such inheritance from their parents and instead adopted a male heir on their parent's behalf to inherit the estate and carry on the family name. Such writing provided justification for the frequent intervention of agnates to appoint posthumous heirs and disinherit daughters. Contrary to Learning of the Way ideals, Sung law responded with detailed rules dividing property between natal daughters and a posthumous male heir that gave daughters the lion's share. (Chu Hsi's model women presumably relinquished their rights to such shares.)

Women's private property within marriage also violated Learning of the Way principles. Personal property, held by men or women, undermined patriarchal authority and broke down communal consciousness. It damaged harmony between brothers, it was argued, and led to early family division. A wife's private property upset both gender and generational hierarchies. Accordingly, funerary inscriptions for women written by Learning of the Way men and others began to record with increasing frequency in the Southern Sung cases of wives donating their dowries to their husbands' households. The fact that eulogies praised such generosity as a special virtue shows that it was by no means typical, and that women still had the authority *not* to relinquish their property. Nevertheless, by promoting dowry donations, these inscriptions contributed to a gradual change in attitude that made a woman's private assets and her control over these less acceptable.

At the same time, the aggressive separation of "inner" and "outer" in Learning of the Way philosophy gave women enormous responsibility in the household. It was the duty of the woman to take over nearly all responsibility for the household, to release her husband from quotidian worries and allow him to pursue "outside" affairs (including scholarship and personal cultivation). This had the effect of increasing the importance of women in the household, even as it relegated the domestic to a morally lower status than the nondomestic realm of men. A senior wife held the position of female head of house, and this could entail considerable authority over the human and material resources of an elite family's estate. Providing clothing by spinning and weaving and preparing food were obvious tasks for poor and rich women alike, and were labeled "women's work." But in a large household, the female head of house would have significant managerial responsibilities, including managing servants, arranging funerals, providing allowances from the common funds, or keeping track of all income and expenditure. Mothers were often the ones who arranged marriages for both sons and daughters. In the case of widows, we find Learning of the Way men praising wives for hiring farmhands, supervising workers, and buying and selling land. So-called domestic responsibilities could reach far into the community as seen by exemplary women involved in public building projects or famine relief. (In one example we were told how a wise mother prevented peasant unrest by opening up the family storehouses and selling rice at low prices.) Supporters of the Learning of the Way like Chen Te-hsiu lauded women who had the "strength" and "intelligence" to take on these multifarious activities.

Widows played a crucial role in maintaining the household and preserving the patriline, for which they were morally obligated to stay loyal and chaste in their husband's home. When a man died, his widow had to provide the missing link in the eternal patrilineal chain. A woman who conquered adversity and raised an heir to maturity could rescue a patriline from oblivion. Therefore the Chu Hsi school and later Confucians idealized the image of the strong, hardworking widow who saved her family from destitution and reestablished a line of male descendants. Widow remarriage, they felt, destroyed patrilines and threatened the familial and cosmic moral order.

The Learning of the Way vision for family and society had no room for large dowries, private property in marriage, or widow remarriage; nevertheless, Chu Hsi and others in his day seemed to take all of these for granted. They articulated ideals to which one could aspire in prescriptive texts, but in other writings they accepted the practical solutions of those around them. Judges who opposed remarriage nonetheless upheld property law that encouraged it and defended the right of widows to remarry. Even Chu Hsi acknowledged that sometimes widow remarriage was unavoidable, and he accepted dowry property and its special legal treatment within marriage as a given. Attitudes began to harden, however, among Chu Hsi's later followers.

Chu Hsi's disciple and son-in-law Huang Kan (1152–1221) directly attacked women's property rights and the desire of widows to remarry. In his judicial verdicts, Huang announced his disregard for established practice and declared his intent to change customs to make them conform more to Learning of the Way ideals. As a magistrate he ordered wives to share the fruits of their dowry property with their husband's family and allow the head of the household to manage their dowry lands. He called on widows to preserve their own and their husband's property for their children, and he forced widows to live in their husband's home, rather than return home. Such an ideal contravened the autonomy Chinese widows were used to, and whereas Huang wanted widows to stay chaste, he did allow that if they had no children, they could remarry and could take their dowry property with them. He wanted women to show greater commitment to their husband's family and off-spring, but he did not countenance breaking the bond between a woman and her dowry completely. Despite his aggressive attempts at reform, Huang did not advocate separating a woman from her property, even beyond death, and he accepted a certain degree of personal autonomy for widows and divorcées.[3]

Over the century after Huang Kan's death, his teachings spread north and eventually took hold among both Chinese and Mongol Confucians at the Yüan royal court. Just as the Yüan rulers reinstated the civil service examinations in 1313 in a simplified form based on Chu Hsi's commentaries, new laws on marriage and property were implemented in the early fourteenth century that supported all of Huang Kan's ideas and in some cases went even beyond them. The intent of Learning of the Way Confucians was to generate social structures that would preserve the patriline, and the Yüan government implemented new laws that helped them do this. This could not have happened, I argue, had it not been for the confrontation between Chinese and Mongol culture in the thirteenth and early fourteenth centuries that broke down ideas of ethnic distinction and created a transformation of gender relations.

The Mongol occupation of China disrupted the gender-property regime that had operated in China for centuries. Fundamental assumptions that had governed property relations until that time were upset, and long-established legal precedents were overturned. Inheritance practices, the institution of private property within marriage, and the rights of widows were all qualitatively transformed in the direction of Confucian patrilineal ideals. This came about by two complementary processes. First, the Mongol challenge to traditional Chinese law and practice opened up the opportunity for Learning of the Way adherents at court to push their radical agenda. Second, the interests of the Mongol government coincidentally overlapped with certain aspects of patrilineal principles.

Marriage and property relations among the Mongols, a nomadic-steppe people, were in many respects conceptually opposite the Chinese, resembling what Goody has described as the African mode of production and reproduction rather than the Eurasian system of China. The African model was characterized by a lack of property transmitted through women and more complete incorporation of a woman into her husband's lineage. The levirate kept widows from returning home. In

---

3 In the interesting case of a man trying to retrieve the dead body of his previous wife for her dowry, it was none other than Huang Kan who ruled that the woman's body and her property belonged to the household where she had fled after her three marriages broke up.

the case of inner-Asian nomads, it was often impossible for a woman to return to her natal family, which could be far away in an unknown part of the steppe. Mongol ideas of governance and taxation were also very different. The Mongols emphasized control over people rather than control over land, and their tax system reflected this. They instituted hereditary soldier households and other hereditary occupational groups, relied heavily on male corvée labor, and tended to tax households rather than land. It is no coincidence that the challenge to women's property rights and personal autonomy came in confrontation with steppe society.

First, Mongol law attached property to the male line far more than it had been under Sung and earlier Chinese law. Parents could still give their daughters dowry, but when parents died without sons, their estate no longer went automatically to their daughters to be taken into a marriage. Instead, a daughter could claim the property only if she married uxorilocally and thus maintained her father's household as a viable economic unit and fulfilled his corvée obligations. In hereditary soldier households, succession to property was explicitly tied to succession to military duty. Women were excluded from inheritance in these households because they could not take over a father's military service. Such practices influenced civilian households as well. There are no references to any half-share rule under the Yüan or later dynasties, and we no longer find the qualitative similarity between a daughter's and a son's inheritance that had characterized the previous centuries in China. Inheritance was regarded in far more gendered terms. These changes were stimulated by the Mongol government's concern for maintaining taxable households and keeping up a hereditary soldier population, as opposed to maintaining patrilineal ancestral sacrifices. But the result was unprecedented material support for the agnatic patrilineal in accordance with Confucian ideals.

Second, the bond between a married woman and her dowry property was broken. In the Sung and before, we saw how women could take their dowries into second and third marriages, and how even after death dowry was treated separately to benefit an individual woman. By contrast, a Mongol bride arrived with little or no dowry, but received personal property from the husband's family. The practice of the levirate kept both a widow's person and her property in the home of the husband, and saved families of moderate means from considerable hardship. In 1303, after the levirate had operated in South China for just over thirty years, the Yüan government decreed that a woman could no longer take her dowry out of a marriage, whether she was widowed or divorced, but had to leave all assets behind for "the family of her former husband." The decision, proposed by a Mongol official, was in response to complaints that families were getting impoverished when widows or divorcées left the household taking their dowries with them. The same note had been sounded in 1299, when a Chinese official complained that when officials died who were serving in faraway places like Kwang-tung, their wives and concubines quickly remarried taking away all the property of the household (their own and their husband's). The Yüan government issued a law forbidding widows and concubines of officials serving in Kwangtung to remarry, and it required local authorities to send them back at government expense to the first husbands' family. These rulings reveal a profound shift in concern away from the problem of elite women getting stripped of property and falling into servile status, which we see in the Sung, toward the new issue of a man's family suffering financially at the hands of a woman.[4] Gone is the concept that dowry was attached to a woman to maintain her within marriage, beyond it, and even in death. The new Yüan laws, adopted by all later dynasties, transferred control of a woman's assets from the woman and her natal family to the first husband and his family.

Such a limit on financial autonomy was unheard of for elite women of the Sung and before, who had always kept their dowry for life. Not surprisingly, once dowry provided less benefit to the woman herself and would not return to the natal family even if the woman herself did, its size and quality were reduced. Dowries never reached the same size after the Sung, and daughters in all parts of China rarely if ever received land. This further contributed to an inheritance regime that reduced a daughter's inheritance and kept property in the male line.

Third, control of a woman's person was also stripped from her and her natal family and transferred to her husband and his parents. Again, after an encounter with the levirate of more than a generation in the South, and 200 years or more in parts of the North, traditional Chinese ideas of personal autonomy had faded away. The Sung custom whereby women routinely returned home after widowhood or divorce and entered remarriages arranged by themselves or their natal parents was

---

4 This change in legal language is paralleled by a shift in discourse in miscellaneous notes and other sources. The theme prevalent in the Sung of elite orphan girls falling into concubinage and a life of suffering for lack of dowry is replaced by criticism of women who are seen to control too much property. For random examples of the former, see *I-chien-chih*, i-chih 20:360–1; and *Tung-hsüan pi-lu*, 12:90–1. For a striking example of the latter, see *Chih-cheng chih-chi* (Shanghai: Ku-chi ch'u-pan she, 1987) by K'ung Ch'i, and discussion in Paul Smith, "Fear of Gynarchy in an Age of Chaos: Kong Qi's Reflections on Life in South China under Mongol Rule," *Journal of the Economic and Social History of the Orient* 41:1 (1998): 1–95. The prevalence of uxorilocal marriage, which as I have shown was encouraged by Yüan law, may also have contributed to this discourse.

made illegal in many cases by the levirate, which Khubilai applied to all Chinese at the end of 1271. Khubilai's decree allowed that any eligible levir could force a widow into a marriage with him (even over the objections of the first husband's parents in some cases), and such a levir could be almost any junior relative of the husband, including a distant cousin. At first, the levirate took precedence over all other marriage law, including such traditional Chinese prohibitions against having two principal wives or marrying while underage. Such a blanket enforcement of the levirate reflected Mongol marriage customs. But it threw marriage law into confusion and generated a flood of lawsuits by Chinese women and their natal families who resisted these radical new restrictions on a woman's autonomy. The levirate law was not repealed, but from the late 1270s on, chastity emerged as a legal alternative to a forced levirate marriage. A widow could choose to stay chaste instead of marrying the levir, but she still had to stay in her first husband's household. Only widows in households without levirs could return to their natal families and remarry as before. In this form, the levirate operated for Chinese until 1330. During all of this time, a widow was forbidden to return home and remarry as long as an eligible levir existed.

In 1309, the authorities took the further step of establishing that if a woman did remarry (in the absence of a levir), she had to have the permission of her in-laws, and her in-laws would keep any betrothal gifts received. This eliminated control by the woman and her natal parents over her remarriage and transferred it to her husband's family. The legal recourse that women had previously availed themselves of was severely restricted, when in 1313, women lost the right to bring cases to court. The order was aimed especially against widows, who were accused of filing lawsuits to display their charms and attract new husbands. As with the loss of property rights, such a loss of personal autonomy would have been unimaginable for elite women of the Sung and before, but it was entirely consistent with steppe attitudes and practices.

Fourth, the Yüan government established new and unprecedented support for widow chastity. In addition to the restrictions on property rights and personal autonomy that limited widow remarriage, the government took concrete steps to encourage widow chastity. In 1304 the emperor ordered local officials to provide grain to help support impoverished widows. Later the same year, the Ministry of Rites set down an official definition of chaste widows for the first time in Chinese history, and it established systematic imperial recognition and rewards for such widows. To qualify as a chaste widow, a woman had to have been widowed before she was 30, to have made a public vow of chastity, and to have stayed chaste until she was over 50 years old.

Both regulations reveal some of the tensions generated by the new marriage laws. The decree ordering local officials to support widows also stated that widows must not be forced into remarriages; and the clarification of who qualified as a chaste widow was in response to the proliferation of petitions from self-proclaimed families of chaste widows seeking state rewards. Nevertheless, the governments of the Ming and Ch'ing dynasties adopted the new provisions on chaste widows and the laws restricting women's property, and put their weight behind the cult of widow chastity, even as they harshly outlawed levirate marriage. The cult spread quickly, and widow behavior was soon widely accepted as a litmus test of Confucian morality. In the words of one modern scholar, female chastity came to be "a metaphor for community honor."[5]

Most remarkable about these developments is the extent to which they overlapped with the aims of Learning of the Way Confucians in the Sung. Consistent with the influence of Huang Kan's teachings at the Mongol court, the new Yüan laws corresponded largely to the more radical proposals of Chu Hsi's son-in-law Huang Kan. Chu Hsi and others wanted to reduce women's inheritance and the private property they took into marriage. Yüan law achieved this, though in the case of cut-off households Yüan law encouraged uxorilocal marriage as opposed to agnatic adoption. Chu Hsi and his followers wanted women to contribute their dowry property to their husband's households, thereby relinquishing their rights to take it out of a marriage. Yüan law prevented women from taking any property out of a marriage and thus broke the centuries-old bond between women and their property in China. (In this regard it went beyond even Huang Kan's proposals.) Finally, Huang Kan wanted to force widows to stay chaste in the home of their in-laws, and Yüan law provided an array of incentives and penalties that encouraged just that.

In language reminiscent of Huang Kan's in the previous century, which shows that the government knew it was going against common practice, the Ministry of Rites in 1304 explicitly cited the need "to encourage the reform of greedy habits and by example promote the adoption of generous and worthy customs" when it rewarded widow chastity.[6] These laws aimed at preventing widows from returning to their natal families are all the more remarkable when we consider that 100 years earlier such behavior was seen as an ethnic marker that distinguished the Chinese from their steppe neighbors. Behavior that was once seen as defining non-Chinese peoples was transformed into an example of ancient Chinese Confucian virtue.

5 Susan Mann, "Widows in the Kinship, Class, and Community Structures of Qing Dynasty China," *Journal of Asian Studies* 46:1 (Feb. 1987): 43.
6 YTC 33:13a.

As can be expected of new laws that violated centuries of traditional practice, people did not necessarily change their behavior overnight to conform to the law. This may account for an apparent disconnection between women's formal property rights and social practice in the late imperial period, as demonstrated by Japanese survey data, which provide a picture of widely differing practices, sometimes conforming with, sometimes conflicting with written law. The new structures that supported widows and made remarriage taboo also generated serious tensions within families. If a widow was not herself the head of the household, the family gained economically if she remarried. Under the new laws of the Yüan dynasty, the first husband's family could keep her original dowry plus receive the betrothal gifts from the new husband. Widows were often forced into remarriage or made to suffer if they refused. For some widows, suicide became the only way to preserve one's honor and escape forced remarriage. As Shiga Shūzō has noted, government rewards and the cult of chastity were designed to protect women who opted to stay in their husband's house and enjoy the economic benefits found there. But while government encouragement of widow chastity was meant to prevent abuse, it could only contribute to the rise of popular customs toward the end of the imperial era that afflicted widows with mistrust, superstition, and even deadly violence.

The Yüan transformation of marriage and property law complemented the rise of agnatic lineages. Attempts at establishing corporate lineage estates in the Sung were notoriously unsuccessful. Instead, affinal kin seem to have played a far more important role in providing the services and opportunities that agnatic lineages were intended to provide. The changes that came about in the Yüan had the long-term effect of funneling resources and power from the affinal to the agnatic line. They also weakened a woman's ties to her natal family and strengthened her bonds to her marital family. These developments reinforced lineage authority and together with new Ming laws set the stage for the growth of lineages over the next few centuries into powerful corporate entities, which existed throughout the South by late imperial times. This resulted in a loss of control of resources and personal autonomy by individuals, both men and women, and an increase in authority of lineage elders.[7] Learning of the Way Confucian teachings justified the rise of lineages and contraction of personal property rights in the Ming as they had the changes in marriage and property law of the Yüan. Together these developments brought about lasting social change.

7 Buddhist temples in the South, which had been heavily patronized by women, similarly lost large amounts of property to lineage organizations, and many were abandoned in the Ming.

The Yüan dynasty must be seen as a major turning point in Chinese history. Yüan developments deprived women (and eventually men) of property rights, economic independence, and personal autonomy. The resulting shift toward greater patrilineality in Chinese society was also influenced by Learning of the Way Confucian philosophy and the rise of corporate lineages. But in many regards indigenous Chinese developments could not have taken effect had it not been for new laws enacted under the Yüan dynasty and the change in thinking that were all stimulated by the Chinese encounter with Mongol rule. What many Chinese looked back on as developments in the direction of timeless Confucian values were in fact the product of a singular experience of foreign occupation and cultural confrontation.

Bibliography

Primary sources are listed by their short title, as cited in the footnotes, followed by complete title if different, author, and publication information. Secondary sources are listed by author.

Primary Sources

Ai-hsüan chi 艾軒集 [Collected works of Lin Kuang-ch'ao], 9 ch. Lin Kuang-ch'ao 林光朝 (1114–1178). SKCS chen-pen ed. (1st series).

Chan-yüan ching-yü 湛淵靜語 [Quiet words that plumb the deep], 2 ch. Po T'ing 白珽 (1248–1328). Pai-pu ts'ung-shu chi-ch'eng ed.

Chang-tzu ch'üan shu 張子全書 [Complete works of Chang Tsai]. Chang Tsai 張載 (1020–1077). Kuo-hsüeh chi-pen ts'ung-shu ed. Taipei: Shang-wu yin-shu kuan, 1968.

Ch'en Liang chi. Ch'en Liang chi tseng-ting pen 陳亮集增訂本 [Revised and enlarged edition of Ch'en Liang's collected works], 2 vols. Ch'en Liang 陳亮 (1143–1194). ed. Teng Kuang-ming 鄧廣銘. Peking: Chung-hua shu-chü, 1987.

Ch'eng-chai chi 誠齋集 [Collected works of Yang Wan-li], 133 ch. Yang Wan-li 楊萬里 (1127–1206). SPTK ed.

Ch'i-tung yeh-yü 齊東野語 [Random talk East of Ch'i]. Chou Mi 周密 (1232–1308). Photo reprint of Han-fen lou ed., *Sung-jen hsiao-shuo* no. 10. Shanghai: Shanghai shu-tien, 1990.

Chia-fan. Ssu-ma Kuang chia-fan 司馬光家範 [Ssu-ma Kuang's Family principles], 10 ch. Ssu-ma Kuang 司馬光 (1019–1086). 1626 ed. Reprint, Taipei: Chung-kuo tzu-hsüeh ming-chu chi-ch'eng, 1978.

Chia-hsün pi-lu 家訓筆錄 [Record of family instructions], 1 ch. Chao Ting 趙鼎 (1084–1147). Orig. 1144. TSCC ed.

Chiang-hu wen-chi. Chiang-hu ch'ang-weng wen-chi 江湖長翁文集 [Collected works of the old man from Chiang-hu]. Ch'en Tsao 陳造 (1133–1203). SKCS chen-pen ed. (5th series).

Chiang-su chin-shih chih 江蘇金石志 [Compilation of inscriptions from Kiangsu], 24 ch. Compiled by Miao Ch'üan-sun. N.p.: Chiang-su t'ung-chih chü, 1927.

297

Reprint, *Shih-k'o shih-liao hsin-pien*, Ser. 1, Vol. 13. Taipei: Hsin-wen feng ch'u-pan kung-ssu, 1979.

Chiao-ch'i chi 腳氣集 [Essays on beri-beri], 2 ch. Ch'e Jo-shui 車若水 (13th century). Pai-pu ts'ung-shu chi-ch'eng ed.

Chieh-tzu t'ung-lu 戒子通錄 [Comprehensive collection of warnings for children]. Liu Ch'ing-chih 劉清之 (1130–1195). SKCS chen-pen ed. (1st series).

Ch'ien-fu lun 潛夫論 [Discourses of a man in hiding]. Wang Fu 王符 (ca. 90–165). TSCC ed.

Chien-yen i-lai hsi-nien yao-lu 建炎以來繫年要錄 [Record of essential matters since the Chien-yen period (1127–1130)]. Li Hsin-ch'uan 李心傳 (1166–1243). Wen-yüan ko SKCS ed.

Chih-cheng chih-chi 至正直記 [Frank recollections of the Chih-cheng period (1341–1368)]. K'ung Ch'i 孔齊 (ca. 1310–after 1365). Shanghai: Ku-chi ch'u-pan she, 1987.

Chih-chiang chi. Chih-chiang Li hsien-sheng wen-chi 直講李先生文集 [Collected works of Li Kou]. Li Kou 李覯 (1009–1059). 37 + 3 ch. SPTK ed.

Chin shih 金史 [Chin dynastic history]. T'uo-t'uo 脫脫 (1313–1355) et al. Reprint, Peking: Chung-hua shu-chü, 1975.

Chin-ssu lu 近思錄 [Reflections on things at hand]. Chu Hsi 朱熹 (1130–1200). Orig. 1173. Kuo-hsüeh chi-pen ts'ung-shu ed. Taipei: Shang-wu yin-shu kuan, 1968.

Ch'ing-ming chi (CMC). *Ming-kung shu-p'an ch'ing-ming chi* 名公書判清明集 [Collection of decisions by famous judges to clarify and enlighten]. Anon. Orig. 1261. Reprint of 1569 ed., Peking: Chung-hua shu-chü, 1987.

Ch'ing-yüan t'iao-fa shih-lei 慶元條法事類 [Classified laws of the Ch'ing-yüan period (1195–1200)]. Reprint, Taipei: Hsin-wen feng ch'u-pan kung-ssu, 1976.

Ch'iu-chien wen-chi. Ch'iu-chien hsien-sheng ta-ch'üan wen-chi 秋澗先生大全文集 [Complete collected works of Wang Yün]. Wang Yün 王惲 (1227–1304). SPTK ed.

Chu-hsi chüan-chai chi. Chu-hsi chüan-chai shih-i kao hsü-chi 竹溪鬳齋十一藁續集 [Continuation of collected works of Lin Hsi-i], 30 ch. Lin Hsi-i 林希逸 (ca. 1210–1273). Wen-yüan-ko SKCS ed.

Chu-tzu ta-ch'üan 朱熹大全 [Complete works of Master Chu], 100 + 11 + 10 ch. Chu Hsi 朱熹 (1130–1200). SPPY ed.

Chu-tzu wen-chi 朱子文集 [Collected works of Master Chu]. Chu Hsi 朱熹 (1130–1200). TSCC ed.

Chu-tzu yü-lei 朱子語類 [Classified conversations of Master Chu]. Chu Hsi 朱熹 (1130–1200). Peking: Chung-hua shu-chü, 1986.

Chu Wen-kung wen-chi. Hui-an hsien-sheng Chu Wen-kung wen-chi 晦菴先生朱文公文集 [Collected works of Literary Master Chu Hui-an (Chu Hsi)]. Chu Hsi 朱熹 (1130–1200). SPTK ed.

Ch'üan T'ang wen 全唐文 [Complete literature of the T'ang], 1,000 ch. Tung Kao 董誥 (1740–1818) et al. Peking: Chung-hua shu-chü, 1983.

CMC. See *Ch'ing-ming chi.*

Erh Ch'eng ch'üan-shu 二程全書 [Complete writings of the two Ch'engs]. Ch'eng Hao 程顥 (1032–1085) and Ch'eng I 程頤 (1033–1107). SPPY ed.

Fan Wen-cheng kung chi 范文正公集 [Collected works of Fan Chung-yen]. Fan Chung-yen 范仲淹 (989–1052). SPTK ed.

Fei-jan chi 斐然集 [Collected works of Hu Yin], 30 ch. Hu Yin 胡寅 (1098–1156). SKCS chen-pen ed. (1st series).

Han Fei-tzu. Han Fei-tzu chiao-chu 韓非子校註 [*The Han Fei-tzu* with corrections and commentary]. Han Fei 韓非 (ca. 280–233 B.C.). Yang Ching-chao et al. ed. Chiang-su province: Jen-min ch'u-pan she, 1982.

Han-mo ch'üan-shu. Hsin-pien shih-wen lei-chü han-mo ch'üan-shu 新編事文類聚翰墨全書 [Newly compiled complete guide to letter writing with brush and ink arranged topically]. Liu Ying-li 劉應李 (d. 1311). 1307 ed.

Han shu 漢書 [History of the Former Han]. Pan Ku 班固 (A.D. 32–92). Peking: Chung-hua shu-chü, 1962; reprint 1975.

HCP. See *Hsü tzu-chih t'ung-chien ch'ang-pien.*

Ho-nan Ch'eng-shih i-shu 河南程氏遺書 [Writings by the Ch'engs of Ho-nan]. Ch'eng Hao 程顥 (1032–1085) and Ch'eng I 程頤 (1033–1107). In *Erh Ch'eng ch'üan-shu* 二程全書 [Complete works of the two Ch'engs]. SPPY ed.

Ho-shan chi. Ho-shan hsien-sheng ta-ch'üan chi 鶴山先生大全集 [Complete works of Wei Liao-weng], 110 ch. Wei Liao-weng 魏了翁 (1178–1237). SPTK ed.

Hou Han shu 後漢書 [History of the Later Han]. Fan Yeh 范曄 (5th cent.). Peking: Chung-hua shu-chü, 1965; reprint 1973.

Hou-ts'un chi. Hou-ts'un hsien-sheng ta-ch'üan-chi 後村先生大全集 [Complete works of master Hou-ts'un (Liu K'o-chuang)], 196 ch. Liu K'o-chuang 劉克莊 (1187–1269). SPTK ed.

Hsi-shan chi. Hsi-shan hsien-sheng Chen Wen-chung kung wen-chi 西山先生真文忠公文集 [Collected works of master Chen Hsi-shan (Chen Te-hsiu)]. Chen Te-hsiu 真德秀 (1178–1235). SPTK ed.

Hsiao-hsüeh. Hsiao-hsüeh chi-chieh 小學集解 [Elementary learning with collected commentaries]. Chu Hsi 朱熹 (1130–1200). Edited by Chang Po-hsing (1651–1725). Kuo-hsüeh chi-pen ts'ung-shu ed. Taipei: Shang-wu yin-shu kuan, 1968.

Hsin-kan hsien-chih 新淦縣志 [Gazetteer of Hsin-kan county], 10 ch. 1873 ed.

Hsin Yüan shih 新元史 [New history of the Yüan]. K'o Shao-min 柯劭忞 (1850–1933). Reprinted in *Yüan shih erh-chung* 元史二種 [Two works of Yüan history]. Shanghai: Ku-chi ch'u-pan she, 1989.

Hsü-kung chi. Hsü-kung wen-chi 徐公文集 [Collected works of Hsü Hsüan], 30 ch. Hsü Hsüan 徐鉉 (916–991). SPTK ed.

Hsü tzu-chih t'ung-chien 續資治通鑑 [Continuation of the Comprehensive Mirror for Aid in Government], 220 ch. Pi Yüan 畢沅 (1730–1797). Peking: Ku-chi ch'u-pan she, 1957.

Hsü tzu-chih t'ung-chien ch'ang-pien (HCP) 續資治通鑒長編 [Outline for a continuation of the Comprehensive Mirror for Aid in Government]. Li T'ao 李燾

(1115–1184). Sung-shih yao-chi hui-pien. Shanghai: Ku-chi ch'u-pan she, 1986.

Hua-yang kuo-chih 華陽國志 [Gazetteer of Hua-yang (Szechwan)], 12 ch. Ch'ang Ch'ü 常璩 (4th cent.). TSCC ed.

Hui-an hsien-sheng Chu Wen-kung wen-chi. See *Chu Wen-kung wen-chi.*

I-chien chih 夷堅志 [Record of I-chien the listener]. Hung Mai 洪邁 (1123–1202). Edited and punctuated by Ho Chuo. Peking: Chung-hua shu-chü, 1981.

I-ch'uan chi 伊川集 [Collected works of Ch'eng I]. Ch'eng I 程頤 (1033–1107). In *Erh Ch'eng ch'üan-shu* 二程全書 [Complete works of the two Ch'engs]. SPPY ed.

Kao-feng chi. Kao-feng wen-chi 高峰文集 [Collected works of Liao Kang], 12 ch. Liao Kang 廖剛 (1071–1143). SKCS chen-pen ed. (1st series).

Kuei-shan chi 龜山集 [Collected works of Yang Shih]. Yang Shih 楊時 (1053–1135). SKCS chen-pen ed. (4th series).

Kung-k'uei chi 攻媿集 [Collected works of Lou Yüeh], 112 ch. Lou Yüeh 樓鑰 (1137–1213). TSCC ed.

Le-ch'üan chi 樂全集 [Collected works of Chang Fang-p'ing], 40 ch. Chang Fang-p'ing 張方平 (1007–1091). SKCS chen-pen ed. (1st series).

Li-chi. Li-chi chi-shuo 禮記集說 [Record of rites with collected commentaries]. Edited by Ch'en Hao. Reprint of Shih-chieh shu-chü ed., 1937. Shanghai: Ku-chi ch'u-pan she, 1987.

Liang-che chin-shih chih 兩浙金石志 [Compilation of inscriptions from Liang-che], 18 + 1 ch. Juan Yüan 阮元 (1764–1849). Reprint, *Shih-k'o shih-liao hsin-pien*, Ser. 1, Vol. 14. Taipei: Hsin-wen feng ch'u-pan kung-ssu, 1979.

Liang-ch'i chi. Liang-ch'i hsien-sheng wen-chi 梁谿先生文集 [Collected works of Li Kang], 180 ch. Li Kang 李綱 (1083–1140). Reprint of Ch'ing edition in National Central Library. Taipei. 1970.

Lin-chiang fu chih 臨江府志 [Gazetteer of Lin-chiang prefecture], 32 ch. Ch'ang-po Te-hsin 長白德馨. 1871 ed.

Lin-ch'uan chi. See *Wang Lin-ch'uan chi.*

Lu Chiu-yüan chi 陸九淵集 [Collected works of Lu Chiu-yüan], 36 ch. Lu Chiu-yüan 陸九淵 (1139–1193). Peking: Chung-hua shu-chü, 1980.

Lu-t'ing shih-shih 虜廷事實 [Facts from the land of the caitiffs]. Anon. In *Shuo-fu san-chung* 說郛三種 [Three works of Shuo-fu], by T'ao Tsung-i 陶宗儀 (fl. 1360) et al. Shanghai: Ku-chi ch'u-pan she, 1988.

Lü Tung-lai wen-chi. Lü Tung-lai hsien-sheng wen-chi 呂東萊先生文集 [Collected works of Lü Tsu-ch'ien], 20 ch. Lü Tsu-ch'ien 呂祖謙 (1137–1181). TSCC ed.

Lung-yün chi. Lung-yün hsien-sheng wen-chi 龍雲先生文集 [Collected works of Liu Yen], 32 ch. Liu Yen 劉弇 (1048–1102). Yü-chang ts'ung-shu ed., 1915.

Man-t'ang chi. Man-t'ang wen-chi 漫塘文集 [Collected works of Liu Tsai], 36 ch. Liu Tsai 劉宰 (1166–1239). SKCS chen-pen ed. (9th series).

Meikō shohan seimeishū 名公書判清明集 [Collection of decisions by famous judges to clarify and enlighten]. Orig. 1261. Reprint of Sung ed. of *Ch'ing-ming chi* held in Seikadō library, Tokyo, Japan. Tokyo: Koten kenkyūkai, 1964.

Meng-ch'i pi-t'an 夢溪筆談 [Notes from dream brook]. Shen Kua 沈括 (1030–1095). SPTK ed.

Meng-liang lu 夢梁錄 [Record of dreams of happiness]. Wu Tzu-mu 吳自牧 (ca. 1256–1334). Orig. 1274. In *Tung-ching meng-hua lu wai ssu chung* 東京夢華錄外四種 [Dreams of the glory of the Eastern Capital (and four other works)]. Shanghai: Chung-hua shu-chü, 1962.

Mien-chai chi 勉齋集 [Collected works of Huang Kan], 40 ch. Huang Kan 黃幹 (1152–1221). SKCS chen-pen ed. (2nd series).

Min-chung li-hsüeh yüan-yüan k'ao 閩中理學淵源考 [Treatise on the origins of the Fukien school of Neo-Confucianism (*li-hsüeh*)]. Li Ch'ing-fu 李清馥. Orig. 1749. SKCS chen-pen ed. (2nd series).

Ming hui-tien 明會典 [Collected statutes of the Ming dynasty]. 1587. Reprint, Peking: Chung-hua shu chü, 1989.

Ming-kung shu-p'an ch'ing-ming chi. See *Ch'ing-ming chi.*

Ming-lü chi-chieh fu-li 明律集解附例 [The Ming code with explanations and precedents appended]. Orig. 1367. Reprint of 1908 ed., Taipei: Ch'eng-wen ch'u-pan she, 1969.

Ming-tao chi 明道集 [Collected works of Ch'eng Hao]. Ch'eng Hao 程顥 (1032–1085). In *Erh Ch'eng ch'üan-shu* 二程全書 [Complete works of the two Ch'engs]. SPPY ed.

Mu-yeh chi 楳埜集 [Collected works of Hsü Yüan-chieh], 12 ch. Hsü Yüan-chieh 徐元杰 (1194–1245). SKCS chen-pen ed. (Suppl. series).

Nan-chien chia-i kao 南澗甲乙稿 [Draft of collected works of Han Yüan-chi], 22 ch. Han Yüan-chi 韓元吉 (1118–1187). Wu-ying tien Chü-pen pan-shu ed., 1828. (References also provided in notes for SKCS chen-pen ed.)

Nan-Sung shu 南宋書 [History of the Southern Sung], 68 ch. Ch'ien Shih-sheng 錢士升 (Ming dynasty). Reprint of 1797 ed.

Ou-yang chi 歐陽集 [Collected works of Ou-yang Hsiu]. Ou-yang Hsiu 歐陽修 (1007–1072). In *Ch'üan Sung wen* 全宋文 [Complete writings of the Sung], vols. 16–18. Ch'eng-tu, Szechwan: Pa-shu shu-she, 1991.

P'ing-shan chi 屏山集 [Collected works of Liu Tzu-hui], 20 ch. Liu Tzu-hui 劉子翬 (1101–1147). SKCS chen-pen ed. (4th series).

Seimeishū. See *Meikō shohan seimeishū.*

Shih chi 史記 [Records of the historian]. Ssu-ma Ch'ien 司馬遷 (145–90? B.C.). Peking: Chung-hua shu-chü, 1959; reprint, 1982.

Shih-ching 詩經 [Book of Songs]. In *Shih-san ching chu-shu* 十三經註疏 [The thirteen classics with commentaries]. Ed. Juan Yüan 阮元 (1764–1849). Reprinted in 2 vols., Peking: Chung-hua shu-chü, 1980.

Shih-lin kuang-chi 事林廣記 [Expanded compilation of myriad matters]. Ch'en Yüan-ching 陳元靚 (ca. 1200–1266), with later anon. additions. Photo reproduction of Yüan, chih-shun (1330–1333) ed. Kyoto: Chūbun shuppansha, 1988.

Shih-san-ching chu-shu 十三經注疏 [The thirteen classics with commentaries]. Ed. Juan Yüan 阮元 (1764–1849). Reprinted in 2 vols., Peking: Chung-hua shu-chü, 1980.

SHT. See *Sung hsing-t'ung.*

SHY. See *Sung hui-yao.*

Shui-tung jih-chi 水東日記 [Daily record of east of the water], 177 ch. Yeh Sheng 葉盛 (1420–1474). Wen yüan-ko SKCS ed.

Shuo-fu 説郛 [Writings on matters near and far]. T'ao Tsung-i 陶宗儀 (b. 1316). Reprint in *Shuo-fu san-chung* 説郛三種 [Three works of Shuo-fu]. Shanghai: Ku-chi ch'u-pan she, 1988.

Ssu-k'u ch'üan-shu ts'ung-mu 四庫全書總目 [Complete catalogue of the Four Treasuries]. Orig. 1782. Peking: Chung-hua shu-chü, 1965; reprint 1987.

Ssu-ma chi. Wen-kuo Wen-cheng Ssu-ma kung wen-chi 溫國文正司馬公文集 [Collected works of Ssu-ma Kuang], 80 ch. (1132). Ssu-ma Kuang 司馬光 (1019–1086). SPTK ed.

Ssu-ma ch'uan-chia chi. Ssu-ma Wen-cheng kung ch'uan-chia chi 司馬文正公傳家集 [Collected works of Ssu-ma Kuang as transmitted in his family], 80 ch. Ssu-ma Kuang 司馬光 (1019–1086). Kuo-hsüeh chi-pen ts'ung-shu ed. Taipei: Shang-wu yin-shu kuan, 1968.

Ssu-ma shih shu-i 司馬氏書儀 [Letters and etiquette of Mr. Ssu-ma], 10 ch. Ssu-ma Kuang 司馬光 (1019–1086). TSCC ed.

Su Tung-p'o chi 蘇東坡集 [Collected works of Su Shih]. Su Shih 蘇軾 (1036–1101). Shanghai: Shang-wu yin-shu kuan, 1958.

Su-wei chi. Su-wei kung wen-chi 蘇魏公文集 [Collected works of Su Sung], 72 ch. Su Sung 蘇頌 (1020–1101). SKCS chen-pen ed. (4th series).

Sung hsing-t'ung (SHT) 宋刑統 [Collected penal laws of the Sung]. Tou I 竇儀 (914–966) et al. Peking: Chung-hua shu-chü, 1984.

Sung hui-yao (SHY). *Sung hui-yao chi-kao* 宋會要輯稿 [Draft version of the Important Documents of the Sung]. Ed. Hsü Sung 徐松 (1781–1848). Peking: Chung-hua shu-chü, 1957; reprint 1987.

Sung shih 宋史 [History of the Sung]. T'o T'o 脱脱 (1313–1355) et al. Peking: Chung-hua shu-chü, 1977.

Sung shih hsin-pien 宋史新編 [New compilation of the history of the Sung], 200 ch. K'o Wei-ch'i 柯維騏 (fl. 16th cent.). Reprint of 1831 ed. Taipei: Wen-hai ch'u-pan she, 1974.

Sung-Yüan hsüeh-an (SYHA) 宋元學案 [Case studies of Sung and Yüan Confucians], 4 vols. Huang Tsung-hsi 黃宗義 (1610–1695) and Ch'üan Tsu-wang 全祖望 (1705–1755). Peking: Chung-hua shu chü, 1986.

Sung-Yüan hsüeh-an pu-i 宋元學案補遺 [Continuation of Case studies of Sung and Yüan Confucians]. Wang Tzu-ts'ai 王梓材 (Ch'ing dynasty). Ssu-ming ts'ung-shu ed. Taipei: Kuo-fang yen-chiu yüan, 1966.

SYHA. See *Sung-Yüan hsüeh-an.*

Ta Ch'ing lü-li 大清律例 [Statutes and precedents of the great Ch'ing]. Orig. 1740. Shanghai ta-hsüeh fa-hsüeh yüan. T'ien-chin: Ku-chi ch'u-pan she, 1993.

T'ang hui-yao 唐會要 [Important documents of the T'ang]. Wang P'u 王溥 (922–982). Kuo-hsüeh chi-pen ts'ung-shu ed. Taipei: Shang-wu yin-shu kuan, 1968.

T'ang lü shu-i (TLSI) 唐律疏議 [The T'ang Code with subcommentary and explanations]. Ch'ang-sun Wu-chi 長孫無忌 (d. 659). Peking: Chung-hua shu-chü, 1983.

Tao-ming lu 道命錄 [Record of the fate of the way], 10 ch. Li Hsin-ch'uan 李心傳 (1166–1243). Chih-pu-tsu chi ts'ung-shu ed.

T'ao-shan chi 陶山集 [Collected works of Lu Tien], 16 ch. Lu Tien 陸佃 (1042–1102). TSCC ed.

TCTK. See *T'ung-chih t'iao-ko.*

T'ieh-an chi. Sung Bao-chang ko chih-hsüeh-shih Chung-hui T'ieh-an Fang-kung wen-chi 宋寶章閣直學士忠惠鐵庵方公文集 [Collected works of Mr. Fang Ta-ts'ung], 45 ch. Fang Ta-ts'ung 方大琮 (1183–1247). Photo reproduction of 1513 ed. in Seikadō Library, Tokyo.

Tso-i tzu-chen 作邑自箴 [Self-exhortations of a magistrate]. Li Yüan-pi 李元弼 (ca. 12th cent.). Author's preface 1117. SPTK Supplemental series.

Tuan-ming chi 端明集 [Collected works of Ts'ai Hsiang], 40 ch. Ts'ai Hsiang 蔡襄 (1012–1067). SKCS chen-pen ed. (4th series).

Tung-ching meng-hua lu 東京夢華錄 [Dreams of the glory of the Eastern Capital (K'ai-feng)], 10 ch. Meng Yüan-lao 孟元老 (fl. 1126–1147). In *Tung-ching meng-hua lu wai ssu chung* 外四種. Shanghai: Chung-hua shu-chü, 1962.

Tung-hsüan pi-lu 東軒筆錄 [Notes from the eastern pavilion], 15 ch. Wei T'ai 魏泰 (ca. 1050–1110). Orig. ca. 1090. TSCC ed.

Tung-t'ang chi 東塘集 [Collected works of Yüan Shuo-yu], 20 ch. Yüan Shuo-yu 袁說友 (1140–1204). SKCS chen-pen ed. (1st series).

T'ung-chih t'iao-ko (TCTK) 通制條格 [Statutes from the comprehensive regulations (of the Yüan)]. Orig. 1323. Edited and punctuated by Huang Shih-chien 黃時鑑. Hangchow: Chekiang ku-chi ch'u-pan she, 1986.

Wang Lin-ch'uan chi. Wang Lin-ch'uan ch'üan-chi 王臨川全集 [Complete works of Wang An-shih], 100 ch. Wang An-shih 王安石 (1021–1086). Hong Kong: Kuang-chih shu-chü, 1974.

Wei-nan wen-chi 渭南文集 [Collected works of Lu Yu], 50 ch. Lu Yu 陸游 (1125–1210). In *Lu Yu chi* 陸游集 [Writings of Lu Yu], Vol. 5. Peking: Chung-hua shu-chü, 1976.

Wen-chung chi 文忠集 [Collected works of Chou Pi-ta], 200 + 5 ch. Chou Pi-ta 周必大 (1126–1204). SKCS chen-pen ed. (2nd series).

Wen-hsien t'ung-k'ao 文獻通考 [Comprehesive investigations of important documents]. Ma Tuan-lin 馬端臨 (1254–1325). Kuo-hsüeh chi-pen ts'ung-shu ed. Taipei: Hsin-hsing shu-chü, 1959.

Wu-hsing chin-shih chi 吾興金石記 [Record of inscriptions from Wu-hsing (Hu-chou)]. Lu Hsin-yüan 陸心源 (1834–1894). Reprint in *Shih-k'o shih-liao hsin-pien*, Ser. 1, Vol. 14. Taipei: Hsin-wen feng ch'u-pan kung-ssu, 1979.

Wu-i chi. Wu-i hsin chi 武夷新集 [New collected works of Yang I], 20 ch. Yang I 楊億 (974–1020). SKCS chen-pen ed. (8th series).

Wu-wei chi 無為集 [Collected works of Yang Chieh], 15 ch. Yang Chieh 楊傑 (late 11th cent.). SKCS chen-pen ed. (5th series).

Yeh Shih chi 葉適集 [Collected works of Yeh Shih]. Yeh Shih 葉適 (1150–1223). Peking: Chung-hua shu-chü, 1961.

YTC. See *Yüan tien-chang.*

YTCHC. See *Yüan tien-chang hsin-chi.*

Yü-chüeh chi 玉玦記 [Story of the jade pendant]. 1581. Reprint in Chung-kuo hsi-chü yen-chiu tzu-liao. Taipei: T'ien-i ch'u-pan she, 1983.

Yüan-feng kao. Nan-feng hsien-sheng Yüan-feng lei-kao 南豐先生元豐類藁 [Classified draft of Tseng Kung's collected writings], 50 + 1 ch. Tseng Kung 曾鞏 (1019–1083). SPTK ed.

Yüan shih 元史 [Yüan dynastic history]. Sung Lien 宋濂 et al. Orig. 1370. Peking: Chung-hua shu-chü, 1976; reprint, 1992.

Yüan-shih shih-fan 袁氏世範 [Mr. Yüan's precepts for social living], 3 ch. Yüan Ts'ai 袁采 (fl. 1140–1195). Orig. 1179. Chih-pu-tsu chai ts'ung-shu ed. Reprinted in TSCC.

Yüan-tai fa-lü tzu-liao chi-ts'un 元代法律資料輯存 [Collection of Yüan legal materials]. Edited and punctuated by Huang Shih-chien 黃時鑑. Hangchow: Chekiang ku-chi ch'u-pan she, 1988.

Yüan tien-chang (YTC). *Ta-Yüan sheng-cheng kuo-ch'ao tien-chang* 大元聖政國朝典章 [Statutes and precedents of the sacred administration of the great Yüan dynastic state]. Orig. 1322. Photo reprint of Yüan edition: Taipei: Ku-kung po-wu kuan, 1976.

Yüan tien-chang hsin-chi (YTCHC). *Ta-Yüan sheng-cheng tien-chang hsin-chi chih-chih t'iao-li* 大元聖政典章新集至治條例 [New collection of statutes and precedents of the Yüan from the *chih-chih* period (1321–1323)]. Supplement to *Ta-Yüan sheng-cheng kuo-ch'ao tien-chang* (YTC) 大元聖政國朝典章 [Statutes and precedents of the sacred administration of the great Yüan dynastic state]. Orig. 1322. Photo reprint of Yüan edition: Taipei: Ku-kung po-wu kuan, 1976.

Yüan wen-lei 元文類 [Writings of the Yüan dynasty]. Orig. published as *Kuo-ch'ao wen-lei* 國朝文類 [Writings of the dynastic state]. Su T'ien-chüeh 蘇天爵 (1294–1352). Orig. 1336. Reprint, Taipei: Shih-chieh shu-chü, 1962.

Secondary Sources

Allsen, Thomas. "The Rise of the Mongolian Empire and Mongolian Rule in North China." In *The Cambridge History of China*, Vol. 6, *Alien Regimes and Border States, 907–1368*, ed. Herbert Franke and Denis Twitchett. Cambridge: Cambridge University Press, 1994, pp. 321–413.

Baker, Hugh. *Chinese Family and Kinship.* New York: Columbia University Press, 1979.

Beattie, Hilary. *Land and Lineage in China: A Study of T'ung-ch'eng, Anhwei, in the Ming and Ch'ing Dynasties.* Cambridge: Cambridge University Press, 1979.

Bernhardt, Kathryn. "The Inheritance Rights of Daughters: The Song Anomaly?" *Modern China* 21:3 (July 1995), pp. 269–309.

————. "A Ming-Qing Transition in Chinese Women's History? The Perspective from Law." In *Remapping China: Fissures in Historical Terrain*, ed. Gail Hershatter et al. Stanford, Calif.: Stanford University Press, 1996, pp. 42–58.

————. *Women and Property in China, 960–1949*. Stanford, Calif.: Stanford University Press, 1999.

Bielenstein, Hans. "The Chinese Colonization of Fukien until the End of the T'ang." In *Studia Serica Bernhard Karlgren Dedica*, ed. Soren Egerod and Else Glahn. Copenhagen: Ejnar Munksgaard, 1959, pp. 98–122.

————. "Chinese Historical Demography: A.D. 2–1982." *Bulletin of the Museum of Far Eastern Antiquities* 59 (1987), pp. 1–288.

Birge, Bettine. "Chu Hsi and Women's Education." In *Neo-Confucian Education: The Formative Stage*, ed. Wm. Theodore de Bary and John Chaffee. Berkeley: University of California Press, 1989, pp. 325–67.

————. "Women and Property in Sung Dynasty China (960–1279): Neo-Confucianism and Social Change in Chien-chou, Fukien." Ph.D. dissertation, Columbia University, 1992.

————. "*Zur Sozialgeschichte der Chinesischen Familie im 13. Jahrhundert: untersuchungen am Ming-gong shu-pan qing-ming ji*, by Gudula Linck" (review article), *Journal of Sung-Yuan Studies* 24 (1994), pp. 269–85.

————. "Review of Chu Hsi's Family Rituals: A Twelfth-Century Manual for the Performance of Cappings, Weddings, Funerals, and Ancestral Rites, trans. by Patricia Ebrey." *Chinese Literature: Essays, Articles Reviews* 16 (1994), pp. 157–60.

————. "Levirate Marriage and the Revival of Widow Chastity in Yüan China," *Asia Major* 8:2 (1995), pp. 107–46.

————. "Women and Confucianism from Song to Ming: the Institutionalization of Patrilineality." In *The Song-Yuan-Ming Transition in Chinese History*, ed. Paul Smith and Richard von Glahn. Berkeley: University of California Press, forthcoming.

————. "Age at Marriage of Sung Women." M.A. thesis, Columbia University, 1985.

Bol, Peter K. "Chu Hsi's Redefinition of Literati Learning." In *Neo-Confucian Education: The Formative Stage*, ed. Wm. Theodore de Bary and John Chaffee. Berkeley: University of California Press, 1989, 151–85.

————. "The Sung Examination System and the *Shih*." *Asia Major*, 3rd series, 3:2 (1990), pp. 149–71.

————. *"This Culture of Ours": Intellectual Transitions in T'ang and Sung China*. Stanford, Calif.: Stanford University Press, 1992.

Bossler, Beverly J. *Powerful Relations: Kinship, Status, and the State in Sung China (960–1279)*. Cambridge, Mass.: Harvard University Press, 1998.

Bray, Francesca. *Technology and Gender: Fabrics of Power in Late Imperial China*. Berkeley: University of California Press, 1997.

Burns, Ian. "Private Law in Traditional China (Sung Dynasty): Using as a Main Source of Information the work *Ming-kung shu-p'an ch'ing-ming chi*." Ph.D. dissertation, University of Oxford, 1973.

Carter, Thomas. *The Invention of Printing in China and Its Spread Westward.* New York: Columbia University Press, 1925; reprinted 1931.

Chaffee, John. "Education and Examinations in Sung Society." Ph.D. dissertation, University of Chicago, 1979.

———. *The Thorny Gates of Learning in Sung China: A Social History of Examinations.* Cambridge: Cambridge University Press, 1985 (2nd ed., Albany: State University of New York Press, 1995).

———. "The Marriage of Sung Imperial Clanswomen." In *Marriage and Inequality in Chinese Society,* ed. Rubie Watson and Patricia Ebrey. Berkeley: University of California Press, 1991, pp. 133–69.

Chan, Hok-lam, and Wm. Theodore de Bary, eds. *Yüan Thought: Chinese Thought and Religion under the Mongols.* New York: Columbia University Press, 1982.

Chan Wing-tsit [Ch'en Jung-chieh] 陳榮捷. "Chu-tzu ku ch'iung" 朱子固窮 [Chu Hsi's poverty]. *Shu-mu chi-k'an* 15:2 (1981). Reprinted in *Chu-hsüeh lun-chi* 朱學論集 [Collected Essays on Chu Hsi Studies], by Chan Wing-tsit [Ch'en Jung-chieh]. Taipei: Hsüeh-sheng shu-chü, 1982, pp. 205–33.

Chan, Wing-tsit. "Chu Hsi." In *Sung Biographies,* ed. Herbert Franke. Wiesbaden: Franz Steiner Verlag, 1976, pp. 282–90.

———. "Chu Hsi and Yüan Neo-Confucianism." In *Yüan Thought: Chinese Thought and Religion under the Mongols,* ed. Hok-lam Chan and Wm. Theodore de Bary. New York: Columbia University Press, 1982, pp. 197–231.

———. *Chu Hsi Life and Thought.* Hong Kong: The Chinese University Press, 1987.

———. "Chu Hsi's Poverty." In *Chu Hsi New Studies,* by Wing-tsit Chan. Honolulu: University of Hawaii Press, 1989, pp. 61–89.

———. "Chu Hsi and the Academies." In *Neo-Confucian Education: The Formative Stage,* ed. Wm. Theodore de Bary and John Chaffee. Berkeley: University of California Press, 1989, pp. 389–413.

———, ed. *Chu Hsi and Neo-Confucianism.* Honolulu: University of Hawaii Press, 1986.

———, trans. *Reflections on Things at Hand: The Neo-Confucian Anthology Compiled by Chu Hsi and Lü Tsu-ch'ien.* New York: Columbia University Press, 1967.

Chang Pang-wei 張邦煒. "Sung-tai fu-nü tsai-chia wen-t'i t'an-t'ao" 宋代婦女再嫁問題探討 [An investigation of the question of remarriage of women in the Sung]. In *Sung-shih yen-chiu lun-wen chi* 宋史研究論文集 [Collected essays on Sung history], ed. Teng Kuang-ming 鄧廣銘 and Hsü Kuei 徐規. Hangchow: Chekiang jen-min ch'u-pan she, 1987, pp. 582–611.

Ch'ang Pi-teh 昌彼得, et al. *Sung-jen chuan-chi tzu-liao so-yin* 宋人傳記資料索引 [Index to Sung biographical materials]. Taipei: Ting-wen shu-chü, 1973.

Ch'en Chih-ch'ao 陳智超. "Ming k'o-pen *Ming-kung shu-p'an ch'ing-ming chi* shu-lüeh" 明刻本名公書判清明集述略 [A brief description of the Ming edition of the *Ch'ing-ming chi*]. *Chung-kuo shih yen-chiu,* no. 4 (1984), pp. 137–52.

———. "Ming k'o-pen *Ming-kung shu-p'an ch'ing-ming chi* chieh-shao" 明刻本名公書判清明集介紹 [An introduction to the Ming edition of the Ch'ing-ming chi]. Appendix to *Ming-kung shu-p'an ch'ing-ming chi* (CMC). Peking: Chung-hua shu-chü, 1987, pp. 645–86.

Ch'en Ku-yüan 陳顧遠. *Chung-kuo ku-tai hun-yin shih* 中國古代婚姻史 [History of marriage in ancient China]. 1927. Reprint, Shanghai: Shang-wu yin-shu kuan, 1933.

Ch'en, Paul Heng-chao. *Chinese Legal Tradition under the Mongols.* Princeton, N.J.: Princeton University Press, 1979.

Ch'en P'eng 陳鵬. *Chung-kuo hun-yin shih-kao* 中國婚姻史稿 [A draft history of Chinese marriage]. Peking: Chung-hua shu-chü, 1990.

Ch'en Tung-yüan 陳東原. *Chung-kuo fu-nü sheng-huo shih* 中國婦女生活史 [History of the life of Chinese women]. Peking, 1937. Reprint, Taipei: Shang-wu yin-shu kuan, 1986.

Ch'eng T'ien-ch'üan 程天權. "Hun-yin yü ch'in-shu" 婚姻與親屬 [Marriage and kinship]. In *Chung-kuo min-fa shih* 中國民法史 [History of Chinese civil law], ed. Yeh Hsiao-hsin 葉孝信. Shanghai: Jen-min ch'u-pan she, 1993.

Ch'i Hsia 漆俠. "Sung-Yüan shih-ch'i P'u-yang Cheng-shih chia-tsu chih yen-chiu" 宋元時期浦陽鄭氏家族之研究 [A study of the Cheng family of P'u-yang in the Sung and Yüan periods]. In *Ryū Shiken hakushi shōju kinen Sōshi kenkyū ronshū* [Collected studies in Sung history dedicated to Professor James T. C. Liu in celebration of his seventieth birthday], ed. Kinugawa Tsuyoshi. Tokyo: Dōhōsha, 1989, pp. 159–66.

Chia, Lucille. "Printing for Profit: The Commercial Printers of Jianyang, Fujian (Song-Ming)." Ph.D. dissertation, Columbia University, 1996.

Chiang-hsi sheng wen-wu k'ao-ku yen-chiu so 江西省文物考古研究所, et al. "Chiang-hsi Te-an Nan-Sung Chou-shih mu ch'ing-li chien-pao" 江西德安南宋周氏墓清理簡報 [Brief report of tomb of Madam Chou of the Southern Sung in Te-an, Chekiang]. *Wen-wu* (Sept. 1990), pp. 1–13.

Chikusa Masaaki 竺沙雅章. *Chūgoku bukkyō shakaishi kenkyū* 中國佛教社會史研究 [Studies in the social history of Chinese Buddhism]. Kyoto: Dōhōsha, 1982.

———. "HokuSō shidaifu no shikyo to baiden: omoni Tōba sekitoku o shiryō toshite" 北宋士大夫の徙居と買田主に東坡尺牘を資料として [Land purchases and local residence of Northern Sung *shidafu*, using as a main source the letters of (Su) Tung-p'o]. *Shirin* 54:2 (1971).

———. "Kanseki shihai monjo no kenkyū" 漢籍紙背文書の研究 [A study of writing on the backs of the pages of Chinese books]. *Kyoto daigaku bungakubu kenkyū kuyō* 14 (1973), pp. 1–54.

———. "Sōdai kanryō no kikyo ni tsuite" 宋代官僚の寄居について [Temporary sojourning of Sung officials]. *Tōyōshi kenkyū* 41:1 (1982), pp. 28–57.

———. "SōGen bukkyō ni okeru an dō" 宋元佛教における庵堂 [Cloisters and halls in Sung and Yüan Buddhism]. *Tōyōshi kenkyū* 46:1 (1987), pp. 1–28.

Ching, Julia. "Chen Te-hsiu." In *Sung Biographies*, ed. Herbert Franke. Wiesbaden: Franz Steiner Verlag, 1976, pp. 88–90.

Chu, Ron-guey. "Chen Te-hsiu and the Classic on Governance." Ph.D. dissertation, Columbia University, 1988.

————. "Chu Hsi and Public Instruction." In *Neo-Confucian Education: The Formative Stage*, ed. Wm. Theodore de Bary and John Chaffee. Berkeley: University of California Press, 1989, pp. 252–73.

Ch'ü-chou shih wen-kuan hui 衢州市文管會. "Che-chiang Ch'ü-chou shih Nan-Sung mu ch'u-t'u ch'i-wu" 浙江衢州市南宋墓出土器物 [Items excavated from a Southern Sung tomb in Ch'ü-chou, Chekiang]. *K'ao-ku*, no. 11 (1983), pp. 1004–11, 1018.

Ch'ü, T'ung-tsu. *Law and Society in Traditional China*. Paris: Mouton and Co., 1965.

————. *Han Social Structure*. Edited by Jack Dull. Seattle: University of Washington Press, 1972.

Clark, Hugh. *Community, Trade, and Networks: Southern Fujian Province from the Third to Thirteenth Century*. Cambridge: Cambridge University Press, 1991.

Cleaves, Francis, trans. *The Secret History of the Mongols*. Cambridge, Mass.: Harvard University Press, 1982.

Cohen, Myron. "Developmental Process in the Chinese Domestic Group." In *Family and Kinship in Chinese Society*, ed. Maurice Freedman. Stanford, Calif.: Stanford University Press, 1970.

————. *House United, House Divided: The Chinese Family in Taiwan*. New York: Columbia University Press, 1976.

————. "Lineage Organization in North China." *Journal of Asian Studies* 49 (Aug. 1990), pp. 509–34.

Dardess, John W. *Conquerors and Confucians: Aspects of Political Change in Late Yüan China*. New York: Columbia University Press, 1973.

Dawson, Christopher, ed. *The Mongol Mission: Narratives and Letters of the Franciscan Missionaries in Mongolia and China in the Thirteenth and Fourteenth Centuries*. London: Sheed and Ward, 1955.

de Bary, Wm. Theodore. "A Reappraisal of Neo-Confucianism." In *Studies in Chinese Thought*, ed. Arthur Wright. Chicago: University of Chicago Press, 1953, pp. 81–111.

————. *Neo-Confucian Orthodoxy and the Learning of the Mind and Heart*. New York: Columbia University Press, 1981.

————. *The Liberal Tradition in China*. Hong Kong: The Chinese University Press, and New York: Columbia University Press, 1983.

————. "Introduction." In *The Rise of Neo-Confucianism in Korea*, ed. Wm. Theodore de Bary and JaHyun Kim Haboush. New York: Columbia University Press, 1985, pp. 1–58.

————. "Chu Hsi's Aims as an Educator." In *Neo-Confucian Education: The Formative Stage*, ed. Wm. Theodore de Bary and John Chaffee. Berkeley: University of California Press, 1989, pp. 186–218.

————. "Uses of Neo-Confucianism: A Response to Professor Tillman." *Philosophy East and West* 43 (Jan 1993), pp. 541–55.

————. "Reply to Hoyt Cleveland Tillman." *Philosophy East and West* 44:1 (1994) pp. 143–4.

de Bary, Wm. Theodore, and John Chaffee, eds. *Neo-Confucian Education: The Formative Stage*. Berkeley: University of California Press, 1989.

Dennerline, Jerry. "Marriage, Adoption, and Charity in the Development of Lineages." In *Kinship Organization in Late Imperial China, 1000–1940*, ed. Patricia Ebrey and James Watson. Berkeley: University of California Press, 1986, pp. 170–209.

de Pee, Christian. "Cases of the New Terrace: Canon and Law in Three Southern Song Verdicts." *Journal of Sung-Yuan Studies* 27 (1997), pp. 27–61.

de Rachewiltz, Igor, et al. "Turks in China under the Mongols: A Preliminary Investigation of Turco-Mongol Relations in the 13th and 14th Centuries." In *China among Equals*, ed. Morris Rossabi. Berkeley: University of California Press, 1983, pp. 281–310.

———. *In the Service of the Khan: Eminent Personalities of the Early Mongol–Yüan Period (1200–1300)*. Wiesbaden: Otto Harrassowitz Verlag, 1993.

Deuchler, Martina. *The Confucian Transformation of Korea*. Harvard-Yenching Institute Monograph no. 36. Cambridge, Mass.: Harvard University Press, 1992.

Dull, Jack. "Marriage and Divorce in Han China." In *Chinese Family Law and Social Change*, ed. David Buxbaum. Seattle: University of Washington Press, 1978, pp. 23–74.

Eberhard, Wolfram. *Social Mobility in Traditional China*. Leiden: E. J. Brill, 1962.

———. *Settlement and Social Change in Asia*. Hong Kong: Hong Kong University Press, 1967.

Ebisawa, Tetsuo. "Bondservants in the Yüan." *Acta Asiatica* 45 (1983), pp. 27–48.

Ebrey, Patricia Buckley. *The Aristocratic Families of Early Imperial China: A Case Study of the Po-ling Ts'ui Family*. Cambridge: Cambridge University Press, 1978.

———. "Women in the Kinship System of the Southern Song Upper Class." In *Women in China: Current Directions in Historical Scholarship*, ed. Richard Guisso and Stanley Johannesen. Youngstown, N.Y.: Philo Press, 1981, pp. 170–209.

———. "Conceptions of the Family in the Sung Dynasty." *Journal of Asian Studies* 43:2 (Feb. 1984), pp. 219–46.

———, trans. *Family and Property in Sung China: Yüan Ts'ai's Precepts for Social Life*. Princeton, N.J.: Princeton University Press, 1984.

———. "The Women in Liu Kezhuang's Family." *Modern China* 10:4 (1984), pp. 415–40.

———. "Early Stages in the Development of Descent Group Organization." In *Kinship Organization in Late Imperial China, 1000–1940*, ed. Patricia Ebrey and James Watson. Berkeley: University of California Press, 1986, pp. 16–61.

———. "Concubines in Sung China." *Journal of Family History* 11 (1986), pp. 1–24.

———. "Women, Marriage and the Family in Chinese History." In *Heritage of China: Contemporary Perspectives on Chinese Civilization*. ed. Paul Ropp. Berkeley: University of California Press, 1990, pp. 197–223.

———. "Shifts in Marriage Finance." In *Marriage and Inequality in Chinese Society*, ed. Rubie Watson and Patricia Ebrey. Berkeley: University of California Press, 1991, pp. 97–132.

————, trans. *Chu Hsi's "Family Rituals": A Twelfth-Century Manual for the Performance of Cappings, Weddings, Funerals, and Ancestral Rites.* Princeton, N.J.: Princeton University Press, 1991.

————. *Confucianism and Family Rituals in Imperial China: A Social History of Writing about Rites.* Princeton, N.J.: Princeton University Press, 1991.

————. "Women, Money, and Class: Ssu-ma Kuang and Sung Neo-Confucian Views on Women." In *Papers on Society and Culture of Early Modern China.* Taipei: Institute of History and Philology, Academia Sinica, June 1992.

————. "Property Law and Uxorilocal Marriage in the Sung Period." In *Family Process and Political Process in Modern Chinese History.* Taipei: Institute of Modern History, Academia Sinica, 1992, pp. 33–66.

————. *The Inner Quarters: Marriage and the Lives of Chinese Women in the Sung Period.* Berkeley: University of California Press, 1993.

Ebrey, Patricia Buckley, and James Watson, eds. *Kinship Organization in Late Imperial China, 1000–1940.* Berkeley: University of California Press, 1986.

Elman, Benjamin A. *A Cultural History of Civil Examinations in Late Imperial China.* Berkeley: University of California Press, 1999.

Elvin, Mark. *The Pattern of the Chinese Past.* Stanford, Calif.: Stanford University Press, 1973.

————. "Female Virtue and the State in China." *Past and Present* no. 104 (Aug. 1984), pp. 111–52.

Endicott-West, Elizabeth. *Mongolian Rule in China.* Cambridge, Mass.: Harvard University Press, 1989.

————. "The Yüan Government and Society." In *The Cambridge History of China,* Vol. 6, *Alien Regimes and Border States, 907–1368,* ed. Herbert Franke and Denis Twitchett. Cambridge: Cambridge University Press, 1994, pp. 587–615.

Erickson, Amy Louise. *Women and Property in Early Modern England.* London: Routledge, 1993.

Farmer, Edward. *Zhu Yuanzhang and Early Ming Legislation: The Reordering of Chinese Society Following the Era of Mongol Rule.* Leiden: E. J. Brill, 1995.

Farquhar, David. *The Government of China under Mongolian Rule: A Reference Guide.* Münchener Ostasiatische Studien, Vol. 53. Stuttgart: Franz Steiner Verlag, 1990.

Fei, Hsiao-tung. *Peasant Life in China.* London: Routledge and Kegan Paul, 1939; reprint 1980.

Fogel, Joshua. *Politics and Sinology: The Case of Naitō Konan.* Cambridge, Mass.: Harvard University Press, 1984.

Franke, Herbert, ed. *Sung Biographies.* Wiesbaden: Franz Steiner Verlag, 1976.

————. "Women under the Dynasties of Conquest." In *La Donna Nella Cina Imperiale e Nella Cina Repubblicana,* ed. Lionello Lanciotti. Florence: Leo S. Olschki Editore, 1980, pp. 23–43.

————. "Jurchen Customary Law and the Chinese Law of the Chin Dynasty." In *State and Law in East Asia: Festschrift Karl Bünger,* ed. Dieter Eikemeier and Herbert Franke. Wiesbaden: Otto Harrassowitz, 1981, pp. 215–33.

————. "The Legal System of the Chin Dynasty." In *Ryū Shiken hakushi shōju kinen Sōshi kenkyū ronshū* [Collected studies in Sung history dedicated to Professor James T. C. Liu in celebration of his seventieth birthday], ed. Kinugawa Tsuyoshi. Tokyo: Dōhōsha, 1989, pp. 387–409.

————. "The Chin Dynasty." In *The Cambridge History of China*, Vol. 6, *Alien Regimes and Border States, 907–1368*, ed. Herbert Franke and Denis Twitchett. Cambridge: Cambridge University Press, 1994, pp. 215–320.

Franke, Herbert, and Denis Twitchett, eds., *The Cambridge History of China*, Vol. 6, *Alien Regimes and Border States, 907–1368*. Cambridge: Cambridge University Press, 1994.

Franke, Herbert, and Hok-lam Chan. *Studies on the Jurchens and the Chin Dynasty.* Variorum Collected Studies Series: CS591. Aldershot, England: Ashgate Publishing Ltd., 1997.

Freedman, Maurice. *Lineage Organization in Southeastern China.* London School of Economics Monographs on Social Anthropology, no. 18, 1958; reprint London, New York, 1965.

————. *Chinese Lineage and Society: Fukien and Kwangtung.* London School of Economics Monographs on Social Anthropology, no. 33. London: Athlone Press, 1966; reprint 1971.

Fu-chien sheng po-wu kuan 福建省博物館, ed. *Fu-chou Nan-Sung Huang Sheng mu* 福州南宋黃昇墓 [The tomb of Huang Sheng of Fu-chou in the Southern Sung]. Peking: Wen-wu ch'u-pan she, 1982.

Fung, Yu-lan, *A History of Chinese Philosophy* 2 vols. Trans. Derk Bodde. Princeton, N.J.: Princeton University Press, 1952–3 (Vol. 1 orig. 1937).

Gallin, Bernard, and Rita Gallin. "The Chinese Joint Family in Changing Rural Taiwan." In *Social Interaction in Chinese Society*, ed. S. L. Greenblatt, R. W. Wilson, and A. A. Wilson. New York: Pergamon Press, 1982.

Gardella, Robert. *Harvesting Mountains: Fujian and the China Tea Trade, 1757–1937.* Berkeley: University of California Press, 1994.

Gardner, Daniel. *Learning to be a Sage: Selections from the "Conversations of Master Chu, Arranged Topically."* Berkeley: University of California Press, 1990.

Gates, Hill. "The Commoditization of Chinese Women." *Signs* 14:4 (Summer 1989), pp. 799–832.

Gernet, Jacques. *Daily Life in China on the Eve of the Mongol Invasion 1250–1276.* Trans. H. M. Wright. Stanford, Calif.: Stanford University Press, 1962 (orig. Paris, 1959).

Giles, Lionel. *Descriptive Catalogue of the Chinese Manuscripts from Tunhuang in the British Museum.* London: British Museum, 1957.

Golas, Peter. "Rural China in the Sung." *Journal of Asian Studies* 39:2 (Feb. 1980), pp. 291–325.

Goody, Jack. *Production and Reproduction: A Comparative Study of the Domestic Domain.* Cambridge: Cambridge University Press, 1976.

————. "Inheritance, Property and Women: Some Comparative Considerations." In *Family and Inheritance: Rural Society in Western Europe, 1200–1800,* ed. Jack Goody, Joan Thirsk, and E. P. Thompson. Cambridge: Cambridge University Press, 1976, pp. 10–36.

———. *The Development of Family and Marriage in Europe.* Cambridge: Cambridge University Press, 1983.

———. *The Oriental, the Ancient and the Primitive: Systems of Marriage and the Family in the Pre-industrial Societies of Eurasia.* Cambridge: Cambridge University Press, 1990.

Goody, Jack, and S. J. Tambiah. *Bridewealth and Dowry.* Cambridge: Cambridge University Press, 1973.

Goody, Jack, Joan Thirsk, and E. P. Thompson, eds. *Family and Inheritance: Rural Society in Western Europe, 1200–1800.* Cambridge: Cambridge University Press, 1976.

Guisso, Richard. "Thunder over the Lake: The Five Classics and the Perception of Woman in Early China." In *Women in China*, ed. Richard Guisso and Stanley Johannesen. Youngstown, N.Y.: Philo Press, 1981, pp. 47–61.

Hansen, Valerie. "Popular Deities and Social Change in the Southern Song Period (1127–1276)." Ph.D. dissertation, University of Pennsylvania, 1987.

———. *Changing Gods in Medieval China, 1127–1276.* Princeton, N.J.: Princeton University Press, 1990.

———. *Negotiating Daily Life in Traditional China: How Ordinary People Used Contracts, 600–1400.* New Haven, Conn.: Yale University Press, 1995.

———. *The Beijing Qingming Scroll and Its Significance for the Study of Chinese History.* Albany, N.Y.: Journal of Sung-Yuan Studies, 1996.

Hartwell, Robert. "A Revolution in the Chinese Iron and Coal Industries." *Journal of Asian Studies* 21 (1962), pp. 153–62.

———. "Markets, Technology, and the Structure of Enterprise in the Development of the Eleventh-Century Chinese Iron and Steel Industry." *Journal of Economic History* 26:9 (1966), pp. 29–58.

———. "The Evolution of the Early Northern Sung Monetary System." *Journal of the American Oriental Society* 87 (1967), pp. 280–9.

———. "Demographic, Political, and Social Transformations of China." *Harvard Journal of Asiatic Studies* 42 (1982), pp. 383–94.

———. "New Approaches to the Study of Bureaucratic Factionalism in Sung China: A Hypothesis." *Bulletin of Sung and Yüan Studies* 18 (1986), pp. 33–40.

Hazelton, Keith. "Patrilines and the Development of Localized Lineages." In *Kinship Organization in Late Imperial China, 1000–1940*, ed. Patricia Ebrey and James Watson. Berkeley: University of California Press, 1986, pp. 137–69.

Hervouet, Yves, ed. *A Sung Bibliography.* Hong Kong: The Chinese University Press, 1978.

Hirschon, Renée. "Introduction." In *Women and Property – Women as Property*, ed. Renée Hirschon. New York: St. Martin's Press, 1984, pp. 1–22.

Ho, Ping-ti. "Early Ripening Rice in Chinese History." *Economic History Review*, 2nd series, 9:2 (1956), pp. 200–18.

———. *The Ladder of Success in Imperial China: Aspects of Social Mobility, 1368–1911*. New York: Columbia University Press, 1962.

———. *An Estimate of the Total Population of Sung and Chin China*, Etudes Song, 1st series, no. 1. The Hague: Mouton, 1970, pp. 33–53.

Hoang, Pierre. *Le Marriage Chinois au Point de Vue Legal*. Shanghai: Catholic Mission Press, 1915.

Holmgren, Jennifer. "Economic Foundations of Virtue: Widow Remarriage in Early and Modern China." *Australian Journal of Chinese Affairs* 13 (1985), pp. 1–27.

———. "Observations on Marriage and Inheritance Practices in Early Mongol and Yüan Society, with Particular Reference to the Levirate." *Journal of Asian History*, 20:2 (1986), pp. 127–92.

Honig, Emily, and Gail Hershatter, eds. *Personal Voices: Chinese Women in the 1980s*. Stanford, Calif.: Stanford University Press, 1988.

Hsiao, Ch'i-ch'ing. *The Military Establishment of the Yüan Dynasty*. Cambridge, Mass.: Harvard University Press, 1978.

———. "Mid-Yüan Politics." In *The Cambridge History of China*, Vol. 6, *Alien Regimes and Border States, 907–1368*, ed. Herbert Franke and Denis Twitchett. Cambridge: Cambridge University Press, 1994, pp. 490–560.

Hsing T'ieh 邢鐵. "Sung-tai te ts'ai-ch'an yi-chu chi-ch'eng wen-ti" 宋代的財產遺囑繼承問題 [The question of inheritance by testament in the Sung]. *Li-shih yen-chiu* 6 (Dec. 1992), pp. 54–66.

———. "Sung-tai te lien-t'ien ho mu-t'ien" 宋代的奩田和墓田 [Dowry land and grave land in the Sung]. *Chung-kuo she-hui ching-chi shih yen-chiu*, no. 1 (1993), pp. 36–53.

Hsü, Cho-yün. *Ancient China in Transition*. Stanford, Calif.: Stanford University Press, 1965.

Hsu Dau-lin, "Separation between Fact-finding (Trial) and Law-finding (Sentencing) in Sung Criminal Proceedings." *Sung Studies Newsletter* 6 (Oct. 1972), pp. 3–18.

Hucker, Charles O. "Introduction." In *A Dictionary of Official Titles in Imperial China*, by Charles Hucker. Stanford, Calif.: Stanford University Press, 1985.

Hulsewé, Anton F. P. "Contracts of the Han Period." In *Il Diritto in Cina*, ed. Lionello Lanciotti. Florence: Leo S. Olschki Editore, 1978, pp. 11–38.

———. *Remnants of Ch'in Law: An Annotated Translation of the Ch'in Legal and Administrative Rules of the 3rd century B.C. Discovered in Yün-meng Prefecture, Hu-pei Province, in 1975*. Leiden: E. J. Brill, 1985.

Hung Chin-fu 洪金富. "Yüan-tai te shou-chi hun" 元代的收繼婚 [Levirate marriage in the Yüan]. In *Chung-kuo chin-shih she-hui wen-hua shih lun-wen chi* 中國近世社會文話史論文集 [Papers on Society and Culture of Early Modern China]. Taipei: Academia Sinica, Institute of History and Philology, 1992, pp. 279–314.

Hymes, Robert P. *Statesmen and Gentlemen: The Elite of Fu-chou, Chiang-hsi, in Northern and Southern Sung*. Cambridge: Cambridge University Press, 1986.

————. "Marriage, Descent Groups, and the Localist Strategy in Sung and Yüan Fu-chou." In *Kinship Organization in Late Imperial China, 1000–1940*, ed. Patricia Ebrey and James Watson. Berkeley: University of California Press, 1986, pp. 95–136.

————. "Lu Chiu-yüan, Academies, and the Problem of the Local Community." In *Neo-Confucian Education: The Formative Stage*, ed. Wm. Theodore de Bary and John Chaffee. Berkeley: University of California Press, 1989, pp. 432–56.

————. "Review of *The Inner Quarters: Marriage and the Lives of Chinese Women in the Sung Period*, by Patricia Ebrey." *Harvard Journal of Asiatic Studies* 57:1 (June 1997).

Hymes, Robert P., and Conrad Schirokauer, eds. *Ordering the World: Approaches to State and Society in Sung Dynasty China*. Berkeley: University of California Press, 1993.

Ihara Hiroshi 伊原弘. "Sōdai kanryō no kon'in no imi ni tsuite" 宋代官僚の婚姻の意味について [On the meaning of marriage for Sung bureaucrats]. *Rekishi to chiri* 254 (1976).

————. "NanSō Shisen ni okeru teikyo shijin: Seidofu ro, Shishū ro o chūshin to shite" 南宋四川における定居士人：成都府路，梓州路を中心として [Elites with fixed residences in Southern Sung Szechwan: focusing on Ch'eng-tu-fu circuit and Tzu-chou circuit]. *Tōhōgaku* 54 (1977).

————. *Chūgoku chūsei toshi kikō* 中國中世都市紀行 [A journey to cities of medieval China]. Chūkō shinsho series no. 897. Tokyo: Chūō kōronsha, 1988.

————, ed. *Yanagida Setsuko sensei koki kinen Chūgoku no dentō shakai to kazoku* 柳田節子先生古稀記念中國の傳統社會と家族. [Traditional Chinese society and family: a festschrift in celebration of the seventieth birthday of Professor Yanagida Setsuko]. Tokyo: Kyūko shoen, 1993.

————. "Sōdai shakai to zeni: shomin no shisanryoku o megutte" 宋代社會と錢—庶民の資産力をめぐって [Sung society and money: the economic resources of the common people]. Special issue entitled, *Sōzeni no seikai: TōAjia no kokusai tsūka* 宋錢の世界—東アジアの國際通貨 [The world of Sung money: the international currency of East Asia]. *Ajia yūgaku* No. 18 (July, 2000), pp. 4–18.

Ikeda, On. "T'ang Household Registers and Related Documents." In *Perspectives on the T'ang*, ed. Arthur Wright and Denis Twitchett. New Haven, Conn.: Yale University Press, 1973, pp. 121–50.

I-lin-chen 亦鄰真. *Yüan-tai ying-i kung-tu wen-t'i* 元代硬譯公牘文體 [The language of directly translated official documents of the Yüan]. *Yüan-shih lun-ts'ung* no. 1. Peking: Chung-hua shu-chü, 1982, pp. 164–78.

Itabashi Shin'ichi 板橋真一. "Sōdai no kosetsu zaisan to joshi no zaisanken o megutte" 宋代の戶絕財產と女子の財產權をめぐって [Property of extinct households and daughters' property rights in the Sung]. In *Yanagida Setsuko sensei koki kinen Chūgoku no dentō shakai to kazoku* 柳田節子先生古稀記念中國の傳統社會と家族. [Traditional Chinese society and family: a festschrift in cel-

ebration of the seventieth birthday of Professor Yanagida Setsuko], ed.
Ihara Hiroshi. Tokyo: Kyūko shoen, 1993, pp. 365–82.

Jamieson, George. *Chinese Family and Commercial Law*. Shanghai: Kelly and Walsh
Ltd., 1921; reprint, Hong Kong: Vetch and Lee Ltd., 1970.

Jeffcott, Colin. "Government and the Distribution System in Sung Cities." *Papers
on Far Eastern History* 1 (March 1970), pp. 119–52.

Johnson, David. *The Medieval Chinese Oligarchy*. Boulder, Colo.: Westview Press,
1977.

———. "The Last Years of a Great Clan: The Li Family of Chao Chün in Late
T'ang and Early Sung." *Harvard Journal of Asiatic Studies* 37:1 (June 1977),
pp. 5–102.

Johnson, Wallace. *The T'ang Code*, Vol I, *General Principles*. Princeton, N.J.:
Princeton University Press, 1979.

Judd, Ellen. "*Niangjia*: Chinese Women and Their Natal Families." *Journal of
Asian Studies* 48:3 (Aug. 1989), pp. 524–44.

Kato, Shigeshi. "On the *Hang* or the Associations of Merchants in China, with
Special Reference to the Institution in the T'ang and Sung Periods."
Memoirs of the Research Dept. of the Tōyō Bunko no. 9 (1936), pp. 45–83.

Kawamura Yasushi 川村康. "Sōdai zeisei shōkō" 宋代贅婿小考 [A short study of
uxorilocal sons-in-law in the Sung]. In *Yanagida Setsuko sensei koki kinen
Chūgoku no dentō shakai to kazoku* [Traditional Chinese society and family: a
festschrift in celebration of the seventieth birthday of Professor Yanagida
Setsuko], ed. Ihara Hiroshi. Tokyo: Kyūko shoen, 1993, pp. 347–63.

Keightley, David. "Early Civilization in China: Reflections on How It Became
Chinese." In *Heritage of China: Contemporary Perspectives on Chinese Civilization*. ed. Paul Ropp. Berkeley: University of California Press, 1990, pp.
15–54.

Kelleher, Theresa. "Reflections on Persons at Hand: The Position of Women in
Ch'eng-Chu Neo-Confucianism." Paper presented at Annual Meeting of the
Association for Asian Studies, March 22–4, 1985. Philadelphia.

———. "Confucianism." In *Women in World Religions*, ed. Arvind Sharma. Albany:
State University of New York Press, 1987, pp. 135–59.

Kessler, Adam. *Empires beyond the Great Wall: The Heritage of Genghis Khan*. Los
Angeles: Natural History Museum of Los Angeles County, 1993.

Kinugawa Tsuyoshi 衣川強. "Sōdai no hōkyū ni tsuite: bunshin kanryō o chūshin
toshite" 宋代の俸給について文臣官僚を中心として [Sung dynasty salaries:
with emphasis on civil officials]. *Tōhō gakuhō* 41 (1970).

———. "Kanryō to hōkyū: Sōdai no hōkyū ni tsuite zokkō" 官僚と俸給宋代の俸給
について續考 [Officials and salaries: further research on Sung dynasty
salaries]. *Tōhō gakuhō* 42 (1971).

———. "Shushi shōden" 朱子小傳 [A short biography of Chu Hsi]. *Kōbe shōka
daigaku jinbun ronshū* 神戶商科大學人文論集 [Essays in the humanities, Kobe
College of Commercial Science] 15:1 (1979).

——— ed. *Ryū Shiken hakushi shōju kinen Sōshi kenkyū ronshū* 劉子健博士頌壽紀
念宋史研究論集 [Collected studies in Sung history dedicated to Professor

James T. C. Liu in celebration of his seventieth birthday]. Tokyo: Dōhōsha, 1989.

Ko, Dorothy. *Teachers of the Inner Chambers: Women and Culture in Seventeenth-Century China.* Stanford, Calif.: Stanford University Press, 1994.

Kobayashi Takashiro 小林高四郎 and Okamoto Keiji 岡本敬二, eds. *Tsūsei jōkaku no kenkyū yakuchū* 通制條格の研究譯註 [Translation and commentary of the *T'ung-chih t'iao-ko*], 3 vols. Tokyo: Kokushohan kōkai, 1964–1976.

Kracke, E. A. *Civil Service in Early Sung China: 960–1067.* Cambridge, Mass.: Harvard University Press, 1953.

———. "Family versus Merit in Chinese Civil Service Examinations under the Empire." *Harvard Journal of Asiatic Studies* 10 (1947), pp. 105–23.

Kuhn, Dieter. "Decoding Tombs of the Song Elite." In *Burial in Song China,* ed. Dieter Kuhn. Heidelberg: Edition Forum, 1994, pp. 11–160.

Kulp, Daniel. *Country Life in China: The Sociology of Familism.* New York: Teacher's College, Columbia University, 1925.

Kuo Tung-hsü 郭東旭. "Sung-tai ts'ai-ch'an chi-ch'eng fa ch'u-t'an" 宋代財產繼承法初探 [Preliminary study of inheritance law in the Sung]. *Ho-pei ta-hsüeh hsüeh-pao,* no. 8 (1986), pp. 113–121.

———. "Sung-tai chih sung-hsüeh" 宋代之訟學 [The study of suing in the Sung Dynasty]. In *Sung-shih yen-chiu lun-ts'ung,* ed. Ch'i Hsia 漆俠. Pao-ting: Ho-pei ta-hsüeh ch'u-pan she, 1990, pp. 133–47.

Lanciotti, Lionello, ed. *Il Diritto in Cina: Teoria e Applicazioni Durante le Dinastie Imperiali e Problematica del Diritto Cinese Contemporaneo.* Florence: Leo S. Olschki Editore, 1978.

———, ed. *La Donna Nella Cina Imperiale e Nella Cina Repubblicana.* Florence: Leo S. Olschki Editore, 1980.

Lang, Olga. *Chinese Family and Society.* New Haven, Conn.: Yale University Press, 1946.

Laslett, Peter. *World We Have Lost.* London: Methuen and Co., 1979.

Latham, Ronald, trans. *The Travels of Marco Polo.* New York: Penguin Books, 1980.

Lau Nap-yin [Liu Li-yen] 柳立言. "Ch'ien-t'an Sung-tai fu-nü te shou-chieh yü tsai-chia" 淺談宋代婦女守節與再嫁 [A brief discussion of chastity and remarriage of Sung women]. *Hsin shih-hsüeh* 2:4 (1991), pp. 37–76.

———. "Sung-tai t'ung-chü chih-tu hsia te suo-wei 'kung-ts'ai'" 宋代同居制度下的所謂共財 [So-called 'common property' under the co-residence system of the Sung]. *Chung-yang yen-chiu yüan, li-shih yü-yen yen-chiu so chi-k'an* 65:2 (1994), pp. 253–305.

Lee, Thomas H. C. *Government, Education, and Examinations in Sung China.* Hong Kong: Chinese University Press, 1985.

———. "Neo-Confucian Education in Chien-yang, Fu-chien, 1000–1400: Academies, Society and the Development of Local Culture." In *Kuo-chi Chu-tzu hsüeh-hui i-lun wen-chi* 國際朱子學會議論文集 [Proceedings of the International Chu Hsi Conference]. Taipei: Chung-yang yen-chiu yüan,

Chung-kuo wen-che yen-chiu so [Academia Sinica, Institute of Literature and Philosophy], 1993, pp. 945–96.

Legge, James, trans. *Li Chi: Book of Rites.* 2 vols. New York: University Books, 1967. (Orig. *Li Ki,* Oxford University Press, 1885, as Vols 27 and 28 of *Sacred Books of the East*).

———, trans. *The She King or Book of Poetry,* Vol. 4 of *The Chinese Classics.* Oxford University Press, 1871; reprint, Hong Kong: Hong Kong University Press, 1961.

Levy, Howard. *Chinese Footbinding: The History of a Curious Custom.* New York: Walton Rawls, 1966.

Linck, Gudula. *Zur Sozialgeschichte der Chinesischen Familie im 13. Jahrhundert: Untersuchungen am "Ming-gong shu-pan qing-ming ji"* [Toward a social history of the Chinese family in the thirteenth century: research on the *Ming-kung shu-p'an ch'ing-ming chi*]. Stuttgart: Franz Steiner Verlag, 1986.

Liu Ching-chen 劉靜貞. "Nü wu wai-shih? Mu-chih-pei-ming chung suo-chien chih Pei-Sung shih-ta-fu she-hui chih-hsü li-nien" 女無外事？墓誌碑銘中所見之北宋士大夫社會秩序理念 [Women do not attend to outside affairs? Northern Sung literati concepts of social order as seen in funerary inscriptions]. *Fu-nü yü liang-hsing hsüeh-k'an* 婦女與兩性學刊 no. 4 (March 1993), pp. 21–46.

Liu, James T. C. *Reform in Sung China: Wang An-shih (1021–1086) and His New Policies.* Cambridge, Mass.: Harvard University Press, 1959.

Mann, Susan. "Widows in the Kinship, Class, and Community Structures of Qing Dynasty China." *Journal of Asian Studies* 46:1 (Feb. 1987), pp. 37–56.

———. *Precious Records: Women in China's Long Eighteenth Century.* Stanford, Calif.: Stanford University Press, 1997.

McDermott, Joseph. "Charting Blank Spaces and Disputed Regions: The Problem of Sung Land Tenure." *Journal of Asian Studies* 44:1 (Nov. 1984), pp. 13–41.

———. "The Chinese Domestic Bursar." *Ajia kenkyū kai* (Tokyo), no. 2 (Nov. 1990), pp. 267–84.

———. "Family Financial Plans of the Southern Sung." *Asia Major* 3rd series, 4:2 (1991), pp. 15–78.

———. "Equality and Inequality in Sung Family Organization: Some Observations on Chao Ting's *Family Instructions*." In *Yanagida Setsuko sensei koki kinen: Chūgoku no dentō shakai to kazoku* [Traditional Chinese society and family: a festschrift in celebration of the seventieth birthday of Professor Yanagida Setsuko], ed. Ihara Hiroshi. Tokyo: Kyūko shoin, 1993), pp. 1–21.

McKnight, Brian. *Village and Bureaucracy in Southern Sung China.* Chicago: University of Chicago Press, 1971.

———. "From Statute to Precedent: An Introduction to Sung Law and its Transformation." In *Law and the State in Traditional East Asia,* ed. Brian McKnight. Honolulu: University of Hawaii Press, 1987, pp. 111–32.

————. *Law and Order in Sung China.* Cambridge: Cambridge University Press, 1992.

————. "Chinese Law and Legal Systems: Five Dynasties and Sung." Draft chapter for *Cambridge History of China* (1989 version). Cambridge: Cambridge University Press, forthcoming.

————. *The Washing Away of Wrongs: Forensic Medicine in Thirteenth-Century China.* Ann Arbor: Center for Chinese Studies, University of Michigan, 1981.

————. "Mandarins as Legal Experts: Professional Learning in Sung China." In *Neo-Confucian Education: The Formative Stage*, ed. Wm. Theodore de Bary and John Chaffee. Berkeley: University of California Press, 1989, pp. 493–516.

————. "Divorce in Sung China." In *Proceedings of the Second Symposium on Sung History (Ti-erh chieh Sung-shih hsüeh-shu yen-t'ao hui lun-wen chi* 第二屆宋史學術研討會論文集). Taipei: Chung-kuo wen-hua ta-hsüeh shih-hsüeh yen-chiu so, 1996.

————. "Who Gets It When You Go: The Legal Consequences of the Ending of Family Lines (*juehu*) in the Song Dynasty (960–1279)." *Journal of the Economic and Social History of the Orient* 43:3 (2000), pp. 314–63.

McKnight, Brian, and James T. C. Liu, trans. *The Enlightened Judgments: Ch'ing-ming Chi, The Sung Dynasty Collection.* Albany: State University of New York Press, 1999.

McMullen, David. "Bureaucrats and Cosmology: The Ritual Code of T'ang China." In *Rituals of Royalty: Power and Ceremonial in Traditional Societies.* ed. David Cannadine and Simon Price. Cambridge: Cambridge University Press, 1987.

————. *State and Scholars in T'ang China.* Cambridge: Cambridge University Press, 1988.

McMullen, James I. "Non-Agnatic Adoption: A Confucian Controversy in Seventeenth and Eighteenth Century Japan." *Harvard Journal of Asiatic Studies* 35 (1975), pp. 130–89.

Min shang-shih hsi-kuan tiao-ch'a pao-kao lu 民商事習慣調查報告錄 [Report of an investigation of business practices among the people]. N.p.: Chung-hua min-kuo ssu-fa hsing-cheng pu, 1930.

Miyazawa Hisayuki. "An Outline of the Naitō Hypothesis and Its Effects on Japanese Studies of China." *Far Eastern Quarterly* 14:4 (1955), pp. 533–52.

Miyazaki Ichisada 宮崎市定. "Sōdai kansei josetsu: Sōshi shokkan shi o ika ni yomubeki ka" 宋代官制序説—宋史職官志を如何に讀むべきか [An introduction to the bureaucratic system of the Sung: how should one read the Monograph on Bureaucracy of the *Sung Dynastic History*?]. In *Sōshi shokkanshi sakuin* 宋史職官志索引 [Index to the Monograph on Bureaucracy of the *Sung Dynastic History*], ed. Saeki Tomi. Kyoto: Kyōto daigaku Tōyōshi kenkyūkai, 1963, pp. 1–57.

————. "Sōdai igo no tochi shoyū keitai" 宋代以後の土地所有形體 [Forms of landholding from the Sung on]. In *Ajiashi kenkyū* アジア史研究

[Studies in Asian history]. Vol. 4. Kyoto: Tōyōshi kenkyūkai, 1964, pp. 87–129.

————. "SōGen jidai no hōsei to saiban kikō: Gentenshō seiritsu no jidaiteki shakaiteki haikei" 宋元時代の法制と裁判機構——元典章成立の時代的社會的 背景 [The structure of law and trial prodecure in the Sung and Yüan: the historical and social background of the *Yüan tien-chang*]." In *Ajiashi kenkyū* アジア史研究 [Studies in Asian history] Vol. 4. Kyoto: Dōhōsha, 1975; 170–305. (Orig. *Tōhō gakuhō* 1954)

————. "The Administration of Justice during the Sung Dynasty." In *Essays on China's Legal Tradition*, ed. Jerome Cohen, Randle Edwards, and Fu-mei Chang Chen. Princeton, N.J.: Princeton University Press, 1980, pp. 56–75.

Morgan, David. *The Mongols*. Oxford: Blackwell, 1986.

Morita Kenji. "SōGen jidai ni okeru shūfu" 宋元時代における修譜 [The compilation of genealogies in the Sung-Yüan period]. *Tōyōshi kenkyū* 37:4 (1979), pp. 27–53.

Morohashi Tetsuji 諸橋轍次. *Dai kanwa jiten* 大漢和辭典 [Comprehensive Chinese-Japanese Dictionary]. 13 vols. Tokyo: Taishūkan, 1960.

Mote, Frederick W. "Chinese Society under Mongol Rule, 1215–1368." In *The Cambridge History of China*, Vol. 6, *Alien Regimes and Border States, 907–1368*, ed. Herbert Franke and Denis Twitchett. Cambridge: Cambridge University Press, 1994, pp. 616–64.

————. *Imperial China 900–1800*. Cambridge, Mass.: Harvard University Press, 1999.

Moule, A. C., and Paul Pelliot, trans. and eds., *Marco Polo: The Description of the World*. London: Routledge and Sons, 1938.

Nagasawa Noritsune 長澤規矩也. "Hampon kaisetsu" 版本解説 [An explanation of the edition]. Postface to *Meikō shohan seimeishū* 名公書判清明集 [Collection of decisions by famous judges to clarify and enlighten], pp. 1–2. Reprint of Sung ed. of *Ch'ing-ming chi* held in Seikadō library, Tokyo, Japan. Tokyo: Koten kenkyūkai, 1964.

Nagata Mie 永田三枝. "NanSōki ni okeru josei no zaisanken ni tzuite" 南宋期 における女性の財産權について [Women's property rights in the Southern Sung]. *Hokudai shigaku* 北大史學 31 (Aug. 1991), pp. 1–15.

Naitō Torajirō 內藤虎次郎. "Gaikakuteki TōSō jidai kan" 槪括的唐宋時代觀 [Some general observations about the T'ang-Sung period]. *Rekishi to chiri* 9:5 (1922), pp. 1–12.

Nakada Kaoru 中田薫. "TōSō jidai no kazoku kyōsan sei" 唐宋時代の家族 共産制 [The communal property system of the family in the T'ang and Sung]. In *Hōseishi ronshū* 法制史論集 [Collected essays on legal history], Vol. 3 Pt. 2. Tokyo: Iwanami Shoten, 1943; reprint 1985, pp. 1295–360.

————. *Hōseishi ronshū* 法制史論集 [Collected essays on legal history], 4 vols. Tokyo: Iwanami Shoten, 1943; reprint 1985.

Nakagawa Tadahide 中川忠英. *Shinzoku kibun* 清俗紀聞 [Accounts of Ch'ing customs]. Tokyo: 1799. Copy held by Marquand Library of Art and Archaeology, Princeton Univerisity Library.

Neskar, Ellen. "The Cult of Worthies: A Study of Shrines Honoring Local Confucian Worthies in the Sung Dynasty (960–1279)." Ph.D. dissertation, Columbia University, 1993.

Niida Noboru 仁井田陞. *Tōsō hōritsu bunsho no kenkyū* 唐宋法律文書の研究 [Studies of T'ang-Sung legal documents]. Tokyo: Tōhō bunka gakuin, 1937; reprint Tōkyō daigaku shuppankai, 1983.

————. *Tōryō shūi* 唐令拾遺 [Collected remnants of the T'ang statutes]. 1933; reprint, Tokyo: Tōkyō daigaku shuppankai, 1983.

————. *Chūgoku mibunhō shi* 中國身分法史 (original title: *Shina mibunhō shi* 支那身分法史) [History of personal status law in China]. 1942; reprint, Tokyo: Tōkyō daigaku shuppankai, 1983.

————. *Chūgoku hōseishi kenkyū* 中國法制史研究 [Studies in Chinese legal history]. Vol. 1: *Keihō* 刑法 [Criminal law]. Tokyo: Tōkyō daigaku shuppankai, 1959: reprint 1991.

————. *Chūgoku hōseishi kenkyū* 中國法制史研究. Vol. 2: *Tochihō, torihikihō* 土地法，取引法 [Law of land, law of transactions]. Tokyo: Tōkyō daigaku shuppankai, 1960; reprint 1991.

————. *Chūgoku hōseishi kenkyū* 中國法制史研究. Vol. 3: *Dorei nōdohō, kazoku sonrakuhō* 奴隷農奴法，家族村落法 [Law of slave and serf, law of family and village]. Tokyo: Tōkyō daigaku shuppankai, 1962; reprint 1991.

————. *Chūgoku hōseishi kenkyū* 中國法制史研究. Vol. 4: *Hō to kanshū, hō to dōtoku* 法と慣習，法と道德 [Law and custom; law and morality]. Tokyo: Tōkyō daigaku shuppankai, 1964; reprint 1991.

————. "Eiraku Taitenbon *Seimeishū* ni tsuite" 永樂大典版清明集について [On the *Yung-lo ta-tien* edition of the *Ch'ing-ming chi*]. In *Chūgoku hōseishi kenkyū*, Vol. 4: *Hō to kanshū; hō to dōtoku*, pp. 437–41.

————. "Hoppō minzokuhō to Chūgokuhō to no kōshō (1): Kindai keihō kō" 北方民族法と中國法との交渉（一）: 金代刑法考 [The relation between Chinese law and the law of the Northern peoples (1): a study of Chin dynasty penal law]. In *Chūgoku hōseishi kenkyū*, Vol. 1: *Keihō*. Tokyo: Tōkyō daigaku shuppankai, 1959; reprint 1991, pp. 453–524.

————. "Gentenshō no seiritsu to Daitokutenshō" 元典章の成立と大德典章 [The *Ta-te tien-chang* and the origins of the *Yüan tien-chang*]. In *Chūgoku hōseishi kenkyū*, Vol. 4. Tokyo, 1964, pp. 181–99.

————. "*Meikō shohan seimeishū* kaidai" 名公書判清明集解題 [Explanatory notes on the *Ch'ing-ming chi*]. Postface to *Meikō shohan seimeishū* 名公書判清明集 [Collection of decisions by famous judges to clarify and enlighten], pp. 3–6. Reprint of Sung ed. of *Ch'ing-ming chi* held in Seikadō library, Tokyo, Japan. Tokyo: Koten kenkyūkai, 1964.

Ocko, Jonathan. "Women, Property, and Law in the People's Republic of China." In *Marriage and Inequality in Chinese Society*, ed. Rubie Watson and Patricia Ebrey. Berkeley: University of California Press, 1991, pp. 313–46.

Ogawa Tamaki et al. 小川環樹 *Shinjigen* 新字源 [A new Origin of Characters]. Tokyo: Kadokawa shoten, 1968.

O'Hara, Albert. *The Position of Women in Early China: According to the* Lieh-nü chuan *"The Biographies of Eminent Chinese Women."* Westport, Conn.: Hyperion Press, 1945; reprint 1981.

Ortner, Sherry. "Is Female to Male as Nature Is to Culture?" In *Women, Culture, and Society*, ed. Michelle Rosaldo and Louise Lamphere. Stanford, Calif.: Stanford University Press, 1974, pp. 67–87.

Oshima Ritsuko 大島立子. "Genchō no 'josei' ni tsuite" 元朝の女婿について [On uxorilocal sons-in-law in the Yüan]. *Shiron* 43 (1990), pp. 76–90.

Overmyer, Daniel. *Folk Buddhist Religion.* Cambridge, Mass.: Harvard University Press, 1976.

Peterson, Charles A. "Old Illusions and New Realities: Sung Foreign Policy, 1217–1234." In *China among Equals*, ed. Morris Rossabi. Berkeley: University of California Press, 1983, pp. 204–39.

Ratchnevsky, Paul. "The Levirate in the Legislation of the Yuan Dynasty." In *Tamura hakushi shoju tōyōshi ronso* [Asiatic studies in honour of Dr. Tamura Jitsuzō on the occasion of his sixty-fourth birthday]. Tokyo: Dōhōsha, 1968, pp. 45–62.

———. *Un Code des Yüan*, 4 vols. Paris: Collège de France, Institut des Hautes Etudes Chinoises, 1972–1985 (Vol. 1 orig. Paris: Ernest Leroux, 1937).

———. *Genghis Khan: His Life and Legacy.* Trans. by Thomas Haining. Oxford: Blackwell, 1991.

———. "Jurisdiction, Penal Code, and Cultural Confrontation under Mongol-Yüan Law." *Asia Major*, 3rd series, 4:1 (1993), pp. 161–79.

Riasanovsky, Valentin. *Fundamental Principles of Mongol Law.* Indiana University Publications, Uralic and Altaic Series, Vol. 43, 1965.

Rockhill, William, trans. *The Journey of William of Rubruck to the Eastern Parts of the World, 1253–55, as Narrated by Himself.* Nendeln, Liechtenstein: Kraus Reprint Ltd., 1967 (orig. London: Hakluyt Society, 1900).

Rosaldo, Michelle. "Women, Culture, and Society: A Theoretical Overview." In *Women, Culture, and Society*, ed. Michelle Rosaldo and Louise Lamphere. Stanford, Calif.: Stanford University Press, 1974, pp. 17–42.

Rossabi, Morris. "Khubilai Khan and the Women in His Family." In *Studia Sino-Mongolica: Festschrift für Herbert Franke*, ed. Wolfgang Bauer. Wiesbaden: Franz Steiner Verlag, 1979.

———. *Khubilai Khan: His Life and Times.* Berkeley: University of California Press, 1988.

———, ed. *China among Equals: The Middle Kingdom and Its Neighbors, 10th-14th Centuries.* Berkeley: University of California Press, 1983.

Rubruck, William of. See Rockhill, trans.

Sa, Sophie. "Marriage among the Taiwanese of Pre-1945 Taipei." In *Family and Population in East Asian History*, ed. Susan Hanley and Arthur Wolf. Stanford, Calif.: Stanford University Press, 1985, pp. 277–308.

Sadachi Haruto 佐立治人. "Seimeishū no 'hōi' to 'ninjō:' Soshō tōjisha ni yoru hōritsu kaishaku no konseki" 清明集の'法意'と'人情' ——訴訟當事者による

法律解釋の痕跡 ['Law' and 'human feelings' in the *Ch'ing-ming chi*: Evidence for the interpretation of the law by the parties to a lawsuit]. In *Chūgoku kinsei no hōsei to shakai* 中國近世の法制と社會 [Law and society in early modern China], ed. Umehara Kaoru. Kyoto: Kyōto Daigaku Jinbun Kagaku Kenkyūjo, 1993, pp. 293–334.

Schafer, Edward. *The Empire of Min.* Rutland, Vt.: Charles E. Tuttle, 1954.

Schirokauer, Conrad. "Neo-Confucians under Attack: The Condemnation of *Wei-hsüeh.*" In *Crisis and Prosperity in Sung China,* ed. John Winthrop Haeger. Tucson: University of Arizona Press, 1975, pp. 163–98.

———. "Chu Hsi and Hu Hung." In *Chu Hsi and Neo-Confucianism,* ed. Wing-tsit Chan. Honolulu: University of Hawaii Press, 1986, pp. 480–502.

———, and Robert Hymes. "Introduction." In *Ordering the World: Approaches to State and Society in Sung Dynasty China,* ed. Robert Hymes and Conrad Schirokauer. Berkeley: University of California Press, 1993, pp. 1–58.

Schottenhammer, Angela. "Characteristics of Song Epitaphs." In *Burial in Song China,* ed. Dieter Kuhn. Heidelberg: Edition Forum, 1994, pp. 253–306.

Schurmann, Herbert F. *Economic Structure of the Yüan Dynasty: Translation of Chapters 93 and 94 of the* Yüan shih. Harvard-Yenching Institute Series, Vol. 16. Cambridge, Mass.: Harvard University Press, 1956.

Scogin, Hugh. "Between Heaven and Man: Contract and the State in Han Dynasty China." *Southern California Law Review* 63:5 (July 1990), pp. 1325–1404.

Scott, Joan. *Gender and the Politics of History.* New York: Columbia University Press, 1988.

Serruys, Henry. "Remains of Mongol Customs in China during the Early Ming Period." *Monumenta Serica* 16 (1957). Reprinted in *The Mongols and Ming China: Customs and History.* London: Variorum Reprints, 1987.

Shammas, Carole, Marylynn Salmon, and Michel Dahlin. *Inheritance in America from Colonial Times to the Present.* New Brunswick, N.J.: Rutgers University Press, 1987.

Shiba Yoshinobu 斯波義信. *Sōdai shōgyōshi kenkyū* 宋代商業史研究 [A study of Sung commerce]. Tokyo: Kazama shobō, 1968.

———. *Commerce and Society in Sung China.* Trans. and ed. Mark Elvin. Ann Arbor: Center for Chinese Studies, University of Michigan, 1970.

———. "Urbanization and the Development of Markets in the Lower Yangtze Valley." In *Crisis and Prosperity in Sung China,* ed. John Haeger. Tucson: University of Arizona Press, 1975, pp. 13–48.

———. *Sōdai Kōnan keizaishi no kenkyū* 宋代江南經濟史の研究 [Studies in the economy of the lower Yangtze in the Sung]. Tokyo: Tōkyō daigaku Tōyōbunka kenkyūjo, 1988.

Shiga Shūzō 滋賀秀三, *Chūgoku kazokuhō no genri* 中國家族法の原理 [Principles of the Chinese family system]. Tokyo: Sōbunsha, 1967; reprint 1981.

———. "Chūgoku kazokuhō hokō" 中國家族法補考 [A supplementary study of the Chinese family system]. *Kokka gakkai zasshi* 4 parts. 67:5 (Nov. 1953), pp. 1–31; 67:9 (Aug. 1954), pp. 54–83; 67:11 (Oct. 1954), pp. 89–123; 68:7 (March 1955), pp. 33–57.

———. "Family Property and the Law of Inheritance in Traditional China." In *Chinese Family Law and Social Change*, ed. David Buxbaum. Seattle: University of Washington Press, 1978, 109–50.

Skinner, G. William. "Introduction: Urban Development in Imperial China." In *The City in Late Imperial China*, ed. G. William Skinner. Stanford, Calif.: Stanford University Press, 1977.

Smith, John M. "Mongol and Nomadic Taxation." *Harvard Journal of Asiatic Studies* 30 (1970), pp. 46–86.

Smith, Paul. *Taxing Heaven's Storehouse: Horses, Bureaucrats, and the Destruction of the Sichuan Tea Industry 1074–1224*. Cambridge, Mass.: Harvard University Press, 1991.

———. "Fear of Gynarchy in an Age of Chaos: Kong Qi's Reflections on Life in South China under Mongol Rule." *Journal of the Economic and Social History of the Orient* 41:1 (1998), pp. 1–95.

So, Billy Kee-long. "Economic Developments in South Fukien, 946–1276." Ph.D. dissertation, Australian National University, 1982.

Steele, John, trans. *The I-li or Book of Etiquette and Ceremonial*, 2 vols. London: Probsthain & Co., 1917.

Stone, Lawrence. "The Education Revolution in England, 1560–1640." *Past and Present* 28 (July 1964), pp. 41–80.

Sudō Yoshiyuki 周藤吉之. *Sōdai kanryōsei to daitochi shoyū* 宋代官僚制と大土地所有 [The Sung bureaucracy and large land holding]. Tokyo: Nihon hyōronsha, 1950.

———. *Chūgoku tochi seidoshi kenkyū* 中國土地制度史研究 [Studies of the history of the Chinese land system]. Tokyo: Tōkyō daigaku shuppansha, 1954.

———. *Sōdai keizaishi kenkyū* 宋代經濟史研究 [Studies on Sung economic history]. Tokyo: Tōkyō daigaku shuppankai, 1962.

———. *Tō Sō shakai keizaishi kenkyū* 唐宋社會經濟史研究 [Studies in the social economy of the T'ang and Sung]. Tokyo: Tōkyō daigaku shuppankai, 1965.

Sun, E-tu Zen, and J. de Francis, eds. *Chinese Social History: Translations of Selected Studies*. Washington, D.C.: American Council of Learned Societies, 1956.

Swann, Nancy Lee. *Pan Chao: Foremost Woman Scholar of China*. New York: Century Co., 1932.

Tai Yen-hui. "Divorce in Traditional Chinese Law." In *Chinese Family Law and Social Change*, ed. David Buxbaum. Seattle: University of Washington Press, 1978, pp. 75–106.

Takahashi Yoshio 高橋芳郎. "Oya o nakushita musumetachi: NanSōki no iwayuru joshi zaisanken ni tsuite" 親を亡くした女たち―南宋期のいわゆる女子財産權 について [Daughters whose parents have died: so-called property rights of daughters in the Southern Sung period]. *Tōhoku daigaku: Tōyōshi ronshū* 6 (Jan. 1995), pp. 343–72.

Tanaka Kenji 田中謙二. "Gentenshō bunsho no kōsei" 元典章文書の構成 [The composition of the documents in the *Yüan tien-chang*]. *Tōyōshi kenkyū* 23:4 (March 1965), pp. 92–117.

———. "Gentenshō ni okeru Mōbun chokuyakutai no bunshō" 元典章における 蒙文直譯體の文章 [Direct translation from Mongolian in the *Yüan tien-chang*] In Yoshikawa Kōjirō and Tanaka Kenji, *Gentenshō no buntai* 元典章の文體 [The language of the *Yüan tien-chang*]. Kyoto: Kyōto daigaku jinbun kagaku kenkyūjo, 1964, pp. 47–161. (This book is published as a supplement to *Gentenshō keibu dai issatsu* [The Ministry of Punishments section of the *Yuan tien-chang*, Vol. One], ed. Iwamura Shinobu and Tanaka Kenji. Kyoto: Kyoto Daigaku Jinbun kagaku kenkyūjo, 1964.)

Tao Jing-shen [T'ao Chin-sheng] 陶晉生. "Pei-Sung fu-nü te tsai-chia yü kai-chia" 北宋婦女的再嫁與改嫁 [Remarriage and second marriage for women in the Northern Sung]. *Hsin-shih hsüeh* 6:3 (1995), pp. 1–28.

Tao, Jing-shen. *The Jurchen in Twelfth Century China.* Seattle: University of Washington Press, 1976.

———. *Two Sons of Heaven: Studies in Sung-Liao Relations.* Tucson: University of Arizona, 1988.

ter Haar, Barend J. *The White Lotus Teachings in Chinese Religious History.* Leiden: E. J. Brill, 1992.

Tietze, Peter. "The Liao." In *The Cambridge History of China,* Vol. 6, *Alien Regimes and Border States, 907–1368,* ed. Herbert Franke and Denis Twitchett. Cambridge: Cambridge University Press, 1994, pp. 43–153.

Tillman, Hoyt Cleveland. *Confucian Discourse and Chu Hsi's Ascendancy.* Honolulu: University of Hawaii Press, 1992.

———. "Intellectuals and Officials in Action: Academies and Granaries in Sung China." *Asia Major* 3rd series, 4:2 (1991), pp. 1–14.

———. "A New Direction in Confucian Scholarship: Approaches to Examining the Differences between Neo-Confucianism and *Tao-hsüeh*." *Philosophy East and West* 42:3 (July 1992), pp. 455–74.

———. "The Uses of Neo-Confucianism, Revisited: A Reply to Professor de Bary." In *Philosophy East and West* 42:1 (1994), pp. 135–42.

Tillman, Hoyt Cleveland, and Stephen H. West, eds. *China under Jurchen Rule.* Albany: State University of New York Press, 1995.

Ting Hsüeh-yün 丁學芸. "Chien-kuo kung-chu t'ung-yin yü Wang-ku pu i-tsun" 監國公主銅印與汪古部遺存 [The seal of the princess regent and the ancient remains of the Onggut tribe]. *Nei-Meng-ku wen-wu k'ao-ku* 3 (1984).

Twitchett, Denis. "The Fragment of the T'ang Ordinances of the Department of Waterways Discovered at Tun-huang." *Asia Major,* 2nd series, 6:1 (1957), pp. 23–79.

———. "The Fan Clan's Charitable Estate, 1050–1760." In *Confucianism in Action,* ed. David Nivison and Arthur Wright. Stanford, Calif.: Stanford University Press, 1959, pp. 97–133.

———. *Land Tenure and the Social Order in T'ang and Sung China.* London: Oxford University Press, 1962.

―――. "Merchant, Trade, and Government in Late T'ang." *Asia Major* 14:4 (1968), pp. 63–93.

―――. *Financial Administration under the T'ang Dynasty.* Cambridge: Cambridge University Press, 1963; reprint 1970.

―――. *Printing and Publishing in Medieval China.* New York: Frederic Beil, 1983.

―――. *The Writing of Official History under the T'ang.* Cambridge: Cambridge University Press, 1992.

Twitchett, Dennis, and Herbert Franke, eds. *The Cambridge History of China*, Vol. 6, *Alien Regimes and Border States, 907–1368.* Cambridge: Cambridge University Press, 1994.

Ueda, S. "Li Kou." In *Sung Biographies*, ed. Herbert Franke. Wiesbaden: Franz Steiner Verlag, 1976, pp. 574–5.

Uematsu, Tadashi. "*Institutions of the Yüan Dynasty* and Yüan Society." *Gest Library Journal* 5:1 (Spring 1992), pp. 57–69.

Umehara Kaoru 梅原郁. "NanSō Kainan no tochi seido shitan – eiden, tonden o chūshin ni" 南宋淮南の土地制度試探――營田屯田を中心に [On landownership in Huai-nan under the Southern Sung: civil land and military land]. *Tōyōshi kenkyū* 21:4 (March 1963), pp. 26–57.

―――. "Chang Yung." In *Sung Biographies*, ed. Herbert Franke. Wiesbaden: Franz Steiner Verlag, 1976, pp. 48–50.

―――. *Sōdai kanryō seido kenkyū* 宋代官僚制度研究. [A study of the bureaucratic system in the Sung]. Kyoto: Dōhōsha, 1985.

―――, ed. *Chūgoku kinsei no hōsei to shakai* 中國近世の法制と社會 [Law and society in early modern China]. Kyōto: Kyōto Daigaku Jinbun Kagaku Kenkyūjo, 1993.

―――, trans. *Meikō shohan seimeishū yakuchū* 名公書判清明集譯注 [Translation with notes of the *Ch'ing-ming chi* (CMC)]. Kyoto: Dōhōsha, 1986.

Vittinghoff, Helmolt. "Lu Tien." In *Sung Biographies*, ed. Herbert Franke. Wiesbaden: Franz Steiner Verlag, 1976, pp. 687–91.

von Glahn, Richard. "Community and Welfare: Chu Hsi's Community Granary in Theory and Practice." In *Ordering the World: Approaches to State and Society in Sung Dynasty China*, ed. Robert Hymes and Conrad Schirokauer. Berkeley: University of California Press, 1993, pp. 221–54.

―――. *Fountain of Fortune: Money and Monetary Policy in China, 1000–1700.* Berkeley: University of California Press, 1996.

Waley, Arthur, trans. *Book of Songs*. 1937. Reprint, New York: Grove Press, 1960.

Waltner, Ann. "Widows and Remarriage in Ming and Early Qing China." In *Women in China*, ed. Richard Guisso and Stanley Johannesen. Youngstown, N.Y.: Philo Press, 1981, pp. 129–46.

―――. *Getting an Heir: Adoption and the Construction of Kinship in Late Imperial China.* Honolulu: University of Hawaii Press, 1990.

Walton, Linda. "Kinship, Marriage, and Status in Sung China: A Study of the Lou Lineage of Ningbo c. 1050–1250." *Journal of Asian History* 18:1 (1984), pp. 35–77.

Wan Kuo-ting. "The System of Equal Land Allotments in Medieval Times." In *Chinese Social History: Translations of Selected Studies*, ed. E-tu Zen Sun and J. de Francis. Washington, D.C.: American Council of Learned Societies, 1956.

Wang Gungwu. "The Rhetoric of a Lesser Empire: Early Sung Relations with Its Neighbors." In *China among Equals*, ed. Morris Rossabi. Berkeley: University of California Press, 1983, pp. 47–65.

Wang Yün-hai 王雲海. *Sung hui-yao chi-kao k'ao-chiao* 宋會要輯稿考校 [An Examination of the *Sung hui-yao*]. Shanghai: Ku-chi ch'u-pan she, 1986.

Watanabe Hiroyoshi. "Junki matzunen no Kenneifu: shasōgome no konrai to tairyō to" 淳熙末年の建寧府——社倉米の昏賴と貨糧と [Chien-ning-fu in the late 12th century: abuses in the borrowing and lending of community granary rice]. In *Nakajima Satoshi sensei koki kinen ronshū* 中島敏先生古稀記念論集 [Studies on Asian history dedicated to Prof. Satoshi Nakajima on his seventieth birthday] Vol. 2. Tokyo: Kaimeidō, 1981, pp. 195–217.

———. "Local *Shih-ta-fu* in the Sung." *Acta Asiatica* no. 50 (1986), pp. 54–72.

Watson, James. *Emigration and the Chinese Lineage: The Mans in Hong Kong and London*. Berkeley: University of California Press, 1975.

Watson, Rubie. "Women's Property in Republican China: Rights and Practices." *Republican China* no. 10 (1984), pp. 1–12.

———. "Afterword: Marriage and Gender Inequality." In *Marriage and Inequality in Chinese Society*, ed. Rubie Watson and Patricia Ebrey. Berkeley: University of California Press, 1991, pp. 347–68.

Wei T'ien-an 魏天安. "Sung-tai 'hu-chüeh t'iao-kuan' k'ao" 宋代戶絕條貫考 [An examination of "regulations on cut-off households" in the Sung]. *Chung-kuo ching-chi shih yen-chiu* no. 3 (Sept. 1988), pp. 31–8.

Wilbur, C. Martin. *Slavery in China during the Former Han Dynasty*. Chicago: Field Museum of Natural History, 1943.

Wilkinson, Endymion. *The History of Imperial China: A Research Guide*. Harvard East Asian Monographs, no. 49. Cambridge, Mass.: Harvard University Press, 1973.

Wilson, Thomas. *Genealogy of the Way: The Construction and Uses of the Confucian Tradition in Late Imperial China*. Stanford, Calif.: Stanford University Press, 1995.

Wittfogel, Karl A., and Feng Chia-sheng. *History of Chinese Society, Liao (907–1125)*. Philadelphia: American Philosophical Society, 1949; reprint 1961.

Wolf, Arthur. "Women, Widowhood, and Fertility in Premodern China." In *Marriage and Remarriage in Populations of the Past*, ed. Jacques Dupâquier et al. London and New York: Academic Press, 1981.

Wolf, Margery. *The House of Lim: A Study of a Chinese Farm Family*. Englewood Cliffs, N.J.: Prentice-Hall, 1968.

———. *Women and the Family in Rural Taiwan*. Stanford, Calif.: Stanford University Press, 1972.

Wong, Sun-ming. "Confucian Ideal and Reality: Transformation of the Institution of Marriage in T'ang China." Ph.D. dissertation, University of Washington, 1979.

Wright, Hope. *Alphabetical List of Geographic Names in Sung China.* Matériaux pour le Manuel de L'Histoire des Song. Paris: École Pratiques des Hautes Études, 1956.

Wrigley, Anthony, and Roger Schofield. *Population History of England.* Cambridge: Cambridge University Press, 1989.

Wu T'ing-hsieh 吳廷燮. *Nan-Sung chih-fu nien-piao* 南宋制撫年表 [Year-by-year record of Southern Sung administrators]. Orig. 1918. Reprint combined with *Pei-Sung ching-fu nien-piao,* ed. Chang Ch'en-shih 張忱石. Peking: Chung-hua shu-chü, 1984.

Yanagida Setsuko 柳田節子. "Sōdai tochi shoyūsei ni mirareru futatsu no kata: senshin to henkyō" 宋代土地所有制にみられる二つの型—先進と邊境 [Two types of landholding seen in the Sung: advanced and frontier]. *Tōyō bunka kenkyūjo kiyō,* 29 (1963), pp. 95–130.

———. "NanSōki kasan bunkatsu ni okeru joshōbun ni tsuite" 南宋期家產分割における女承分について [Women's inheritance resulting from the division of family property during the Southern Sung]. In *Ryū Shiken hakushi shōju kinen Sōshi kenkyū ronshū* [Collected studies in Sung history dedicated to Professor James T. C. Liu in celebration of his seventieth birthday], ed. Kinugawa Tsuyoshi. Tokyo: Dōhōsha, 1989, pp. 213–42.

———. "Sōdai joshi no zaisanken" 宋代女子の財產權 [Women's property rights in the Sung]. *Hōseishi gaku* 42 (1990).

———. "Shohō: Nagata Mie, 'NanSōki ni okeru josei no zaisanken ni tzuite'" 書評：永田三枝—"南宋期における女性の財產權について [Review of Nagata Mie, "Women's property rights in the Southern Sung"]. *Hōseishi kenkyū* 42 (1993), pp. 300–1.

———. "Sōdai no joko" 宋代の女戶 [Female households in the Sung]. In *Yanagida Setsuko sensei koki kinen Chūgoku no dentō shakai to kazoku* 柳田節子先生古稀記念中國の傳統社會と家族 [Traditional Chinese society and family: a festschrift in celebration of the seventieth birthday of Professor Yanagida Setsuko], ed. Ihara Hiroshi. Tokyo: Kyūko shoen, 1993, pp. 89–106.

———. "Gendai joshi no zaisan shōkei" 元代女子の財產承繼 [Women's inheritance in the Yüan]. In *SōGen shakai keizaishi kenkyū* 宋元社會經濟史研究 [Studies in the social economy of the Sung and Yüan]. Tokyo: Sōbunsha, 1995, pp. 261–76.

Yang Chung-i. "Evolution of the Status of 'Dependents.'" In *Chinese Social History: Translations of Selected Studies,* ed. E-tu Zen Sun and J. de Francis. Washington, D.C.: American Council of Learned Societies, 1956, pp. 142–56.

Yang I 楊毅. "Shuo Yüan-tai te shou-chi hun" 說元代的收繼婚 [Levirate marriage in the Yüan period]. *Yüan-shih lun-ts'ung* no. 5 (1993), pp. 273–81.

Yang, Lien-sheng. *Money and Credit in China: A Short History.* Cambridge, Mass.: Harvard University Press, 1952.

Yang, Xianyi, and Gladys Yang, trans. *The Courtesan's Jewel Box: Chinese Stories of the Xth to XVIIth Centuries*. Peking: Foreign Languages Press, 1981.

Yoshikawa Kōjirō 吉川幸次郎 and Tanaka Kenji 田中謙二. *Gentenshō no buntai* 元典章の文體 [The language of the *Yüan tien-chang*]. Kyoto, 1964.

Yao, Esther S. Lee. *Chinese Women: Past and Present*. Mesquite, Texas: Ide House, 1983.

Yao Ta-li 姚大力. "Yüan-ch'ao k'o-chü chih-tu te hsing-fa chi ch'i she-hui pei-ching" 元朝科舉制度的行發及其社會背景 [The operation of the Yüan examination system and its social context]. *Yüan-shih chi pei-fang min-tzu shih yen-chiu chi-k'an*, no. 6 (1982), pp. 26–59.

————. "Chin-mo Yüan-ch'u li-hsüeh tsai pei-fang te ch'uan-po" 金末元初理學在北方的傳播 [The dissemination of Neo-Confucianism in north China during the late Chin and early Yüan dynasties]. *Yüan-shih lun-ts'ung* 2 (1983), pp. 217–24.

Yeh Ch'ien-chao 葉潛昭. *Chin-lü chih yen-chiu* 金律之研究 [Studies of the Chin code]. Taipei: Shang-wu ch'u-pan she, 1972.

Yeh Hsiao-hsin 葉孝信 et al. *Chung-kuo min-fa shih* 中國民法史 [History of Chinese civil law]. Shanghai: Jen-min ch'u-pan she, 1993.

Yüan Li 袁俐. "Sung-tai nü-hsing ts'ai-ch'an-ch'üan shu-lun" 宋代女性財產權述論 [A discussion of women's property rights in the Sung period]. Hangchow, 1988. Reprint in *Chung-kuo fu-nü shih lun-chi hsü-chi* 中國婦女史論集續集 [Continuation of collected essays on the history of Chinese women], ed. Pao Chia-lin 鮑家麟. Taipei: Tao-hsiang ch'u-pan she, 1991, 173–213.

Glossary-Index